SEI

ENCYCLOPEDIA
FOR CHURCH
GROUP LEADERS

ENCYCLOPEDIA

FOR CHURCH

GROUP LEADERS

EDITED BY LEE J. GABLE

ASSOCIATION PRESS

NEW YORK

INTRODUCTION

"I REMEMBER a teacher I had" . . . "I remember a pastor" . . . "There was a superintendent." So begin the replies when people are asked what they remember from their childhood experiences in the church. Then follow true stories of men and women who worked with boys and girls. Usually they are stories of true appreciation, recalling dedicated Christian work. Sometimes they are stories tinged with regret, recalling missed opportunity, or responsibilities too lightly assumed. One inescapable conclusion, however, is that the church group leader has far-reaching influence in the work of a Protestant church.

The church group leader does not work alone. He works in partnership with other leaders and with members of the group. It is true that every leader must sometimes draw apart for evaluation, planning, reading, and spiritual renewal. His work is not all done in groups. When he draws apart, however, it is so that he may return to the group again in better partnership.

The leader often sees farther and more clearly than members of the group who have not paid the price of study, thought, and spiritual discipline that the leader has paid. It becomes his task then to help them see farther and more deeply than they would see without him. This the preacher does in his sermons, and the teacher or discussion leader in the background presentation that must precede discussion. Sometimes he must help them see farther and more deeply than they want to see! This may set him apart for a while. Yet, if his leadership is to have lasting value, he must exercise it within the group as partner, not outside the group as dictator. To keep these two phases of leadership in clear and honest focus is one of the most difficult responsibilities of the church worker. Much of this book bears on this problem. Chapters 3 and 7 deal with it specifically.

A tremendous amount of material has been written for church group leaders to help them understand the mission of the church and the ways in which they and their groups may work together in it. This is good, but it creates a problem. No volunteer worker has access to all of this material, or can take the time to sort it out and read what would help him most. It is the purpose of this book to help solve this problem by bringing together into one volume many writings that would be difficult for any worker to assemble for himself.

These writings were chosen primarily for volunteer leaders who work with groups in their own churches. For experienced workers, the book offers review and a broadening of vision. For new or prospective workers, the book offers a broad orientation to educational work in the church. These primary uses suggest a number of others. Administrators of church work, such as superintendents, pastors, and directors of Christian education, will find here a convenient summary of significant writings for their own use as well as resources to use in the training and supervision of volunteer workers. College and seminary students will find these materials a useful compilation for their own review of church work, and a book which they may later use with volunteer church workers. Several copies might well be placed in the church library where they can be consulted readily.

The reader will probably begin with the chapters that deal with the things he needs to know, and this is good. Or he may read first about the age group with which he works. This is also good, but he should not stop there. Much that is written about the age group just above and just below his own will speak to him too. Also, when he reads about other age groups, he finds general principles which apply to all ages. Certainly, he should read Part I, in order to be confronted again with the foundations on which his work in the church must stand. Others may wish to read the book, chapter by chapter, for it is arranged in logical sequence.

No quotation or idea should be accepted uncritically. Before the reader adopts an idea, let him ask some penetrating questions. Would this idea help our group to strengthen the Christian work and witness of our church? Why do I favor (or oppose) the idea? How should the idea be changed if our group were to accept it? How should I present the idea? When? To whom?

It is hoped that no one will stop with reading this book, but will go on to read some of the books and periodicals from which this material is taken. If the quoted portion brings special help, the entire publication is certain to bring greater value.

The selection of quotations posed a number of problems. There was much more good material than could possibly be used. Sometimes it was necessary to choose one out of a number of equally good readings, almost arbitrarily. Sometimes it was necessary to omit an excellent article or chapter because it partly duplicated another, or because it did not fit into the progression of ideas. Following are a few of the principles of selection which the editor used:

- Deal with essential tasks and main concerns of the church group leader.
- Provide materials which help answer the basic questions of why, what, and how.
- Use quotations that stand "on their own," and are not dependent on other parts of the publication from which they come.
- Include, in each chapter, writings about as many age groups

as are required in order to take proper account of age-group differences.

• Aim at maximum helpfulness by selecting material that is difficult enough to be stimulating, yet easy enough to be useful.

The term "Christian nurture" is used frequently. In what sense is it different from "Christian education"? To the editor, there is no basic difference in meaning. There is a sense, however, in which the two terms are differently understood. This book is concerned with the growth of persons of all ages toward Christian maturity and with the total effort of church and home to assist that growth. This is the meaning we ought to find in "Christian nurture." This, of course, is the meaning of "Christian education" too. The difficulty is that, to some people, Christian education has come to mean the work of only a part of the church. They apply it to the Sunday school alone, or to the Sunday school plus one or two other agencies of the church. Or they think of it as that part of the work of the church for which a particular board of the denomination or of the congregation is responsible. The implication is that the rest of the denomination or of the congregation need not be concerned about Christian education. We must think in broader terms than these. Christian growth of persons of all ages must be the concern of the *whole* church. The use of "Christian nurture" is to encourage breadth of vision.

To the Corinthian Christians, Paul wrote, "I planted, Apollos watered, but God gave the growth" (1 Cor. 3:6, RSV). It matters little which of us is the modern Paul or the modern Apollos. What does matter, and matter greatly, is that our work with church groups be of such quality that God can bless it with growth.

Preparation of such a book as this requires the help of many people. To list all of them would be an endless task, yet some of them must be mentioned, at least by categories. The editor is indebted to Association Press for inviting him to undertake a stimulating task and for dealing patiently with him all along the way.

He is indebted primarily to the publishers and authors who permitted the use of portions of their publications.

The Scripture quotations in the portions of the book written by the editor are from the *Revised Standard Version of the Bible,* copyright 1946 and 1952 by the Division of Christian Education, National Council of Churches, and used by permission. Scripture quotations included in the various readings follow the original publications in the versions quoted and in the forms of acknowledgment used.

The editor is indebted also to the fifty or more people who examined the tentative outline and gave their counsel on the selection of material. First and last, are the three ladies in the editor's family who helped and encouraged as the occasion required. To all of these—grateful appreciation.

LEE J. GABLE

TABLE OF CONTENTS

PART II : SOME BASIC QUESTIONS ABOUT
CHRISTIAN NURTURE

PART I

BASIC

TRUTHS

FOR

CHURCH

GROUP

LEADERS

1. CHRISTIAN FOUNDATIONS

"... YOU ARE FELLOW CITIZENS with the saints and members of the household of God, built upon the foundation of the apostles and prophets, Christ Jesus himself being the chief cornerstone, in whom the whole structure is joined together and grows into a holy temple in the Lord; in whom you also are built into it for a dwelling place of God in the Spirit" (Eph. 2:19b–22, RSV).

This is the foundation on which twentieth-century Christians are privileged to build their own Christian lives and the life and work of the church. We are not left with our own resources alone, but have the benefit of centuries of God's self-revelation and of man's response to God. This is a privilege which every church worker should understand and recognize.

As always, privilege involves responsibility, and this responsibility belongs especially to the church group leader. For himself, he must undertake sufficient study to understand the priceless heritage which comes to us from God and through the church. He must interpret the Christian heritage to the people of the church, for it is their heritage and they should understand it. He must encourage self-examination in the church, to determine to what extent our life and work fit the foundation and the structure which have come to us from the past.

21

Since the leader's task is to help people build their own structures of life and thought, taking into account the heritage from the past, the leader must understand people. Therefore, this chapter on foundations deals not only with our beliefs, the Bible, and the church, but also with man. He who would serve the church well must understand all of these.

You Teach Theology

Every time a Christian teacher teaches, he is dealing with theology. He may not read many books in theology. He may be quite unfamiliar with traditional theological language. Yet as he tells about God and his ways of working in the world, he is talking theology. As he leads his pupils into an understanding of God's revelation, he relates theology to life.

Often the teacher is unaware of his theological role. Consequently, he may not have reflected on the Christian faith enough to be able to present a consistent theology. He may be teaching, therefore, theological ideas which are as confusing to the student as to himself.

To communicate the Christian Gospel effectively, the teacher must understand his role in relation to theology. He must examine his own Christian beliefs to be able to lead his students. Indeed, beliefs about God, Christ, the Church, and the Christian life, are at the heart of Christian teaching.

There has been a reawakening of theological interest in recent years. Books on theology are being written for laymen, not merely for professional theologians. Evidence that this rekindled interest in theology has influenced Christian education lies in the counsel Christian educators have sought from professional theologians. Church school curricula are examined to see that there is a consistent and sound approach through the church school literature.

Staff article, *International Journal of Religious Education*, February, 1955, pp. 18–20. Used by permission.

One of the significant developments in denominations is a unified theological approach in the entire church school curriculum.

The Christian teacher must constantly examine his theology in relation to the theological affirmations of his own denomination, for his own thinking as well as that written into the literature is inevitably reflected in his teaching. It is vitally important that he have a clearly consistent theology and an inquiring mind. Discussion of theological questions with the pastor and parents helps bring about a unified theological witness.

Among many professional theologians today there is agreement on many ideas that profoundly affect Christian education. In some instances, the acceptance of these ideas would change the nature and content of present teaching. Christian education operates in a climate where these ideas flourish. Four ideas which have special relevance for Christian education are: "Word of God," "the nature of man," "faith," and "the Church."

The Word of God

Where does the Christian go for authority? Does he simply consult his own experience to discover his relation with God and God's activity in life? Does he accept the dogmatic interpretations of an infallible Pope? Or does he find authority in an infallible Scripture? In wrestling with this question, theologians have rediscovered the Protestant concept of the "Word of God." God's Word is neither an infallible book or Pope, nor individual experience. It is God's action in human life, revealed partially in all human experience and fully in Jesus Christ. The Bible has authority insofar as through it God's living Word is spoken to men. The Church has authority only as it speaks God's Word.

According to this view, the Bible is a book which historical criticism must analyze. It witnesses to the fact that "God was in Christ reconciling the world to Himself." The Christian is not bound to particular words as "God's Word." The Bible is not simply history, but the record of God's mighty action in history. It is no mere textbook in ethics, but the record of changed lives.

It is the dramatic story of God's effort on behalf of man. The Bible is read in order to hear God speaking in personal and social experience. Behind the words of Scripture or the words of the Church lies the Word of God. This is the sole authority for the Christian. This Word became flesh in Jesus Christ.

What significance does this view have for Christian education? In the first place, it emphasizes the primary importance of both the Church and the Bible in Christian education. God speaks his living Word through the Bible and in the Church to the experience of men in their hopes and fears, their dreams and frustrations. The authority of the Bible and the Church rests in neither words nor creeds, but in their witness to the mighty act of God in Christ.

Second, this view calls upon Christian teachers to help persons develop the power to recognize and acknowledge God's Word in their lives. As experiences in the life of Paul are studied the person listens to God's Word for his own life. As one studies the creeds of the Church, he listens to God speaking to his own situation. As the Hebrew prophets are examined, he listens for God's judgment upon his own people. The Bible and the Church are means through which the Holy Spirit bears witness to God's Word and through which men are helped to receive power to do God's will.

Third, this view sees Bible study as a means both of preparing a person for faith in God and of understanding that faith. The source of faith is God, not the Bible or the Church. Bible study helps a student both to prepare for meaningful faith in God and to understand the meaning of that faith in all of life.

The Nature of Man

A central affirmation in Christian theology is that God is creator; man is his creature. Only in this faith can we understand what life is all about, and what the purpose for living is. One of the great problems of our time is the denial that man is dependent upon anything outside himself for his life. Man is considered the measure of all things; custom and legislation are thought to be the source of morality and correct living. The Christian faith, however, affirms that man is dependent upon God for his very life. God created man in his own image for fellowship with himself. No matter what a person does, he is still God's son, and precious in his sight.

God gave men freedom to choose among alternative courses of action. Freedom includes even the ability to deny dependence upon God. Man misuses freedom by separating himself from God. He bows before other gods than God, the Father of our Lord Jesus Christ. He worships idols rather than God. He tries to control his own destiny, denying his dependence upon God.

Such misplaced allegiance is sin. Sin is not simply the sum total of evil acts which are committed. It is a negative relationship to God which man by himself is powerless to overcome. No person has within himself the latent power to save himself. Sin is such that only God can take the initiative in raising men again to fellowship and faith. There can be no room for pride, for "all have sinned and come short of the glory of God."

Particular sins flow from the negative relationship with God. To be sure, the Christian faith is concerned about these sins. Faith does not come, however, as the result of a series of good deeds to replace evil ones. It comes only when in faith men respond to God's love. Faith, showing itself in works of love, is the mark of a Christian.

From this point of view, how would the church school teacher approach persons? He would start from the fact that apart from God, man cannot rebuild a right relation with God. He does not have within himself the latent capacities to save himself, if only he can be instructed and trained in the right direction. Lives are transformed not by instruction, but by faith.

What effect does this concept have when accepted by Christian education? In the first place, Christian education would interpret life to men as children of God who without faith are separated from God. It would seek to bring to themselves those who live away from the Father. The task of Christian education would be, then, far more than teaching what is right, for even perfect knowledge is insufficient for doing the right. It would prepare persons for a meaningful faith.

This is not to say that Christian education would be unconcerned about conduct and morality. The Christian faith is concerned with the whole of life. Faith makes a difference in life. It constantly changes the way people act and think. Christian education, therefore, would lead people to make intelligent ethical choices, always in faithful response to God's love.

Faith

Faith is a relationship with God involving trust, love, forgiveness, and obedience. This is no static experience, but a dynamic, growing relationship.

Faith grows out of the encounter of God with man. God takes the initiative in establishing the relationship. In the encounter, man responds faithfully to God. On God's part, the relationship involves acceptance, forgiveness, and love; on man's, loyalty, trust, and obedience.

The whole man is involved in the relationship, the emotions, the intellect, and the will. Faith is not simply an emotional experience or intellectual exercise. It is a growing, active relationship which is expressed in a person's every act.

This concept is more than a "growing to maturity." The Christian life is more than an unfolding of latent inner resources which need to be trained and conditioned. A new dimension is added to life. God is the source of freedom, forgiveness and guidance. The Christian faith is a living encounter with a loving and active God who has revealed himself in Jesus Christ.

From this view of faith, Christian education would both prepare men for encounter and help interpret this relationship in individual and social life. It would prepare persons by helping them to understand the nature of God and his ways of working with men. It would interpret faith by studying man's need and exploring God's will for his children.

What would this idea mean in teaching children? Teaching would certainly be relevant to the child's experience. Parents and teachers would try to demonstrate in their relationship with a child what are the fruits of faith. However, the teacher must point beyond human experience to the perfect love of God. The child would be led to see that even the most ideal human love is but a pale reflection of the love of God in Christ. Christian teaching would prepare the child to receive through faith that love which God has poured out for him.

Although faith certainly involves responsible actions in relation to other people, no standard of goodness or virtue is taught as the condition for faith. Right relations with people flow out of a growing awareness of God's love and will.

Far more important, then, than content of curriculum materials is the relationship of teacher and pupils, a relationship characterized by acceptance, forgiveness, love and trust.

Faith is no static, isolated experience. It is a continually growing response to God. The Christian teacher is a means of helping persons develop and enlarge their faith, not only by his use of curriculum content but by his love and concern for persons.

The Church

What is the Church? What place does the Church have in the Christian life? These are questions which have increasingly demanded answers in theological discussion. One of the most important discussions in current theology is the question of the nature of the Church.

There is probably greater diversity in the concept of the Church than on any other single theological doctrine. Whatever the differences in basic understanding of the Church, there are still broad areas upon which there is agreement.

The Church is more than simply a company of folks bound together in a common cause. The Church is a community with a

Lord who is its head. The Church is God's community, into which every Christian is incorporated. It is the sphere through which the Holy Spirit operates to proclaim the Gospel and to build the faith. The Bible cannot be understood except through the historical witness of the Church. The encounter of God and man is no isolated event involving simply a person and God. Faith is always the encounter of God and man in the community of the Church. The Church is the community of those who respond to that encounter in faith. The Church is an organism, not an institution. It is the Body of Christ, the "household of God."

Such a view of the Church means that the Christian teacher would see his role as one member of the Body of Christ. He has a teaching function alongside those other functions which constitute the total ministry of the Church. The Christian teacher never teaches in isolation. The class is never simply "his class." He and his pupils are together participants in the Body of Christ. The teacher performs one function within that Body.

Such a view of the Church would reverse our thinking, which tends to start from the local Church and the denomination, finally getting to the ecumenical Church. To be sure, the Christian teacher functions within a specific worshiping congregation, in which he gives expression to his membership in the Body of Christ. But the local congregation must be interpreted in the light of the whole Body, not the Body as the sum total of its individual parts.

The Christian teacher has a profound opportunity. He guides persons, young and old alike, into meaningful acceptance and expression of the Christian faith. He must know the Gospel which is his content. He will constantly re-examine his own faith to be able to perform his task. Only in a deep faith of his own can the Christian teacher invite his students to, "Come and see what the Lord has done."

What a Christian Ought to Know and Believe

BY W. NORMAN PITTENGER

Many, of course, will say that the best statement of "what a Christian ought to know and believe" will be found in the Apostles' (or perhaps the Nicene) Creed. I should not wish to dispute this, if we are looking for a traditional statement of the basic affirmations of the Christian Church. On the other hand, there are many who recognize that the Apostles' Creed, and the Nicene Creed as well, are themselves in need of interpretation for contemporary Christians. The former has much symbolic phrasing, the latter is highly theological (especially in the long section dealing with the person of Jesus Christ). In any event, what these documents really intend to say is susceptible of statement in other words. And there are a goodly number of men and women who quite evidently wish for another and more immediately contemporary statement of what one might call the essence of the Christian position.

Let me try to put this in a somewhat schematic form, recapitulating the several points in a concluding paragraph.

1. *God, the Father of mankind, Creator and Sovereign Ruler of all things.* This is the basic Christian affirmation, on which all else must rest. Christians put their trust in God. The God in whom they trust is no impersonal force, no cosmic energy, but the living God of the Old and New Testaments, whose fatherly

W. Norman Pittenger, *The Christian Century*, December 14, 1955, pp. 1463–1465. Also appeared, in altered form, in *Tomorrow's Faith Today* (New York: Exposition Press, 1957). Used by permission.

care includes all men in its embrace. He is the divine Reality whose creative energy is in and through all things, yet unexhausted by his working in them. He is the sovereign Lord, whose power is sufficient for the fulfillment of his purposes and who can make "even the wrath of man to serve him." In nature and in history he reveals himself, for they are the work of his hands. Above all, in the community of Israel he has moved to make himself known to his children, preparing the way for a climactic self-manifestation in one historical personality.

2. *Jesus Christ, God's Son, our Lord, in whom True God dwells in a true man.* Central to the Christian faith is the person of Jesus Christ. In this Man of Nazareth, Christians find the crucial disclosure of the reality of God. He is God's Son, in a supreme and special sense; although he is this without denying the sonship to God which is true of all men. He is our Lord, the one whom we may love and serve and follow, finding in him "the way, the truth and the life." As that one in whom God truly dwells, in focal fashion, he is to be worshiped and adored, for in the rich fullness of his human life he brings God near and makes him a vivid and compelling reality for us. He is the "Incarnate Word"— the human expression of the outward-moving power and love of God in the concrete terms of our human experience.

3. *Jesus Christ for us men and for our wholeness lived with us as man, died for our sakes, rose from the dead, and is alive forevermore.* This Lord of men, this Self-Expression of God in our human life, has done something for men which they could not do for themselves. Living with us as one of us, taking upon him the burden of human sin and suffering and death, he has shared our full experience. By the "mighty act of God," who wrought this work in and through him, Jesus conquered death and sin. He is no dead hero of two thousand years ago; he is the living Lord, who remains forever the way in which we know God most directly, find his presence most real, and are enabled to serve him

most fully. Whatever may have been the detailed facts of his birth, life and conquest of death, the great fact remains: Jesus came and lived and loved and taught and worked and suffered and died and was known again as living in the hearts and lives of his followers. He thus has established—or God has established through his whole impact on men—an at-one-ment between God and men such as is not known elsewhere or otherwise.

4. *The Spirit of the Father and the Son, worshiped together with them in unity of Godhead.* As the response to the total fact of Jesus Christ, there has been released into the lives of his followers a new power and strengthening which has bound them into a unity of life and love. So rich, so real, so personal in its working is this power and strengthening that men have been obliged to speak of it as "he," not as "it." They have seen it as the very power and strengthening of God himself; their response to Jesus Christ has been itself a divinely given and divinely active response. Thus they relate this Spirit to God himself; this Spirit is divine, as the action of God in Jesus is divine. In consequence, the Christian thinks of God not as a bare and isolated monad, but as one who possesses in himself the richness of the three modes of existence in which he has revealed himself: Father, Son, Holy Spirit. Nor are these confined in their operation to the Christian experience alone. Wherever God is self-expressed, there the "Word of God" is at work; wherever response is made to what is known of God, there the Spirit is at work. It is a definitive, not an exclusive, operation that Christians affirm to have been accomplished in the historical Jesus and in the Spirit known in Christian life.

5. *One holy church, one baptism into Christ, one Eucharist, one fellowship of the faithful in heaven and earth.* Christians are knit together, in their response to Jesus Christ, in a community which they have called "the church." That community, now divided, is in truth one, for it adores, loves, serves, and follows one Lord. It is holy, not because it is always in an empirical sense per-

fect but because it is enabled, by God's grace, to make men holy—that is, surrendered and consecrated to the service of God and his purpose in Christ. The church is Christ's body, as St. Paul puts it; it is his instrument for continuing self-expression in the world of men and therefore it shares in Christ's holiness, despite its obvious weakness, its imperfection, the sinfulness of its members and its institutional forms.

Admission to membership in it is by baptism, with water and the gift of the Spirit; through that act of baptism, it initiates into its ongoing life those "who are being saved" and incorporates them into Christ's family. The central action of worship of the community is the Lord's Supper. Holy Communion, Eucharist (or whatever other name may be given the rite), in which the presence of Christ is known and received, his sacrificial death remembered, and his disciples knit once again—and again and again—into unity with one another and with God in him. Nor is the community confined to this world of space and time, for it includes in "one fellowship in heaven and earth" all who have followed the Christian way, accepted the faith in Christ, and lived as men and women "in Christ."

6. *The life of the world to come, God's victory over sin, evil and death, and his kingdom which shall have no end.* The Christian believes that death is not the end of human life, but that in some fashion beyond our present understanding, God who in the first instance created and constituted our human nature can and does recreate and reconstitute it to live in his presence and by his power. This is no natural "immortality of the soul," which may or may not be so; it is the "resurrection of the dead"—not in their flesh and blood, not as a matter of chemicals, but as the persistence of man's true being in its full reality but in a mode appropriate to another realm than this world's materiality. That giving of life "from the dead" is God's gracious working, however it be conceived; and it is part of the accomplishment of his purpose, by which death itself, as well as the sin and evil that have ap-

peared in the creation, will be overcome in a great victory of the love and glory of God who is sovereign ruler of all things. Thus God's rule—his kingdom of charity, truth, and peace—is "in the end" sure and certain.

It is our task, here and now in this present world, to be "fellow workers with him" in establishing for men and women and children as they live in the world as much of that charity, truth and peace as can be established. We are to labor as "colonists of heaven" to conform this world, by God's grace, to the pattern which has been shown us as his will for his people. Thus, as Emil Brunner has so vividly phrased it, "God's grace is our task."

In Summary

Such, as I see it, is "what a Christian ought to know and believe, to his soul's health." Anything else which has been taught or thought about the Christian position is perhaps important, perhaps useful, perhaps a significant implementation of the central affirmations; although it may be that much which has been taught or thought is but human error or the result of man's attempt to know more than is open to him to know. There is room, then, for charity and sympathy and mutual understanding in these secondary or peripheral matters; in essentials, unity; in unessentials, agreement to differ; in all things, charity.

Those of us who have shared in the great ecumenical enterprise of our day, and especially those who have talked deeply with others about the profound realities of our faith, have increasingly come to feel that some such affirmations as I have here written down are indeed our bond of unity in Christ. But it is not the *words* that unite us; it is our common *life* as Christians, of which such words as these may, or may not, be an adequate expression. We have theological differences, we subscribe to differing philosophies, we worship in varying ways, we understand the moral implications of Christian faith and life in dissimilar fashion. But we are still one in the things that basically matter. May it please God that we shall soon be one in a great reunion of the Christian community, which will thus be able to manifest to the world the fact of our oneness in Christ.

This, then, is the sort of answer which I give to those who ask "what a Christian ought to know and believe, to his soul's health." He ought to know and believe in God, Father of all mankind, and Creator and Sovereign Ruler of all things. He ought to know and believe in Jesus Christ, God's Son, our Lord, in whom True God dwells in a true man. He ought to live in the light of that Lord's living among us as one of us, dying, rising again, living forevermore. He ought to know and believe in, and open himself to, the Spirit of the Father and the Son, worshiping Godhead as Father, Son and Holy Spirit. He ought to share in the life of the holy church through baptism into Christ, to worship at the Lord's Supper where Christ is present and his saving work made available. He ought to rejoice in his membership in the one fellowship of the faithful in heaven and earth. He ought to look in strong hope for the life of the world to come, confident that God will be victorious over sin and evil and death. And he ought to labor and work, "as much as lieth in him," that God's will may be done on earth as it is in heaven, gladly giving himself to the spreading of the gospel and the establishment among men, by God's grace, of the kingdom of love, of truth, and of peace.

What Is the Bible?

BY ROBERT C. DENTAN

It is the conviction of Christians that God revealed Himself in history. The Bible is the record of that revelation. It is not primarily a book about men, but about God; its chief value is not that it contains great literature, but that it shows us what God is like and what God has done.

The Bible as the Revelation of God

The God whom the Bible reveals is not an impersonal force, not a vague, remote Absolute whom we might call the Supreme Being, not a mere law of nature, like the principle of gravitation. He is a personal God, One who loves, plans, creates, and reveals Himself. This does not mean that God has a physical body; nor does it mean that His will and emotions and plans are always changing like those of human personalities. No words used to describe human personality can have quite the same sense when applied to God. God is infinite and His personality is not changeable, as our limited human personalities are; His plans and purposes are eternal and His love is unchanging and unlimited. The God of the Bible is personal because persons, beings who can think, will, create, and love, are the highest things we know in all creation, and God must be at least as great as the greatest things which He has made. His nature must somehow include all those qualities which go to make human personality the noblest and most valuable thing we know.

Robert C. Dentan, "The Approach to the Bible," *The Holy Scriptures* (Greenwich: Seabury Press, 1949), pp. 5–24. Used by permission.

It is important to understand this clearly because God Himself is the principal character in the Bible story, and all through the Bible He is revealed as acting like a person. He is not abstract and shadowy, but a living God who thinks, speaks, and acts. He made the world by the decree of His Will and has a plan for that world and has revealed His plan to His creatures. The Bible pictures the personal activity of God so vividly that it often seems to make Him act exactly as human beings do. It sometimes speaks of Him as having arms and hands and fingers. It even speaks of God repenting of what He has done. Such expressions are not to be taken literally, but are simply vivid ways of making us realize that God is intensely real and that our relationship with Him is not with some ill-defined idea in our own minds nor with some force of nature, but is the relationship of persons with a Person. The God of the Bible is not an It to be impersonally discussed; He is a Thou, who at every point confronts us with an invitation to believe and a command to obey.

How God Reveals Himself

Because God is personal and has made us "in His image" (Genesis 1:26) to be His children, He desires to reveal Himself to us in order that we may know and love Him. For those whose minds and hearts are prepared to receive it, the revelation of God is unmistakable. It takes place in three general ways.

First of all, God reveals Himself in *Nature,* not because Nature is the same thing as God, but because God created and controls it. From Nature one can learn that God exists, and, since Nature was created by God, it shows something of the character of its Creator. In the beauty and orderliness and dependability of the natural world we can see reflected the beauty and order and dependability of God.

In the second place, God reveals Himself in certain great acts in *History.* As Christians, we are chiefly concerned with this revelation, since it is the belief that God has manifested Himself in history which distinguishes the Christian and Jewish religions from most other religions.

In the third place, God reveals Himself through the inspired insights of great men whom we call *Prophets*. This is really just another side of God's revelation in history, because we should not understand the meaning of sacred history if there were no one capable of explaining it. Ordinary men look at the events of history and see in them only the operation of chance or of mechanistic laws; the prophet looks at these same events and sees in them the unfolding of God's eternal purpose. The prophet speaks, of course, primarily, to his own contemporaries, but because he deals with eternal things his message has enduring significance. It is because of the great prophetic personalities of the Old and New Testaments that we are able today to understand the meaning of the story which the Bible tells. It should be understood, of course, that the word prophet used in this sense is not limited to those who are technically called prophets; it includes all great religious teachers who help men better to understand the wonderful works of God.

God's Special Revelation in the Bible

In some sense, no doubt, God reveals Himself in all history, but the Bible is the story of a particular section of history in which God chose to make Himself known in an unmistakable way. This is the history of Israel: the Old Israel of the Hebrew nation and the New Israel of the Christian Church. In this history, we see how God chose one nation to be the agent of His revelation to all men everywhere. We see how God made Himself known to this nation by redeeming them out of the land of Egypt; how He guided and moulded them through the centuries that followed; and finally, how He finished His work of revelation by another great redeeming act, the victory of Christ over sin and death, and created the Church to proclaim the Good News to all humanity.

In the Bible we see God actually at work, creating, guiding, and redeeming. When we read the Bible, it is not as though we were in the classroom, listening to one teacher after another tell us things about God. It is rather as though we were in a theater and were seeing God engaged in the performance of His mighty acts. The drama of the redemption of mankind is a long and magnificent one and the various chapters of Biblical history are the acts of the play. But we must always remember that, even though we call it a drama, it is a drama that really happened. In all essential details, the history which is told in the Bible is true history.

The Bible as the Word of God

Since the Bible is the record of how God revealed Himself to mankind, it is properly called the Word of God. This is clear when we understand that here Word simply means communication or message. When we want to communicate our thoughts to others, we make use of words to do so. Sometimes we use the expression "word" in the singular to mean a sentence or a whole message, as when we say, "His last word to me was such and such," meaning someone's last connected thoughts. It is in this sense that the Bible is God's Word to man. In the Bible, we find God's own message about Himself. The Bible story contains that communication of the truth about Himself and about His purposes for the world which God desired mankind to have.

It is important to notice that when we say the Bible is the Word of God, we do not mean that it is so many different words of God, as though every separate word or verse, taken by itself, had God for its author. There is much in the Bible which clearly refers only to particular times or situations in the past. There is much that was true and valid for certain stages in the development of man's understanding, but is no longer valid once men have passed beyond that stage. There is much that is included in the Bible only because it helps us to understand the progress of the story. Some passages of Scripture are hard to interpret and some even offend our sense of Christian morality. But we are not intended to read the Bible in piecemeal fashion, interpreting every verse and chapter by itself. Many serious doctrinal and moral errors have arisen because people have drawn far-reaching conclusions from particular chapters or verses of the Bible without trying to see how that particular fragment fits into the larger pattern. The particular words must be seen in the light of the Word as a whole.

From the Bible story as a whole we learn: what God is like; whence man came; what God intended man to be; how man, by rejecting God's plan and choosing his own, has brought himself to his present tragic state; and how God Himself has provided the means of release which make it possible for men to realize the glorious destiny of divine sonship for which they were created. This story, in all its sweep and grandeur, is God's Word to man.

The Inspiration of the Bible

Everyone would agree that the Bible is an inspired book, but not all would agree as to what inspired means. In common speech, the word is often used in quite loose fashion to mean something that is extraordinarily fine, as when we say that Shakespeare is an inspired poet. Some would explain the doctrine of the inspiration of the Bible as nothing more than an extension of this use of the term. The Bible, they would say, is inspired in the same sense in which all great literature is inspired, only more so. When the Church, however, uses the term she means something much more than this. She means that, in some quite definite and unique way, the Bible is the work of God the Holy Spirit.

The Bible is inspired, first of all, because it has an inspired story to tell. It is a unique story which is not just the history of a particular nation or an interesting group of people, but a story in which God is the principal actor. Behind the whole great drama with its colorful events and its richly human characters, we see God directing its course and shaping the end toward which it moves.

But it is also the Church's faith that God, who presides over the story, presided also in some way over the writing down of the story, so that the essential meaning was not distorted by human misunderstanding and thus lost to future generations. God the Holy Spirit has watched over the growth and preservation of this book so that we can trust it as a reliable record of what God has done for us, and can accept its general view of the world as a dependable basis for our own faith and conduct.

This does not mean that we are bound to believe that every single word and verse in the Bible has been dictated by God and is therefore unfailingly true (the doctrine commonly called *verbal infallibility*). There are many things in the Bible which would make it difficult to hold this view: contradictions, incidental errors of fact, and ideas which are clearly of human origin. More important than these considerations, however, is the fact that such a view would make the Bible an unreal, almost magical book, and would seem to represent God as acting in a way which is unlike the way in which He works elsewhere.

In the Bible story, we find God always working through men, real, human, fallible men like ourselves. The great characters of the Biblical drama are warm, human, and lovable. The Bible never hesitates to show their faults as well as their virtues. Even in the stupendous event of the Incarnation, which is the central event of Scripture and of all history, God did not choose to reveal Himself through a demigod, one far removed from our common humanity, but through One who was perfectly Man, "in all things . . . made like unto his brethren" (Hebrews 2:17). So when God gave us the Bible and made use of human beings as its authors, we should not expect that He would take away their natural human qualities from them: their special interests, their own style of writing, even their capacity to make mistakes. God did not overpower their minds and hands so that they ceased to be creative writers and became, instead, merely His secretaries. The work of inspiration was rather that of a gentle influence which guided their work as a whole and made sure that the total picture was not false or distorted and that nothing essential was omitted.

The Unity of the Bible

The Bible is divided into two parts, the Old and the New Testaments, and each part is essential for the Christian Faith. Sometimes one part has been overemphasized at the expense of the other. Some of our religious ancestors were inclined to depend too much upon the Old Testament and to slight the distinctive teaching of the New. Today, we are tempted to do the opposite and think of the Old Testament as merely a Jewish book which is not really necessary for Christians. There are those who set the Old Testament against the New as though it taught a dreadful kind of religion from which we have now been happily delivered. This is not the teaching of the New Testament itself nor has such a view ever been accepted by the Church.

According to the Christian view, the Bible is a single, organic whole which, though it is composed of many books by many authors, has a single story to tell. It is like a play in two great acts, neither of which can be understood without the other. If one read the Old Testament without going on to the New, he would miss the climax of the drama and the point of the whole story, since the New Testament contains the necessary conclusion of the story which the Old Testament starts out to tell. On the other hand, to read the New Testament without the Old would be like trying to understand the last chapter of a long novel without bothering to read the earlier part of the book, which sets the scene, introduces the characters, and describes the basic conflicts which are to be resolved.

The Background of Old Testament History

Since the chief danger today is a neglect of the Old Testament, it is necessary to set forth in somewhat fuller detail the reasons for including it among the things about which a Christian should know "to his soul's health." There are two directions in which an understanding of the Old Testament is especially required for an understanding of the New.

First of all one must know the general outline of Old Testament history in order to understand the historical situation which is pictured in the New Testament, and the allusions to that history which the New Testament writers make on nearly every page. Just as one could not hope to understand the American people without knowing in general what their history has been from the founding of the colonies down to the present, so one cannot hope to understand the Jews, from among whom Jesus came and to whom He addressed His message, unless one has some knowledge of the long history which formed their character and created their peculiar problems. From one point of view, the events related in the New Testament may really be considered the last chapters in the heroic story of ancient Israel. These events are the high point of that story: the one great goal toward which it had really been moving from the very first.

If we look at the Gospel of St. Matthew, we discover a striking example of this in the very first chapter. More than half the chapter is merely a list of names taken from the Old Testament, names which would be meaningless to a person unfamiliar with Old Testament history. It seems a dull way to begin a book, but the writer evidently felt that it was necessary right at the outset to show Jesus Christ in His proper place as the end and fulfilment of the whole long history which had gone before.

The other New Testament writers had a similar point of view. There is hardly a page of the New Testament that does not have something to say about the men or events of the Old. The Old Testament was the sacred book of Jesus and Paul and the other men of New Testament times, the only Bible they knew. They constantly make casual references to Abraham, Moses, David, and the prophets and do not trouble to explain these things in detail, because they rightly assumed that the people to whom they were speaking already had a thorough knowledge of the Old Testament story. For this reason, if for no other, we can hardly hope to understand their message unless we also know that story.

The Background of Old Testament Ideas

In addition to the general background of Old Testament history which the New Testament assumes that we know, there is also a great background of concepts, ideas, and attitudes with which the New Testament writers take it for granted that we are familiar. There are many subjects on which the New Testament has little to say, not because it is indifferent to them, but because it assumes that Christians already will be thoroughly acquainted with the thought of the Old Testament and will have absorbed such ideas there.

In the New Testament, for example, there is surprisingly little of what is called the doctrine of God. The New Testament assumes that the Christian will know what God is like from reading the Old Testament. There he will learn:

that God is personal
that He is the Creator
that He loves the world which He has created
that He has a plan for mankind
that He rules over the forces of history
that He demands justice and brotherhood among His children
that He punishes wickedness and rewards goodness
that He is a God who saves and redeems.

All these things must first be understood before we can understand the special features which the New Testament has to add to that general picture.

Even what is often regarded as the most characteristic New Testament idea about God, that He is a Father, is rooted in the Old Testament and is clearly suggested in the teaching of such prophets as Hosea, Jeremiah, and Malachi. What is remarkable in the New Testament is not the doctrine itself, but the new emphasis which is placed upon it.

To take another example, the New Testament has little to say about God's demands for justice and brotherhood in social relationships. This does not mean that the New Testament writers were not interested in such things, but that they took it for granted that their readers were already familiar with the pronouncements of the Hebrew prophets on this subject.

New Testament Essential to Understanding Old

Just as the Old Testament is necessary for understanding the New, so, for Christians, the New Testament gives the necessary key for understanding the Old. When one comes to the end of any story, things which were said or done in earlier episodes take on a depth of meaning which they did not have when the reader first encountered them. When one reads through any book a second time, if the book is worth reading, one sees an inner relationship between seemingly disconnected events and subtle shades of meaning in speeches made by the characters which one did not see at first reading. The story has a new logic and the meaning of particular events is illuminated by the new-found logic of the whole. When we, as Christians, use the Old Testament in our worship and in our meditation, there is hardly a passage in it which does not take on some new meaning because we know that God's perfect revelation in Christ is the end of the story. The great poetry of the Psalms, the work of the prophets, the tales of the heroes of Israel, the ethical ideas of Israel's teachers, all receive a new illumination when seen in the light of Christian experience. The Christian can never be content merely to interpret the Old Testament in the light of the times in which it was written. For him, it is a Christian book and its true significance is disclosed only when it is bound up in a single volume with the New Testament and interpreted in the light of the final and perfect revealing act of God which the New Testament describes. This inner and essential relationship between the two Testaments is what we mean by the unity of Bible.

The Old Testament: Preparation for the Gospel

The Old Testament may be defined, from a purely human and objective point of view, as the literature of ancient Israel. In one of the popular editions of the classics, the volumes containing the Old Testament are called Ancient Hebrew Literature. But even from this standpoint it differs from other collections of literature coming down from antiquity, since Israel was different from all other ancient peoples. The ancient Hebrews had a concern for God which sets them apart from the rest of the ancient world and their literature is marked by an almost exclusive preoccupation with religious ideas and behavior.

For Christian believers, this complete absorption of the writers of Israel in God and in His plan for man is something more than national or racial genius. It is evidence of the election (that is, the Divine Choice) of Israel to fulfil a high and unique destiny. When God began the great work of redeeming His Creation He chose for Himself, as the Bible says, "a peculiar people" who were to be His servants and messengers. However, as with any servants, there had to be a period of preparation, and the Old Testament is the story of this preparatory stage.

There were certain attitudes which the people of Israel had to acquire; certain ideas of God and Man which had to be deeply impressed upon them. Perhaps most important of all, they had to learn the profound meaning of human sin and man's inability to realize his great possibilities and to attain his deepest desires by his own efforts. So Old Testament history is largely the story of a deepening sense of national frustration and tragedy. Through the teaching of the great prophets the people of Israel were brought to understand the meaning of their own, and of all, tragedy. The spiritual leaders of the nation were brought to a point where they realized that the hope of man was not in himself, but in God. They came really to understand that, apart from God's willingness to aid and lift him out of the mire in which he is sunk, man's cause is hopeless.

The people of Israel were reminded constantly that God once had saved them out of the dark bondage of Egypt. Later they experienced a similar deliverance from the Babylonian exile. Those who understood the meaning of these things could never really doubt either God's power or His willingness to save. What God had done in the past, they were sure He would do again. So the Old Testament closes in a mood of eager expectation, a belief that God would soon intervene once more to save His people (Isaiah 60:1–3; Malachi 3:1). There were some even who saw that what was needed was not merely deliverance from external bondage, but from sin, which was the real root of their trouble (Psalm 130:8; Isaiah 53:4–5). This new great act of God, they believed, would be the last, for by it God would establish His eternal Kingdom (Daniel 7:27).

The New Testament begins just where the Old Testament leaves off. In the first chapter of the Gospel of St. Mark, the first of the gospels to be written, it says, *Jesus came into Galilee, preaching the gospel of the kingdom of God and saying, "The time is fulfilled, and the kingdom of God is at hand."* The Old Testament looks forward to a redemption yet to come; the New Testament looks back on a redemption already accomplished.

The Old Testament, then, is the story of the first long stage in the history of Israel, the people of God. In its first stage, Israel was a nation and membership in it was determined chiefly by the accident of birth. This was the only kind of spiritual community which could have been established under the conditions of the ancient Semitic world. With the beginning of the New Testament period, however, the old, national Israel had fulfilled its mission. Humanity was ready for a great new, creative movement in the drama of redemption. This did not mean that Israel was eliminated or that the idea of a holy nation was no longer important. It was still God's purpose to do His work through a spiritual community, a society, a brotherhood, which should be everywhere in the world, yet not of the world; a leaven which should gradually permeate the life of humanity. So out of the Old Israel and continuous with it, there grew the New Israel, the Christian Church. This body was no longer restricted in membership by requirements of race and nation, but was freely open to all: to Greek and Jew, to barbarian and Scythian, to slave and free citizen (Colossians 3:11).

In the New Testament and the history of the Church we continue to read the history of Israel, for the idea of the Church as the New Israel is basic to any understanding of what the Church claims to be. The Old Testament is not, therefore, just the history of some curious, ancient people who somehow provided the historical and physical environment in which our Lord and his apostles worked. It is our own history, the first chapter in the story of that great spiritual and redemptive movement which began with the Exodus from Egypt and which continues to the present day. We are a part of that movement.

The Apocrypha: a Necessary Link

Between the Old and New Testaments, many Bibles do, and all Bibles should, contain a section called The Apocrypha. These are books which appear only in the Greek version of the Old Testament, the Septuagint, and not in the Hebrew. They, therefore, were regarded by the Jews of Palestine as of inferior worth and not treated as a part of Holy Scripture.

The Christian Church has not been entirely agreed as to what the status of these books should be. Some, notably the Roman Catholics, regard them as fully canonical, while others reject them entirely. The position of the Episcopal Church (as expressed in the sixth of the Articles of Religion) is that they are good and useful books, which ought to be read, but which are not to be used to prove any point of doctrine. This is certainly a sane and reasonable point of view. While none of these books reaches the heights which the Old Testament reaches at its greatest, yet the Apocrypha contains fascinating and sometimes inspiring stories like those of Tobit and Judith, excellent moral and ethical literature like the Wisdom of Solomon, and important history such as First Maccabees. The Apocryphal literature is extremely important for helping to understand the historical and religious developments which took place between the Testaments.

The New Testament: Proclamation of the Gospel

Like the Old Testament, the New is a collection of writings of different types and of different degrees of interest and value. It is not a systematic treatise on Christian doctrine. It is a very much smaller book and less complex than the Old Testament; it covers a much smaller period of time, and contains a smaller variety of literary types.

Its books fall into four divisions: accounts of the life of Jesus (the Gospels), the early history of the apostolic Church (Acts), letters of St. Paul and other great figures of the apostolic age (the Epistles), and an apocalypse (Revelation). These books were not written originally with the intention of making them part of a new Christian scripture, since the Christian Church already had what it considered a sufficient scripture in the Old Testament. They were intended to meet the needs of particular times and places such, for example, as:

> The need to preserve in written form the life and teachings of Jesus when the age of the eye-witnesses began to draw to a close.
>
> The need to deal with situations which arose in the new churches which had been founded in Galatia, Corinth, Colossae, etc.
>
> The need to give some guidance for the crisis created by the beginning of persecution.

These writings were all intended for specific situations and can be understood properly only if those situations are kept in mind.

In the early ages of the Church, there were many such writings, but with the rise of heresy (false and dangerous beliefs), it became necessary to make a selection among them to safeguard the faith. The books now included in the New Testament were finally recognized by general agreement within the Church as safe and trustworthy accounts of the faith of Christian believers during the first generation. In this way, the Church eventually developed a body of Christian scriptures roughly parallel to the older scriptures. They were given the name New Testament since they describe the means by which God's New Covenant was established, and the way in which it was understood by the generation which stood closest to the events.

The books of the New Testament were written under the overruling influence of God's Holy Spirit and provide a reliable standard for Christian belief and practice. Once again it must be emphasized that we are not to interpret individual passages by themselves, torn out of their context, nor may we just select certain passages we like and ignore others. That which is important in the New Testament is not the beauty or historical accuracy of certain particular verses or chapters, but the whole faith to which the whole New Testament bears witness.

Underlying all the obvious differences in point of view in the different books, the New Testament bears unified witness to one great fact, that God the Son has completed the great work of revelation and redemption, and that men are saved only as they joyfully accept what God has done. This message is called the Gospel (Good News). While there always will be considerable discussion as to the value of this or that particular passage, or the historical factuality of some particular incident, there can be no doubt as to the nature of the faith which the whole New Testament affirms, nor need there be any doubt as to the correctness in all essential matters of the story which it tells.

The Devotional Use of the Bible

As we turn from considering these basic facts about the Bible and begin to study the Bible itself, it is important to remember that it is not merely a source of sacred history and of inspired ideas, for this would make it just a record of God's revelation in the past. This might lead us to think that the Word of God is a dead thing, something once spoken but now preserved in fossil form within the covers of a book. But God's Word is a living Word and Christian people have always believed that God makes use of the

Bible to speak directly to the heart and conscience of the individual in every age. The Bible is a sacramental thing by means of which God gives His Word to everyone who comes to it in a spirit of prayer and humility. For the Christian it is never enough to read the Bible as great literature or even as the record of dramatic and significant events of the past. He must also read the Bible in a devotional way, asking for the guidance of God's Holy Spirit and expecting that, from time to time, he will hear God speaking from its pages in words clearly addressed to his own needs. When we read the Bible in this fashion, it takes on a new meaning. It becomes a living, present-day revelation: God's word to us.

What Is the Church?

BY ROBERT MC AFEE BROWN

> *The Church is first and foremost a divine reality. This distinguishes it from all other realities.* . . . *For those who, by faith, affirm it and belong to it, it is the whole family of God in heaven and on earth, it is the work of God in the world.*—Professor J. Coert Rylaarsdam.

It is time to pull our lines together, and summarize ways in which the word "church" has been used by Christians.

The commonest definition is that the church is *a local congregation,* housed in a specific building. The church is the place you go to on Sunday, or the building you pass on Saturday (and perhaps on Sunday) on your way to the golf course. It has a minister, an organ, some bizarre windows, and a mortgage.

But it is also a place where people have been sustained in times of tragedy, where they have prayed to God and felt his presence, where they have gone to offer themselves up in service for others. The Church may be much more than a local gathering of people, but it must always be at least that. No "invisible" Church is worth talking about unless it receives concrete embodiment in a specific group of persons. The "local church" may be the despair of those with a great vision for the Church, but unless they identify themselves with it, they are spiritual parasites.

Others describe the Church as a *denomination.*

Robert McAfee Brown, *The Significance of the Church* (Philadelphia: Westminster Press, 1956. Copyright by W. L. Jenkins), pp 45–53. Used by permission.

Q: What Church do you belong to?

A: I am an Episcopalian (or Lutheran, or Presbyterian, or Two Seed in the Spirit Baptist).

There are creative aspects to denominational life; within Christendom the "wholeness" of the Church can be maintained through the varieties of denominational life. Thus, to risk some generalizations, Congregationalism witnesses to the importance of the "gathered community"; Episcopalianism witnesses to the significance of the sacramental life; Presbyterianism witnesses to the centrality of the Bible and the Word. It is only when a denomination claims to be the exclusive road to the Kingdom of God that denominationalism becomes an unmitigated evil. Paul's horror-struck question to the Corinthians, "Is Christ divided?" as they split into factions over allegiance to Paul and Apollos and Cephas, is a relevant question to people who split into factions over allegiance to Luther and Calvin and Hooker and even Mary Baker Eddy.

These are two tangible definitions of the Church. But there are more significant images and figures which can be drawn together in the lines of a hymn about the Church.

The Church as the "Body of Christ"

> The Church's one Foundation
> Is Jesus Christ her Lord;
> She is His new creation
> By water and the Word.

The Church is the continuator of the Messianic ministry of Jesus, called, like him, by service and suffering, to spread the Reign of God to the ends of the earth, till all men are reconciled to him through Christ.—*Archibald Hunter's interpretation of T. W. Manson's interpretation of Paul's interpretation of the Church.*

Now you are the body of Christ.

> —*Paul, speaking for himself.*

In authentic Christian thought there is no way of separating the realities "Christ" and "the Church." Christ does not just leave "changed individuals," he leaves a community, the Church. To think of Christ is necessarily to think of the Church; he is "the Church's one Foundation." Conversely, to think of the Church is necessarily to think of Christ; the Church is "his new creation." It rests on him, not on the whims of men. And the work of the Church today, however fractured and imperfect, is *his* work. Through it his purposes are carried out in the world.

This raises a question: Did Jesus mean to found a Church? Recent Biblical studies have re-established the close connection between Jesus and the Church. The famous bone of contention between Catholics and Protestants, Jesus' charge to Peter, "You are Peter, and on this rock I will build my church" (Matt. 16:18), is now accepted by many scholars as an authentic statement. Many claim that the "rock" is Peter's faith in Christ (Jesus' statement comes in response to Peter's declaration, "You are the Christ"). This means that faith in Christ is the foundation of the Church—a Protestant contention if there ever was one. Even if it is assumed that the "rock" is Peter himself, Protestants assert that this does not justify the Catholic contention that Peter's successors are Christ's vicars on earth to whom men must give allegiance. To the Catholic contention, *"Ubi Petrus ibi ecclesia"* (Where Peter—or his successor—is, there is the Church), the Protestant stoutly replies, *"Ubi Christus ibi ecclesia"* (Where Christ is, there is the Church).

The Church as the "Bride of Christ"

From heaven he came and sought her
To be His holy Bride.

The hymn now describes the Church as Christ's bride. The figure is infrequent in the New Testament, but it recurs often in the history of the Church. Feminine readers will not like the figure very much, because it is a symbol of obedience. Just as the wife was supposed to be obedient to the husband in Biblical times, so the Church is to be obedient to Christ, who is the "head of the household." The figure thus reminds us of the subservience of the

Church to her master. The Church acts in his name, not in her own; her message is of him, not of herself.

The Church as Dependent Upon the "Work" of Christ

With His own blood He bought her
And for her life He died.

The mention of "blood" strikes most modern readers as repulsive. And yet Christian faith asserts that in the death of Jesus something "happened" which affected the relationship of God and men. In order to demonstrate God's love, Christ was willing to die that men might know the extent of this love. Since he was killed by sinful men, we can say that in the crucifixion, men's sin and God's love were locked in mortal combat. And Christian faith, linking the cross with the resurrection, asserts that the powers of sin and death could not hold Christ captive, but that through him God overcame those powers. It is out of this triumph that the Christian Church was born.

Thus it is a sober reporting of the facts to say that Christ "bought" the Church with his blood (i.e., with his very "life") and that when he died he did so for "her life," so that the Church might exist to witness to the victorious God. Because of his death, the Church lives.

The Church as the "People of God"

Elect from every nation,
Yet one o'er all the earth,
Her charter of salvation
One Lord, one faith, one birth.

We have seen how God chose Israel as his special people, electing her to be "a light unto the Gentiles," and how the Early Christian Church felt herself the inheritor of this task and looked upon herself as the "new Israel" to evangelize all nations. We have seen how "her charter of salvation" is faith in one Lord, Jesus Christ. In a later chapter we shall discuss "one birth" (baptism).

It is true at all times that the Church is never "chosen" because

of her greatness, but simply because God loves her, in spite of her
brokenness, arrogance, and sin. The claim to be the "people of
God" leads, not to pride, but to repentance, and the promised
newness of life which can flow from God's mercy. This means
that the people of God must not only proclaim the good news, but
embody it in their own life. If God forgives them, they are to
forgive one another. If God loves them in spite of their unworthiness, then they are to "love the brethren" in spite of the brethren's
unworthiness. If God gives good gifts to them, then they are to
share those gifts with one another and all mankind. The people
of God must therefore always be a missionary people, an evangel-
izing people, seeking to engraft the gospel in the hearts of all men
and nations, that the God to whom they give allegiance may become the God to whom all men give allegiance.

The Church as a Sacramental Community

One holy Name she blesses,
Partakes one holy food.

"Protestants" often leave the sacramental side of the Church's
life to "Catholics" and assume that there is something suspicious
about the whole business. This is a betrayal of the Reformers, for
whom "partaking of one holy food" was the highest and most
joyful moment in the entire life of the Church.

The Church itself can be sacramental of the divine love poured
out for mankind, as it concerns itself in love with the lives of men.
It can be a place where the deep experiences of human life are
brought into the presence of God. The individual within the community who knows that he is forgiven by God may be more ready
to forgive his neighbor; and the one who, within the sacramental
fellowship, has been forgiven by his neighbor, may find in that a
deeper knowledge of what God's forgiveness is. The joining of two
people in marriage is given a sacramental character as it is blessed
by the Church, under God. The fact of death is seen in the light
of God and the assurance of "the life everlasting." All the high

moments of life can become "windows to eternity," or sacraments, as they are related to the life of the Church.

The Church as a Foretaste of the Kingdom of God

And to one hope she presses,
With every grace endued.

ᘒ

In Protestant churches
There's been a dearth
Of living as "strangers
And pilgrims on earth."

—*Saint Hereticus.*

And it's a great loss. For the Church should look forward to the consummation of "one hope." It should be a "pilgrim people," a band that is on the march, its face set toward the coming Kingdom of God, not as something that will be "built" by muscular Christians, but as a gift that God will give in his own good time. Christians live as "strangers and pilgrims on earth." They look "forward to the city which has foundations, whose builder and maker is God." They have not received what was promised, "but having seen it and greeted it from afar," they "make it clear that they are seeking a homeland." (See Heb., ch. 11.)

To borrow a phrase from Paul, they are "a colony of heaven" (Moffatt). A colony exists far away from the homeland, but the members give allegiance not just to the colony, but chiefly to the homeland. And the church as a "colony of heaven" is thus a foretaste or "earnest" of what is one day to be true for all.

This sounds strange, and yet this is the dimension of the Church's life that distinguishes it from all other groups. Christians are reminded at the Lord's Supper that they show forth the Lord's death "till he come." "The return of Christ" is a difficult symbol in any case, but at least it stands for the fact that history —and the life of the Church—moves toward *him,* rather than toward chaos or the devil. The Church then must live expectantly, waiting in hope and promise for God's activity in history. It lives between the time when God appeared in Christ and the time when all things shall be in subjection unto him.

The Church as the Communion of Saints

Yet she on earth hath union
With God the Three in One,
And mystic sweet communion
With those whose rest is won.

O God, our heavenly Father, who hast given us the blessed assurance that the dead as well as the living are in Thy care; we give Thee thanks for all dear and loved ones who have passed away from our earthly fellowship. *Keep us, with them, in the everlasting fellowship of Thy Church,* and bring us at last, cleansed and purified, to the glory and beauty of Thine eternal presence; through Jesus Christ our Lord. Amen.—*A prayer from the Book of Common Order of the Church of Scotland.*

Here is another emphasis for Protestants to recover. The "communion of saints" is the ultimate expression of the *koinonia* we talked about in an earlier chapter. It has two significant dimensions.

It refers to the fellowship of Christians in all places where the Christian community exists. When you break bread at the Lord's Table in Omaha, you are in communion with Christians in Chartres, Bangalore, and even Kansas City. The partitions, the divisions, are broken down. And the communion of saints is very real for those who pray together, who engage in acts of love and service for one another, and who share deep sorrow and deep joy.

Yet there is a further dimension to the communion of saints, for Christians claim to be in a communion that transcends time. In their intermittent worship on earth they join in the unending life of praise which the redeemed in heaven offer to God. They unite "with angels and archangels and *all the company of heaven*" in uttering the praises of God. In prayer, Christians come close to God and to all who are close to God, whether alive or not. Those who have died do not "leave the Church" but become those in the Church who have an unclouded vision of the God who is God both of the dead and of the living.

This cannot be described in cold type or even in warm prose. But it can be a part of the experience of any of the people of God. Those who have passed through "the valley of the shadow of death" themselves will know it best.

What Is Man?

BY GEORGIA HARKNESS

The poet who wrote the eighth psalm, overwhelmed by the greatness of the physical universe and his own littleness in it, cried out to God:

> When I consider thy heavens, the work of thy fingers,
> The moon and the stars, which thou hast ordained;
> What is man, that thou art mindful of him?

Had he known what we know of astronomical space and island universes millions of light-years away, which the great telescopes reveal, he might have been all the more impressed with man's insignificance. He found the answer to his question and put it in the next words:

> For thou hast made him but little lower than God,
> And crownest him with glory and honor.
> Thou makest him to have dominion over the work of thy hands;
> Thou hast put all things under his feet.

Our problem is, Can we still say this of man? Not only has astronomy greatly enlarged our view of the physical world in which man seems but a tiny midget, but the mutual slaughter of millions of men has greatly deflated our confidence in man's ability to master himself or the world. Yet it is basic to Christian faith to see in man dignity, greatness, and kinship to God.

The reason why it is not easy to say clearly just what man is, is the fact that when one begins to describe one aspect of man's

Georgia Harkness, *Understanding the Christian Faith* (Nashville: Abingdon Press, 1947), pp. 92–105. Used by permission.

nature, another apparently contradictory but equally real aspect presents itself. Then unless both sides are included, the description becomes not only fragmentary but false. The Christian understanding of man can best be stated in four of these paradoxes:

> Man is both nature and spirit.
> Man is both free and bound.
> Man is both child of God and sinner.
> Man is both transient and eternal.

We shall attempt in this chapter to suggest the meaning of the first three.

Man as Nature and Spirit

To say that man is nature is simply to say what few people have ever denied—that we each have a body. This body is composed of physical and chemical elements, very intricately related. It has much in common with the bodies of the higher animals, and has a long biological past. Each human body is marvelously equipped with organs of sensation, muscular movement, digestion, circulation, respiration, reproduction, self-repair of injury, and other functions that we seldom think about unless they get out of order. The human body takes longer to mature than the bodies of most of the lower animals, and it will endure an amazing amount of strain, but it wears out in seventy or eighty years.

If we ask whether our bodies are the product of nature or of God, it is a false alternative, for everything in nature is the handiwork of God. That God has been fashioning the human organism through billions of years of creative labor should not make us think less, but more, highly of it. And the more one learns through biology or physiology of the way it is put together to serve our need, the more we can say with the psalmist:

> I will give thanks unto thee; for I am fearfully and wonderfully made:
> Wonderful are thy works;
> And that my soul knoweth right well.

But is the body all? Christian faith affirms vigorously that it is not. In the majestic epic of creation with which Genesis begins, there are three key sentences: "In the beginning God created . . . And God saw that it was good . . . And God created man in his own image, in the image of God created he him." This conviction that man is a living soul made in the divine image is central to our understanding of ourselves and our fellow man. Let us add to this witness from the Old Testament, Jesus' unvarying estimate of the worth of every human soul as a child of God—however weak, sinful, or outcast by men one might be—and we have the foundations of the Christian view of man and his destiny.

The term "soul" has gone out of fashion in many quarters, particularly among psychologists. This is not wholly loss, for it is inaccurate to speak of the soul as a third thing about us that is not mind or body—a mysterious something that cannot be discovered or defined. Nevertheless, when the soul is understood as spirit, or as mind or consciousness in the broadest sense, it means something very real. Perhaps the best way to get at what it means is to think of the difference between the human spirit and all lower forms of animal life. A man can weigh moral issues and make moral decisions, can strive after truth and beauty, can learn from the past experience of the human race and project his aspirations into the long future, can form fellowships with other men for mutual enrichment, can worship God and come into fellowship with him. These capacities make of man a "living soul" in a sense not shared by any other creature, and justify us in assuming with the author of Genesis that man is God's supreme creation made in the divine image.

Man as Free and Bound

If we undertake to select one attribute which above all distinguishes human personality from animal life and from the world of physical nature, it is man's freedom. If we glance again at the characteristics named above which make him a soul, we see it

is only because man has some freedom of choice that he can decide between good and evil, employ his intelligence to discover
truth, become sensitive to beauty, appropriate meanings from
the past or project them as goals into the future, increase the
values in a society, or come into conscious fellowship with God.
God might have chosen to make us automatic puppets or mechanically determined robots, but he chose to make us men with
freedom to achieve or mar our destinies.

Freedom is God's supreme gift, though with it comes inevitably
the possibility of misuse. Without freedom there would be no sin,
for "sin lies at the juncture of nature and spirit." Without freedom we should have no responsibility for ignorance or error.
But without freedom we should be human machines instead of
sons of God. It is freedom that makes us moral beings bearing
the divine image.

Nevertheless, we are never wholly free, and it is as serious a
mistake to overlook our limitations as to deny the fact of our
freedom. Our heredity, our social environment, and our own previous experience have set for us certain paths that are easier to
follow than others, though in normal persons the grooves are seldom so fixed that we cannot possibly get out of them. Our bodies,
useful servants that they are, are subject to fatigue and disease;
they have to be fed and clothed; they will not do all that in our
more ambitious moments we ask of them. We live in a physical
world which in its basic order cannot be changed, and which in
the arrangement of its parts is subject—but never wholly so—to
control by human wills. We live in a society of which many aspects
—but not every aspect at once—can be altered. On any project
we work at, whether it is getting a meal, reading a book, driving a
car, controlling the use of atomic energy, or making world peace,
human freedom can be exercised effectively only when our limitations, as well as the possibilities open to us, are taken into account.

Some of these limiting factors are established by God in the
creation of the world. Such things as gravitation in the physical

world, the eventual death of a living organism, the inevitable collapse of a society built on hate and greed, are elements in the way things are made. We had better accept them, for protest will not change them. Others, such as preventable disease, ignorance, poverty, strife, and all manner of social evils, are man-made limitations and by a right use of human freedom can be removed. A large part of what is meant by the coming of God's Kingdom on earth is the lifting of such limitations so that all men, as God's sons, may be free.

Man as Child of God

This brings us to the third great paradox. Man is the child of God, as Jesus taught us to regard him. Otherwise the words "Our Father" would be meaningless. Man is of infinite worth as God's child. But man also is a sinner. Which note shall we put uppermost?

It is essential that we keep a right balance in our judgment of man's nature. Religious humanism and the more extreme forms of liberalism have sometimes made so much of man's power and self-sufficiency that God almost vanished from the picture. Or, if God did not disappear, the difference between God and man became so slight that humility about our status tended to disappear. In contrast with this assumption of the divineness of human nature, the new orthodoxy puts its emphasis on the difference between God and man, and on the sinfulness which always and everywhere corrupts human nature. There is truth in both these positions, and error in both if carried to extremes. We must never forget that it is God who has made us, and not we ourselves; that our lives are in his keeping; that the only appropriate attitude for the Christian is humble worship of God and dependence on our Creator.

Sinners we are, and sinners we remain save for the unmerited, forgiving mercy of God. Nevertheless, we are children of God, and *all* men are his children—made in his image with the stamp of divinity upon their souls.

To hold this belief about man is vital to our Christian outlook and action. Upon it hinge many issues. Take, for example, democracy. Whatever the political system, there can be no real democracy except that which is founded on the conviction that all human beings, of whatever race, or color, or class, or sex, are of supreme worth in God's sight and ought therefore to be treated as persons. This conviction is the only real leverage by which to combat race prejudice, economic exploitation, mass unemployment, forced labor, or other forms of slavery. Only on the basis of the equality and inherent worth of men and women, adults and children, old persons and young, can family fellowship exist. Not until this principle is extended to include the persons of all nations in the family of God, great nations and small, white and colored, victor and vanquished, shall we have an international order founded on the ideal of justice for all—and without this foundation we shall not have peace.

Within our churches our programs of missions, religious education, evangelism and most of the other activities would be meaningless except for the conviction that all persons are precious to God and are at the same time in need of salvation and capable of being brought to new life in Christ. When Paul wrote, "There is neither Jew nor Greek, there is neither bond nor free, there is neither male nor female: for ye are all one in Christ Jesus," he uttered truth of far-reaching consequences.

If this is true of our basic human relations, what man thinks of himself is equally important to personal living. The undermining of a sense of meaning and destiny for one's life is one of the most serious aspects of our contemporary scene. From it has come much cynicism, despair, and loss of nerve. Whatever happens, one ought to live with courage, dignity, and hope. One can so live if he thinks of himself as a child of God and, in spite of tragic sin and folly, knows himself to be the object of God's continuing love and care. Lacking this conviction, one is apt to find his stamina slipping and inner resources crumbling before the avalanche of misery that has engulfed our time. Only the union of humility with an awareness of human dignity that is not of our own making but the gift of God, can enable us to transform confusion and chaos into "a time for greatness."

Man as Sinner

But not only is it necessary to preserve a sense of man's dignity as God's child; it is equally, and perhaps even more, necessary to see all men including ourselves as sinners. What, then, do we mean by sin? [1]

There is no single definition of sin, and no list of sins that could be drawn up would be complete. What is ordinarily thought of as sin, such as lying, stealing, drinking, gambling, may be sinful; but to name such practices does not get anywhere near to the heart of the trouble. That opinions of Christians differ as to the sinfulness of such recreations as card playing and dancing shows the need of something that goes much deeper than the practice itself if we are to judge what is sinful.

In the first place, any act or attitude that is sinful runs counter to the nature of God and the righteous will of God. This is the truth that lies in the often distorted doctrine of human depravity. When we measure even our best acts and aspirations by the standard of God's holy will as revealed in Christ, we all have sinned and come short of the glory of God. The eclipse of the concept of sin during the brief ascendancy of humanistic liberalism was a direct outgrowth of our failure to take seriously God's holiness and the rigor of his moral demands. When man becomes the measure of all things, we talk of "cultural lags" and "antisocial behavior." When God is restored to his rightful place of primacy in human thought, sin, our ancient enemy, again is seen to be our ever-present and most malignant foe.

In the second place, any sin, whether of overt act or inner attitude, presupposes freedom to do or to be otherwise. To the extent that a person really does what he must do or is what he must

---

[1] Several paragraphs in this section are reprinted from the chapter entitled "The Burden of Our Sin" in *The Dark Night of the Soul.*

be, *and cannot help himself,* to that extent he is victim and not sinner. As nobody is wholly free, so nobody is wholly depraved. But the other side of this comforting truth is that one rarely, if ever, is wholly helpless and therefore free from guilt. In almost every situation there is freedom enough left to do better than one does. Certainly if we view life, not as separate incidents, but as a whole, nobody ever reaches the upper limits of his freedom. In those large areas of choice which God has given us but within which we do not choose according to his will, we sin and stand under his righteous judgment.

In the third place, sin presupposes a knowledge of good and evil adequate to form a basis of choice. According to the ancient but wonderfully meaningful story of the Fall, there was no sin in Eden until our first parents, discontented with their human lot and desiring to be "as God," ate from the tree of knowledge of good and evil. Such knowledge is at once our bond of kinship with divinity and our undoing. The demand of our faith is not ignorance, but humble dedication of such knowledge as we have to God and action by it in accordance with his will.

And in the fourth place, sin, according to the Christian frame of thought, involves at the same time relation to our neighbor and to God. As the Christian requirement of love links love of God and love of neighbor in a twofold Great Commandment from which neither element can be dropped, so sin against neighbor through lack of human love is sin against God. The distinctive character of Jesus' ethics lies in the fact that for him religion and morals were all of one piece. To do the will of his Father and to serve those in need were for him not two requirements but one, a supremely costly but supremely joyous adventure in self-giving love.

When these four requirements are put together, at least the outlines of the meaning of sin become clear. There is a sinful state of pride and rebellion against God from which not even the most saintly soul is wholly clear. There are sinful attitudes and acts, such as anger, avarice, lust, killing, stealing, adultery, in which a person free enough so that he could feel and do otherwise chooses to obey evil impulses instead of good. There are sins of omission that arise, not so much from positive sinful impulses as from something that may be even more serious because more subtle—from indifference; from moral dullness, laziness, and flabbiness; from lethargy and complacency where we ought to be sensitive to the needs and feelings of others; from ignorance at points where we could know what we ought to do if we took pains to try to know.

There are also what are usually called social sins, such as race prejudice, economic injustice, tyranny, persecution, and war. In such situations one may not feel like much of a sinner, for the sin is so commonly practiced and its effects so spread out that one's sense of guilt is dulled. Nevertheless, the consequences of such sins are often far more serious than of private and more easily recognized sins, for the effects are multiplied manyfold in complex social relations. Actually no clear distinction can be drawn between individual and social sins, for every sin proceeds from the attitude of an individual, and every sin in its consequences affects somebody else besides the sinner.

All sin roots in self-love, in preferring to have our own way when we ought to love God and our neighbor. Everybody knows what this means—or ought to, for we all do it! The moral life even for the best of men is a continual struggle against selfishness. This simple but serious fact throws light on some otherwise difficult theological ideas.

There is born in all of us, not "original sin" as a hereditary corruption passed on from Adam's guilt, but a biological tendency to self-centeredness. This is as natural and unsinful in little children as is the impulse to eat or sleep or cry from discomfort. It is a useful endowment, not only for self-preservation, but for the growth of personality through the relating of all experience to the self. But such self-centeredness, though very necessary, is very dangerous, and in adult life easily passes over into willful selfishness. If uncurbed, it becomes the self-love which is the root of all other sins and of most of our unhappiness.

The forms such self-love takes, in the ordinary events of living, are manifold. It shows itself in desire to have our own way regardless of the wishes or rights or needs of others; in the narrowing of interests to what immediately touches us; in thirst for personal recognition, compliments, and applause; in eagerness in conversation or action always to occupy the center of the stage; in jealousy of others who secure recognition or privileges or goods we want; in self-pity; in peevishness and petty complaint when things do not go as we would have them. These are, at best, unlovely traits when we see them in others. As indications that we love ourselves more than we love our neighbor or our Lord, they are evidences of sin so life strangling that God alone can give release.

So firmly do the chains of self-centeredness enmesh us that we cannot by will power break their hold. Whether selfishness takes the form of callous indifference or of positive self-seeking, being ashamed of it will not release us. Shame may be a step toward repentance, but it cannot of itself deliver us and may serve only to increase our despair. This is the way Paul felt about it when he exclaimed:

> The good which I would I do not: but the evil which I would not, that I practise. . . . I find then the law, that, to me who would do good, evil is present. For I delight in the law of God after the inward man: but I see a different law in my members, warring against the law of my mind, and bringing me into captivity under the law of sin which is in my members. Wretched man that I am! who shall deliver me out of the body of this death? [2]

God alone can save us. But can God? Only if we yield our wills to him and in repentance and faith lay hold upon his forgiveness. If we do not, our self-love is "unpardonable," not because God does not desire to pardon us, but because we do not make the commitment of faith which alone opens the way to his forgiving mercy. God cannot meet us if we block the path. The "sin of

---

[2] Romans 7:19–24.

unbelief" is no theoretical rejection of God's existence; it is the deadlier atheism of preferring our way to his, of choosing to live by our own desires and standards to the rejection of his righteous will. If persisted in, it means the death of our higher life and of all that is potentially best within us.

God gives release. When Paul asked the question, "Who shall deliver me from the body of this death?" he answered it in his next words, "I thank God through Jesus Christ our Lord." By the beginning of the next chapter he was saying: "There is therefore now no condemnation to them that are in Christ Jesus. For the law of the Spirit of life in Christ Jesus made me free from the law of sin and death." [3] And at the end of the chapter he pours out his spirit in one of the most glorious paeans of victory in all literature: "Who shall separate us from the love of Christ? shall tribulation, or anguish, or persecution, or famine, or nakedness, or peril, or sword? . . . Nay, in all these things we are more than conquerors through him that loved us." [4]

---

[3] Romans 8:1–2.
[4] Romans 8:35–37.

2. PEOPLE GROW AND CHANGE

BASIC TRUTH remains the same, though there is always more truth to be discovered and our incomplete understandings of truth may at any time be replaced by fuller and better understandings. But people change. In body, mind, and spirit they change. In skills and abilities, wants and needs, they change. Week by week and year by year they change. The degree of truth they can understand changes as they grow. The way in which they grasp truth and make use of it varies from childhood to youth to adulthood.

The church group leader deals both with truth that is unchanging and with people who change continually. He must understand both. The same God is Father to the youngest child and to the oldest adult. But there is a vast difference between their understandings of God and their ways of responding to God. Therefore church work with children is vastly different from church work with adults. It is obvious that the church group leader who would contribute to Christian nurture must know the age group with which he works.

He should understand other ages too. He should know the experiences which members of his group had in previous classes and departments. He should also know the experiences they will have in years to come. He must help them build foundations for those later years. Furthermore, no group stands by itself, alone. Each group needs to know the feelings and work of other groups if they are to be mutually supporting parts of the Body of Christ.

The first five readings present basic information which will help a church group leader understand the children, youth, or adults with whom he works. The developmental charts which conclude the chapter give specific information about each age group. Charts of this type have at least two values. They summarize the results of much research and study. They help us to see a particular age group in relation to the groups that precede and follow it. They also have at least one limitation. They lose the individual in the "average." There is no such person as an "average" five-year-old or an "average" adolescent. Any person is above or below average in many respects. He is not necessarily superior or inferior, however, just because he happens to deviate from the norm given on a chart.

Children Are Not Small Adults

BY JENKINS, SHACTER, AND BAUER

Children are not small adults. They do not think, feel, or react as grown-up people do. Physically, mentally, and emotionally each child is a growing, changing person with needs and potentialities which are his alone.

Often the child who is difficult, whose behavior is not desirable, who is labeled "naughty" or "badly behaved," is only a child who has not been understood by the adults about him. Sometimes they have pushed him too hard and expected too much from him; sometimes they have not known enough about boys and girls to realize that he is acting like other children of his age, that he is not deliberately naughty, but is having "growing pains" and trying to assert himself as a person. The first responsibility of parents and teachers who sincerely want to help a child grow to his fullest capacity is to try to understand all children's needs and patterns of growth, and particularly those of their own children.

Sometimes we think of a newborn baby as a completed individual, as though all he has to do is grow up. This is not so. A baby brings with him the potentialities for completed development, but at birth even his heart, lungs, and digestive tract do not function as they will when he is older. The nerves, which are the pathways from his brain to his muscles and the contact for sense impressions from the outside world, are not yet completed in their development. The skeletal development of the child is different

Gladys Gardner Jenkins, Helen Shacter, and William W. Bauer, *These Are Your Children* (Chicago: Scott, Foresman and Co., copyright, 1949), pp. 10–17. Used by permission.

from that of the adult. He has to do much growing and continued developing before he becomes a "grown-up."

At each stage, the behavior of a child is directly influenced by his physical development. The active fifteen-month-old child who touches, feels, and puts in his mouth everything about him is responding to a growth need, not just being a nuisance and "in to everything." The restless six-year-old finds it difficult to sit still because of his tremendous drive toward activity. The child who is passing through the growth spurt of preadolescence may be awkward and trip or drop things, not from carelessness, but because of the uneven growth of his body. We need to know the general stages of development through which our children are passing if we are to understand their behavior.

It is essential also to know the individual child, to understand his heritage, his potentialities, and his own particular pattern of growth. Although normal children are essentially similar in their sequence of growth, no two children, even in the same family, are alike in the way in which they pass through this sequence. Some meet life with eagerness, head on; others are more phlegmatic, less easily excited. Some are easily guided from birth; others seem full of an independent aggressiveness from an early age. Some have great vigor and vitality; others seem to have less stamina, less ability to meet whatever comes. It is difficult to distinguish between environmental factors and tendencies with which the child was born, but whatever their source, there are sharp individual differences in make-up which cannot be overlooked.

Within the range of "normal" some children will develop physically much more rapidly than others, some much more slowly. Yet in the total progress of growth each child will reach normal adulthood. In every group there will be some children ahead of the others of their age physically, mentally, and emotionally, and some who are behind in one or all aspects of development. It is important in understanding the child to know the individual rate of development—is this child a fast-maturing child or a slow one?

The faster-maturing child may need opportunities to go ahead of his age group. The slower one may need to be watched for fear he will be pushed too hard or overstimulated in an effort to keep him with the majority of his age group. We are usually aware of the need for the mentally retarded child to be allowed to take things at a different pace from his age group. We are not always so keenly aware of such special needs among children in the normal group who merely mature slowly.

Nor do children always grow evenly in all aspects of their development. Some children seem to grow more smoothly than others, so that at any given age they are mentally, emotionally, and physically at an equal level. There are indications that these children may have less difficulty in growing up and show fewer behavior problems than those who grow rapidly in one area and more slowly in another. A child may develop rapidly mentally so that he seems ahead of his actual age group, but at the same time may be immature in his social growth. It would not be fair to judge such a child by one area in which he is advanced, and scold him for not living up to the same level in all his activity. We must know all sides of a child's development if we are to understand him and meet his needs.

Growth does not always go smoothly ahead. It is always continuous, but it is not always steady. Sometimes there will be weeks or even months during which the child seems to stand still in his development. At other times the child may even seem to go backwards; he may not seem as independent today as he did last month. Sometimes these slowing-up periods come before a new spurt in growth. There is a pause in growth, for instance, before the growth spurt which marks the beginning of the adolescent period. In order to get a true picture of the growth of the child we should not look at the immediate present, comparing this week with last week, or today with yesterday, but take the long view— look back six months or a year or two years and observe the growth which has steadily taken place. The nine-year-old may baffle adults with his bad language and his untidy appearance, but he knows more about truthfulness and honesty than he did at six or even seven; he is more cooperative in his work and play, and he is more self-reliant.

Numerous clinics and research centers have contributed to our understanding of the normal stages of child development. One of the best known is at Yale, under the leadership of Dr. Arnold Gesell. The insight and understanding which he has brought to us concerning developmental growth is both helpful and significant. His books *The Infant and Child in the Culture of Today* and *The Child from Five to Ten* are recommended to all thoughtful parents and teachers who would further their insight and understanding.

Among the other centers adding to our knowledge of children, their needs and their development, are the Institute of Child Welfare at the University of California; the Experimental School at the University of Michigan; the Child Welfare Research Station at the University of Iowa; the Institute of Child Welfare at the University of Minnesota; the Merrill Palmer School, Detroit; the Brush Foundation at Western Reserve University; and the Fels Foundation at Antioch College. Most of the studies which have been undertaken by these and other research centers follow two types of patterns: "cross-sectional" studies and "longitudinal" studies. "Cross-sectional" studies involve comparing and studying large groups of children and isolating those characteristics which seem to appear almost always at certain age levels. The "longitudinal" studies are those which follow individual children over a period of years, so that their patterns of growth are charted, and certain patterns of growth are observed. Both types of study have made valuable contributions to our understanding and knowledge.

Another approach to the understanding of children's development and problems is that of the psychiatrists, clinical psychologists, and social workers. They are concerned not so much with what behavior to expect as with why these reactions occur, and why growth is sometimes slowed up in a child, not from any factors in his own make-up, but from environmental causes. Thus they add to our understanding of both normal emotional growth patterns and unhealthy ones. They work both with children who have problems and with parents who need help in guiding their children.

From the many specialized workers in this field has come valuable information on how children feel, on their relationships with their parents, with brothers and sisters, with teachers, and with children of their own age. From case studies of individual children there has come to us a body of material more subjective and less easily measured than that which has come from the laboratories of child development, but of great importance in understanding the point of view and the reactions of our boys and girls. This material has been gathered through interviews between the worker and the child in which the child has been helped to talk of his feelings, his memories, and his reactions to the experiences of his life. From such revelations we have been given greater understanding of the basic needs of children and of the manner in which tensions and anxieties can temporarily block growth or distort it.

Among the outstanding child-guidance clinics of the country are the Judge Baker Foundation of Boston, which was established under the direction of William Healy; the Philadelphia Child Guidance Clinic, under Dr. Frederick Allen; and the Institute for Juvenile Research in Chicago, the first and oldest clinic of this type in the country. Dr. David Levy of New York and Anna Freud and Susan Isaacs of England have made significant individual contributions, as have Dr. C. A. Aldrich and Dr. Benjamin Spock of Mayo Clinics, and Dr. Fritz Redl of Wayne University.

We need both types of understanding—the one to give to us the general pattern of development and the individual variations within that pattern, and the other to help us understand the emotional life of the child and the interplay between this life and the growth process.

If a child's growth seems to differ greatly from that of most children of his age, it is wise to pause and look for the reasons. Children cannot be made to grow, but growth can be encouraged by good physical and emotional care. Growth itself comes from an inner force and is inevitable. The child will grow in some measure and in some fashion whatever care is provided for him, but he may not fulfill his growth possibilities unless he receives adequate care. He will grow best if his home and school provide an environment of affection, in which he can feel that he belongs, that he is loved and needed. A child needs to feel that the adults about him like him and are interested in him. If this feeling is lacking and if the child feels unwanted or unloved, growth may be retarded.

The child needs good physical care, for we know that a fatigued child, a poorly nourished child, or a physically ill child cannot develop as fully as he might otherwise. Good food, fresh air, protection from disease, the correction of physical defects, plenty of exercise and outdoor play, balanced by relaxation and rest—all these are essential for the best development of a child's personality.

The child also needs opportunities to reach ahead, to take the next step, the right amount and kind of stimulation at the right time. He cannot learn either reading or independence until he has reached a stage in his growth at which he is ready to learn these things. If he is pushed ahead too soon, if too much is expected of him before he is ready, the discouragement may react against growth instead of helping it. On the other hand the child may be slowed up in his growth if his parents or teachers do not recognize when he has reached a point of readiness for the next step. If the child is kept dependent when he has shown a desire to be independent, he may either rebel and take the independent step himself, or hold back and lose interest. The little child who reaches for his spoon shows a readiness to take a first step toward independence from Mother in feeding himself. If Mother will not give him the spoon because he is "messy" in using it, the child may later refuse to feed himself when Mother decides he is ready to do so. If a child is ready for the next step in arithmetic, and is kept back until the slowest member of the class is ready, he may lose interest in trying to take the next step, and fool away his time.

Growth is influenced by many environmental factors. Sometimes the child may be experiencing too much competition with older brothers or sisters, so that he is discouraged at the comparisons and ceases to try to compete. Sometimes there is a new baby in the family, and the child is feeling the burden of being the oldest or is feeling a bit less loved. Sometimes, by even well-meaning parents or teachers, he has been criticized and scolded for his mistakes and failures, without enough balancing praise for his successes. If a child is tense, anxious, unhappy, out of harmony with his parents or his environment, his growth will not proceed as fully or as well as if he were emotionally secure and happy.

In the following sections we have tried to give to parents and teachers pictures of normal children as they grow from year to year and go from kindergarten through the elementary school. This is a guide to help you know what to expect of your children from year to year, what their needs will be, so that you may be ready to meet them. Through case studies we have attempted to suggest the variations within the pattern, the problems of the individual child, or the interactions between the child and others around him. We have tried to bring an awareness of the individual differences between children, differences in environment, background, endowment, and emotional needs. Alert teachers and parents will always keep the individual child foremost in their minds, seeing him against the background of the normal developmental picture. Sometimes if the child seems very far from this picture, both teachers and parents will feel the need to use the resources of their community or state to help the child adjust and work through his problems. We need to be aware that some problems are due to a particular phase of development and that others have a serious emotional basis. The nine-year-old boy who is noisy and untidy may just be trying to show his independence, to be like the other fellows; but the boy who is aggressive to the point of being unable to get along with other children, or the boy who withdraws into himself and cannot make friends, is in need of special help.

As a child enters kindergarten, then, we need to be aware that he is still growing, developing, and maturing and that as he changes from year to year, his needs and potentialities will change too. He is *not* merely an adult in miniature.

Much of the behavior that is typical of normal children is exasperating and irritating to adults. We object to the six-year-old's being quite so noisy and boisterous, and we wish he wouldn't fidget so. And when our preadolescent loses all the good habits of orderliness and cooperation that we have worked so hard to build up, we find it very discouraging. But if we can learn what may legitimately be expected, we will save ourselves and our children much unnecessary heartache and bewilderment. We will not make the mistake of regarding as wrong or abnormal, behavior that is perfectly normal for the child's age and level of development. If, in addition, we study the special needs and growth patterns of the individual child, we can help guide his development against the background of our knowledge of the whole sequence of growth. We cannot make children grow, but we can understand their growth needs and cooperate with growth.

What Three-Year-Olds Are Like

BY PHOEBE M. ANDERSON

Careful observation of a group of three-year-olds for an hour on Sunday morning reveals not only a great deal about this age in general; but it also is the best way to come to know one child in particular. By observing a group of children we can see the wide variations in motor skills, intellectual understanding, emotional maturity, social awareness, and development of religious personality. We also can see, over a period of time, the specific development in these areas of any particular child. As teachers, we need to know our children. Yet we often find ourselves so busy with the program for the day that *we fail to observe the children* with keenness and understanding.

Let us look for a moment at some of the characteristics of three-year-old children, both as a group and as individuals, that Alice Todd observed and pondered over as she wrote of the children in her journal.

> The general tone of happiness in the hall indicates that the children enjoy the church experience and are glad to be here again. I suppose three-year-olds generally enjoy being with other three-year-olds even if they actually do very little together. I wonder what "church" means to each of these children? To Ronnie is it a sports car; to Katie, a dish cupboard that always needs putting in order; to Carol, a picture file; to Leslie and Shelley, smooth building blocks; to Charles, dry clothes? These are the things the children might tell their parents about their church. But I think their happy feelings on the inside spring from ex-

Phoebe M. Anderson, *Religious Living with Nursery Children* (Boston: The Pilgrim Press, copyright, 1956), pp. 8–15. Used by permission.

81

periences they can't tell about. The words would be too hard to find, words for feeling glad about growing into a too-big dress, feeling secure and able to be alone without mother, discovering that it's fun to do things with other children, feeling relieved to find that "accidents" are acceptable.

Almost every child can recognize "his" picture identifying the hook for his clothes and can remember it from week to week. What other things can a child remember for a week? Songs? Stories? Or must he be personally involved in the experience in order to remember it . . . like planting the seed himself instead of hearing about seeds. In my teaching, am I counting too much on what the children remember as a measure of what they learn?

What ideas do the children have about money and its importance? . . . I'm thinking about Mrs. Ray's remark to Alan not to lose his money. Should I be doing something with the money the children bring besides turning it over to the church school treasurer? What should it be?

There is considerable difference among nursery children in how they enter a group. Katie and Carol needed emotional support; Ronnie probably knew he was going to play with the sports car as soon as he entered the door; Jimmy began in the quiet part of the room where the books and puzzles were. Are these children growing in their feeling of security in the group? How much time does Katie spend in her little corner by the dish cupboard? What else does Ronnie do besides run his favorite car? What are the other children doing? *I must pay more attention.*

These children grow fast. Katie's too-big dress and Betsy's too-short one betray the same characteristic. They have heard about how big they are growing, which probably accounts for the interest in the growing story and for Henry's remark at the end. I wonder if any of the children is concerned about how big he or she is?

Much of the play is a clear imitation of the adult activity which they see and understand. Most of this play centers around the mother's activity at home. With what part of their fathers' lives can—or do—these boys identify? Do they play men's roles from firsthand experience or from make-believe and story material? They knew some things about the doctor. What do they know of "office daddies," or "factory-working daddies"?

There is great variation in physical skill. No one can color within an outline; only two can cut. The children enjoy pasting and clay activities. These have a nice squishy feel, but no one has yet intended any design with paste except Henry. His creation this morning was purposeful, a thing to be shared and treasured. Some children can manipulate puzzle pieces into the right places, some can't; some can build towers and balance blocks, some can't; some can dress the dolls—even fasten the snaps, some cannot.

In singing and rhythms there also is considerable difference. Some children can carry a tune, march in time, jump, hop, or gallop to a tune. Most cannot do these things. . . . I think we will give our scissors to the kindergarten; they are frustrating to most of these children. . . . Could we devise any more large muscle activity? We need more.

Is the nursery group so stimulating and exciting an experience that the children have to be toileted more often than usual? I wonder if Charles' accidents are frequent and how they are treated at home. I must go to see *Charles*—not just his new baby sister. I'll call Mrs. Kent for an appointment, let her know that I plan to devote most of the time to Charles, and why. Wonder how she feels Charles is getting along at this point. She may need help.

There are several indications of intellectual ability: skill with puzzles; imagination that can devise a story; attention span that sometimes stretches to fifteen minutes in a group activity; ability to understand concepts like growing. What sense of time do these children have? They can understand, "in a few minutes," and, "after the story is over." How do they understand tomorrow, and the next week, and next Sunday, or last Sunday? And long ago when Jesus lived?

There was much learning about human relationships this morning. Katie learned that taking Michael's cups made Michael object. I hope she also learned that the teacher will help children straighten things out. Come to think of it, Katie and Michael are the smallest ones in the group. Was Katie, in the "too-big" dress, trying to build up her own self-esteem by "picking on" Michael? . . . Through her experience this morning Marcella *should* have learned to ask for Jimmy's puzzle instead of taking it. Did she learn *that* through Miss Jane's "teaching," or did she merely feel adult disapproval without a very clear understanding of why or of how Jimmy felt or of the rights of others? . . . Leslie and Shelley learned that building blocks *together* is fun.

Did the children today find the teachers helpful to them in what *the children* wanted to do, understanding of their difficulties before they understood them themselves, always ready to treat them as persons, allowing them to make their own decisions, choose their own activity, create their own picture or block play or housekeeping situation, hang up their own clothes?

It is easy to see from these few observations of a Sunday morning session that the usual way of describing nursery children in terms of their *physical, emotional, social,* and *intellectual* development doesn't wholly describe a child. None of these concepts of development is a separate entity that can be untangled from the others, brushed off, laid bare, and measured like the mercury column on a thermometer. They are descriptive terms, not definitive or exact ones, and a child grows in all these ways at the same time, and in more, too. *Psychological* and *religious* growth are two other aspects of growth just as impossible to measure, but equally valuable as descriptive terms.

Take Carol, for example. We may know that she is 39 inches tall and weighs 41 pounds, has just learned to ride her "trike," and seems to prefer her left hand. Emotionally, she seems not very happy and cries loud and long at the slightest scratch or unintentional bump. Socially, she seems fearful of extending herself to anyone, teacher or fellow pupils. She plays alone most of the time. She seems bright, can accurately count from four to six objects, works new puzzles quickly, knows all the colors including light and dark shades, asks endless questions of the teacher all the time.

But when Carol comes hesitantly into the nursery room in her nylon organdy dress and patent leather shoes, bedecked with locket, bracelet, and gold baby ring, and says to you, "My daddy isn't working today and he came to church with us," you find that none of the information you have does you much good. You know lots of things about Carol, but you do not know Carol. For she is the complex sum or whole of all you have observed, plus every experience she has had, every person she has dealt with, and every interpretation she has given to those experiences and persons in her long three and one-quarter years. No one will ever completely know Carol, for she is unique in all the world. But for a teacher to appreciate just this much about a child, his uniqueness, there is none other like him, is to take the road to discovering that every Carol and every Henry is perfectly delightful, a person to be treasured, cared for, and understood.

Yes, Carol is more than the sum of all the facts we can garner about her. We need to know this "more." What is going on inside the brown-eyed lass in the perky organdy walking slowly into the room? What kind of person does she think she is? What kind of place is she discovering the church to be? What kind of persons has she decided her teachers and the other children are? Unless we can discover at least partial answers to these questions, we cannot effectively establish a personal (therefore, a teaching) relationship with her.

The Developmental Task—The Clue to Effective Teaching

What is going on inside Carol? What is the big thing in her life that she needs to get done?

What is this for you—for me?

Each of us is a person of particular motivations and yearnings that underlie all that we say and do, that make us unique, different from everyone else. There is a great struggle going on inside each of us, and lots of lesser struggles, too: to possess something we have wanted for a long time; to master a new skill; to complete a training course; to attain certain educational goals; to get along with one's superiors (or spouse); to succeed at a new job; to become a better mother; to find a faith that will hold life together.

Our lives are organized around tasks such as these. We are purposeful creatures who act in terms of values we hold, seeking to acquire or accomplish some goal we see before us. The person whose life is not organized around some such intentional activity feels useless, unwanted, lost. Such a person seems to have lost his "aliveness," he is weary, energy-less; he does not want nor is he able to "get into the swim" of life about him. He is ill and needs help.

Children, like adults, have a great deal of similar unfinished business before them: to learn to ride their "trike"; to do the things of which their parents approve; to understand and get along with adults; to be able to do the things the other children do; to establish their right to make decisions; to have ideas; to become independent; to find out what the world is like—light switches, angleworms, muddy puddles, icicles, and snow. The list is endless, and the items are not mutually exclusive. Any child can have a considerable hidden agenda of things to be done, worlds to be explored and conquered, people to be understood, problems to be worked out.

This "unfinished business" or "struggle going on" has more accurately been called "developmental task." For each child there is a unique task, a job-to-be-done, that concerns no one else as it does him. This task arises from three sources, usually working together: one, the child's body develops and his muscles must do new things; two, he himself chooses (often unconsciously) to accomplish the task; three, society (his parents, or friends or teacher, or all other people) expects him to accomplish the task. If the child successfully completes his developmental task, he is happy and is able to move on to others. If he does not complete it, he is unhappy, feels social disapproval, and often has difficulty with the tasks that arise at a later age. As the phrase implies, the specific nature of the developmental task changes with age, growth, and development; but developmental tasks are characteristic of all human life, be it preschool, adolescent, or old age.

For an example at the nursery level, let us look at Carol's behavior on Sunday morning.

First, she is three and one-quarter years of age, sturdy, physically competent, able to keep up with a group of nursery children. Second, she wants to belong to the group. Her mother reported that Carol could hardly wait for Sundays to come around so she could get her pretty clothes on and go to church school. Third, her parents and the teacher expected her to join the group happily, without tears or fears.

One of Carol's developmental tasks, therefore, is to be able to get along happily with a group of almost strangers without feeling fearful, lost, deserted, or inadequate. Physically, she is ready to do it; by personal choice she *wants* to do it; the people important to her *expect* her to do it.

On this particular Sunday morning Carol, with the teacher's help, took another step along the road of accomplishing this task. If Carol continues to get along happily in the nursery without her mother, she will be free to face other tasks involving her growing independence from her mother, and she will probably succeed in accomplishing them. If she fails here, the next time she faces this task—perhaps at kindergarten—she will come to the situation with feelings of inadequacy and anxiety that will make the task even harder. She may accomplish physical separation from her mother and never achieve emotional independence. Such is the new wife who leaves her husband for her mother after the first quarrel.

Understanding this concept of the developmental task, which each child has on his hands, is most important for *all* teachers. For only if we are wise enough to understand the clues the child gives as to the nature of his task, and skilled enough to provide whatever help the child needs at the moment for accomplishing the task, have we truly, and in the most real sense, become his teacher.

The child will then have the thrilling experience of being understood by one who helps him accomplish something he wants very much to do. Consequently, this experience will become the basis for mutual trust and love between the child and you, his teacher. Having once been understood, the child can then forgive you when you fail to understand. And, amazingly enough, the trust and love and forgiveness he experiences in relation to you, his first teacher and frequently the first adult he comes to know well outside the family, become the attitudes with which he meets and extends himself to all other people. This is the way love is learned: "We love, because he first loved us."

Some developmental tasks, such as learning to put on one's clothes, are relatively easy, and once mastered they pretty much stay mastered. Others are more difficult, and are achieved by degrees over a long period of time, even a lifetime, such as learning to be a sensitive, responsible member of the family of man. Most of us dress ourselves with little thought about how to do it. Few, if any of us, are able always to live and work and act with concern and sensitivity toward our fellows, even with considerable thought.

Children of nursery age all have some developmental tasks in common; but the clues any child gives about himself and his concerns, and the methods he uses to achieve what he needs to do, are uniquely his own. Our job as teachers is to read the clues aright and to help the child in his struggle to achieve—as Mrs. Todd did for Carol. The child's growing edges are at this point of his developmental tasks. Here is where learning takes place— personal, vital, important learning. Here is where the nursery leader becomes the child's teacher as well as his friend, for how the child feels about himself after he has struggled with his concern is what he has learned.

For example, suppose Carol had not been ready to stay without her mother. Suppose that Mrs. Todd with all her skill had not been able to help her feel secure and wanted in the three-year-old group. What would Carol have learned? No one, of course, can say definitely. Carol may have learned, "The nursery is a place with nice toys and a nice teacher where mothers leave their children. If you don't want to stay, the teacher will find your mother and she will take you home."

Or had she stayed and rocked the cuddly dog in the rocking chair for the whole hour, she would have learned something different but every bit as vital. This is the kind of learning that affects personality, that becomes part of a child's behavior. By comparison, the story of "Jesus, the Children's Friend," the song of church bells, the prayer would have been, for Carol, superficial. Instead,

Carol discovered in Alice Todd an understanding friend. Is it not possible that out of that experience, the story of "Jesus, the Children's Friend," and the conversation and prayer about the doctors who are children's friends, had real meaning and personal significance for Carol because Carol had herself experienced this meaning?

Toward a Better Understanding of Older Boys and Girls

BY DOROTHY LA CROIX HILL

"What makes Johnny show off all the time?"

"I don't believe that Sally learns a thing."

"All that Anne cares about is sitting next to Roberta and giggling at what the boys say."

"Gerald feels left out, but the other boys and girls seem to like him well enough."

"Why is Allen always late? Why doesn't he say a word or do a thing without prodding and urging?"

"What makes Pete tell such whoppers?"

"Why can't Mark enter into plans of the class? Why does he always prefer to be a 'committee of one'?"

"Why should Jim constantly make fun of other pupils' ideas, yet never offer one of his own?"

"Is there a reason why Margaret talks every minute?"

"Why does the class choose Bob or Mary or Sue for everything, whether or not they can do the job well?"

"Why can't this class settle down to intelligent planning?"

The "whys" and the "whats" show that teachers who ask such questions either consciously or unconsciously recognize a truth basic to our understanding of boys and girls, basic indeed to our

Dorothy LaCroix Hill, "Toward a Better Understanding of Our Boys and Girls," *Working with Juniors at Church* (Nashville: Abingdon Press, 1955), pp. 56–69. Used by permission.

understanding of all persons, including ourselves: "There is always a reason for everything we do, for everything we are."

If there is always a reason, our first step in solving a problem is to discover the reason, not to attack the behavior directly. It does no good to order Johnny to stop showing off or to ask Mark why in the world he cannot co-operate. It harms, rather than helps, to call attention to Anne's silliness, Peggy's sullenness, or the group's lack of wisdom in choosing a popular person instead of an able one for responsibilities.

Our reason for noting and questioning the behavior in the first place determines in large part how effectively we will deal with it. Do we want to alter the behavior so that we will not be annoyed and so that we can more easily persuade the class to do the things we have decided are important? Is our concern centered in the fact that these kinds of behavior hinder the growing, the changing, the learning, both of individuals and of the group? Do we feel that the ways certain boys and girls act and react indicate immaturity with which we must be patient? Or do they indicate an unhappy, unhealthy state which we would like to help them overcome because we love them and want the best for them?

The teacher who frequently feels annoyed and frustrated may well examine his teaching procedures. He may need to discover how to stimulate the curiosity and purposing of boys and girls, how to plan with the group instead of for them. Perhaps he needs to guide them into wider experiences where there will be opportunity for pupils to choose from a variety of activities and to make contributions to the class plans in a variety of ways. Because we are all different, we like to do different things, we learn in different ways, and we feel that some kinds of learning are more valuable than others. The teacher who regularly purposes to have the whole class learn the same thing, at the same time, and in the same way, simply because he thinks they should, is likely to find his sessions with juniors strenuous and unrewarding.

Even teachers who normally follow a better kind of teaching procedure may find their boys and girls reacting in unpleasant and unpredictable ways when for one reason or another they hurry or push the group, or play the role of dictator. By the way in which we teach juniors we often bring troubles upon ourselves.

We deal more reasonably and more effectively with the behavior of boys and girls when our concern is for them, rather than for ourselves. The very word "discipline" has its origin in the Latin word meaning "pupil," or "learner." Hence the important kind of discipline is that which helps individual boys and girls, and the group as a whole, to learn more richly, more deeply, and with greater satisfaction to themselves.

Two kinds of study will aid us in helping our children to learn and to grow into happy, useful Christian persons—the study of individual boys and girls, and the study of their behavior in groups. For the teacher who discovers how such study can increase his effectiveness and his satisfaction in his work, there will always be new books and new magazine articles to read, new points of view in the field of child study to find out about. Best of all, there will be new children to know and new groups which challenge him to find skillful and helpful ways of guiding them.

For You to Do

Write some "whys" or "whats" about the behavior of juniors whom you know. After each question leave space to write possible reasons for this behavior as you discover them in the reading of this book or in the leadership course you are taking. Note possible ways to help these juniors, or the group, change to ways of behaving which will contribute more to their learning.

Why Are All Boys and Girls Different?

The inborn characteristics of each child are the product of one combination of parent cells out of the countless combinations which might have been possible. Since birth each of these children has had a multitude of varied experiences. Because he is himself, and only himself, he has responded to these experiences differently from anyone else, even from the brothers and sisters who have shared in some of them. This in itself is enough to make him an individual.

However, the ways in which each child is different from any other are not constant, to be known and understood once and for all. From week to week the child changes. The things which have happened to him this week, or even this morning before he came to our class, may make him more or less ready to learn. The differences important to us as teachers are those which either help or hinder his purposeful activity in the group.

Differences That Are Important to Our Teaching

Once we are convinced that a child learns best through his own purposeful activity, we know that our job is to help each one participate as fully as possible in learning experiences which he finds important. We can accomplish this only as we recognize individual differences and make provision for them in our planning. We can accomplish it only as we find ways to know and understand each boy and girl.

It does not greatly matter that Ben's eyes are blue instead of brown, but it does matter that Ben is a nervous lad for whom a lengthy period of sitting or of trying to concentrate on quiet study is sheer torture. We will think about Ben as we plan our unit and its sessions. We will remember that when the group studies, Ben does better when we are near enough to direct and guide his attention more than is necessary for other boys and girls. We will remember that he needs experiences with concrete objects, things he can touch, materials he can manipulate. When they study "The Homeland of Jesus," Ben and other juniors may wish to create dioramas, showing the shepherd life of early Palestine and the agricultural life of its later years. Ben will learn as he consults pictures and simple Bible dictionaries, so that he can create such scenes accurately from clay and wood, stones and real grain, clothespins and cloth.

It may not be especialy important that Frank is a bit taller than other ten-year-olds, but it is important that he reads on a ninth-grade level. For Frank we will have ready a Bible encyclopedia, a good concordance, storybooks for junior-high-school boys and girls, so that he can go about his learning in ways that are stimulating and satisfying to him. Johnny's reading ability lies at the other extreme, on a third-grade level. This is important to his learning experience in our group. For him we will provide many pictures, objects to handle, and very simple storybook and picture-book material related to the unit.

When George frequently comes dragging into class after the session is half over, we will remember that all is not well in his home. This is a difference important to learning. We will not add further to the child's troubles by a sharp reprimand, but will welcome him warmly, so that he may feel loved and needed here. We will not scold or urge him to work on the Sunday when the boys and girls are anxious to finish their frieze of missionaries, and George puts down his crayon, shakes his head, and says miserably, "I just can't work on it today. I don't feel like it." We allow him to sit and watch his committee until finally he relaxes in the atmosphere of good fellowship and takes up his crayon for a few minutes before the session closes. After the others have gone, George feels free to talk a bit about his trouble. We are glad for a chance to remind him that as long as there have been people and families, some have had troubles like those of his home; but when there seemed nothing anyone could do, many have found help in remembering that God always knows, always cares, and is ready to help when people will let him.

There are sensitive children who cannot learn when sharp words linger in their minds. One day Betsy dropped her bracelet. The teacher, hearing the jangle in the midst of other confusion, asked sharply, "Who did that?" Betsy raised a timid hand, and the teacher said unreasonably, "Betsy! I didn't expect that sort of thing from you!" Jane would have been resentful, but she would have disposed of the incident with a shrug. Betsy's eyes were pools of misery throughout the morning.

When Mary or David offer to give other juniors their parts in a play, the teacher who knows individual differences may not be especially happy at this seeming display of generosity. This teacher knows that Mary and David, so often unsure of their ability to do well, at first did want very much to be in this play. They need a chance to succeed, not to withdraw. Had it been Ross and Esther who offered their parts, it might have represented growth in their concern for other members of the class. The teacher would have been glad for them.

We will never, of course, expect all the juniors to reach the same levels of religious insight and understanding. Some from their past experiences with religion in church and home will be more able to see and to put together what they are learning now with what they have experienced in the past to make new relationships, new learnings. Knowing how limited Joe has been in a home almost completely uninterested in religion, we will be thrilled with the wonder in his eyes and voice as he says, "Just think! Some men live seventy-five or eighty years and never do anything that people remember. But Jesus only taught and preached about three years, and here we are reading about him almost two thousand years later."

How a boy or girl feels about himself in relation to the group is another kind of difference important to his learning experience.

For the first two sessions of a laboratory class George sat impassive, his arms folded across his chest, his eyes cast down. He did nothing, said nothing, and paid little attention to other boys and girls. When the class worked, he moved about aimlessly. The juniors were engaged in a unit planned to help them have a growing knowledge of God through discoveries of his love and goodness in the world about them. When committees were formed to make investigations outdoors, George declined to join any of them. He went out to sit silent and alone on the church steps. The teacher joined him, but her efforts at conversation met with little response. The boy's thoughts seemed to be far away—a daydreamer, the teacher guessed.

Three committees grew out of the study, each to report on how men have worked with God to make homes, or to provide food, or to furnish transportation for mankind. Again George did not wish to participate, but a friendly boy in the second committee urged him to join this group. The members, all but George, decided that each would tell how one kind of food is the result of men working with God.

"You could tell about cheese," friendly Art suggested.

"I can't give no report," said George. "I'm dumb."

"Who says so?" asked Art.

"Everybody says so," George replied. "And I'm a mean kid, too. Everybody says so."

The teacher sat down with George, suggesting that others on the committee begin work on their reports. George seemed ready to talk a little. He assured her that he could not give a report, but something about his insistence made her feel that he would like to try. She brought simple picture books on food and homes and transportation. His reading was halting, his grammar very poor, and it seemed impossible for him to organize or even to recall information to which the teacher called his attention.

While transportation interested him more, George kept coming back to Art's suggestion that he report on how men had worked with God to make cheese. It was evident that he would like to find favor with this boy and with the committee.

The teacher helped him to think through three simple sentences about the grass and water needed by cows to produce milk, about the care that men give to their herds and their pastures, and about the knowledge and skill necessary for the scientific manufacture of cheese. The processes of cheese making, however, were clearly beyond George's understanding unless he could have visited a cheese factory and seen the operation for himself.

That afternoon the teacher saw him on the beach alone, silent. She joined him as he was putting on his shoes. They talked about the lake and the boats. Not a word was said about cheese. The next morning George was the first child to arrive. He was filled with anxiety.

"I can remember those two things about grass and cows," he said, "but I just can't get that about men making cheese."

"You do want to give the report?" asked the teacher.

"Art said I should," he answered simply; and the teacher saw how much Art's friendship and approval meant to him.

Alone with Art, she said, "George wants to give that report about cheese, but he just can't remember what to say. How can we help him? Could your committee help him?"

"Sure," said Art. "We'll tell him what to say. He can write it down and read it. We'll all help him."

When it was time for reports, George was the first to volunteer. He was eager to get his part done. Flanked by two committee members who held pictures illustrating his report on cheese, George read haltingly four simple sentences.

Because his committee listened courteously, the other boys and girls did, too. The teacher thanked him simply, just as she would have thanked any other child; and George went back to his seat with evident relief, wearing the first smile anyone had seen.

From that moment he "came alive" in the group. Now he felt that it was possible for him to learn, to do what the others did. When they read in unison, George tried to join in. He participated in a choral reading from Psalms. He brought in two contributions for the exhibit prepared by his committee. Sometimes he sang with the group. He joined Art and other boys at the lake and had fun, for he was a good swimmer. He ceased to be a solitary child.

In the laboratory class he was no longer silent and unobtrusive. Indeed, his behavior was sometimes disturbing. However, the teacher and those who were helping and observing rejoiced that his acceptance in the group had made it possible for George to start learning and growing. He could begin to believe in the love of God, for he had found a measure of love and welcome in this small group studying about God's goodness and finding ways to express their gratitude for it.

Knowing Our Juniors as Individuals

A beginning step is a conscious effort to learn the juniors' names and thereafter to call them by name. Someone has said that to influence any person for good, we must be able to speak his name.

A second step is to make ourselves available to children. In the twenty minutes before or after a class session we discover what juniors are thinking about, what they are interested in doing. As they become sure of our warm interest and understanding, they bring many things to show us, many plans and ideas which may never materialize, but which are exciting to think about and talk about. The teacher who wants to know boys and girls will not merely "listen." He will respond to their interests, asking intelligent questions, sharing similar experiences of his own.

Within class sessions we will be alert to incidents and remarks which may help us understand why boys and girls are the kinds of persons they are, for we know that *there are always reasons for what each one is and does.* In our teaching we encourage individuals to express their ideas, their preferences, and their wishes. We pay close attention as the group plans activities, knowing that by their choices they will be telling us the ways in which they like to learn. As the boys and girls work, we will be interested in what each one is doing. Through questions and comments we may help individuals to keep their goals always before them and to consider their own work in relation to the plans and purposes of the class.

We will be interested in juniors' conversations with one another. We will observe them wherever we see boys and girls, welcoming chance contacts on the bus, at the library, in the store. Occasionally we will plan with them the kinds of parties juniors consider fun—a potluck supper after a late afternoon of carol singing, a roller-skating party, a hike or picnic—not forgetting that whenever juniors are together to work or to play, they will be learning and growing from the Christian fellowship which a leader helps to guide.

Knowing their families and homes helps us to understand why our boys and girls are as they are. Jerry, his teacher discovered, was the only son and grandson, the only male cousin. A visit in his home disclosed that a grandmother and an aunt lived with the family. With fond complacency all the adults permitted him to monopolize the conversation and interrupt at any time. Now the teacher began to understand why he interrupted other children in class discussions, why he seemed impelled to be always in the limelight. She ceased to think of him as a rude and annoying boy and saw him as a child with a problem, which might be gradually worked out in the class since all were friendly persons. To like Jerry she needed to know much more about him. As she cultivated his friendship, she was delighted with his keen mind, with the freshness of his viewpoint about people and situations. She admired his skill in sports and his tenderness toward animals. Little by little she discovered special contributions he could make to class plans and so win recognition from the group in constructive ways.

Mickey, too, talks and talks. So does Margaret, but we know that this is a highly sociable age. We know that these boys and girls are all growing in ability to express themselves and that they take great pleasure in doing it. We observe how games often turn into talkfests, with people arguing loudly. There is little waiting a turn, little patient courtesy. We remember that this is an age when self-control, although it is growing, is still imperfect. When talking seems to hinder the progress of class thinking and planning, we encourage the boys and girls to consider this problem. The solutions they offer are likely to be very good ones and very specific, for juniors do not think in generalities:

Listen, so you won't repeat what someone else said.
Don't keep saying the same thing over, just because you think
  it is a good idea.
Take turns.

If you have said a lot, let someone talk who hasn't said anything yet.

Tell your idea to the class, not to your neighbor.

Stick to the subject.

The teacher recognizes honest efforts to abide by the rules and encourages the boys and girls to do so. He is good-humored and patient. That helps the members of the class to be good-humored and patient, too. And so together they create a relaxed atmosphere of friendliness and approval in which even the sensitive and nervous ones can learn and grow.

Knowing About the Group

Some classes are steady and hard-working, with well-defined goals. They enjoy the opportunity to help plan and direct their own learning. Others, like individual juniors, are less mature and need a different kind of guidance. Here, again, there are always reasons. The reasons, if we can discover them, indicate ways to guide that will be most helpful in the Christian growing of the group.

Some classes have had little experience with solving their own problems and setting up their own goals for learning. They need a gradual introduction to independence, with larger and larger opportunities for choices and for self-direction, as they show themselves ready. We would not expect this kind of group to decide upon the making of a movie with pictures and script as the most interesting way to learn about the life of Jesus. They probably could not carry such a prolonged activity through to a satisfying conclusion, even if the idea appealed to them. Instead we might challenge the group imagination with vividly told incidents from the life of Jesus, then most informally "pretend" that we are the people of that land and day. How would we feel about Jesus? Has he done something special to help each of us? What would we say about him? How would we tell our families and friends about the things we had heard Jesus say or had seen him do? Through the use of "imaginative play" we would guide this less mature group to think purposefully, to give their full attention to a problem. We would use the Bible, pictures, and interesting, well-illustrated books on Bible background to help the juniors make their imagining more real, more true to the facts and the times. We might help them to choose a few incidents which in their opinion give the best picture of Jesus, and work on these until they can share them as simple dramatizations with another group. A hymn, a poem, a choral reading, of the teaching found in Matthew 5:43–48 would round out the dramatizations. Through such group activities these boys and girls would grow in ability to set up purposes and work together toward their realization.

A key to understanding our class of juniors may be the discovery that they are following a certain kind of leader or that the group has certain standards which determine whether a boy or girl shall be accepted. In one group the person admired and followed was a boy who openly flouted adult guidance at home, at school, and at church. Needless to say, it was a group difficult to guide until the teacher began to win his friendship and to help all the juniors to recognize and value some other kinds of leadership. No teacher can depose one boy or girl leader and set up another in his place. Instead he must help each member of the group to contribute his best to class experiences, and then help the members of the group learn to appreciate one another's strong points.

Each group has a social pattern made up of what are sometimes simple and sometimes intricate relationships among the members. Knowing the pattern helps us to understand and guide the boys and girls. Who are the members of the small groups within the larger one? Which children always sit together and visit together? Who are the most sought-after persons? Who are the left-out ones? Who are favorite working companions? Who are never chosen or are a last choice? By what standards are boys and girls awarded popularity in the group? Are these worthy standards? Does the group need to find some others that are intelligent, more just, more Christian? How can the left-out members of the group be helped to find approval from others? How may some of the well-accepted ones be guided to understand the problems, needs, and desires of those who are not accepted, and to help them into more satisfying relationships within the group?

All efforts of the teacher to understand and guide both individuals and groups have strong roots in the teachings and practice of Jesus. When the rich young ruler sought him out, eager to claim eternal life but not knowing how to find it, Jesus looked into the goals uppermost in the young man's experience and pointed out the way. For all the lowly, common folk of Palestine whose practice of religion could not meet the standards set up by the scribes and the Pharisees, Jesus gave another set of standards for "belonging" in the kingdom of God—the Beatitudes.

When we help boys and girls to establish within their own group a warm fellowship where every member is liked for himself and appreciated for what he contributes to the class experience, our teaching is following that of Jesus. We are developing the "good climate" in which each child, and the whole group, can grow toward the goals of Christian education. In such a climate the curriculum comes to life in the experience of the learners.

Toward a Better Understanding of Young People

BY OLIVER DE WOLF CUMMINGS

Youth is a flexible period of life which does not arrive all at once on a certain birthday or cease at a given moment. It varies as to age with different individuals, and is dependent on factors which vary in the experience of different persons and localities. But for practical purposes it is necessary both in the public schools and in the churches to formulate general principles to serve as a basis for assigning people to groups.

Among the more important considerations which affect the transition from childhood to youth are the following: 1, physical maturing, as experienced in the glandular, muscular and other changes associated with puberty; 2, intellectual maturing, usually evidenced by public school promotion; 3, social maturing, revealed in part by the gang, the set or the personal companions with whom the individual associates. Girls usually reach puberty earlier than boys, and often are taller and larger at age twelve than boys of that age. Boys do not catch up with girls in size for several years, but ultimately they may be several inches taller. The rapid physical and emotional changes account for the awkwardness and moodiness of early adolescence.

Intellectually and socially, girls at age twelve frequently are ahead of boys. Temporarily they think more quickly and clearly and are more aware of sexual differences. The physical, emo-

Oliver DeWolf Cummings, "Our Commission Requires an Understanding of Youth," *Guiding Youth in Christian Growth* (Philadelphia: Judson Press, 1954), pp. 18–19, 22–26. Used by permission.

tional and intellectual changes taking place so rapidly throughout adolescence make age-groupings desirable.

Among the considerations which affect the transition from youth to adulthood are the following:

• Completion of formal schooling.
• Acquiring and holding a full-time job.
• Financial independence.
• Separation from family ties by establishing separate residence —often in an entirely new locality.
• Political and legal maturity (the right to vote, to have full control of property, etc.).
• Marriage.
• Military service.
• Personal attitude (psychological and social associations).

Young People Differ Widely

If it be true that God has so made this universe that no two snowflakes, no two blades of grass, no two flowers are exactly alike, there assuredly is basis for acceptance of infinite variation in God's highest creation—man. Certainly no two brains and no two personalities, not even of identical twins, are alike. In fact, the leader of youth must recognize the peril of ready generalizations and snug classifications. Denominational lesson plans recognize this and encourage adaptations to fit each individual.

It is helpful, however, to recognize the factors or experiences which account for the more obvious differences in young people. Among the more important are the following:

• *Education*—grade school (7th and 8th grade intermediates), junior high, senior high, junior college, college or university, graduate school; trade school, church-related college, state university; commuting daily or weekends by train, streetcar or auto; dormitory or rooming house.
• *Social groupings*—the family's economic and social status,

privileged or poor neighborhood, the gang or set, clubs, sororities, fraternities.

* *Specialized skills and interests*—athletics, drama, music, art, science, mechanics, reading, vocational training, hobbies.
* *Employment*—full or part-time, rural, industrial, white collar, individual or co-operative, working with things or with people.
* *Military service*—the army, navy, air corps, overseas or domestic, conscientious objector.
* *Religious background*—parental religious heritage, previous church, church school, and Youth Fellowship experience, personal prayer life, knowledge of and use of the Bible, commitment to Christ, church membership.

Young People Have Varied Interests

It is of importance to know "what makes young people tick." As we use denominational lesson materials and plan special activities, we must be aware of the things which have general appeal to youth and special attraction to the individuals we lead.

The range of interest is broad and rapidly changing. For example, in the intermediate there is marked difference from month to month. Some interests change with the seasons; others, like dating, are more or less constant. Still others, like fads in clothing, arise out of whims of the gang or set, or out of a wholly unrelated hunch of an individual.

The resourceful leader is able to identify and utilize many of the more typical interests which cast their spell upon young people. We shall examine a few of them here, and suggest the maintaining of an idea book in which to note others as they appear.

Young people are interested in *friendship*. This rates high on every opinion poll of youth. Closely associated are popularity, fellowship, social events, love, sex, dating, marriage.

Young people are interested in *physical activity*—sports, hiking, parties, picnics, work projects, hobbies, "hot-rods."

Young people are interested in *self-expression*. This takes widely different forms. Music, drama, art, mechanics, craft work and television are among the examples.

Young people are interested in *experimentation* and *discovery*. They insist on trying out ideas and plans for themselves and venturing in new and untried directions, sometimes disastrously, yet often creatively.

Young people are interested in *discussion*. The college "bull session," the street-corner conversation, the Youth Fellowship class—all are evidences of the interest in "swapping ideas."

Young people are interested in *vocation*. Some of the interest in experimentation arises out of the desire to discover a vocational field. Many of youth's problems center in their attitudes toward work and achievement—the discovery of meaning in life.

Young people are interested in *religion*. But they demand that it be a religion which incorporates all the interests of life, not one that is concerned merely with a few special practices associated with Sunday and the church. Religion as belief must be balanced by religion as experience and action, by religion as self-expression, experimentation and discovery; it must be the undergirding and integrating factor in daily living and vocation.

Young People Have Many Problems

In each of several areas young people are likely to face problems—their relationship to *themselves,* to their *parents,* to *other young people and adults,* to their *school* or *job,* to their *community,* and to *God.*

Dwight L. Moody said, "I have more trouble with myself than with any other man I know." During early adolescence many young people have trouble with themselves. They become self-conscious and often quite moody. This is understandable in view of the physical and emotional changes taking place within them. Throughout adolescence they are aware of the large gap between their attainments and what they want to be and do. Their need is for self-realization and the self-confidence which comes from being wanted and respected.

Nellie's problem is her waistline; Harriet's, her complexion; Ed's, his awkwardness; George's, his grades in math; Don's, his inability to get the family car for dates; Ethel's, her inability to get dates; Frank's, his inability to hold a job.

Parents are a problem to many adolescents. "They expect so much." "They are always harping on things." "They keep trying to make you quit reading the comics and watching television, so you can get your homework done." "They won't let you use the car for a date." "They won't buy for you the right kind of dress." "They always want you to get home early." "They don't seem to realize that all the kids stay out late nowadays." "You'd think they never were young once themselves."

What really counts with most young people is the opinion of other young people. "What will the gang think?" "I wonder what Sue or Bob will say." The basic need is for a sense of security, of being accepted and liked. Many of the problems of adolescence center here. Attitudes toward smoking, drinking, petting and clothing tend to be determined by the demand for conformity, which is part of the tremendous force of social pressure. Hence, there often is great disappointment for parents and teachers, whose opinions and experiences may not be rated so high as those of the crowd or of some special friend.

Young people face problems in achieving a secure personal faith. For some the easy acceptance of God which characterized their childhood has been rudely undermined by courses in science, history or psychology. Bill, a junior high boy, said to his mother: "I'm not going to Sunday school any more. I've been studying science and have learned that there isn't any God. So I'm not going to Sunday school." In saying this, he revealed a confusion common to adolescents in their transition to a more secure faith.

Many of youth's problems concerning God arise out of the confusion created by the different points of view held by adults. Susan, a junior high girl, expressed it thus, "How are you going to know what to believe about God when you read and hear so many different opinions?"

An even greater problem, however, is the basic human one of spiritual inadequacy as manifested in the struggle of the lower and the higher natures, confused standards of sex morality, failure to do that which is felt to be right—in short, the problem of sin and salvation. At this point the Christian leader who is to be a true physician of the soul should make the fullest use of the rich heritage of the Christian faith.

Many Characteristics of Youth Affect Christian Teaching

If the teacher is truly interested in young people, he will be concerned about their real interests and problems. Each characteristic of each young person needs study to determine its bearing on abundant Christian life. Each problem calls for understanding and for skill in discovering ways of dealing with it. If the real problem of Janet and Ed is that they are having trouble deciding how far to go on a date, a purely logical exhortation on personal purity may not be so effective as a story or illustration expressing positive Christian attitudes and loyalties in the experience of others.

One teacher of high school girls was having difficulty in enlisting class participation. She got a clue to the trouble when a member of her class said: "Well, why shouldn't I drink a little if the rest of the girls in my crowd do?" Since the characteristic involved was conformity, and since social pressure was such a large factor, she changed the mood of discussion by proposing a different question. Would the members of the class help her to weigh the reasons why she, their teacher, should or should not drink? Though reasons were advanced on both sides, the girls found it difficult to justify drinking except on the basis that "other people do and why should you seem to be 'a queer'?" This led to a profitable discussion of conformity and of the responsibility of Christians to take the lead in setting standards.

Toward a Better Understanding of Adults

BY IDRIS JONES

Young Adults

Seven experiences are regarded as transforming youth into adulthood. These experiences include leaving school, self-support, getting married, permanently leaving the parental home, political maturity, service in the armed forces, and chronological age. These provide valuable clues to the needs of young adults. Departure from school, for example, frequently leaves the young adult an isolated individual. He seeks fellowship. The church should seek to insure that the fellowship is Christian. Another need of young adults to which the church can minister is that their minds shall be kept stimulated with studies, biblical and otherwise, that will challenge their capacities and interests.

As the young adult becomes financially self-supporting, he needs to find a Christian orientation to his work, to see it as a Christian vocation with Christian responsibilities. The implications of Christian stewardship for the ways in which he gets and distributes his money are of vital concern in this new experience of economic independence.

Marriage and preparation for it provide the church with an opportunity to help the young couple in their relationships with each other, in the establishment of a Christian home, in finding their place in the Christian fellowship of the church and in community life.

Leaving the parental home may or may not imply financial in-

Idris Jones, *Our Church Plans for Adult Education* (Philadelphia: Judson Press, 1952), pp. 9–11. Used by permission.

dependence. It usually brings, however, problems of personal adjustment in which the church, through counseling and Christian fellowship, can be of help. Stability is needed. In the midst of so many destructive social pressures, the Christian fellowship of the church can truly be a lifesaver.

Political maturity and service in the armed forces bring into focus the responsibilities of Christian citizenship and of related areas of Christian social righteousness.

Middle-aged Adults

Adults in this middle group are reaching their maximum vocational achievement. They face physical adjustments that affect their personal relationships with others. Many of them are interested in the bearing of their Christian faith upon the public issues of the day. A growing number openly avow their personal need of God's guidance and help for daily living. Despite their seeming material success, many of this group have a sense of personal loneliness that leads them to acquiesce in, and frequently to share in, the unchristian practices of the social community of which they are a part.

These adults need, as do all persons, a vital Christian fellowship that will help to strengthen their Christian living. They need a consciousness of spiritual stability and security in a period when responsibilities can frequently be overwhelming. They need the challenge to a Christian stewardship that will help them see their "successful achievements" as obligations as well as opportunities.

Older Adults

A sense of usefulness and vocational productivity will continue for many older adults until the day of their death. For others, however, the later years may bring retirement, adjustments from vocation to avocation, financial dependence, physical disability, or a constant longing for departed loved ones.

Many of these older adults are free, when retirement days come, to give a large part of their time in various channels of Christian service. They can help the church and the church can help them. All of these older adults need fellowship. Some are able to come to the church or to church homes where groups of interest to them gather. Others will have to be reached in their own homes.

The most significant need of those in this group is an assurance of their personal usefulness. By the nature of things, this usefulness may take a different form from that in their earlier years. The church can be of help to them in making this adjustment. Thus, adult characteristics need to be considered in the creation of an adequate and attractive program. Adults do not stop growing or changing when they have reached maturity. Extensive projects outside as well as inside our churches have shown the rich possibilities of adult education, when adults are given the proper motivation and adequate opportunity for learning.

What do adults need from the church? In general, they need opportunities for Christian fellowship, worship, study, witnessing, and service. Some of these experiences are churchwide, others find their effective expression through various adult groups within the church, and still others through the community and elsewhere. Sunday church school classes, for example, provide many opportunities for Christian fellowship and service, as well as for study. In many ways, these experiences are as educational as the formal study program of the church. The most effective educational program strives for a thorough integration of these experiences in the Christian life and growth of its members. The educational program of the church should enrich the Christian knowledge and understanding of adults, train them for service and leadership, and explore with them the devotional disciplines that expand and strengthen the Christian commitment in daily living.

Among young adults (twenty-five to thirty-five years of age), the vocational decision, the choice of a life partner, and the adjustments to parenthood with its responsibilities loom large. Among those of middle age (thirty-six to sixty-five years), vocational success or frustration, maturity of abilities and powers, the pressure of family and community affairs, and health become important. Beyond sixty-five, an increasing number of adults face the problem of constructive adjustment to retirement, and in some cases to dependency. As a church studies its adults and notes their specific needs, it cannot help but see the tremendous challenge they present. The Christian gospel is full enough and vital enough to give the Christian answer to every adult need. This is not only the evangelistic task, but also the educational task of the church.

A Chart of Normal Development of Children and Youth

Infancy—Preschool Years

Physical Development

Most rapid growth rate of any period.

Mastery of walking, running, climbing, jumping, skipping, using tricycle.

Learning by touching, tasting, feeling.

Desirable habits of eating, sleeping, elimination, usually well established.

Motor coordination gradually developing, permitting cutting, pasting, coloring.

Four-year-olds beginning to wash and dress themselves, lace shoes, brush teeth.

Characteristic Reactions

At one—sociable, beginning to explore environment; enjoys nursery rhymes, pat-a-cake, and simple rhythmic play.

At two—often negativistic, ritualistic, more responsive to humor or distraction than to discipline; increasing understanding of and beginning use of language; solitary or parallel play; possessive.

At three—more conforming, anxious to please, better motor control, interested in other people, cooperative, less rigid or

Gladys Gardner Jenkins, Helen Shacter, and William W. Bauer, *These Are Your Children* (Chicago: Scott, Foresman and Co., copyright, 1949), front and back inside cover pages. Used by permission.

113

ritualistic, highly imaginative, beginning to share, responsive to verbal guidance.

At four—lively, highly social, talkative, much out-of-bounds behavior, expressive, high motor drive, imaginative, dramatic, versatile, constantly asks "Why?"

Special Needs

Sureness of parental support and love.

Consistency and patience from adults.

Regular daily schedule which fits needs of individual child; plenty of sleep.

Chances for self-help, but without pressure.

Companionship of other children.

Play equipment to develop large muscles and challenge creative imagination.

Opportunity for plenty of activity.

At Five

Physical Development

Has entered period of slow growth.

Girls are usually about a year ahead of boys in physical development.

Good general motor control, though small muscles not so fully developed as large ones.

Sensory-motor equipment not ready for reading; child apt to be farsighted.

Speech has very little infantile articulation.

Handedness established by five.

Characteristic Reactions

Stable—good balance between self-sufficiency and sociality; home-centered.

Beginning to be capable of self-criticism, eager and able to carry some responsibility.

Noisy and vigorous, but his activity has definite direction.

Shows purposiveness and constructiveness; knows what he's going to draw before he draws it.

Uses language well; loves dramatic play.

Can wash, dress, feed, and toilet himself, but may still need
occasional help.

Individuality and lasting traits beginning to be apparent.

Interested in group activity.

Special Needs

Assurance that he is loved and valued at home and at school.

Opportunity for plenty of activity; equipment for exercise of
large muscles.

Opportunity to do things for himself; freedom to use and develop his own powers.

Background training in group effort, sharing, give and take, and
good work habits that he will need next year in first grade;
kindergarten experience if possible.

At Six

Physical Development

Growth proceeding more slowly; a lengthening out.

Large muscles better developed than small ones.

Eyes not yet mature; tendency toward farsightedness.

Permanent teeth begin to appear.

Heart is in period of rapid growth.

Characteristic Reactions

Eager to learn, exuberant, restless, overactive and easily fatigued.

Self-assertive; aggressive; wants to be first; less cooperative
than at five; keen competition and much boasting.

Whole body is involved in whatever he does.

Learns best through active participation.

Inconsistent in level of maturity evidenced—regresses when
tired; often less mature at home than with outsiders.

Inept at activities using small muscles.
Relatively short periods of interest.
Has difficulty making decisions.
Group activities popular; boys' and girls' interests beginning to differ.
Much spontaneous dramatization.

Special Needs

Encouragement, ample praise, warmth, and great patience from adults.
Ample opportunity for activity of many kinds, especially for use of large muscles.
Wise supervision with a minimum of interference.
Concrete learning situations and active, direct participation.
Some responsibilities, though without pressure, and without his being required to make decisions and choices or achieve rigidly set standards.

At Seven

Physical Development

Growth slow and steady.
Losing teeth; most sevens have their six-year molars.
Better eye-hand coordination.
Better use of small muscles.
Eyes not yet ready for much near work.

Characteristic Reactions

Sensitive to feelings and attitudes of both peers and adults; especially dependent on approval of adults.
Interests of boys and girls diverging; less play together.
Full of energy but easily tired; restless and fidgety; often dreamy and absorbed.
Very little abstract thinking yet; seven learns best in concrete terms and where he can be active while learning.

Cautious and self-critical; anxious to do things well; likes to use hands.

Talkative, exaggerates; may fight with words instead of blows; highly competitive.

Enjoys songs, rhythms, fairy tales, myths, nature stories, comics, radio, movies.

Able to assume some responsibility; concerned about right and wrong, though often prone to take small things.

Rudimentary understanding of time and money values.

Special Needs

The right combination of independence and encouraging support.

Chances for active participation in learning situations with concrete objects.

Must make adjustment to rougher ways of playground; needs adult help to do this without becoming too crude or rough.

Warm, encouraging, friendly relationship with adults.

At Eight

Physical Development

Growth still slow and steady; arms lengthening, hands growing larger.

Eyes ready for both near and far vision; nearsightedness may develop this year.

Permanent teeth continuing to appear.

Large muscles still developing, small muscles better developed too.

Poor posture may develop during this year.

Characteristic Reactions

Often careless, noisy, argumentative, but alert, friendly, interested in people.

More dependent on Mother again, less so on teacher; sensitive to criticism.

New awareness of individual differences.

Eager, more enthusiasm than wisdom; higher accident rate.

Gangs beginning; best friends of same sex.

Allegiance to peer group instead of to the adult in case of conflict.

Greater capacity for self-evaluation.

Much spontaneous dramatization; also ready for simple classroom dramatics.

Understanding of time and use of money.

Responsive to group activities, both spontaneous and adult-supervised.

Fond of team games, comics, radio, adventure stories, collections of all kinds.

Special Needs

Much praise and encouragement from adults.

Must still be reminded of his responsibilities.

Wise guidance and channeling of his interests and enthusiasms, rather than domination or overcritical standards.

A best friend.

Experience of "belonging" to peer group; opportunity to identify with others of same age and sex.

Adult-supervised groups also; planned after-school activities.

Exercise of both large and small muscles.

At Nine

Physical Development

Slow, steady growth continues; girls forge further ahead, some children reach the plateau preceding growth spurt of pre-adolescence.

Lungs and digestive and circulatory systems almost mature; heart especially subject to strain.

Teeth may need straightening; first and second bicuspids appearing.

Eye-hand coordination good; hands ready for crafts and shop work.

Eyes almost adult size; ready for near work with less strain.

Characteristic Reactions

Decisive, responsible, dependable, reasonable, strong sense of right and wrong.

Individual differences distinct and clear; abilities apparent.

Capable of prolonged interest; often makes plans and goes ahead on his own.

Gangs strong and of one sex only, of short duration and changing membership.

Perfectionistic; wants to do well, but loses interest if discouraged or pressured.

Interested less in fairy tales and fantasy, more in his community and country and in other countries and peoples.

Loyalty to his country and pride in it.

Much time spent in talk and discussion; often outspoken and critical of adults.

Much arguing over fairness in games.

Wide discrepancies in reading ability.

Special Needs

Active rough and tumble play.

Friends and membership in a group.

Training in skills, but without pressure.

Reasonable explanations; no talking down to him; definite responsibility.

Frank answers to questions about the coming physiological changes.

In Preadolescence

Physical Development

A "resting period," followed by a period of rapid growth in height and then growth in weight; this usually starts somewhere between 9 and 13; boys may mature as much as two years later than girls.

Secondary sex characteristics beginning to develop.

Rapid muscular growth.

Uneven growth of different parts of the body.

Enormous but often capricious appetite.

Characteristic Reactions

Wide range of individual differences in maturity level among this age group.

Gangs continue, though loyalty to the gang stronger in boys than in girls.

Interest in team games, pets, radio, comics; marked interest differences between boys and girls.

Much teasing and antagonism between boy and girl groups.

Awkwardness, restlessness, and laziness common as result of rapid and uneven growth.

Child approaching adolescence often becomes overcritical, changeable, rebellious, uncooperative.

Interested in activities to earn money.

Special Needs

Knowledge and understanding of the physical and emotional changes about to come.

Skillfully planned program to meet needs of those who are approaching puberty as well as those who are not.

Warm affection and sense of humor in adults; no nagging or condemnation or talking down to him.

Sense of belonging and acceptance by peer group; increasing opportunities for independence.

In Adolescence

Physical Development

Rapid weight gain at beginning of adolescence; enormous appetite.

Sexual maturity, with accompanying physical and emotional changes; girls are usually about two years ahead of boys.

Sometimes a period of glandular imbalance.

Bone growth completed; adult height reached; improved muscular coordination.

Heart growing rapidly.

Characteristic Reactions

Going to extremes; emotional instability with "know-it-all" attitude.

Return of habits of younger child—nail biting, tricks, impudence, daydreaming.

High interest in philosophical, ethical, and religious problems; search for ideals.

Preoccupation with acceptance by the social group; fear of ridicule and of being unpopular; oversensitiveness; self-pity.

Strong identification with an admired adult.

Assertion of independence from family as a step toward adulthood.

High interest in physical attractiveness.

Girls usually more interested in boys than boys in girls, resulting from earlier maturing of the girls.

Special Needs

Conformity with and acceptance by the peer group.

Adequate knowledge and understanding of sexual relationships and attitudes.

Adult guidance which is kindly, unobtrusive, and does not threaten the young person's feeling of freedom.

The assurance of security; adolescents seek both dependence and independence.

Opportunities to make decisions and to earn and save money.

Provision for constructive recreation and if possible a "worthy cause."

Developmental Task Chart for Adults

Developmental Task	Young Adults	Middle Age	Old Age
Vocation	Choosing a vocation Preparation Getting started Living on income Motives and standards	Improving in vocation Evaluating motives Changing if dissatisfied Inability to change Developing avocation	Retirement Insecurity Adjusting to new situation Living on income
Church Relationship	Motive of service Preparation for service Time to serve Finding place of greatest ability	Assumption of mature responsibility Too many activities Re-evaluation of service activities Growth in service	Insecurity in place of service Less ability to serve but more time Adjusting to others taking place of leadership Failure to keep growing
Family	Choosing a mate Adjusting to family life Setting home standards Child training and care	Personal relationships in the home Members of all ages Adolescent problems and guidance	Relation to grown children and in-laws Grandchildren Husband-wife relationship

Irene Smith Caldwell, *Adults Learn and Like It* (Anderson: Warner Press, 1955), p. 30. Used by permission.

Developmental Task	Young Adults	Middle Age	Old Age
Family (*cont.*)		Need to free children Financial strain Rethinking standards	Loss of companion Changing home situation Feeling unneeded Dependence
Spiritual Growth	Acceptance of basic philosophy Setting patterns of worship Group pressures on individual conscience Bible as guidebook	Staying true to accepted philosophy Growing and improving Relaxing in effort Giving in to group pressures Bible as a challenge	Continuing true to accepted philosophy Still looking forward Keeping sweet in disposition Adjusting to new standards Bible as a comfort

3. LEADER AND GROUP—A TEAM

THE TITLE of this chapter suggests a change that has taken shape gradually in Christian nurture. No longer can it be thought that the leader is a person who stands apart, selecting the goals that he thinks best and leading his followers toward them. Rather, leader and group are a team, working at tasks that belong to both of them. This idea will usually be accepted by the chairman or the parent as describing the relationship in which they can best work.

The idea of the leader working with his group in a teamwork relationship may not be so readily accepted by the teacher, but it applies here too. When the good teacher is teaching, and the good pupil is learning, they work together. Someone has wisely said that teaching is "guiding pupils while they learn." Teacher and pupils are a team. This is not to say that teacher and pupils are alike. The teacher usually knows more than the pupil and is the more mature Christian. He has traveled a road much like the one he now wants the pupil to travel. But in a very real sense he must travel with the pupil. How to walk with the pupil, helping him find the way, without *showing* him the way, is one of the most difficult problems of leadership. The leader often wishes he could simply *tell* his group, and spare them the necessity of traveling the hard road of experience. But there are no short cuts to Christian maturity. Each of us must learn the lessons of life for himself—sorrow and how to endure it, success and how to live with it, failure and how to survive it, challenge and how to meet it. The leader can help, but each member of the group must do the learning and the growing himself.

This view of the role of the leader calls attention to a truth which we have known vaguely for a long time but which we have taken far too lightly. One of the leader's greatest assets is his relationship with his group—the way he feels about them, the way he works with them. This may be far more important than the knowledge he has or the skills he knows how to use. He must not only know the people with whom he works but must understand the conditions, or "climate," within which their Christian nurture may best take place. He, himself, is an important part of that "climate."

The first three readings deal with the place of the leader in the teaching-learning-growing process. Two of them were written for leaders of adult groups, yet they are challenging for workers with any age. Workers with children may wish at this point to read the second quotation in chapter 5, for it shows how small children develop through relationships with teachers. The last reading in this chapter deals with the conditions for Christian nurture and lays a foundation for a teamwork view of leadership.

The Teacher's Role

BY FERRIS E. REYNOLDS

The best place for any teacher who wants to understand his task to begin is with himself. Any forward step that he takes will necessarily be a step from where he is. He may profitably begin by asking: "How do I feel about myself in my role as teacher?" "Do I pose as an authority?" "Do a few years' seniority or experience qualify me for such a position?" "Does the fact that I have been asked to teach a class automatically set me up as a specialist in religion?"

Socrates, one of the world's most effective teachers of ethics, never permitted himself to be called a teacher. He liked to think of himself as a gadfly whose business it was to go about stinging dull minds into activity, arousing thought, or as a midwife whose task it was to deliver noble thoughts from productive minds. Rather than call the young learners around him "students" or "pupils," he insisted upon calling them "associates." Would it be practical for us to hold an attitude similar to that of Socrates toward ourselves and our work with those in our classes?

If he desires it, almost any group will allow the leader to do the thinking for all its members. While this may be flattering to the leader, it is hardly the best way to help the members of the group, for they are thus surrendering the joy of exploring new areas of thought merely to avoid the expenditure of effort needed to set forth on their own individual quests for new truth.

Ferris E. Reynolds, "A Look at the Teacher," *An Adventure with People* (Philadelphia: Christian Education Press, 1954), pp. 22, 23. Used by permission.

A teacher must avoid yielding to this unspoken conspiracy on the part of the group to let him do their thinking for them. Instead, he must devote much of his time and ingenuity to devising means for helping the members of his class to do their own thinking. The teacher should spare no expenditure of effort toward this end, for once their natural reluctance to throw themselves into the classwork is overcome, teacher and associates alike will enjoy the experience of learning together.

Three Leadership Types—Boss, Overseer, Catalyst

BY PAUL F. DOUGLASS

For purposes of this discussion leaders may be classified in three categories: the boss, the overseer, and the catalyst. Each of these types of leadership tends to determine the climate of the group and the participant pattern. The reactions of members to leadership may range from obedience and dependence, as Figure 13 points out, to continuing growth in initiative, the capacity to bear responsibility, and the awareness of values.

When a leader is a *boss,* for example, dictating plans and making decisions, group members tend to become his minions. They work under his orders and await his commands. They act as machines. When the switch is turned on, the people go into motion; when it is pulled, they cease to operate. Group members thus become puppets and automatons. Instead of experiencing growth, individuals wither; instead of discovering and inventing, they acquiesce.

Another type of leader acts as an *overseer* solicitously caring for the welfare of the group. Under this kind of leadership, the members of a group tend to become timid and defenseless, expecting that the leader will always attend to their good. Like slaves serving under the boss, they experience no inner growth. Rather, they are likely to become complacent, unresourceful, unimaginative, acquiescent routineers.

A third kind of leader is the *catalyst.* He encourages participation and reaction. He seeks the kind of group pattern that provides

Paul F. Douglass, *The Group Workshop Way in the Church* (New York: Association Press, 1956), pp. 127–134. Used by permission.

"space" for people to grow in. Under the catalyst type of leadership, people mature as participants. The human power which lies as a potential within the group is released and given direction. The group "multiplier" is put to work. The leader, in the catalyst role, becomes just the one member of the group who bears the heaviest responsibility for seeing to it that all the members work—and work together. Work in this context means wholehearted participation of all the members in the achievement of the common purpose. They are fully involved. They have a stake in the outcome. They are committed.

Catalytic Leadership and Productivity

While bosses and overseers are everywhere present in group life, research indicates that the catalyst-type leader contributes most to productivity, participant satisfaction, and personal growth. Such a leader works to keep the channels of communication open so that all the relevant resources of all the different people in the group can flow into the meeting. Such a leader *facilitates change.* He guides and stimulates group performances toward the achievement of its purposes. A catalytic leader has at least eight characteristics:

1. The leader possesses *technical competence in the area of the group's interest.* Colonel Bernard S. Waterman says bluntly that there are two parts to leadership: "knowing your stuff— or technical proficiency which helps you to choose the right goal; and the human skill to get people to want to do their best." [1]

2. The leader performs a *gatekeeping function.* He must be alert to identify facts, technologies, and sets of agreements as relevant or irrelevant to the discussion. In other words, he must act to evaluate input, feedback, and production in general.

---

[1] Col. Bernard S. Waterman, "Don't Let 'Management' Trick You," *The Army Combat Forces Journal,* September, 1955.

Figure 13.

GROUP PRODUCTIVITY UNDER DIFFERENT
TYPES OF LEADERSHIP

<u>TYPE OF LEADER</u>

<u>CHARACTER OF GROUP WORK PERFORMED</u>

THE CATALYST
releases human potential,
encourages reaction
and participation

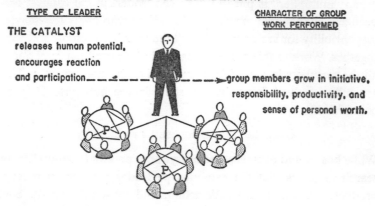

group members grow in initiative,
responsibility, productivity, and
sense of personal worth,

THE OVERSEER
cares for the details
of people's welfare
solicitiously

group members become complacent,
unresourceful, unimaginative,
acquiescent routineers.

THE BOSS
dictates plans and
makes decisions

group members tend to become his
slaves—obedient, dependent,
often resentful, and frequently
grumbling clandestinely.

3. The leader maintains the activity of the group as *exploratory, experimental, and free from dogmatic rigidities.* The genius of the group activity lies in the thoroughness and objectivity with which the members explore the nature of their problems and weigh the consequences of alternative courses of action.

The leader has the responsibility for guiding and focusing the exploration in the way most adequate to mobilize individual resources to achieve efficient progress toward the goal.

4. The leader exercises a power that facilitates the group process by attention to the flow of *communication and timing*. He pays attention to scheduling resource input. He arranges for Mr. X to talk with Mr. Y. He proposes buzz sessions. He is sensitive to points where role playing can be helpful. He can suggest materials to be read, points of view to be studied. The catalytic leader's concern with communication is not for the purpose of manipulating or dominating. Rather it comes from the sincere desire to make thorough explorations relevant to the problem and helpful to group production in creating a shared framework of ideas, purposes, and reciprocal relationships. It is this movement toward understanding that forges the individuals into an organic unit. The shared ideas, beliefs, expectations, and aspirations which each group member translates into his own performance produce what Frank appropriately calls an "active dynamic togetherness." [2]

5. The leader has a responsibility for steering the group, especially by rehearsing the consequences that may result from alternative courses of action. His activity may be described as "steering by consequences." A group moves toward a goal by a program of thought and action in a sequence of identifiable steps. Each step is taken by discussing alternative courses of action and selecting the one most advantageous course at that particular choice point or "forking of the roads." Since acts are related in a time sequence, that is, since one step naturally is taken after another, each movement alters the situation in the context of which the next act is performed. Hence the leader, steering by consequences, seeks to develop the most information available about each alternative course

---

[2] Lawrence K. Frank, *How to Be a Modern Leader* (New York: Association Press, 1954), p. 69.

of action so that the next step can be planned more wisely. In the evolving pattern of the group consensus, the leader has the obligation to see to it that each acceptance is made by taking into consideration full information and weighing all the consequences.

As the group feels its way ahead, the leader and the group members ask themselves a series of running questions. First, they inquire: "What have we learned about the nature of our problem as we have probed into the consequences of alternative courses of action? What have we learned about reality of our own resources? What have we learned about the realities of the situation external to us? In short, to use a vernacular expression, "What are we up against?" Second, the group looks upon its decision in the light of consequences, in terms of the definition of its own responsibilities as they are defined by the course of action taken. Third, the group faces an emotional situation among its own members and in relation to its own morale. That situation is related to what next step is to be taken. Are the members ready to undertake the next step, fully aware of the consequences attached to such action? Do they feel confident in attacking this next stage of the problem? Do they feel that the objective to be attained is worth the cost of achieving it? In short, as Thelen puts it: "How do people now feel with regard to the challenge of the next step?" [3]

6. The leader must be aware that change produced by the acts of his group have *consequences for other groups as well.* "Consequences," Thelen observes, "ramify like the spreading circular ripples on a pond." [4] Because what Group A does may affect what Group B does or may do, Group A needs to determine what part of its experience should be reported to Group B. Again, Group A should think through how the action of Group B can influence its own work. What re-

---

[3] Herbert A. Thelen, *Dynamics of Groups at Work* (Chicago: University of Chicago Press, 1954), p. 190.
[4] *Ibid.*

sources can Group B supply to Group A to make its exploratory work most effective? Here, it is clear, the workshop
group experiences the expanding fact of social interdepend-
ence.

7. The leader has a special responsibility for focusing attention
   on *choice points*. A group comes to attention best in response
   to formulated questions. These questions identify alternative courses of action. To each course there are attached certain inevitable consequences—"If we do A, then we may expect to face situation B."

8. The leader has an obligation to keep the exploratory work
   of the group within the facts of *reality*. He does not propose,
   if he can help it, to let the group discussion become impractical or to base reasoning on hypothetical major premises
   which are fantastic. He keeps the discussion relevant, focused,
   and unambiguous.

From his experience around the world in action programs, John
R. Mott asserted that mankind's supreme need is for great leaders
—leaders who live to the utmost limits of their faith rather than
their doubts. He explained:

> There are too many mechanical men in life, too many routineers,
> too many people going through motions for motion's sake. There
> are too few ready to explore a problem, to think through con-
> sequences, to make fearless breaks with precedent. There are
> too few leaders who live as students of the central strategic factor
> in the hierarchy of priorities.

In emphasizing the need for training leaders, Mott pointed out
what he meant in this way: "You will remember that Samuel
Morley asserted that he who does the work is not so profitably
employed as he who multiplies the doer." He continued:

> Recruiting, training, the wise use of strong men in strategic roles
> to achieve great goals—there you have it. And what is the first
> essential of recruiting? To become alarmed! To awaken to need!
> To be concerned! Every responsible leader should regard this

as incomparably his most important single task: to lay siege to strong personalities. My whole experience has taught me that you cannot command the loyalty of strong men by fractional, casual, and occasional approaches. We stumble and fail in our recruiting because we regard it as a human undertaking. The summons in recruiting is threefold: (1) It is a call to personal discipleship. (2) It is an invitation to undertake a specific task. (3) It is the discovery of the right man to undertake the right role. The rare gift in recruiting is not simply to discover the man, but at the same time to discover hitherto unexplored continents of work and the releasing of the one for the other—the identification of men of talent in order to release them for special work.

John R. Mott had in mind the assignment of men to roles necessary for the achievement of goals that were worthy of their supreme endeavor. Their best was challenged by the greatness of the purpose. He made this final observation:

One of the common failures in leadership performance lies in a neglect of personal evaluation. Early in my career I made it my obligation to sit down quietly after every meeting and write out a criticism of the session. I needed to learn from each experience so that I could do a better job the next time. I have consistently applied to my own life the same rigid measurement. At the beginning of each year I work out a personal balance sheet. I evaluate my own achievements against goals set up. I inventory my responsibilities and opportunities for the next twelve months. I allocate my priorities. I define the chief targets of my strategy. This kind of personal control of life is the obligation of the leader.

In the group workshop church the objective is to mature the group skills and build a culture that will sustain high endeavor. In the activity of a group stimulated by the catalytic skill of the leader, members make their positive contributions. "Inside themselves" they feel free and unanxious. At the same time they feel responsible. Moreover, they have the assurance that their personal worth is appreciated and respected. They discover that what they do or fail to do has ramifications throughout the whole web of the interdependent social structure.

Questions to Test Your Leadership—
Against Research Findings

BY DAVID H. JENKINS

Leading a group is a complicated, difficult job. What can we gain from the way the researchers have approached the study of groups that will help us be more effective leaders and teachers of adults?

Leadership is to be judged in light of the goals and purposes of the group

A commonplace? Wait. When social scientists began to do more than talk about leadership and started to carry out experimental research, they came face to face with a dilemma. Either they had to say that leadership is whatever the person does who is in the *position* of leader, or they had to say that leadership is whatever behavior influences the group. (A few researchers have solved this dilemma by laying aside the concept of leadership because of its varied and confused definitions, and have turned their attention to an examination of the dynamics of the entire group.)

Another approach is to speak of *good* leadership and to call good leadership whatever the leader does that helps the group, and call good membership whatever the members do that help the group. That is all right as long as we realize that the same act may be helpful regardless of whether the leader does it or a member.

David H. Jenkins, "New Questions for Old," *Adult Leadership,* June, 1956, pp. 59–61. (A monthly publication of the Adult Education Association of the U.S.A., 743 North Wabash Avenue, Chicago 11, Illinois.) Used by permission.

A test question we may ask ourselves as we work at being leaders is, "Will what I am about to do help the group in moving toward its goals or purposes?"

But how often we ask other questions instead: "What is the *proper* way to run a meeting?" "Am I losing control of the group?"

As we look back over many past meetings, we may find that we have been following the ritual of procedures: "It has always been done this way." We hesitate to select or create procedures and methods which, at the time of the particular meeting, will be most likely to help the group make progress.

At one time an agenda is necessary, so everyone will have a common starting point (what kind of items get on the agenda is a question worthy of separate exploration). At another time an agenda puts the group in a strait jacket from which they cannot escape in order to work on the problems which really concern them. How many meetings have been killed because "we had to *cover* the agenda?"

Remember the question: "Are the things I am about to do, the procedures and methods I expect to initiate, going to help the group make progress toward its goals?" (Unfortunately, in more groups than we'd like to admit it is well nigh impossible to judge good leadership because no one is clear about what the goals or purposes of the group really are, especially in terms which permit the leader or the members to decide what behavior will be helpful.)

Groups working at different tasks may need quite different kinds of leadership

We cannot expect the same way of doing things to pay off in every group we work with. Sometimes a close personal working relationship between the members and the leader will be effective; under other conditions this relationship will confuse a group. Some groups must accept the responsibility for thinking through problems and making their own decisions; other groups need firm direction from the person in charge.

Now it is easy to say that the group we work with is of a certain type—that it must, for instance, always accept direction from the leader. But its "type" may really be a *stereotype,* and prevent us from making the best contributions to the needs of the group. We may give direction on certain occasions when a group decision is desperately needed. And the reverse is also true: we may seek a group decision when clear direction from the leader is required. *There are no set rules of leadership.*

A leader can be only as effective as his group will let him be

This is not a rationalization for those poor meetings. A group does set limits for its leader—and he shouldn't blame himself for not doing what the group will not let him do. For example, some groups have their own ritual of procedure so tightly prescribed that woe be to the leader who questions it, even though it may be almost completely blocking the group's progress. Or the members will sometimes take out on the leader the resentments they have accumulated toward other members.

Like everyone else in the group, the leader will soon quit trying to help the group if his attempts are met with repeated rejection by the members. Few of us, if any, can stand continuous opposition in any situation. The research findings are pretty clear about this. The converse is also true: if attempts by the leader, or members for that matter, are encouraged and accepted by the group, more attempts to be helpful will be forthcoming.

In most groups, the entire group is responsible for the success or failure of the group

Rarely can it all be blamed on the leader, nor can he be given all the credit. As group members, we'd often like to let our responsibility slide—and we do. But the leader can do little about that.

He can, on many occasions, seriously impede the attempts of members to be helpful to the group. If he believes that he always knows best, then he will not permit suggestions to come from members. He may limit too narrowly what he will allow the members to do, thus preventing them from making the contributions they could make to the work of the group.

Groups usually need help of two kinds: help on making progress toward their working goals, and help on keeping the group in a healthy working condition

This idea has received continuing confirmation both from the study of what members do that helps groups (frequently discussed as "task roles" and "group maintenance roles"), and from the study of leadership behavior (in these articles described as the task leader and the socio-emotional leader).

A sensitive leader is usually intuitively aware of both needs and will attempt to be as helpful as he can in both ways. But much of our everyday thinking about groups and leadership has been predominately centered on "getting the job done" and much less attention has been given to improving the working relationships among members. We are seeing more clearly that "getting the job done" efficiently requires a group that has established effective ways for the members to work and communicate with one another.

Whether, frequently, it would be valuable to have co-leaders for a group, one concentrating on the task to be done and the other concentrating on the working processes of the group, remains to be seen. Perhaps one role or the other has to remain unofficial or informal. But that definite attention needs to be paid by the group to its working relationships, along with its progress on the job, is no longer in question. Yet in much of our behavior as leaders we ignore this requirement.

A special point for attention: it is difficult for the leader to resolve the dilemma posed by these two needs of the group. If he concentrates successfully on the socio-emotional processes of the group, he will tend to be liked. If he concentrates on the task processes, he will tend to be less well liked.

If our position as leader depends on people selecting us, we may avoid risking their displeasure by not pressing the group to work as effectively as they might. It takes no small courage sometimes to require members of a group to work as they must work if the job they are attempting is to be accomplished. The wisdom of the business or army organization is apparent here: the foreman is not responsible to his men for his position, so he is freer to demand work from them. Leaders in voluntary organizations are less fortunate in this regard.

What about Teaching

The points presented above may be most easily interpreted in the case of a group which is attempting to do a job or solve a working problem. But they also have application to the teaching job many of us are trying to do.

Teaching is as complex a job as is leading. In both cases we are attempting to work with a group of people toward the accomplishment of some ends. Ordinarily we think of leading as helping a group make progress on some task important to the group as a whole.

In teaching we are helping the individual members in the group to make some changes in themselves (learn something) which are desired by them. In leading, our primary concern is with the group as a group. In teaching, our primary concern is with the individual members of the group.

Perhaps a new term is needed. If we say that whoever is doing things which help the group is showing leadership, why shouldn't we say that whoever is doing things which help the individual members to learn is showing *teachership?* Have we ignored too long the fact that other people in the class besides the teacher can help other members to learn? So far, we have had no word for it. As we have believed so often that the only person who can be helpful to a working group is the leader, so we have even more strongly believed that the only person who can be helpful in a learning situation is the teacher.

We already know enough about group leadership to know that a narrow concept of leadership prevents the group from making the most use of the resources and skills of the members, with a consequent loss of efficiency. This principle seems equally true for learning groups.

Students, especially adult students, bring substantial resources to any learning situation. Many of them, for example, bring skills based on much experience which can be of great use to the group in building and maintaining good working relationships in the class.

An experiment much worth trying would be one in which the teacher of the class made it clear he was going to give attention primarily to the subject matter of the course or training session, and asked that the adult students take the responsibility for keeping the working processes in the class moving effectively. This would be shared responsibility, using class resources.

And there is the question of selecting suitable teaching methods. It takes different leadership for groups working on different tasks. So, too, does it take different teachership for groups interested in learning in different areas. And different teachership may be needed at different stages in the learning. Do we consider this when we set up a class or a series of training sessions on the "discussion basis" or the "lecture basis?"

Classes set restrictions on teachers in the same manner that groups do on leaders. If they are used to lectures, an instructor who wants to shift to an open discussion meets with resistance. And vice versa. Such classes need special help from the instructor to discover that there are a variety of experiences which can be helpful in learning.

It is his responsibility to see that the most effective methods are used to accomplish the learning which is desired. The proper basis of evaluation of a teacher is not the methods he uses, but the measure of the amount and quality of learning which has been achieved by the students.

Understanding the various elements in leadership gives us some basic tools and insights from which we can, in a creative way, fashion our methods of leading and teaching.

We Teach and Lead through Relationship

BY REUEL HOWE

We have the gift of the new relationship from God in Christ into which baptism is the door. He gave up this gift not for ourselves only, but for all men. The Christian Church exists primarily for those who are not in it, which is to say that our chief aim is missionary. The first meaning of baptism for us is that we are cared for, but its second meaning is that we are called to care for others; first we are ministered unto, but finally we must minister. How easy it is, however, for us to think of the Church as existing primarily for those who are already in; how easy it is for us to be concerned for our parish's success, prestige, and adornment and to forget those to whom we are sent. We may be so forgetful of our mission as to resent any reminders of our responsibility to those outside and to resent, also, their intrusion into our "fellowship" when they appear as a result of others' invitations. On the contrary, the Christian's mark of maturity is his readiness to seek out and care for or minister. All of us having been baptized are ministers of Christ, both laity and clergy.

All natural relationships offer natural opportunities for this ministry, and none more completely than the parental one. And certainly, if the rite of baptism is to be followed immediately by the beginning of the process that is to effect all that was begun, then parents, in the case of infants and children, are key people. When we study the natural role of the parents, we begin to see how profoundly they are ministers and how much depends upon them.

Reuel Howe, *Man's Need and God's Action* (Greenwich: Seabury Press, 1953), pp. 65–76. Used by permission.

In the first place, the relationship is a primary one. With the parent, the child has his first experience of relationship that will profoundly determine his capacity for relationship thereafter. Anyone who has ever worked with people cannot help but see that our capacities and incapacities for living with others grow out of our earlier experiences of relationship, particularly the primary one with our parents. And why not? How else would we learn to live with one another? It is not surprising, for instance, that difficulties in the marital relationship often grow out of difficulties that the partners had in relation to their respective parents. A boy who had been constantly criticized by a perfectionistic mother will be unable as a husband to enter into a relationship of mutual give and take with his wife. He will brood over even just criticisms because he will be unable to discuss them with her. Similarly, difficulties in any relationship go back, in part, to the casual influences of the first relationships. And I would not exclude from this influence of family experiences the individual's future capacity for relationship with God. Of course, God has power to transcend and redeem the effect of these, but relationship on the human level may open or close us temporarily to a relationship with God.

Likewise, the role of a parent in relation to his child is important because in the very early years the child does his most significant learning. Some educators say that all basic learning takes place before the sixth year and that all later learning is but an elaboration of the earlier. We cannot be sure that this is true; but if there is any possibility of its being true, would it not be wise to act as if it were? If it is true, then we will have taught helpfully and well. On the other hand, if it turns out not to be true, no harm will have been done. Certainly, we can agree that during these early years the child acquires indelibly ideas, motives, values, feelings that will have a profoundly determinative effect upon his character, and which in later life will be difficult to change.

An illustration of one of the results of these early influences is that a child acquires a sense of trust and mistrust by the time he is twelve to fifteen months old. Dr. Erik Erikson refers to this as "basic trust which I think is an attitude toward oneself and the world derived from the experiences in the first year of life." [1] Our sense of trust and mistrust is concerned finally with our sense of self in relation to others who are the source determinative in the realization of our being.

Basic trust is fundamental to all trust relationships including those that we call religious. Trust is trust, and who can distinguish between trust and faith? The experience of basic trust in the early years of life is, as we shall see in a moment, a foundation for the later capacity for faith in God. From the beginning of life to the end we must walk by trust or faith (call it what you will) in someone, man or God, and preferably in both.

We see, therefore, how deep a sense as trust is awakened so early in the life of a child. And yet many religious people, many church people, have been heard to say that there is not much that we can do in the way of Christian teaching until a child is old enough to go to school and has a fairly well-developed capacity to use and understand the language of words. If we hold this view, we do not really understand the role of relationship in education, and we put too much stock in what can be accomplished by means of words alone. The assumption that teaching is done primarily through verbal communication is still fairly common. Back of this assumption is another one: that words have meanings within themselves. If this were true, we could engage in a conversation and never have difficulty with the meaning of words. We would always understand one another; and if one of us introduced a word that was new to the other, understanding would not be impaired because the word itself would communicate the meaning or could be explained simply by other words. How wonderful that would be! And yet how ridiculous is the possibility of its being true. We

---

[1] Erik H. Erikson. "Growth and Crises of the Healthy Personality," from *Problems of Infancy*, Hilton J. E. Senn, ed. Josiah Macy, Jr. Foundation (1950), Supplement II. Used by permission.

know how easily a discussion becomes confused because we do not have the same meaning for our words.

Herein is the answer to our problem! The meaning is not just behind the word but also in the understanding of the person using the word. An obvious example is in our different understandings of the word love. The preacher is talking to his people about the love of God. One man who has gone through the depths in his relations with his wife and children and emerged confident, faithful, and accepting, brings his meanings to what he hears about the love of God. Another man is unhappy and sick because he has not yet found someone who can be affectionate with him and not make any demands of him, and therefore he brings very inadequate personal meaning to the understanding of the meaning of love. Also in this congregation is a young girl for whom the word love means a chum. People bring meaning out of their experiences in relationship for their use and hearing of the important words.

Back of the word, therefore, is its meaning; back of its meaning is the experience of men living in relation. The encounter between man and man and man and God produces the experience that has a meaning that demands a word as a permanent symbol by which all like experiences may be identified.

Let us use the child's acquisition of trust as an illustration. In the first place, he did not acquire it through the verbal affirmation and explanations of his mother. She did not sit her child on her knee and say, "Listen, my child, you must understand that I can be trusted. I am really quite trustworthy. There is this evidence and that evidence that I am a trustworthy person. Please believe that I know who you are, what your wants are, that I'll take good care of you. Please say that you know I am to be trusted." All the child would do in response to this frantic verbal attempt to preach the gospel of trust would be to stare uncomprehendingly at his anxious mother and acquire from her not a sense of trust but a sense of anxiety communicated by both her increasingly anxious effort to teach trust and by her failure to provide the very relationship that would awaken his trust. I wonder if we do not do just this when we endeavor to preach the Gospel of Christ by means of verbal affirmations, assurances, and explanations alone?

How then did the mother teach basic trust to her child? First, one does not, cannot *teach* trust. Trust can only be *awakened* in a person. Little is accomplished with untrusting people by talking to them about trust or by giving them books to read on the subject. After the trust is awakened, then they can be instructed through words, books, and other resources.

But how was it awakened in the first place? It was awakened by the mother's demonstration of trustworthiness. The newborn infant is only potentially a person and begins life in a state of complete dependence. He is dependent upon mother, father, and other members of his family. Through them, he is dependent upon the whole culture for food, care, love, and guidance. His first contribution at this time, if not his sole one, is represented by the phrase "I want." If he is to survive, to say nothing of prospering, his wants should receive the response of personal attention. Why should we make such response to the baby's wants? Is this not indulgence and therefore unchristian? This might seem to be the case were it not for the fact that *back of the want* for food, for companionship there is a need and hunger for all that makes possible life and being. We need to see that the calling of an infant into being as a personal self cannot be done apart from meeting his wants. Only in this way can we have meaningful personal encounter with him. When the baby is hungry, therefore, he must be fed. When he is wet and cold, he must be made comfortable. When he is lonely, he must have companionship. Satisfaction of want, at first simple and later more complex, gives the individual a feeling of well-being which leads eventually to a feeling of being loved, and that the loving one is to be trusted. The mother, having a sense of vocation for the well-being of her child, ministers to his needs so dependably that in a very short time he has had an experience the meaning of which he might put this way if he could talk: "I am beginning to know who you are. You are someone upon whom I can depend." In this way there is gradually awakened in him a sense of trust.

On the other hand, the mother is human. She cannot be in two places at once. She has other children and a husband. She has times of weariness and irritation. Accidents happen over which she has no control. Because of these conditions, in addition to other and deeper obstacles to the complete meeting of his need, she is not as dependable as he would like her to be and needs her to be. And out of the experience of deprivation and disappointment and unfulfilled wants of all kinds, come the meanings to which we have to give the word "mistrust." There are many lonely, anxious, and alienated people, who, though they may use the symbols and ceremonies of a religion of reconciliation, do not and cannot enter into a trust relationship with God or man. Years ago a man said wistfully to one of my students: "I wish I could believe that God is God." He expresses for thousands and millions of us the longing of our souls. He uttered a prayer that calls for an answer. Implicit in it is the question, "How do you awaken trust?"

We awake it not by use of the language of words alone but by the use of another language as well, a language which if rightly used is more basic. This is the language of relationship, the language the mother used, the language of mutual address and response, the language of trust and love. It is the language by means of which life provides children with experiences that make it possible for them to respond to the deepest and most complete personal meanings and to call them forth from others. The use of these two languages needs to be correlated because when we have awakened in another the response of trust, anything that we may teach about trust will have meaning for him, and he will be able to learn more about it through verbal instruction.

There is abundant evidence that the Church in carrying on its teaching function has put too much faith in the use of words and used too little the language of relationship. The result is that people are not helped to understand the meaning of their own experiences or to bring these meanings to the understandings of the meanings of the words used in preaching and other methods of formal teaching. The teacher is equally responsible for the relationships out of which come meanings that are essential to the child's future understanding and way of living. Children also need our help to formulate the meanings of their experience so that these will be available for further learning. These personal meanings need to be completed and made more universal by being united with the deeper and larger meanings that have come out of the best experience of men through the centuries. The word should be the instrument by which this is accomplished. A word is a symbol, and it should point to both the meanings possessed by the individual and to the meanings of the race. For example, the religious word faith should be the symbol of the meanings the child can bring out of his experience of basic trust, and also the symbol of the affirmative meanings that come out of the experiences of people in their encounters with God. The child's trust-meanings need the larger, deeper, and more complex meanings that lie back of the word faith in the experience of the people of God. In order for words to have this power of conveying the meaning of the fellowship to the individual, it is necessary for the fellowship to assume relationship responsibility for the meanings the individual should bring to the hearing of the word.

This insight is at the heart of the meaning of the promises of the Church to teach the child the Creed, the Lord's Prayer, and the Ten Commandments. More is intended than mere memorization of the words or even the transmission of the meanings that tradition has given the words and forms. Equally important, because without it the words and their traditional meanings will have no contemporary force, is the necessity for the meaning of the child's experience to be available as a point of contact for the new meanings symbolized by these verbal forms.

Our need today, therefore, is to be able again to speak through the language of relationship as well as through the language of words. I need the grace to *be* in order to help my child, my wife, my friend, my student to *become*. And what do I mean when I suggest that your becoming is dependent upon my being? Simply this: my friendliness helps you to become friendly, my trustworthiness helps you to become trustworthy; or my hostility causes you to become hostile, my anxiety causes you to become anxious. If I affirm, you will become affirmative. This is what I call the language of relationship, the communication that results from living together and which gives us the basic and personal meanings for the words we hear and use. The spirit of the relationship determines the nature of the communication. The partisan, self-righteous spirit, which brings into being a mob, communicates bigotry and hatred for all who do not agree. The Holy Spirit, Who brings into *being* the fellowship of love and reconciliation through that same relationship, provides the experience that causes us to *become reconciled* and to *be reconcilers*.

Thus, the Spirit gives the relationship in which meaningful communication takes place. The Spirit, therefore, makes our relationship a language, a means of engendering being and communicating meaning.

Here is a way of understanding the importance of the parental relationship as a means of teaching and upon which partly depends the realization of the meanings of baptism. Parents are the child's first teachers and the teachers upon whom the child must depend to provide the first and basic instruction. As instruments of the Church's pastoral and teaching function, parents need help in understanding the opportunity inherent in their parental relationship and in accepting their need of the Spirit to help them *to be* in relation to God in order that they may help their children *to become,* in fact as well as in name, "children of God."

PART II

SOME

BASIC

QUESTIONS

ABOUT

CHRISTIAN

NURTURE

4. WHAT IS THE PURPOSE
OF CHRISTIAN NURTURE?

AN IMPORTANT QUESTION that is all too seldom asked has to do with our purpose in Christian nurture. The findings of research suggest that one mark of an effective church group is that its members consider the purpose of the group important. Therefore they join it, attend its meetings, and participate in its work. How many members of the church group you know best really understand the purpose of the group and are committed to it? How many church group leaders understand clearly the purposes of their groups—for the next session, for the coming year, for the next ten years?

This is a difficult subject with which to deal. Who can decide what the purpose of the group should be? In the last analysis, the group itself must do it. But the group must have help. The International Council of Religious Education (now part of the National Council of Churches) developed a set of objectives of Christian education which gave a tremendous amount of help to church workers—national, regional, and local. That set of objectives was necessarily quite general. Children's workers, youth workers, and adult workers found it necessary to develop more specific statements, adapted to age groups. Curriculum writers and program planners found it necessary to develop statements of purpose related to their specific groups and themes. Such statements appear, as a matter of course, in teacher's guides and leader's manuals. Even this is not enough. The church group leader and his group know their own situation and needs better than anyone else. They should decide on the purposes they will try to accomplish. They actually do this (even though they may never prepare a written statement) by the questions they ask, the projects they undertake, and even by their decision to use or not to use a particular curriculum series or program suggestion. Others can help, but leader and group determine the purposes to which they will give themselves.

Why State Our Objectives?

BY JOHN L. LOBINGIER

Those who are asked to be teachers and leaders in the church school need a clear statement of what they are being invited to do. They need to know that the job is no superficial one, but big enough to make demands on the most capable. A clear conception of our real objectives is a challenge to a worker to be and to do his best. It is so far beyond the old idea of "keeping them quiet for an hour," or "just sitting with them and reading a story," that the institution such statements represent and the institution represented by a carefully worked-out list of real objectives are poles apart.

Parents need to be told clearly by the church why it asks them to entrust their children to its care or why they themselves should enter its classes. The fact that it is the traditional thing to "send the children to Sunday school" is not enough for the thoughtful modern parent. He must be convinced that he is sending his children to a church that knows what it is trying to do, has plans for doing it as effectively as possible, and has taken the trouble to outline these plans and to let the parents know what they are.

A clearer understanding of aims is due the pupil also. The older he grows the more critical he becomes of the agencies with which he is identified, whether the day school, a music class, a scout troop, or a church school. He passes judgment on the significance of the program and readily discovers whether the leaders are clear as to the results they seek. There comes a time when pupils themselves evaluate stated objectives. They have a respect and loyalty

John L. Lobingier, *The Better Church School* (Boston: The Pilgrim Press, copyright, 1952), pp. 6, 7. Used by permission.

for those who know what they are trying to do, and they are surprisingly competent judges of the worth of any program.

The church school has a future only to the degree to which it can shift its emphasis from the superficial to the significant. The schools that never stop to ask where they are going, and how they plan to get there, are the ones that keep public attention riveted upon the superficial in Christian education. The schools that give adequate attention to the purposes for which they exist help the public to see something significant in Christian training.

The church itself needs a standard of reference by which to check its progress in Christian nurture. Officers of a church who are alert to see that its funds are managed safely and efficiently ought to be equally alert to see that its educational program operates under a plan that sees clearly where it begins, where it is going, and how it hopes to get there. The church needs a standard for its educational activities, so that when any new plan or procedure is proposed it may check with its standard to decide whether this proposal will retard the realization of its objectives or make their realization more likely. The contest that induces superficial interest but does nothing to bring the school closer to its basic purposes will be frowned upon, whereas a curriculum that results in Christian character and a deeper sense of God will be approved.

A Broad View of Objectives

BY MARY ALICE DOUTY

Tall, slender spire, reaching into the sky—what does it mean? Clangor of bells, pealing from the steeple—what do they say? People hurrying to the church—why do they come? Teacher, greeting his class with warmth—why does he teach?

Knowing our objectives, our purposes, comes first.

A group of leaders was asked to answer in a sentence or two the question, "Why do you teach?" Several of their answers may stimulate our own thinking about our purposes as leaders in the church.

"I teach a class of boys and girls because the teachers I had as a child meant so much to me," wrote one.

Another said, "My own children go to Sunday school, so I figure I have a duty to help with the teaching."

"The church has always been important in my life," wrote a youth counselor, "and I wouldn't feel right without a job."

"I get so much out of it myself," was another answer. "I'm sure church wouldn't mean so much to me without the preparation and responsibility that go with leadership in the church school."

All of these responses are good, but we need to search deeper. Whether our work be teaching, counseling, leading recreation, holding office, or any other of the many jobs of leadership in the church, we must face these questions: What are we trying to accomplish? Why do we teach?

Let us say it boldly. We are giving ourselves to God for the

Mary Alice Douty, "Setting the Framework," *How to Work with Church Groups* (Nashville: Abingdon Press, 1957), pp. 30–32. Used by permission.

fulfillment of Jesus' prayer and ours, "Thy kingdom come." We choose to serve this King who draws us to himself through love. We find our highest joy, our deepest satisfaction, in his law and his will. Parents, teachers, the Church, the Bible, all help to lead us into that relationship with God where he is sovereign in our lives.

The other aspect of the kingdom of God in Jesus' teaching is not so immediate. It is the slow working of yeast in the dough. It is the tiny mustard seed growing into a large tree. It is the disciples of the Master going into the whole world to preach, to teach, and to heal.

We can state our objectives broadly in this way: We are trying to help men and women, boys and girls, to learn and to follow the teachings of Jesus. He gave two commandments! Love God. Love your neighbor. So simply put; yet it takes a lifetime of devotion and practice to learn and to live them!

It is our concern as teachers of the Christian religion to help our students to grow in their understanding of God and of the teachings of Jesus. We search the Bible and study the lives of men of good will. We think and meditate upon what we read and see. We stretch our minds by sharing our thoughts with one another. Alone and together we struggle to develop our beliefs and our philosophy.

By their fruits are they known, said Jesus. And we try to help our students express these beliefs in daily actions and habits. Religious living is not knowledge of facts or memorization of scripture, helpful though these may be. It is the little daily acts of kindness and thoughtfulness that indicate the religion we have learned. It is the attitude we show toward other people. It is our concern for the downtrodden, the sick, the discouraged people about us. And it is the calm, the radiance, the joy that shines on the face of one who walks in fellowship with an all-wise, all-powerful, all-loving God.

We teach toward commitment to God and to the work of God through the Church. We try to develop citizens who look at politics, economics, society, with the teachings of Jesus in mind. Honesty in government, welfare of migrants, rights of minorities, relief to the stricken—these are proper concerns of Christians, both locally and world wide. Our missionaries today study medicine, dentistry, agriculture, economics, education, politics, sociology, and science. It is our creed that God is the Father of all, that all men are brothers. Our brother's need, his disease, his hunger, his subjection, are our concern. We minister to his soul and to his body.

And in our teaching in the Church we think of family life. Here it is perhaps hardest, and should be easiest, to live as Christians. The mother-father relationship toward the children, the parent relationship of boys and girls, should these not be an expression of the God-man relationship? So we believe. Yet how difficult to practice! We are caught up in the changes that have overtaken family life. Father, whether he likes it or not, is no longer the autocrat that Clarence Day knew. Mother is no longer so tied to the houschold chores that she lacks time for other interests. Where is the child who is seen and not heard? Perplexity and confusion are the result in many homes. The Church must help in establishing a new understanding of Christian family life.

All this and more we seek to teach. In whatever work we undertake to do, let us be sure of our objectives.

Goals for the Christian Education of Children

Relationship with God and Ideas of God

The leaders' purpose will be to guide the growing child so that his relationships with God and his ideas of God will develop toward these goals:

- A sense of the reality of God that leads to a comforting, sustaining security; a realization of the care and dependability of God as evidenced in an orderly Universe in which are seen rhythmic changes of seasons, growth, and fruitfulness; an understanding of God's wisdom and greatness through a growing understanding of science; an increasing appreciation of the might and majesty of God, as revealed in nature, in history, and the lives and writings of great religious teachers of the past.

- A sense of fellowship with God who is actively at work in the world for good will, justice, beauty, through persons and through natural and moral law; a growing understanding of God's loving concern for all persons, resulting in a sense of the child's own personal worth, and of his own concern for the welfare of others; a recognition of the righteousness of God and of his demand upon his children for responsive righteousness in personal and social relationships; a growing sensitiveness to the revelations of God as he seeks to make himself known to men today.

Goals for the Christian Education of Children (New York: National Council of Churches, 1945), basic statements of six goals. Used by permission.

- A clarification of thoughts of God, developing away from the narrow idea of him as merely giver of good things, toward a response to him as Spirit; increasingly satisfying experiences of fellowship with God in group worship and in personal meditation.

Relationships with Jesus and Ideas of Jesus

Parents and leaders will have as their purpose the guidance of growing children so that they may experience a relationship with Jesus and clarify their thoughts of Jesus in the direction of these goals:

- A knowledge of the life of Jesus which will give them a definite impression of him as a person who grew normally from infancy through childhood into manhood; one who was friendly, loving, kind to little children, to the hungry, the sick, the lonely; who was just and forgiving; who loved beauty and the out-of-doors; who had courage and was steadfast in standing for the right even when it brought him into conflict with those around him and resulted in terrible suffering; who was not afraid of powerful and cruel opponents; one who lived in close fellowship with God, who was wholly committed to doing the will of God, who was never alone, even when all his friends deserted him, because he knew God was with him; who lived every day as God wants men to live.
- A feeling of affection and admiration for Jesus and a desire and purpose to be like him.
- A growing understanding of Jesus as one who not only lived as God wants men to live but who also revealed to men what God is like, who "showed us the Father."
- An appreciation of Jesus as one who by his life and death made a difference in history and won the right to man's devotion to him as Son of God.
- A growing response to Jesus who by his life and death showed men God's plan for saving them from their sin and bringing them into active participation in his purposes.

- An increasing awareness of the living Christ at work in men and through men today.

The Child and the Church Fellowship

The leader's purpose in the area of the child's church relationships is to guide his experiences so that he shall gradually realize these goals:

- A growing sense of at-home-ness with the persons in his church (teachers, ministers, other children, and adults) and in the building of his church, a feeling of satisfaction in his relationships and activities there; a developing conviction that "It is *good* to be a part of my church."
- A sense of belonging and of loyalty to the church expressed in taking increasing responsibilities for the care of the church property, in contributing to the work which the church is doing, in sharing in the fellowship of the church.
- Growing appreciation of the opportunities for group worship afforded by the church and growing ability to participate in and contribute to these services.
- Developing understanding of the essential nature of the church as a fellowship of persons whose lives are devoted to the doing of the will of God as this has been shown to men through Jesus Christ.
- Appreciation of the necessity for the expansion of the church fellowship to include those who are now outside it, and growing ability to increase the service of the church in its ministry of friendly helpfulness to others.
- Interest in and knowledge of the historical development of the Christian church in general and in the growth of his own communion as a part of the total Christian fellowship.
- Increasing understanding of the relationship of his own local church to other local churches and ability to share in cooperative efforts which serve the community.
- Growing understanding of the functions of the church in the

community and in the world as the institution committed to
the realization of the will of God in all phases of life and
growing ability to increase the effectiveness of the church in
overcoming evils, misunderstandings and group jealousies in
the community and in the world, by increasing cooperation
and good will.

- Appreciation of the church as a world-wide fellowship of
  Christians which transcends barriers of race, nation, class, and
  an increasing sense of being a part of the universal church of
  Christ.
- Ability to combine sincere loyalty and devotion to the church
  with constructive criticism, looking to the changing of its program in the light of changing needs, in order that it may pro-
  gressively reach a more complete achievement of its function.

The Child in His Personal Relationships

Parents and leaders of children will have as their purpose the guidance of boys and girls so that they may grow in the development
of Christ-like character, toward the realization of these goals:

- A developing sense of responsibility for their own conduct.
  An increasing ability to make choices according to Christian
  principles and a willingness to stand by the choices so made,
  even though they involve hardship.
- A growing disposition and ability to think of the needs and
  welfare of others; an increasing concern for the sufferings, in-
  justices and loneliness which others may have to bear; a willingness to share time, abilities, and possessions with them and
  a desire to be of service to them.
- A growing understanding of the teachings and example of
  Jesus and disposition and ability to do what is right and good
  in the spirit of Jesus.
- Awareness of God as the source of life and a developing sense
  of sonship to God, of fellowship with him, of confidence in his
  goodness and love and wisdom, of dedication to his will.

• Recognition of failure to be their best selves, of tendency to sin, to fall short of the high calling, as children of God, and disposition to ask God's forgiveness.

The Child in His Social Relationships

Leaders of children will have as their purpose so to guide the child so that he may grow in his social relationships toward the realization of these goals:

• A growing awareness of other persons, leading gradually to concern for their happiness and welfare.
• A growing understanding of what it means to love one's neighbor as one's self; a sense of respect for the individuality of others, for their right to appreciation and concern.
• Increasing skill in acting as friendly, helpful members of a group, whether it be in the family, neighborhood, school, or community; growing ability in sensing the needs of others, in meeting them in helpful ways, in recognizing and knowing how to relieve loneliness and feelings of inadequacy, in knowing how to work with others in a spirit of real cooperation.
• Increasing ability to put oneself in the place of another in order to understand his feelings and point of view; appreciation of the fact that there are individual differences of opinion and judgment and ability; disposition to deal with such differences fairly and honestly and in good will, ability to find the causes for quarrels and conflict and to know how to go about solving them.
• Growing awareness of social injustice, racial discrimination, and other unfair practices in the community and country; willingness to face the facts and try to understand them; increasing skill in knowing how to attack such problems effectively and without prejudice or bitterness.
• A courageous determination to stand for social justice even at the price of hardship and loneliness.
• A beginning ability and disposition to study the causes of in-

ternational strife, to understand the conditions of realizing world brotherhood, to make some contribution toward this realization.

• Growing sense of fellowship with God in understanding and helping to carry out his purposes revealed to men in Jesus, for a world in which men shall live together as brothers in mutual love and helpfulness.

The Child's Heritage in the Bible

The leader's purpose will be to guide the child in his increasing knowledge and appreciation of the Bible toward these goals:

• A sense of satisfaction in hearing Bible stories, an attitude toward the Bible as an interesting, comforting book.

• A growing knowledge of the content of the Bible: its great stories, its beautiful poetry; its aspirations, prayers, promises of God's nearness and care; its admonitions and laws.

• A knowledge of its great characters to whom God was very near, who found in him forgiveness and comfort and courage and who put the will of God above their own interests and concerns.

• Knowledge of the story of the Bible, how it came to be, how it has been preserved through the ages, how it has been translated into the languages of the world.

• A developing understanding of the nature of the Bible, its unique place among all other books as giving in a peculiar sense a revelation of God and his will, to men; some appreciation of what the Bible has meant to men and to nations; and a growing ability and desire to use the Bible in his own personal and group study and worship.

Junior High Objectives

Christian education seeks to lead junior high boys and girls to know God as Supreme Being, Creator, Sustainer, Ruler and Heavenly Father; to experience a maturing faith in him; to commit themselves joyfully to his will; and to grow into a warm relationship with him.

Christian education seeks to develop in junior high boys and girls an understanding and appreciation of the teachings, life, death, and resurrection of Jesus, the Son of God. This should lead to a growing realization of Jesus Christ as the supreme revelation of God, the acceptance of him as Savior and Lord, and the expression of this Christian faith in daily life and conduct.

Christian education seeks to develop in junior high boys and girls an understanding and appreciation of the nature and destiny of man as a child of God and the resulting responsibilities to God and his fellow men.

Christian education seeks to help junior high boys and girls to live as Christians in the family and in all other relationships of society and to deal with social problems in a Christian manner.

Christian education seeks to develop in junior high boys and girls the desire and ability to participate in the Christian church as loyal members, aware of its heritage, its influence in history, and its continuing fellowship and mission.

Junior High Objectives (New York: National Council of Churches, Department of Youth Work and Department of Curriculum Development, 1954), basic statements of six goals. Used by permission.

164

Christian education seeks to effect in junior high boys and girls a growing knowledge and appreciation of the revelation of God in the Bible; to show them its influence on the life and culture of man; and to help them enjoy the Bible and use it effectively in their own Christian living.

What Adults Want

BY RICHARD E. LENTZ

Adults want to feel increasingly capable of understanding and using the Bible. They want to know how to find what they need in the Bible and how to interpret what they read there.

Adults want to clarify their religious beliefs. They want the peace of absolute conviction and commitment.

Adults want to know the historical beginnings of the Christian religion. This includes a knowledge of Jesus' life and teaching and the main events of Jesus' historical setting.

Adults want the satisfaction of feeling ever more "at home" in the church. They want to know the history of their own religious communion and of their own local church. These they wish to understand in relation to the main streams of Christian history.

Adults want to understand the major Christian symbols and to develop the principal skills of the Christian life, such as worship, prayer, and witness.

Adults want to know the world program of the church as a force in redeeming society.

Adults want to know the relationship between the Christian denominations and the principal aspects of the thrilling ecumenical movement today.

Adults want to deal with moral issues and to gain power from the Christian religion.

Richard E. Lentz, *Making the Adult Class Vital* (St. Louis: Bethany Press, 1954), p. 40. Used by permission.

166

5. HOW DO PERSONS LEARN?

THE LEADER who is to help persons achieve such purposes as were discussed in the last chapter must be concerned about the learning process. This is obviously true of the teacher of a class, for there can be no real teaching unless there is also learning. It is also true of the leader of any church group, for any program that is worthy of church sponsorship aims at some kind of change in persons, and this requires learning.

Three observations may help the reader to make the best use of the material on the following pages:

1. Church work has been hampered by the narrow view that learning is a mental process of accumulating knowledge. A broader view is needed, including the idea of teaching and learning through relationship, as suggested in chapter 3. Implications of this idea for small children are suggested in the third reading following.

True Christian learning involves relationship with God as well as the human relationships of church and home. Therefore a brief quotation is included to show the place of revelation in Christian nurture. This is a difficult quotation, but the profound truth it contains makes it worthy of the reader's careful consideration.

2. When Christian educators have insisted that learning . requires participation in purposeful activity, some critics have charged them with shallow activism. The charge is well-founded *only* if the leader aims at busy-ness for its own sake, without a worthy purpose and without helping people to evaluate their activity and to find meaning in it.

3. A profound understanding of learning is involved in the first quotation. The reader should not be misled by simple style and vocabulary but should discover the implications for church groups in this broad view of learning.

Learning Is Growing—A Broad View as Written for Young People

BY NEVIN C. HARNER

We are thinking here not of body-growth, but rather of personality-growth. A little baby is far from a finished product. As he lies in his crib a few days after birth, he is not as yet a full-fledged person; instead he has been aptly described as a candidate for personality. He has no character, good, bad, or indifferent. He hardly shows as yet any real disposition, either pleasant or unpleasant. He possesses no skills: he can't play a piano, run a typewriter, carry a football. He is moved by no strong feelings about the Jews, the Negroes, the Caucasians, the Russians, the Church, or anything else of larger significance. He finds no meaning whatever at this stage in the three-letter word "God." He can't think. He can't walk. He can't talk. He can't even sit erect.

Fifty years later he will have grown up in all these respects. How does he go from here to there? What are the successive rounds in the ladder of growth? The process may look like a mere hit-or-miss affair, but it isn't that at all. On the contrary, it follows a regular and orderly course from start to finish.

The Life Story of a Habit

A baby has no habits. He has reflexes, which are simple sensory-motor patterns like the blinking of the eye when the light strikes it, but no habits. He has bodily needs and hungers, such as the "desire" to be pleasantly warm and full of food, but no habits.

Nevin C. Harner, "The Ladder of Growth," *About Myself* (Philadelphia: Christian Education Press, 1950), pp. 33–45. Used by permission.

He has some of the raw materials essential to the building of habits, but no habits as yet. For a habit is a learned way of acting, feeling, or thinking. An adult includes hundreds and thousands of them in his personality make-up, but a baby none at all. How does an adult learn his many habits? How are habits formed? The answer comprises two basic principles which are among the most important formulations in all psychology.

The first is *the principle of practice,* which means simply that we form a habit by practicing the same thing over and over again. Let us leave the little baby far behind, and skip over a number of years to find a good example, namely, a high school student learning the touch system on a typewriter. When he first looks down at the four banks of keys, they seem to be nothing but a confused jumble of letters, numerals, and signs. But he goes over them in his mind time after time, and he also goes over them with his fingers. He may begin with simple words which utilize only a few basic letters, and add others one at a time until the whole set of keys is literally at his finger tips. He now knows that "r" lies under the first finger of the left hand on the third row of keys, and "k" under the second finger of the right hand on the second row of keys. Even his fingers know this; indeed they may know it better than his conscious mind. And he can strike these many keys in proper sequence with a speed which one would scarcely believe if he had not actually seen it.

Apparently something is present in his nervous system which wasn't there before. Impulses have traveled over the very same routes so often that they have beaten a path, as it were. It is a little like walking across a ploughed field time after time in the same course until a path is laid down. Of course, there is no change in the nerve cells or fibers which can be seen with the eye or even with a microscope. It is possible that the little tendrils and branches have grown a trifle closer to one another along these routes; or else that the nerve tissue has changed imperceptibly so that an impulse makes its way more easily the fiftieth time than it did the first; but these are only guesses, of which no one is sure.

But one thing is sure: something new has been added to his nervous system, and to him. He may not touch a typewriter for five years, but when his fingers shape themselves over the keyboard again they will begin to "feel" the letters at the right places.

This is the way all habits, without exception, are formed. Has our infant in the span of four or five years become a crybaby, bursting into tears on the slightest provocation? He has done this so often that the tracks are there, ready to be used, whenever a difficulty arises. Does a person as he walks along set one foot before the other without thinking about it, and without knowing how he does it? He has walked so much that walking has become "second nature." Does a man in business turn aside from a chance to pull a shady deal almost automatically? He has practiced this sort of honesty so long and so often that he can scarcely do anything else. Does a girl on a Sunday morning feel an almost irresistible impulse to put on her best clothes and start to church when she hears the bells ringing? She has done this so many Sundays that churchgoing is an inescapable part of her. This is the first principle of habit formation: "We learn what we practice."

The second is *the principle of satisfaction,* which means simply that we form a habit more quickly and easily when the practice of it is accompanied by satisfaction. This should not be too hard to comprehend. When a certain way of acting, thinking, or feeling is enjoyable, we are likely to do it again. Thus we practice it more often. In part, the principle of satisfaction is as simple as that. But there may be something more! It is possible that, when a pleasant feeling-tone goes with an act, the nerve tissue is actually changed through endocrine gland secretions or in some other way, so that fewer runs or trials are required to "beat a path" than would otherwise be the case. Here again we are in the realm of guesswork, but we do know that habits form better when they are practiced with satisfaction.

Take learning to go to church as an example. It isn't enough just to be there fifty-two Sundays a year. If we have disliked it every time, we'll quit going the first Sunday we are old enough to be independent of our parents and to do what we really want to do. But if we found some enjoyment in it—the music, the sermon, the windows, being with people we like, or the quiet contentment which seems to belong to this holy place—that is different! We are likely to form a habit of church attendance which will stay with us as long as we live. "We learn what we practice with satisfaction"—this is the full statement. There are no words in psychology more important than these seven.

Every habit takes shape in accordance with these two principles; we can depend upon it. Are we in the habit of telling lies, white or otherwise, on occasion? The explanation is that we have practiced telling lies, white or otherwise, a good many times, and that the experience proved generally satisfactory. Would we like to become the kind of person who does his homework faithfully? The way to move in that direction is to settle down regularly to the books evening after evening, and hunt around for something pleasant therein—the satisfaction of doing a workmanlike job, or of discovering something new, or of pleasing one's parents, or even of getting a good report card. Do we find ourselves running around with the gang a good deal, and getting quite a kick out of it? We are well on the way to becoming a definite kind of person, the kind who lives principally for running around with the gang. And so on with all we do, think, feel, know, and are!

This discussion of habits raises one question which is worth following up a bit. Do you by any chance have a habit which is distasteful to you, and which you have often thought you would like to shake off? It may be smoking, biting your finger nails, swearing, or something else more or less serious. The question is, How did you ever happen to form a habit distasteful to you, if it is true that we learn what we practice with satisfaction? And why do you keep on doing it now? The answer is quite simple. The habit brought some satisfaction to some part of you, or you would never have learned it. And it continues to bring you some satisfaction, or you would not keep on doing it. The top part of you may find it altogether unpleasant, but farther down in your nature you are getting something out of the habit. The thing to do, then, is to inquire what satisfaction the habit is bringing you, and see if there may not be some other and better way of securing a like satisfaction. Only when you have done this will you make much headway in breaking the habit.

Likes and Dislikes

Our concern under this heading of "Likes and Dislikes" is not with the little ones, such as a fondness for oysters or a distaste for olives. We are thinking of the big ones, such as have to do with family, school, church, Negroes, Japanese, labor unions, and the like. These major likes and dislikes are called attitudes. They are not opinions. They are not judgments. They are primarily feelings. They lie in the realm of the emotions. And they are most important! In large part they make us what we are. And in equally large part they make the world what it is. War and peace, hatred and brotherhood, misery and happiness are in their hands.

Where do these attitudes come from? How do they creep into our lives to color our personalities so deeply, and, when multiplied by a million, to shape the course of world history?

Basically, they develop in the same way as any other habit, because attitudes are nothing but emotional habits. They are habitual ways of feeling about something. And so we learn our attitudes by practicing them with satisfaction. If our home life has been mainly happy, and we have frequently felt a deep sense of attachment to the home and all it stands for, and found satisfaction in feeling this way, we build up in time a tremendous loyalty to our home. Let someone say a word against it, and he has us to reckon with. The house is the finest house, the yard the finest yard, the furnace the finest furnace, and the people the finest people that anyone ever saw. That's the way we feel about it, and that's the way it is. By way of contrast, if during World War II we read a great deal about Japanese atrocities, and on a good many occasions indulged in letting ourselves go against the Japanese and took quite a bit of satisfaction in feeling that way, we come out after a while with a deep-seated prejudice against the Japanese. As far as we are concerned, there is not one good thing about them—no, not one! Their appearance is not attractive, their characters are not trustworthy, their land is not beautiful, their products are not worth having. We simply don't like the Japanese, and that settles the matter. In both of these instances, the attitude is clearly an emotional habit of long standing, built up in the same way as other habits, and now working automatically as all habits do. It is very much like a Jack-in-the-box. Press the spring, and out it pops.

While this is perhaps the chief way in which attitudes develop, there is another way of accounting for them which is quite helpful. When two things reach us wrapped up in the same package, as it were, we often come to feel toward the second the way we originally felt toward the first. For example, none of us like to be unpopular. If we find ourselves unpopular at school, laughed at and never elected to office, we may develop a revulsion against school itself. The two—unpopularity and school—have been so closely interwoven in our experience that we transfer to the second a feeling which was originally directed against the first. We may not be aware that this is happening, but it goes on just the same. This transfer is called "emotional conditioning." We might put its meaning this way: The direction our emotions take is shaped by conditions. A simple illustration may be found in our fear of lightning. The chances are that we are really afraid of the thunder to begin with, because a loud noise is one of the best stimuli for getting a startled reaction in children. But thunder is always accompanied by lightning. Every time we shrank in fear from thunder, a certain condition was present, namely, thunder and lightning together. So in due time the transfer was made, and we became afraid of the lightning. The emotion of fear now took a new direction and was attached to a new object because of this condition.

Many of our attitudes have all too clearly been formed by a process of emotional conditioning. Let us say that in childhood we were bored by church services. We dislike being bored. And so in time we dislike church. Or suppose that one time when we were quite small we were frightened by a Negro, whose unfamiliar face and huge frame towered high above us. Anything big and strange is likely to inspire fear in a child. The whole experience was most unpleasant. We were frightened, and perhaps we were ashamed because we were frightened. And so we wake up one day in adulthood finding ourselves bitterly but unreasonably turned against Negroes. The emotion which we once felt toward a large, strange object has now been directed against a whole people.

One more way of explaining how attitudes begin in the individual life deserves some mention. In a great many cases they are caught from the people we live with. They come to us like measles —by contagion. They sweep over a mass of people like any other epidemic. If our parents and friends all hate and mistrust the Russians, so do we. We have never given much thought to the matter. We have not inquired carefully whether or not the Russians deserve to be hated and mistrusted. Everybody's doing it, and so do we. If everyone around us stands up when the Star Spangled Banner is played, and takes off his hat when the flag passes in parade, and in general shows a deep loyalty to our country, we too stand up and take off our hats and become as patriotic as they are. It may be that we have thought the matter through and arrived at this position out of deep conviction; but more likely than not we simply go along with the crowd.

If these are the ways in which attitudes become a part of us, several rather disturbing conclusions follow. One is that there is no assurance any attitude is telling us the truth about the institution or the people concerned. As we have seen, it may be a mere habit, or the outcome of chance conditions, or a thoughtless borrowing from others. As such, it is not clearly thought through. It is not based upon carefully gathered evidence. It is simply a feeling-tone, an emotional leaning toward or away from someone or something. How sure can you be at this moment that your attitudes toward school, or church, or America, or capitalism, or the Chinese tell you the truth, the whole truth, and nothing but the truth?

Another conclusion is that an attitude is a lazy, inaccurate way of meeting any given situation. If a person is down on the Negroes, he has a ready-made way of dealing with any Negro he meets. He doesn't have to think about the matter. He doesn't have to inquire whether this particular Negro is good or bad, well-educated or illiterate, and work out an approach that fits this individual representative of the race. No, he has a pat approach for the entire race. Push the button, and out pops the Jack-in-the-box. If a person has a fixed prejudice against the Russians, he lumps them all together and treats them all alike. Now there are Russians, and Russians; but that doesn't matter to an attitude. No accuracy of discrimination! No selective judgment! Just a general broadside against all Russians!

It is clear—is it not?—that attitudes are tricky affairs. Every now and then each of us ought to drag his private supply out into the light, and give it a good overhauling in the light of all the facts he can get and all the Christian principles he can discover.

Thinking Things Through

As a general rule, we don't think—that is, really think—unless and until we have to. For true thinking means finding the solution to a problem, or the way through some difficulty. Unfortunately we use the word "think" in a variety of ways in ordinary speech. We may say, "I thought and I thought, but I couldn't recall her name." Properly speaking, that is not thinking at all. It is merely remembering, or trying to remember. Or some sunshiny day we may have drifted off into a mental haze speculating pleasantly on what we would do if we suddenly came into an inheritance of a million dollars. Before our mind's eye moves a splendid procession of mansions, automobiles, yachts, fur coats, and golf clubs. Suddenly an unexpected visitor asks what we are doing, and we reply, "Oh, I was just thinking." That isn't real thinking. It is merely daydreaming. In the true sense of the term, thinking is problem-solving.

Let us suppose that one day you are driving along a country road in an automobile, a sleek, up-to-the-minute convertible. All at once the engine gives a wheeze and a cough, and stops dead. What do you do? Well, you may pass through a brief period of what might be called mild shock. This is so unexpected. You have to shift your mental gears to take in this sudden, drastic change in the situation. A moment ago you were freewheeling along without a care in the world. Now you are motionless and helpless. But soon you begin to assemble your wits, and face things as they are.

Probably your first move is to diagnose the problem, which means that you try to discover where the difficulty lies. How well you do this will depend on how much you know about automobiles. If your knowledge is scanty, your diagnosis may not get much further than an ineffectual "Oh dear, what can the matter be?" But if you are pretty well posted on what takes place under the hood, your diagnosis is considerably better. Is the engine overheated? A car will stop sometimes if the engine temperature mounts too high. No, the thermometer registers only normal temperature. Could it be a broken fuel pump? No, it couldn't be that, for the pump was repaired week before last by a good mechanic. Maybe it's out of gas. Sure enough, the gas gauge stands at "Empty." The day was nice, and the sun was high, and you had lost all track of distance. And so you are out of gas. The problem is diagnosed. You know where the trouble lies.

Your next step, then, is to cast about for solutions of the problem. Is there a farmhouse nearby which might have an extra supply of gasoline? Yes, there is one over there at the foot of the hill, but there are no cars, tractors, or trucks in sight. The prospects are rather poor. It's hardly worth a walk down the lane to find out. Perhaps a passing motorist will be kind enough to stop and allow some gas to be siphoned out of his tank. But, on second thought, that's not such a good idea. In the past ten miles you haven't met a single car, and the chances are against you. Could there be a gas station not too far away? There is none visible on the road ahead, but wait a minute! Wasn't there a gas station about half way up that last hill? Surely there was—on the right-hand side of the road, with two gas pumps, and only about a quarter of a mile away.

Now at last you have it. The problem has been diagnosed. The solution has been found. The only thing that remains is to put this likely solution to the actual test. And so you walk back down the road, find the station open, buy a gallon of gas in a borrowed can, return to your car, start the engine, and the thought-process is over—until the next time.

All real thinking follows this same general pattern. Let us see how it works out in thinking through the very difficult problem of Negro-white relationships in our nation.

The first step is to diagnose the problem. What is the nub of the difficulty? Is it overpopulation, too many people trying to live in a limited area, and getting into one another's way until tension results? Hardly! Even though the number of Americans has been growing rapidly, there is still elbowroom in America. Is it the threat and the fear of intermarriage between the races? In the eyes of many white people this is a real sore-spot, but to Negroes scarcely at all. They do not particularly desire intermarriage, and are not greatly concerned about it. Could the root of the trouble be economic? Perhaps so! We recall that the lynching rate goes up as the price of cotton goes down, and vice versa. Negroes, who are greatly underprivileged, are anxious to get more of this world's goods than they have thus far had. And whites are anxious to keep what they have. The result is rivalry, tension, mistrust, bitterness. For the time being at least, we settle on this as a major part of the problem to be solved.

The next step is to cast about for solutions of this problem. What is to be done about it? Would better education for both Negroes and white people help at all, enabling our citizenry all along the line to fit better into the productive processes of our nation? Would there be any gain in trying to expand the number of bi-racial labor unions, so that the two races might have more opportunity to work things out together? Or should the approach be by way of rehabilitating thousands of acres of land in the South, on which countless people now eke out a slim existence? Or does the solution lie rather in the direction of more bi-racial churches? Among these various solutions, and others which might be included, which is soundest economically? Which is closest to the spirit of Jesus?

The third step—which really goes a bit beyond the thought-process itself—is to try out one or more solutions of the problem in actual practice, and then perhaps revise the strategy, or even start all over again, in the light of the experience gained.

Greatly simplified, this is real thinking. It can be applied to the choice of a vocation, the construction of a budget for one's personal use, the building of a program for a youth fellowship, the problem of boy-girl relationships, the control of atomic power, or any other puzzling issue large or small in the life of the individual or of society. It can be done by a solitary individual or by a number of people in cooperation, in which case it is called group thinking or group discussion. As far as we know, human beings are the only creatures that can really think. It is, therefore, one of our unique and priceless privileges. We ought to do a great deal of it, probably much more than we ordinarily do. It is one of the best ways to climb the ladder from earth to heaven.

Who Made the Ladder?

Forming habits, shaping attitudes, thinking things through—none of these is a mere hit or miss affair. All of them proceed according to definite laws and principles. Who made these laws and principles? All of them, if done well and constructively, represent a steady climb on the ladder of growth. Who set up this ladder?

Clearly we didn't. These processes were going on, and going on just this way, long before we were born. Cromagnon men in the caves of France thousands of years ago formed habits then just as we do today. The ancient Israelites developed attitudes toward the Philistines and the Assyrians in the same way as we develop attitudes toward the Japanese or the Russians. The old Greeks followed exactly the same process of thought as the one we follow, and did very well indeed!

It is equally clear that the psychologists didn't set it up. They have discovered these various laws and principles and processes, but they didn't make them. They simply studied minutely and formulated clearly what was already there. Some psychological laws do indeed bear the name of a man, as, for example, Thorndike's Laws of Learning; but this means only that the man in question reduced them to clear form. He did not create them.

Who then did? God did. He ordained the laws and principles, and wrote them into the structure of things for our own good. He set up the ladder of growth. If we climb it patiently, round by round, it will lead us to him.

We Learn through Relationships—As Written for Workers with Small Children

BY PHOEBE M. ANDERSON

Can children "learn" to be Christian? Surely, if the test of real learning is a change in attitude and behavior, they can. Without saying that nature has nothing to do with a person's becoming a mature Christian, we can assert without fear or equivocation that nurture has a great deal to do with it.[1] The Sunday church school movement is based on this assumption, as are fellowship groups, Christian prayer groups, and, in fact, the church itself. Children can grow up with Christian convictions and practices. The question we keep asking ourselves, our curriculum writers, and our Christian leaders, is: how? How do children grow into mature Christians? What are the steps in this process? How do we teach children to become Christian? If there is something more than songs, stories, projects, and activities, what is it? And how do we do it? These are not easy questions to answer, and yet we must answer them if we are not to fail in our task of Christian education.

The word that is the clue to the answer for each of these questions is "relationship." It is in a relationship of love and trust, respect and forgiveness that a child learns to love and trust, re-

Phoebe M. Anderson, "Christian Growth Through Personal Relationships," *Religious Living with Nursery Children* (Boston: The Pilgrim Press, copyright, 1956), pp. 17–20. Used by permission.

[1] Even the sudden and dramatic conversion that has been the experience of many Christians through the years does not rule out nurture. Nurture-conversion is not an either-or way to mature Christian living. They go along together. Does not each new insight into God's will for one's life involve a conversion?

spect and forgive. Being treated as a person by men and women, parents and teachers who are themselves mature Christian persons is the fundamental experience for growth into Christian maturity. In this relationship of person to person the values, the integrity, the faith, the struggles, the joys of each person are treated with respect and understanding by the other person. Each person finds himself less defensive and fearful and more able to extend himself in an expression of concern to the other.

The word "person" as it is used here in the phrase, "to treat a child as a person," has more than the common-sense meaning of treating him as a member of the human race. Rather it is to think of him as a being of infinite worth. He is not only the child of Harry and Jane Brown; he is also a child of God—winsome, unique, creative—who expresses the nature of his Creator in his laughing, his loving, his forgiving, his boundless energy, his rejection of façade and insincerity. A person is an end in himself. He is not to be used to serve any other end.

Therefore, to treat a child as a person is to live with him as though he were an honored guest for whose life we are responsible. It is to be concerned about his needs, considerate of his moods, respectful of his person and of his possessions. Contrariwise, it is not to use him, manipulate him, or dominate him. There are too many parents and teachers in the world who use children to enhance their own feelings of worth or prestige; or to provide a channel for their own frustrated ambitions; or as an outlet for their own unexpressed hurts; or, by enforcing strict discipline and rigid behavior patterns, to give themselves a sense of power and influential position. A child, in this kind of relationship, becomes an object, a tool in the hands of another, a means to another's end, an "it." For an adult to commit such a sin against a child "it would be better for him if a great millstone were hung round his neck and he were thrown into the sea." A person is a "Thou," a child of God.

The parent or teacher who would treat a child as a person, a "Thou" rather than an "it," must also maintain his own sense of personhood as a member of God's creation. He, too, is a son of God and, therefore, must not be used or thought of as an "it" whose sole function is unflagging service to the child's every whim. The parent or teacher is an "I." Therefore, the relationship of one person to another person is an "I-Thou" relationship; not "I-it," nor "it-Thou," nor, worse, "it-it."

Admittedly, children are likely to be unskilled in this kind of living. But many adults are, too. A child learns to live this way by being valued and regarded as this kind of person. The trouble with us adults who cannot treat children in this fashion is that we, in our growing up, were not treated as persons, and we are still trying to establish our sense of worth and value and prestige in our own eyes by using people to help us do it, especially the children about us, for they are the most vulnerable. There is considerable truth in the observation that most of us tend to treat children pretty much as we were treated by adults when we were children.

This "I-Thou," or person-to-person, relationship with children does not produce rude, undisciplined, self-centered children, *if the adults in the relationship insist on maintaining their personhood.* For example: John's mother respects his right to have, augment, or dispose of his collection of grubby sticks and uninteresting stones; and John must in turn respect his mother's buttons, bows, and various odd things that are available in every single drawer of the old sewing machine. The teacher does not interrupt John when he is talking or make a request of him when he is deeply engaged in something, nor does John interrupt her.

Adults do not take things from children without asking, nor do children take things from adults or from other children without asking. Adults do not tease children, or fool them, or misinform them, nor do children tease each other or "lie" to adults. The same kind of respect, consideration, and thoughtfulness which adults must accord children if adults would treat them as persons, adults must also expect for themselves. If they do not, the child grows into a boorish, unfeeling adult with no concern for the feelings or rights of others. If, on the other hand, adults demand "respect" of children without granting it, and courtesy without extending it, the child either grows into Mr. Milquetoast, the prey of any authoritarian person or idea that accosts him, or he becomes an adult who fights authoritarianism on every hand, dominates all whom he can (wife and children, the neighbors, public servants, and so forth), and has a hard time living with superiors or bosses whom he cannot dominate. To state the matter succinctly: children grow into real persons, whole persons, by being treated as real persons by adults who are themselves real persons, whole persons. Children grow into mature Christian persons through an "I-Thou" or *personal relationship* with mature Christian persons.

Revelation and Christian Nurture

BY LEWIS J. SHERRILL

The doctrine of revelation, from one point of view, is almost as important as the fact of revelation and the reports of revelation; because it has so much to do with what we shall hear and ask others to hear in the Christian community, and so much to do with determining the frame of mind with which we shall begin to respond and open or close the way for others to respond. The doctrine of revelation, then, is a crucial element in the life of the Christian community and in the philosophy of Christian education. Indeed, it could be maintained that it is the determinative element in both. That is to say, any philosophy of Christian education must incorporate a doctrine of revelation in *some* form or other.

The doctrine of revelation which is incorporated into a philosophy of Christian education can take a negative form. Many negative forms of the doctrine of revelation are possible. For example, if there is the presupposition that God can in no way be known and communicated with as Personal Being, the philosophy of Christian education must be constructed around that premise.

The doctrine of revelation as incorporated into the philosophy of Christian education can take a positive form. Again, many variations are possible. But, for example, if there is even so much as an openness of mind toward the possibility that God can be known and communicated with as Personal Being, a philosophy of Christian education can be constructed which is consistent with the doctrine of revelation as confrontation. This in turn would mean

Lewis J. Sherrill, *The Gift of Power* (New York: The Macmillan Company, copyright, 1955), pp. 68–70. Used by permission.

that the educational work of the Christian community could be carried on in such a way as to allow the fact of revelation and the reports of revelation to speak for themselves to the members of the Christian community. What, then, is meant by revelation as confrontation?

To express the concept of revelation as confrontation in one of the simplest ways possible would be to say that God as Self confronts man as a self, and has disclosed himself to man.

To speak thus of "confrontation" means that God as infinite Personal Being faces man as a finite personal being. In terms which we have used earlier, it implies that in any togetherness between God and man there is always also a separateness of selfhood. It implies that man is not himself a god, but faces God; and if in facing God he is drawn toward God he is not absorbed into God. But on the other hand it does *not* need to imply, as some would have it, that God as Personal Being is wholly outside man as a personal being; for the doctrine of the Spirit of God means that God as Personal Being is perceived as present within man as a personal being, present within man yet not identical with man.

To speak of revelation as God's *Self*-disclosure implies that *what* is revealed in the encounter between man and God is not information *about* God, but God *himself* as Personal Being. The reports of revelation may have to be cast in terms that contain information, or that attempt to describe what was perceived in the encounter. But in the encounter itself what is disclosed is some aspect of infinite, perfect Selfhood, being unveiled in some form of relationship with finite, imperfect selves.

To speak of revelation as confrontation implies, further, that human perception is involved in revelation. Revelation is revelation *to human beings*. The capacities of the human self are engaged in receiving what is communicated in revelation. This does not mean that no one benefits from revelation unless he knows he is doing so. It does mean that unless he *perceives* what is disclosed, the disclosure has not yet reached him. For to perceive is more than merely "seeing" what is manifested, and it is more than "hearing" what is uttered. One can see, and not perceive; one can hear, and not understand. Accordingly it is common to find that communication has broken through the confines of what a man already "knew."

After these general statements regarding revelation as confrontation, we may consider some of the more specific questions regarding the nature of revelation.

In the Biblical accounts of revelation there are various media through which God reveals himself to man, and where his disclosure of himself to man is perceived. These media are commonplace, in the sense that they are known, or may readily become known, to the members of the religious community. This means that a great part of God's disclosure of himself is made through what is already known.

Among the chief media employed for this purpose are physical nature, human nature, events in history and, above all, Jesus Christ the living "Word of God," himself the culmination of revelation. The materials taken from such media provide symbols drawn from the realm of that which can be known by the senses. The symbols represent some aspect of God as Personal Being who cannot be fully known since he is infinite, but who yet can be truly known by the aid of the symbols. The symbol then in turn becomes a means of communication in the religious community regarding man's situation, and regarding the corrective, redemptive, and recreative power of God.

We Learn through What We Do—As Written for Workers with Older Children

BY DOROTHY LA CROIX HILL

What Did You Do?

If at the Sunday dinner table instead of, "What did you learn?" father would ask, "What happened today at church? What did you do?" his junior might reply with a torrent of words. For wherever juniors meet, a great deal is happening. The junior who pours out all that "happened," all that he "did," is actually telling us what he learned, if we are able to interpret.

"What did you do at church today?"

"We just sat, and Mrs.—— read out of the quarterly." ("We learned that the church is a place of boredom and inactivity, where people just sit and listen to other people talk or read.")

"What happened at church today?"

"We finished reading the story of Joseph the way it is in the Bible, you know. We can read our new Bibles (Revised Standard Version), but Mrs.—— makes stories sound so exciting that we asked her to read most of it. Then we counted off and made committees of five. Each committee dramatized one part of the story, not saying anything, you know. The others guessed what was being acted out. Our committee showed Joseph's servants finding his cup in Benjamin's sack. I could read that to you. It's toward the end of Genesis."

("We learned that the Bible has stories we can enjoy. We are

Dorothy LaCroix Hill, "What Did You Do?" and "Learning—Good or Bad?" *Working with Juniors at Church* (Nashville: Abingdon Press, 1955), pp. 10–16. Used by permission.

learning to read it and to find our favorite stories and passages in it.")

"What happened at church today?"

"We fellows really had fun! We got the girls crazy, and Miss ——, too. She couldn't do a thing!"

("We learned that the church is a place where one can act like a rowdy. It is not a place where boys and girls work and learn.")

Yes, even when the junior thinks he has learned nothing at church, he has learned much. It may not be what the teacher thinks he has learned. It may not be what he was expected to learn, but he has learned, for all of us are learning all the time. We are learning many different things at once, ways of thinking, feeling, acting. Learning begins in infancy and goes on to our dying day. It is made up of change. We are constantly rubbing up against experiences which force us to change—other people, new ideas, difficult problems and situations, decisions which have to be made, forces of nature. We find ourselves thinking differently, feeling differently, responding in new ways to situations, to what happens, to what people ask of us, to God, and to his will for us.

Some learning helps growth because the person is changing in desirable ways. Some learning interferes with wholesome growth when the learner accepts an untrue or mistaken belief, or becomes the victim of misguided emotions. His response to persons, to situations, to God, can be no better than his thinking and feeling.

A book-loving junior was asked if he were a ballplayer.

"No," he said carefully, "but I am learning."

Both he and his parents had recognized that he was losing out on wholesome fellowship with his own age group because most of the boys in the neighborhood played ball all their waking hours.

"I'm just not good at it," Bill said defensively.

"That's all right, Bill," his father replied. "The fellows who are better at it get to play the most. But any chap can know enough about ball to fill in when a team needs an extra player. A good mitt would help you."

The new mitt did help. So did the evening games in the back yard—all "just for fun"—with the whole family, younger neighbors, and gradually other boys Bill's age all taking a turn at bat and in the field.

Bill found himself learning many things at one time. He was growing not only in skill, but in wholesome feelings toward the game, toward the fellows who played it all the time, and best of all, toward himself.

Bill discovered that learning is changing. He saw himself little by little changing to a fellow who no longer drew back his hand rather than take the sting of a hard-thrown ball, who accepted the offer of a post in left field instead of shaking his head, who felt comfortable on the bench. His parents knew that learning was all these things, and a little more.

It was Bill sounding different and a changed boy when someone asked, "What do the kids in your neighborhood do, Bill?"

"Oh, they mostly play ball," but without any bitterness in the words.

"Are you a ballplayer, Bill?"

"No, but I'm learning," with cheerfulness and a touch of assurance.

The day might never come when Bill could answer, "Yes." He could say that he had learned only when his catching and hitting, running and throwing, would almost always count toward victory for his team. But in the meantime he was *learning*.

Learning—Good or Bad?

Wayne was learning, too. His learning was taking place at church, but it was not good.

When he participated in a laboratory class with boys and girls from several churches, an adult leader said to the instructor, "See if you can find out what is wrong with Wayne. His teacher has so much trouble with him. She says he is mean. She likes children and knows how to work with them, too."

Wayne and his pal were handsome, lively nine-year-olds. The instructor from the first moment kept them too busy for mischief. She liked them, and they liked her. But in the second session something went wrong. Each child had been given a copy of the Revised Standard Version of the Bible, and the class set to work to make some important discoveries about the New Testament. Wayne snatched the Bible from the girl who was passing them. Rapidly he began to thumb through the pages, paying little attention to the teacher's simple directions for finding books, chapters, and verses. Presently he slammed his Bible shut and sat back with folded arms, sullenness settled like a cloud over his bright face. The instructor did not understand what had happened. She said nothing.

The next day the boys and girls found six large teaching pictures in the room, six Bible references on the blackboard. Copies of the Bible, paper, and pencils were ready for use. The juniors were asked to study each picture, copy the titles on a sheet of paper, read the references silently, and write opposite each picture title the name of the Gospel in which they had discovered that story.

Wayne enjoyed looking at the pictures. But once again when he took the Bible, his actions became strange, "frenzied" was the word in the mind of the watching teacher. She sat down beside him and repeated step by step the directions for finding the Gospels. But as she tried to help him, Wayne's attention darted from one child to another. He tried to read the first reference, but his eyes left the page with every few words.

"Read it to me," the teacher invited.

Wayne read well, so that was not the problem. When the first child announced that he had finished, Wayne's face twisted with anger. He slammed his Bible shut and walked to a far chair, his arms folded and his expression sullen. He took no more interest in the session. The Bible seemed to be at the heart of the difficulty. Finally the instructor inquired how the Bible was used with juniors in Wayne's church. Each Sunday when the department met together, a Bible drill was held. Seventy or more children competed to see who could find each reference first and read aloud just enough to show that the right verse had been found. Members of the fourth grade were seldom first, but apparently Wayne could not accept defeat, even by older and more experienced children. His father was a university professor. A good deal was expected of him in the way of scholastic achievement, yet the Bible defeated him Sunday after Sunday. In his passionate efforts to be first he was missing out on the basic learnings which could have helped him become more skillful in handling the Bible. Already the very sight of a Bible was associated in his mind with failure. His emotions began to seethe as soon as copies were distributed. So strong had the pattern of failure become that in this new situation where the Bible was used as a source of needed information, not in meaningless competition, Wayne could not recognize the difference.

Wayne had accepted a wrong idea about the Bible. He thought of it as an instrument of competition. His efforts to use it in this way had created most unwholesome feelings. As a result his response to the Bible, and indeed to the whole of his church-school experience, could not be anything else but disagreeable, both to himself and to his teacher.

Vernon was learning, too. Like Wayne he was learning at church school, and his learning had to do with the Bible.

"What did you do today?" asked his mother.

Vernon's eyes lit up with enthusiasm. The fourth-grade class had started work on a choral reading, Psalms 150, to be shared with the adult classes three Sundays hence.

"It's about musical instruments, you know," Vernon explained. "The girls are the 'strings and pipe,' and we are the cymbals— 'praise him with loud clashing cymbals!' it says."

"You know some of it, don't you?" his mother asked.

"Oh, no!" said Vernon. "We didn't learn it; we just read it."
"How does it begin?" asked his older brother.

"Why"—Vernon pondered a moment, then phrase by phrase, line by line, to his own astonishment he repeated the entire passage. He jumped from his chair in great excitement and ran to get his Bible, "to be sure I got it right." He had it right. He turned to Psalms 95 and read the lines which his class had studied. His mother reminded him that he knew Psalms 100, and he read this with pleasure. His father asked him to read Psalms 23.

Then an idea came to life in Vernon's quick mind. "Say," he said, "whenever we are supposed to read in Psalms for family worship, may I read?"

Vernon's experience with the Bible was helping him to grow in the very ways which his teacher, his church, and his parents desired. It was leading him to want to keep on learning from and using his Bible. It is important to note that when the church learning was lifted up, understood, and appreciated *at home,* Vernon moved forward into a still finer response to the Bible, one which under the guidance and encouragement of his parents might become permanent.

Basic Principles of Learning—As Written for Workers with Adults

BY IRENE SMITH CALDWELL

Mrs. Snodgrass had been teaching the adult class in Jonestown church for more than a dozen years. She was sincere and faithful, and people said she was a good teacher. A teachers' workshop was being held in the village just ten miles away. The pastor urged that every teacher in the Jonestown church participate. Mrs. Snodgrass went out of a sense of duty. She was interested in teaching, and then there was to be a potluck dinner at noon. But she thought she knew how to teach, and it did not occur to her that there was anything new to learn about teaching adults. At first things went as usual, but gradually she felt herself threatened. The group were discussing the topic, "How Adults Learn." They seemed to think that no one learns much by just listening. They thought adults had to participate and be active if they really learned. One woman said, "I've been teaching adults a long time, but if what we're saying here is true, my class hasn't learned very much." Mrs. Snodgrass had a feeling that this might be true of her class too. She felt pretty uncomfortable. Had she wasted all these years? Were they saying she didn't know how to teach? How could you get adults to participate anyway? When she had asked questions her class usually answered with only a word or two, if that. Finally she could stand it no longer so she asked that very question, "How can you get adults to participate?" and she really wanted to know the answer.

Irene Smith Caldwell, "How Adults Learn Best," *Adults Learn and Like It* (Anderson: Warner Press, 1955), pp. 16–19. Used by permission.

This experience suggests several points about adult learning.

1. *The person must have an uncomfortable feeling about not knowing.* When one feels he knows, he is not open to learning. He must have a *desire* to learn (and the church must cultivate this open, eager desire for learning in adults).

2. *In order to learn, one must be involved.* He must be able to see the connection between what is being taught and his own experience. He must feel, "That's my experience," or, "That's what's happening to me," or, "That's my need," or, "Maybe my practice is beneath the Christian ideal," and he must begin the struggle to find the answer. I use "struggle" advisedly, for there is nothing more painful than a new idea.

But Mrs. Snodgrass must go further, and her hardest step is still ahead. She has obstacles to overcome—first, her own habit patterns of more than a dozen years. Then her class have habit patterns too. They are pretty comfortable and may not wish to be disturbed. But in spite of all this, she sets out to make her class period a real learning experience.

3. *Learning requires putting forth an effort.* The learner must do something about ideas. To be challenged with a new idea and not to act accordingly means that personality deterioration sets in. Learning has not taken place when one knows that he should act in a certain way, but only when he changes his attitudes and the proper action results.

A missionary to India stood before a group of college students. He began by saying, "I stand before you in great fear. Not that I have stage fright; but I fear that after I picture the heartbreaking needs of India to you, you will be moved to sympathize, but will go away and continue to live in the same self-satisfied way. If that should be true, it would be better for you never to hear about the needs of India or the world." So learning requires action.

4. *The final step in the learning process is the feeling of satisfaction that comes with accomplishment.* If Mrs. Snodgrass really

improves in her teaching methods and her pupils respond she will be spurred on to greater improvements. We learn best when there is some reward for learning—either our own sense of accomplishment, the words of appreciation of the pastor or class, or our realization that we are more able to help others.

To summarize, then, adults learn best when they have a sense of need, resulting in a desire to learn; when they have a feeling of being personally involved in the issue at hand; when they put forth real effort to put new ideas into practice; and when a feeling of satisfaction results from the learning experience.

When learning is desirable, pleasant, life-centered, and satisfying, then *adults like to learn.*

6. HOW CAN A LEADER KNOW INDIVIDUALS IN A GROUP?

PSYCHOLOGISTS and age-group specialists can tell us about what to expect of people at a given age. They know the stages through which individuals and groups may be expected to pass. They know about what the interests, needs, and abilities of people in a particular age group will be. But they do not know when a specific child will reach a certain stage, or how rapidly he will pass through it to another. Each individual develops at his own rate and in his own way. Therefore the effective group leader needs to know his own particular group and the individuals in it. Only then can he know what they need and how best to work with them. Only then can he sense the reasons for their individual and group behavior and know how to guide them toward Christian maturity.

Some Good Ways of Learning to Know Children

BY ELIZABETH S. WHITEHOUSE

The Need to Know Children

It is Sunday, and the new teacher takes her place in the class at the church school. She studies the faces before her. How shall she guide these boys and girls who look to her to open the way of life to them? Her eagerness to help, her Christian purposes, her knowledge of the Bible—necessary as they are—are not enough for all that must be done. These boys and girls have basic needs. They need to know that God invites them to enter into a deep personal relationship with him. They need to understand that through repentance and trust they may claim God's forgiveness and help because he has promised them these. Just when the child's realization of his need for God will come the teacher cannot know. His confidence must rest upon his knowledge that God is the initiator, that his Spirit is already seeking after each member of the class, continually active, continually present in human life.

So the teacher counts himself a humble co-worker with God in winning the children. In order to be effective in soul winning, the teacher must know these children—Gladys, Robert, Ruth and John—if she is to win their confidence and lead each one to become the best that he or she can be. As Emmett A. Betts says, "We must 'learn' our children before we can teach them." [1] This is doubly true if leaders value individual personality and refuse to

Elizabeth S. Whitehouse, "Getting Acquainted with Children," *The Children We Teach* (Philadelphia: Judson Press, 1950), pp. 15–19 and 25–37 (excerpts). Used by permission.

[1] In *Foundations of Reading Instruction*. Copyright, 1945, by the American Book Company, New York. Used by permission.

accept an assembly line ideal as their goal for children's progress toward goodness.

A teacher must learn to know his children by every means at his command. He must know what they are like, how they learn, and what can be expected of them individually. He must discover their strong points while not overlooking their weak ones. Fortunately, there are a variety of ways by which an adult leader may become acquainted with children.

Finding Out About Children from Their Parents

Usually the person who knows the child best is his mother. Not only has she given him birth, but she has lived with him in closest intimacy for all of his life. A friendly visit to the home can reveal many things—the toys a child likes best, the things he likes to do, his fears, if he has any. Once confidence is established, such a visit can uncover the hopes and ambitions which parents have for their child, the things they worry about concerning him, what it is that makes them proud of him. One can discover the state of the child's health, his present stage and rate of growth, what irritates or embarrasses him, whether or not he reads easily, who are his friends, and, if he is over six, what his achievements at school are. The importance of securing this information will be obvious to every serious-minded teacher.

A visit to the home also throws light on the child's other significant experiences. To how many and what sort of adults does he have to adjust? Is he lost among many brothers and sisters? Is he a pampered only child, or an overburdened oldest child? Is he the only boy among many sisters? Is she the only girl among many brothers? Was he a wanted child? What is his relationship to his mother? His responses and reactions to others in the family? All these matters are important if the teacher is to help the individual child to grow. Such needed facts are casually revealed in tactful conversation to a sympathetic and diplomatic visitor.

A certain teacher was in despair because of her failure to reach Ethel, a junior in her class. Gentleness, opportunities to carry out interesting activities with other class members and to make choices of her own—nothing seemed to make the slightest difference in her unco-operative attitude. It was not until Ethel's teacher had visited the home and had observed how the mother's attention was centered upon a younger boy to the seeming exclusion of Ethel, that the teacher understood. Earlier unsatisfactory experiences with a parent or other adults often set the pattern for later attitudes toward new adult leaders or would-be friends. When the parent-child relationship is not good, the teacher can do little with the child until his confidence has been won.

Observing Children During the Week

Objective observation of children in their home, school, play, and church environment is highly rewarding. This is especially true if observations are made following visits with the parents of children.

To those who have never watched little children at play, the first observation may be a startling experience. Though there are exceptions, most two- or three-year-old children, free to choose their own activities, usually do so without fear. Their need for supervision is obvious. Yet the experienced nursery teacher does not guide their boundless energy with "do's" and "don't's." Instead, she provides opportunities to explore and investigate. She encourages the children to try out materials and equipment, to do what is safe. At the same time she leaves them free to adventure and to experiment with what she has made available.

It is profitable to study the equipment provided by those who know the physical needs of children. Note the large but lightweight blocks, the push-and-pull toys, the big boxes that can be climbed into, that can be filled up, emptied out, pushed over on their sides, all through the use of the larger muscles. Note, too, how careful the teacher is not to cause fear or uncertainty in the venturesome child who is about to scramble up the jungle gym for the first time. She knows that children are often better judges of what they can safely do than are anxious adults. She does not warn, "Look out! You'll fall!" That is a frightening thought to implant in the mind of the little adventurer. Instead, she says, "Go slowly. Hold tight." With these encouraging suggestions the climber reaches the top. "See me!" he shouts in triumph.

Observation of older children is just as rewarding. The older child has greater skill in handling himself. There is evidence of purpose in every act, but he is more cautious in attempting what is new to him. Older children do not reveal their curiosity as frankly as little children do, nor do they call attention to their successes as openly. They are most humiliated by their failures, and often struggle with surprising determination to overcome physical difficulties.

Watch for sign of beginning co-operation in little children. Notice, too, how the understanding leader of older children forestalls difficulties through suggestions for co-operative action. She notices, for example, that Frances has undertaken to move the bookcase away from the wall and that it is too much for her. Before temper blazes, or discouragement stops efforts, the leader suggests to Edith, "Frances needs help. Will you see what you can do?" She turns her attention to a couple of juniors who are growing weary or bored and says, "Let's choose something else to do. Perhaps you and Mildred would like to help clean our supply closet, or would you rather work on our frieze?"

No single trait is more essential for effective Christian living than the ability to live and to work with others co-operatively.

Observing Children in the Church School

Sometimes observation of individual children uncovers special problems with which the child needs help. A director of Christian education in her visit to the Primary Department observed that Floyd was extremely shy, apprehensive of being called upon in class. He did not participate in any of the more active enterprises of the group. She noted also that his color was not good and that he seemed to tire easily. The director encouraged the teacher to call upon Floyd's mother. The teacher discovered that the boy had spent months in bed following a prolonged attack of inflammatory rheumatism. He had never been sturdy enough to take part in the rough-and-tumble play of other children. Because of his illness, his mother had taken an overprotective, worried attitude toward him.

The teacher learned that Floyd was interested in a curio collection. He had been accumulating this for some time, with the help of a generous uncle, who traveled about in strange and unusual parts of the world. Floyd's fund of information about his curios was amazing. When the class began a new missionary unit built around the experiences of boys and girls in a mission school in India, Floyd was invited to bring his curios from India to class and to tell about them. The response of the class to Floyd's presentation was heartwarming. Those who had previously ignored or ridiculed him were now eagerly asking him questions. For the first time the youngster knew what it felt like to be respected as a person in his own right, and to be drawn into group membership.

Spending Time with Children

Playing with Children

The teacher who can play "Farmer in the Dell," or "Run, Sheep, Run," with as much honest enjoyment as the children know, need not worry about the problem of getting acquainted with children.

Talking with Children

Notice that talking *with* children is not the same as talking *to* or *at* them. Sometimes it means forgetting, for awhile, all the important and uplifting words you have to say and concentrating on making it easy for children to talk to you.

A happy child-adult relationship depends upon several things. It depends upon what a child is allowed to talk about, and whether or not he can speak freely. It depends upon adult readiness to accept natural, childlike ways, upon the adult's respect for and liking of children as individuals. It depends upon the ability to see the world as a child sees it, and to like what one sees.

All too often teachers fear rather than welcome spontaneity in their pupils. To be sure, it often needs directing into some worthwhile channel, but spontaneity is nothing of which to be afraid. We cannot hope to know what boys and girls think unless they are permitted to reveal their thoughts.

Of course a "spontaneous" child is not always a polite child, nor always an easy one to handle. He may tell you that he hates Abraham, or is sick and tired of hearing about Moses. Instead of being horrified, why not accept his statement as a fact, and try to discover why Allan is bored by the patriarchs?

Seeing and Feeling with Children

Sally runs into the door, bumps her head and yells angrily. One adult says, "You are too big to cry; it is only a little bump," and all Sally's hurt turns inward to find expression, perhaps, in hurting someone else. Another adult says sympathetically, "I know that hurts, Sally. I am glad you are telling me about it," and accepts without shock what Sally wants to say. Afterward, relieved of tension and hurt, Sally is ready for happier experiences.

Learning with Children

The parent or teacher who feels too old to learn, misses one of the most delightful ways of getting acquainted with children. A teacher and her class of junior boys were out on a picnic. During a lull in the activities, one of the boys brought to her a rock that had been cracked open. The dull, gray-brown exterior of the stone had given no hint of the colorful interior. Teacher and boys examined the stone together. They pointed out its lovely colors and the smooth faceted surfaces. The wonder of it was as apparent on the teacher's face as it was on the faces of her boys.

"What kind of stone is it, Miss Estes?" asked one of the juniors.

"I don't know," answered the teacher. "I wish I did. But we could find out about it." She made suggestions where they might go for help and promised to see what she could discover, too. The group planned to meet early the following Sunday and tell what each had found out. The next Sunday boys and teacher were on hand before class time, each eager to tell what he had discovered. The enthusiasm and shared interest of the group brought them to the class period with a new sense of oneness. Something had been given and something accepted by every one of them, a sharing experience in which each had had a part.

Studying About Children

While never wholly satisfactory apart from actual contact with children, studying about them has its advantages. The study can be carried on individually or in groups. Many churches conduct such study groups, often joining with teachers of other churches in the community for the purpose. Among the many publications in the field of child study are excellent texts prepared for the use of teachers seeking to increase their knowledge of boys and girls. When combined with observation of children in natural situations, such study is of incalculable value.

Learning About Children Through Their Creative Work

Children reveal themselves and their experiences through the things that they make or do. Watch youngsters playing house. Is the "mother" bossy, domineering? Does she punish her play children often? Is her voice loud and scolding? While children like to caricature their parents, their play frequently produces the familiar characteristics of grown-ups. The child may not be revealing what goes on in her own home, but it may be revealing what goes on in some home that she knows.

A little child draws a picture of a house; it is his house. You may not recognize it, but he does. He thinks and talks about his home as he draws. Sometimes children reveal their fears, even their hates, in their drawings.

In a certain school visited by the author, an exasperated teacher showed her a series of pictures which had been made by a pale, nervous child who already had attracted the visitor's attention. Each picture showed the usual square box-like house, with its square-cut windows and door, typical of the drawings of houses made by seven-year-olds. The thing that made the pictures different was the fact that great masses of crayoned flames poured out of every window, and against one of the upstairs windows in each drawing was silhouetted the figure of a little girl. The teacher had been trying to get the child to draw another picture. "Why do you always make the same picture?" she asked. "I do not think it is a very nice one, do you? See if you cannot think of something else to draw."

With the teacher's permission, the visitor talked with the child. "I think this is a very interesting picture," said she, sitting close to the child. "Will you tell me about it?"

"That's me," whispered the child, pointing to the figure in the window. "I dream it every night." That revelation pointed the way for some much-needed help. The teacher's effort to change the drawing had only deepened the child's difficulty. It was the fear-filled thoughts that needed changing.

Children also reveal their responsive selves in the lovely things they make. Into the drawings, poems, songs and prayers, which they write and use so easily under guidance, the children pour out their best thoughts and genuine appreciation.

Learning About Children Through Their Behavior

We know that children tend to repeat the behavior that brings them satisfaction. Because this is true, the alert observer acquires genuine insight into the child's nature and needs and the direction in which he is growing, through studying his behavior.

Alvin, an only child, could not remember the time when he had not had his own allowance. From the first, he had been led by thoughtful parents to lay aside each week a portion of his money as his gift to his church. It was not until Alvin entered the Junior Department that the problem began. His slight build kept him on the sidelines when teams were being chosen. He did not express himself easily in speech. The result was that he was left to his own devices much of the time, an onlooker at the fun the other boys had in day camp and on other occasions. His teacher, who had known him from babyhood, noticed with concern that Alvin no longer had any contribution to make to the department offering.

During the conferences with the boy's mother which followed, the parent showed deep mortification. "But I have seen him take the money each Sunday for the offering," she protested, and took the bank in her hands. It was empty.

Wisely the teacher suggested saying nothing to Alvin immediately. Instead, they both would try to find out what lay back of Alvin's secrecy and his failure to follow his usual plan of giving. With mother and teacher working together, it did not take long to learn that Alvin was very lonely. He had been spending his full allowance each week for candy which he passed out to others, seldom keeping any for himself. When it was gently explained to him that one cannot buy friends, the whole story came out with sobs and tears. With the help of his teacher and Dad, Alvin began making a stamp collection. He soon found that he could make friends by sharing with other boys who also liked stamps, and who were ready to exchange information, trade stamps, pass on the news of a new stamp to him. In such a group Alvin was welcome as a contributing member.

Children Are People, Too

If well-meaning adults would only remember to give children the consideration and respect which they give to their older friends, adult-child relationships would be happier. Children are workers, especially when they are carrying out purposes of their own. They plan and think. They have their own rates of speed in working, and nothing is more disconcerting than to have some adult constantly urging, "Hurry up. The rest are all through."

Children have their own sense of values, and there is nothing adult about it. A blue glass button is more prized by a three-year-old than a quarter would be. The child who found the red disk of glass which had fallen from a bicycle lamp had found the "ruby of great price." Looking through it changed the world for him in the twinkling of an eye. It was his chief treasure, and he was inconsolable when he lost it. Another child walked up to her daddy, holding out her dress on which the child's grandmother had just sewed a colorful patch of generous proportions. "See!" she cried, displaying proudly what an adult would seek to hide. "Nana did it. Nice!" Nor would she permit her new patch to be covered with a bib at dinnertime.

Back of each child is an endless variety of heredity and environment. Before each one are the same endless possibilities for the development of personality. The adult should seek to safeguard that rich promise of variety, encouraging each child to be the best that he can be; not like Daddy or brother Jim, or some other worthy model, but to be his own best self.

A Guide Sheet for Studying a Pupil

Date _____

Pupil's Name _____ Telephone _____

Address _____

Date of Birth _____ Baptized _____ When _____

Birthplace _____ Number of years in church school? _____

Mother's Name _____ Member of what church_____

Is mother employed? _____ Is she active in church? _____

Father's vocation? _____ Is he active in church? _____

Ages of other children in the family? _____

Leisure Time Activities	and	Abilities of the Pupil
1. _____		1. _____
2. _____		2. _____
3. _____		3. _____
4. _____		4. _____

Physical Characteristics: Extremely Fat?__ Thin?__ Tall?__ Short?__

Habits and Attitudes of the Pupil _____

_____

Attends church regularly _____ Irregularly _____

Reasons for regularity: _____ Reasons for irregularity _____

1. _____ 1. _____

2. _____ 2. _____

Comes on time _____ Frequently late _____ Always late _____

To what extent does the pupil participate in the program of the church? _____

Sense of responsibility: High _____ Medium _____ Low _____

Monopolizes conversation _____ Impulsive _____

Quiet _____ Timid _____ Wants attention _____ Respects the rights of others _____ Interested in the successes of his classmates _____

"The Pupil Study Sheet," Utilization Guide to filmstrip, "No Two Alike," *Leadership Education Audio-Visual Kit* (New York: National Council of Churches, 1950), p. 16. Used by permission.

Shows willingness to cooperate _____ Tries to "get even" _____

Is opinionated _____ Indulges in self pity _____ Sense of humor _____

Has emotional stability _____ Needs constant supervision _____

Public school grade _____ Quality of school work _____

Member of what clubs or organizations? _____

Other facts about pupil: _____

_____

_____

Possible points of growth for this pupil:

1. _____

2. _____

3. _____

4. _____

Plans for the accomplishment of this growth:

1. _____

2. _____

3. _____

4. _____

The Pupil Record

BY MILDRED AND FRANK EAKIN

A device which is almost indispensable for such teaching is the pupil record—a notebook kept by the teacher in which one or more pages are reserved for each pupil. The first entry naturally will be the pupil's name. Other items will follow as the information is gained. They should be jotted down as soon as possible after each session, also at other times when something about the pupil has been learned outside of class.

A child's birthday, grade in school, hobbies—such data may well be included. Items about his home situation may prove important. Particularly noteworthy are entries like this, made by a teacher at the close of a Sunday-school session, under the name of Robert: "When Andy began to try to act smart and make a fuss, Robert said, 'Keep quiet; we want to hear this.' And Andy kept quiet." Three months ago Robert's attention had been hard to get. This note by the teacher indicated progress with him.

Persons differ from each other. This is a simple fact which the observant church-school teacher often sees verified—and it is a reason why she should keep pupil records. In a typical group of boys Howard wants to lead, Tom seems uninterested in most of what is said in class but comes to life when the group starts making something. John is eager to do things but doesn't do them well. Harry does better than most of the others but has a poor opinion of his own performances. Roy likes to draw and is some-

Mildred and Frank Eakin, *The Church School Teacher's Job* (New York: The Macmillan Company, copyright, 1949), pp. 2–5. Used by permission.

what rude. George sits off from the group and seems not to want to take part in either discussion or work.

A second fact with a bearing on record-keeping is that boys and girls, in their attitudes and acts, don't "stay put." Last week Howard was peeved. The class had decided to put on a play for old ladies in a near-by Home, but that wasn't the project Howard had favored. What he wanted was for them to buy baseball outfits for boys at the county orphanage. This week, however, his grouch seemed to be gone; he made useful suggestions when the play was being planned. John, who was most enthusiastic last Sunday, had lost some of his ardor meanwhile. This Sunday it was impossible to keep his attention. George sat apart as usual, but he got into the discussion a time or two and his case seemed more hopeful.

Such data as these are basic materials for the teacher who is in earnest about understanding and helping pupils. In the record book she will by and by have a picture of what each pupil is like. Differences will be indicated; from week to week new touches will be added.

Of what practical value will these records be?

One answer is that the teacher who keeps such a record tends to develop the habit of thinking between times of what happened in class, trying to figure out what it meant. No courses of study in teacher training are likely to be as valuable to her as this. Experience is the great teacher, of teachers as well as of everybody else. The trouble is that experience can be so quickly forgotten, its teaching value lost. The record captures and holds it. Much of what is written down may prove to have little value, especially when record-keeping is first tried. But practice will yield facility at spotting the significant happening, and even when the percentage of important items seems low the effort can be rewarding. The records prevent the teacher's thinking about her job from being vague and sporadic, help to give it direction, purpose, effectiveness.

In particular, to list a second kind of value, the records act as a spur to further investigation and discovery. "My class is unruly," the teacher has been in the habit of saying. Or, "My boys don't like to memorize." But record-keeping brings to the fore the fact that this isn't equally true, in either case, of every member of the class. Jimmy and Bill and Jerry tend to get out of hand, but Don, Oliver and Michael are usually well behaved. Moreover the boys with unflattering behavior reputations don't misbehave in the same ways. The week-by-week record shows Jimmy's special ways of being bad. Bill's and Jerry's too. Why these specialties? Scanning the record the teacher asks this question, begins to look around for answers. The home situation? Public school? By and by notations of investigation in these areas begin to appear in the notebook. Teacher is on the way.

As to memorizing, the recorded data may point to special aptitudes, abilities, interests, some of them at least as capable of leading in profitable directions as is a taste for committing to memory. Or they may reveal that when the group was absorbed in work on a play Dick, thought of as a hopeless memorizer, got his lines easily. What does that mean? And then, not at first but later, notations about Don, one of the "good" boys, begin to take on significance. That expression, those eyes, the passive, beaten attitude. To the teacher comes the startling realization that "well behaved" can't be trusted as a final judgment on a child.

A third answer to the question, Why pupil records? is that they help the teacher in handling class situations. She will reap reward for her record-keeping diligence not only in between-sessions thinking and planning and investigating but in the crucial hour when she and the group are together. Record-keeping does not guarantee that everything will go smoothly at every session. No such guarantee is to be had. But the past is the best guide to present understanding and procedures. Experience—specific experience noted down soon after occurrence and later pondered in connection with other items—gradually builds up in one's mind a picture of the persons with whom one has to do, of what they are like, of what is to be expected from them, of what can be done for them; and this in turn can yield a sense of mastery on the part of a leader in a class situation which nothing else can yield.

Mastery is perhaps not the best word. Let us say confidence, sureness of touch. The point is not that the teacher feels she can hold things down no matter what happens; rather it is that she attains a sense of having enough of a key to the natures of these very different persons in her group to make it possible for her, in an hour with them, to exert helpful and satisfying leadership. Jane is restless today. Her inattention threatens to be contagious. But the teacher is not overmuch disturbed. She has come to know Jane, to understand what is back of that restlessness. She has long-range plans for dealing with it. It is not too hard to be patient now. One reason why it is not too hard is because of Mary, who has become so wonderfully cooperative, so unlike the Mary of two months ago.

The next answer—that faithfully kept pupil records help the teacher to gain a cumulative understanding of each pupil's behavior pattern and thus to influence him more effectively—was anticipated in the last two paragraphs. The cumulative understanding pays dividends in the meeting of a session situation. In progress through a series of such situations—with the accompanying observation, record-making, thought, investigation—the value can continue to grow, the influence to deepen and spread. Perhaps one pupil or another baffles the teacher to the end; the pieces of observed and recorded behavior do not seem to fit together. This can be disheartening. But in the case of most of the group the sense of *knowing* them will probably have been attained to a degree that is satisfying. You can really talk with Walter now, you have gained entrance to his world. No triumph in leading a single session can be equal to that.

As a final answer, then, it may be set down that keeping pupil records and making full use of them opens the door to a concept and practice of church-school teaching which can make it, for the teacher herself, a thrilling experience.

Finding Group Interests

BY MALCOLM S. KNOWLES

Program committees composed of people who are well acquainted with the membership often have a great deal of information about what their groups want. Nevertheless, it is always a good idea to start with some planned procedures to determine needs and interests. First of all, guesses by a few people can often be wrong. We are all tempted to think in terms of what people ought to have rather than what they *want*. In addition, asking people what they want involves them in the planning itself and gives them a stake in its success.

There are several ways of finding out what people need and want. For general information on the current interests of people, a little informal "research" can produce some good clues. Some simple procedures are: (1) Watch your newspapers for a month and tabulate the subjects that receive greatest emphasis. (2) Talk with your librarian about what kinds of books and magazines seem to be most popular. (3) Exchange program announcements with other organizations like yours and see what is of interest to their members.

In determining the more specific needs of the people in your group there are of course many more direct avenues to information. Among them are:

Malcolm S. Knowles, *Planning Better Programs* (Chicago: Adult Education Association, 1956), pp. 17–20. Used by permission.

Interviews

Each member of the program committee might take a list of five or ten members to interview by phone or face-to-face. The committee should determine beforehand what questions to ask.

Informal Conversation

We added this category upon receiving a letter from Dorothy Hewitt, Director of the Boston Center of Adult Education and one of the most experienced program planners in the country, which read: "It seems to me that the degree of success we experience as program planners is determined by our ability to put ourselves in the places of as many people as possible. The nearer we come to being a mirror of the inmost desires of the people around us, the nearer we come to success. I find that in just 'passing the time of day' with people I get all sorts of clues and program ideas that I should never get from directly asking them. An ever increasing ability to *listen* to what people say is one of the best sources I know for discovering what people are thinking about."

A Meeting Census

Ask the members to cluster into groups of six or eight. Each cluster should choose a spokesman, then take ten minutes to list their program choices. Then each spokesman can report his list to a central secretary who compiles them into a master list. Interest can be increased by writing the list on a blackboard if one is available. (This is the "buzz group" technique which is useful for many other activities where the direct and active participation of a large group is desired.)

Registration Cards

Have them filled out when people enter. Allow space for indicating background and interests.

Suggestion or Question Boxes

Place them where they are accessible to all and certain to be noticed.

Questionnaires

Vary their pattern according to what you wish to find out. See a sample interest questionnaire on the next page.

An important step in the process of determining needs and interests is interpreting the responses that are received. It is well to keep in mind that none of these techniques can give *conclusive* evidence and that the final test always lies in trying out ideas to see how closely you have come to satisfying *real* needs and interests.

In tabulating questionnaires you might use a rating system which gives, for example, two points to a "very much" response and one point to a "some" response. It is also helpful to:

- Take into consideration the extent to which the responses are representative of the total membership,
- Separate the conclusions that you can be certain of, those that are only probable, and those that provide bases for good hunches only. (By no means disregard the hunches—try them out—experiment with them—but recognize that they are hunches.)
- Study the negative responses carefully. They may shed valuable light on needs and interests.

THE COUPLE'S CLUB

From: Your Program Committee
To: All Members
Subject: *The kind of program you want to have in the coming year.*

If you would like to help us plan this year's program, please fill out this questionnaire and return it today.

		Very Much	Some	Not at All
I.	*I am interested in:*			
	1. Learning more about practical psychology.	____	____	____
	2. Developing hobbies.	____	____	____
	3. Learning more about world affairs.	____	____	____
	4. Doing something concrete to improve our community.	____	____	____
	5. Improving my ability to speak.	____	____	____
	6. Increasing my appreciation of the arts.	____	____	____
	7. Becoming a better parent.	____	____	____
	8. _____			

		Very Much	Some	Not at All
II.	*Our group needs:*			
	1. A stronger treasury	____	____	____
	2. More members	____	____	____
	3. More fellowship	____	____	____
	4. More significant programs	____	____	____
	5. _____			
	6. _____			

III. *The 5 most important problems our community faces are:* *

1. _____   4. _____
2. _____   5. _____
3. _____

* Put a circle around the number of the problem, if any, you think our group ought to do something about.

Signed _____ (optional)

7. WHAT IS IMPORTANT ABOUT
GROUP PROCESS?

MANY SIGNIFICANT STUDIES in group work have been made in the last decade. Outstanding work has been done in study centers on university campuses and in laboratories on group development. As a result, we have more information on group processes than ever before.

In part, this information supports practices that have been familiar to church workers for years. In part, the new information has led to new insights. One has only to compare a recent conference with an earlier one to see how many changed procedures have found their way into practice.

Alert church leaders were aware from the start that the results of this research and experiment had a great deal to offer to the church. Therefore they participated in research and experiment. They saw to it that the newer insights were reflected in church-sponsored gatherings and reported in church publications. Local church workers, however, have adopted these insights slowly. Whether they delayed because of lack of information, or because of fear of trying new techniques, or because many church rooms make group participation difficult, it is of little point to discuss here. Suffice to say that it is important for church group leaders to understand the reasons why people act as they do in groups and to utilize in the church the best group techniques that it is possible to develop.

Two cautions need to be expressed. (1) Group dynamics is a study of the forces that are at work in groups. This study has led to the use of certain techniques. It is wrong, however, to think that these techniques and group dynamics are one and the same. (2) Group processes are not ends in themselves. They are to be used by the church as means to help fulfill its mission.

The Influence of a Group on Its Members
and Leadership

In front of the house three boys were playing. Two of them had bicycles. Presently the two left to ride around the block. Mike, left behind, shouted, "Come back. I'll play like you want. Come on back."

In these words Mike revealed two things: the universal need to be accepted as a member of a group, and the strong influence of the group upon the individual.

There is nothing new in recognizing the effect of the group on its members, for good or for ill. However, in recent years there has been serious study of group phenomena. This has brought to light a good deal of information and has given rise to a new concept of leadership.

As this new knowledge becomes more fully understood and skillfully used, it can have a revolutionary effect on our methods of Christian teaching. It will help us to work "from the inside," with a grasp of what actually makes people change their attitudes and behavior.

Group Purposes and Planning Are Important

Traditionally the teacher has had a goal for his class, but he knew very well that each pupil probably had his own subconscious goal; such as, getting attention from his colleagues, or perhaps just enduring the session until the time when he would be free. One of

---

Staff article, "Individuals Come in Groups," *International Journal of Religious Education,* February, 1955, pp. 13–15. Used by permission.
220

the teacher's first hurdles has been to get the pupils to forget their goals and to accept his own. We now see that a better way is for the group to think through and accept common goals.

Such group purposes often come about as a result of working together on a project. An illustration of this can be seen in a junior high group studying about worship. At first some were bored with the subject; others gave half-hearted attention to it. Then one of the more enthusiastic girls suggested that they "put on a play, with scenery and costumes," to show the rest of the church something of the history of worship. The others immediately responded.

The adult adviser counseled with the boys and girls, made sure they knew where to get the information they needed, and helped them when necessary to evaluate their plans. But he left the responsibility for the pageant in their hands.

Before the dramatization was completed, he saw that the young people were helping one another to grow. Those with more worthy purposes were, by attitudes and words, carrying the others to a higher level.

Some high moments of worship and some deep thinking came about because they were working as a group rather than separately. In the process all of the junior highs grew nearer the goals they had set for themselves and at the same time they approached the more remote goal set by the adult leader.

For years much of our denominational curriculum has stressed pupil participation in planning. Current research is proving that the values coming from group planning are so great as to commend it for consistent use. The influence of the group members upon one another is frequently much greater than the influence of an appointed leader.

Frequently a group that has learned to work together will study harder and make more demands on itself than an appointed leader would ever ask. When a men's class decided to study the church's program for their children they discovered a number of real needs in the various departments.

To meet these needs the men voluntarily set aside two nights a week for several months to make equipment, to talk over plans with the church school workers, and to think through ways they could help at home with the Christian education of their boys and girls. Until that time they had been too busy for any extra-curricular activities.

Everyone Is a Leader

It is evident from the foregoing that no longer can it be accepted as a fact that a group has one leader, who may be the teacher or in some cases the president or chairman. Rather, the influence of every member is recognized—even the person who remains silent.

The leadership roles a person plays may vary from time to time and particular roles may pass from one member to another. A look at one church school class will reveal some roles commonly found among group members:

Joan, a super salesman, is always forcing the group to look at new ideas.

Ann keeps the others from plunging ahead blindly and forces them to evaluate Joan's suggestions.

Jack gets disgusted if discussion or activities drag and lets the group know it is time to "get on the beam."

Martin is the peacemaker who tries to find points of agreement in disagreement or soothes hurt feelings.

Paul is a group disrupter who confidentially tells each one what the others think of him and wish he would do or say. He does this, however, not because he wants to help the situation, but in order to bolster his own place in the group.

Jim remains silent most of the time, often aloof as though uninterested. The others feel anxious over his lack of participation, and their concern hinders the wholehearted accomplishment of their goals.

Each of these persons sometimes leads, sometimes subordinates himself. By encouraging the roles which contribute to group purposes, and redirecting undesirable ones, the teacher and the group help each pupil to develop the most constructive approach possible.

Sometimes in groups there is conflict between members struggling for places of leadership. One may attack another under the guise of being helpful. One who attempts to dominate may give the others a sense of insecurity and make them reluctant to participate fully. All of these factors are disruptive and need to be worked through by the group so that each member has a chance to give his best for the good of all.

The Group Influences Individuals

Trying to change another person's attitudes or behavior is a delicate matter. Each person has an intense desire, largely unconscious, for "status," for acceptance by others as a person of worth. Anything that seems to threaten his status will be resisted.

In spite of this resistance, group pressure can exert a powerful influence on its members. This is frequently illustrated in fraternities. A college student, otherwise uninterested in extra-curricular activities, will go out for the football team or the college paper because of pressure to uphold the fraternity prestige.

Group standards and values also determine behavior. For instance, if in the church school class described above, the members encourage Jack when he begins to show irritation and disgust, his unsocial behavior will be intensified. Displeasure can have the opposite effect. A person's desire to measure up to what the group expects, providing the group does not expect too much, can push him to efforts he might not otherwise attempt.

Encouragement to change for the better can also come from knowing that others make mistakes and have anxieties, too. It is natural to feel resentful when someone else points out one's defects, particularly if he says, "I don't like your attitude." However, one can accept the need for change within himself without nearly so much resentment or feeling of self-depreciation when he is supported by others going through the same experiences.

A youth group had the habit of wasting a good part of the class session with frivolous and irrelevant chatter. One Sunday the teacher concealed a microphone and recorded their conversation for the first ten minutes of the class. He then played it back to them. Hearing themselves in this way, they recognized how foolish they sounded and decided to stop wasting time. This being a group decision, no person felt his own status threatened.

Research has shown that persons tend to accept the ideas of those toward whom they have good feelings and to reject the ideas of those they do not like. They try to see similarity between their own ideas and those of persons they like; or conversely, dissimilarity between their own and those of persons they dislike. If a sense of real fellowship has been established, the members will want each other's help and counsel.

Groups in which tensions exist find worship difficult, whereas members of groups which accept each other's viewpoints find it easy to turn their thoughts together toward God. Emotions either of good will or of hostility flow easily from one person to another.

Granting the strong influence of the group, every person still needs the sense of being an individual, different from every one else, and possessing qualities peculiarly his own. In the group he needs the chance to develop these qualities and to grow in his own way.

The group can help the members evaluate each other's attitudes and actions but does not attempt beyond that to control individuals by coercion. Each member should be privileged and sometimes encouraged to disagree with the majority and know that he still keeps their respect. One person may be a member of several groups, all of which are different, and by maintaining his own integrity grow as a result of his several contacts.

This insight into the meaning and influence of group life recalls the ancient concept of the Church as a Christian fellowship. In this fellowship, Christians who are secure in God's love help one another toward growth, healing, and wholeness. If each small group in every church were to become a miniature fellowship of this kind, the highest purposes of Christian education would be fulfilled.

When Is a Group Mature?

BY GORDON LIPPITT

One of the hypotheses suggested by research workers in the field of Group Dynamics is that *group interaction can go through a process of growth and maturation similar to that of individuals.* In *infancy,* the group, like a new-born baby, is awkward and unco-ordinated in its behavior. It is highly dependent upon the leader. As it grows to *adolescence,* its members struggle with the same conflict of dependence versus independence that the teen-ager goes through. They begin to learn how to do things for themselves and to operate in an efficient manner. The group does not yet know how to handle its emotional crises. Eventually, under the proper conditions, that problem too can be faced and solved in a constructive way, and the group can achieve a state of *maturity* analogous to that of an intelligent and happy individual.

Let us, then, take a look at the *characteristics of a mature group* as listed by Dr. Frank Haiman in his book, *Group Leadership and Democratic Action.*

- A mature group has a clear understanding of its purposes or goals.
- A mature group is able to look ahead and plan ahead.
- A mature group is able to initiate and carry on effective, logical problem-solving.
- A mature group has achieved an appropriate balance between established ways of working together and readiness to change its procedural patterns.

Gordon Lippitt, "Characteristics of a Mature Group," *Religious Education,* November–December, 1952, p. 375. Published by The Religious Education Association, New York. Used by permission.

• A mature group provides for the diffusion and sharing of leadership responsibilities.

• A mature group has a high degree of cohesiveness or solidarity, but not to the point of exclusiveness or to the point of stifling individuality.

• A mature group makes intelligent use of the differing abilities of its members.

• A mature group provides an atmosphere of psychological freedom for the expression of all feelings and points of view.

• A mature group is not over-dominated by its leader or by any of its members.

• A mature group has achieved a healthy balance between cooperative and competitive behavior on the part of its members.

• A mature group strikes an appropriate balance between emotionality and rationality.

• A mature group can readily change and adapt itself to the needs of differing situations.

• A mature group recognizes the value and the limitations of democratic procedures.

• A mature group has achieved a high degree of effective intercommunication among its members.

These characteristics of a mature group, suggested by Dr. Haiman, are indicative of the goals to which we should work in our association group activities. In the light of this goal, we might ask ourselves the following questions:

• Is the Church, through its various groups and activities, developing mature functioning groups, or are many of our groups still in the stage of infancy in terms of operational efficiency?

• Are the groups in operation in the Church program ones which enhance the characteristics listed above?

• To what extent are the characteristics of mature groups related closely to the dimension of the Christian fellowship?

The Group Idea Challenges the Church

BY SARA LITTLE

We must now ask, "What does this have to say to the church?"

There are many groups in the church. Sometimes these groups are genuine fellowships through which the grace of God can reach the participants, casting out fears, healing wounds, and giving purpose and direction for life. But such groups are all too rare. Far more often one finds groups in which most persons engage in activities in a spectator capacity, rather than as a participant understanding and sharing in the purposes of the activities. A person can be lost in the crowd in a large church, known by a few other people and addressed politely but only superficially by most. A person can be exploited by the church in being urged to participate in activities to make them "successful" rather than to find help for himself. Occasionally he may be vaguely stirred by hearing an interpretation of the message of a prophet, or by an elusive idea that almost touches him. But nothing *real* happens. Too concerned about himself and what people think of him to be interested in those other people, sometimes desiring to communicate with others about the central issues of life and yet not knowing how to begin, he moves on, lonely in the midst of many people and anxious about something, he knows not what. One writer has said,

> Our communities and churches are filled with frightened and lonely people who, being afraid to give themselves in personal

Sara Little, *Learning Together in the Christian Fellowship* (Richmond: John Knox Press, 1956), pp. 17–18. Used by permission.

encounter, seek solace in the comfort of things, only to suffer from an increased sense of estrangement and death.[1]

When the sense of security and fulfillment so necessary to human beings is found more through participation in secular groups than in church groups, it is time for the church to be troubled. Many people are finding in nonchurch groups an atmosphere which warms and accepts them, in a way that makes them experience something akin to the love they hear defined in the church. One leader who studied in the Great Books discussion groups states that "the creation of an atmosphere of understanding and acceptance is basic for learning to take place and be assimilated." [2] She sees certain implications for the church. The understanding and acceptance of which public educators and group work agencies speak are, in the church, love and forgiveness. Rejection may be equated with judgment on the human level.

Acceptance may be necessary for learning to take place—but Christian love and forgiveness that should be characteristic of the church bear within them a power which points to God and His redemption, a power which may sustain that individual who responds in faith to the love of God, revealed to him through the fellowship of the church.

It is, therefore, within the church that a person might hope to experience *koinonia,* that fellowship, that sense of community binding Christians together—a fellowship which is, indeed, far more than a sense of "groupness." Baillie says that God's eternal purpose for man was that he might be a part of this fellowship, and that, through the fellowship, he might become what God intended him to be.

---

[1] Reuel L. Howe, *Man's Need and God's Action* (Greenwich, Conn.: Seabury Press, 1953), p. 25. By permission.

[2] Marjorie Felder, "Implications of Group Dynamics for a Philosophy of Christian Education" (unpublished Master's Thesis, General Assembly's Training School, Richmond, Va., 1954), p. 57.

Members One of Another

BY ROSS SNYDER

The greatest picture of what a group is, comes in the letter to the Ephesians, as the writer attempts to state what has happened to the Christians of the first century:

"So then you are no longer strangers and sojourners,"—

(*You are not alien, or "things" to each other.*)

"but you are fellow citizens with the saints and members of the household of God,"—

(*There's a place for you within a people of God, and that fellowship is not limited just to the present people you face.*)

"built upon the foundation of the apostles and prophets, Christ Jesus himself being the chief cornerstone,"—

(*You are growing out of the love and righteousness and redeeming that formed man, and makes all new.*)

"in whom the whole structure is joined together and grows into a holy temple in the Lord;"—

(*You are members one of another, fitly joined together so that the corporateness can upbuild itself in love and each member grow toward maturity in Christ.*)

"in whom you also are built into it for a dwelling place of God in the Spirit."—

(*You are a presence to each other, and God's shaping purpose is present, in the togetherness.*)

This is what—in promise—every church school and every church is.

Ross Snyder, "Members One of Another . . . an Idea Whose Fullness of Time Has Come," *International Journal of Religious Education*, May, 1957, pp. 8, 9. Used by permission.

A Life of Participation

An understanding of the very nature of religion enables us to escape the mistake of believing that it is "knowledge about" that is saving truth. Saving knowledge is rather "participating in" knowledge. "Place yourself at a bound" *inside* the living, moving transactions of love, and the significance of the doctrines of love glows with reality. Teaching—in the religious fashion—does not mean hurling words at persons which they accept or reject, but participating in their lives in a unique way, and participating with them in the reality described in the letter to the Ephesians.

Christian parenthood centrally is becoming capable of a Christian quality of participation in each other's lives, and of participation in a corporate congregation which is a people of God, rather than being trained to "teach religion" to our children, or to instill in them certain character traits.

A Life of Invitation and Revealing

We can participate in another's life or in a joint life with him, only upon his invitation. We cannot force our way in; the hand that opens the door to the depths of another person will always be on the inside of the door. But we can reveal our nature so that he will come to want to open the door, so that transactions may take place. People sense and respond to the spirit revealed in John Woolman's resolve—

A concern arose to spend some time with the Indians, that I might feel and understand their life and the spirit they live in; if haply I might receive some instruction from them, or they be in any degree helped forward by my following the leadings of truth amongst them.

Notice that this life of participation involves a recognition that there will be an otherness—the others will not see, feel, intend the same things. Each is to treat the other as having freedom. Woolman retains his own citadel of decision. He intends to follow the "leadings of truth" while among them, not imitate them.

But here he is reverently "entering into" the lived experience and found truth of other persons. That is a religious participation in their life. The participation here proposed is listening to the experiences and meanings of each other until each understands the other; and, understanding, still respects him.

A gift of life which the Christian church offers its members and the world is the understanding that God, instead of loving vast generalities, loves particular, concrete people in all their individuality and uniqueness. William James once put the implications of this in a very human way.

> Every Jack sees in his own particular Jill charms and perfections to the enchantment of which we stolid onlookers are stonecold. Is he in excess, being in this matter a maniac? Or are we in defect, being victims of a pathological anaesthesia as regards Jill's magical importance? Surely the latter; surely to Jack are the profounder truths revealed; surely poor Jill's palpitating little lifethrobs *are* among the wonders of creation, are worthy of this sympathetic interest; and it is to our shame that the rest of us cannot feel like Jack.[1]

If Jack, in a similar way, could see the hidden potentiality and grace of youngsters and relate to them in an awakening way, what a church school teacher he would be! And the church school would truly be a workshop of humanity. For who of us would have ventured our life pilgrimage if some adult had not seen promise in us, and told us that he recognized it, even if we didn't; had not communicated to us that our life-throbs and our devilment were among the true wonders of creation? So we had courage to stand up and become.

A Shaping and Empowering of Our Life

As the early founders of American democracy believed, there can be no group life unless there is a moral governance within each citizen. Each member must have something transcendently greater than his own impulses and desires to which he feels responsible,

---

[1] *Talks to Teachers,* p. 266. Henry Holt and Co. (Used by permission.)

and before which he brings his own actions and the actions of his group. At the nearest relationship, this is the group itself. And we have all felt this from the other end—that is, we want to feel responsible to some group that is a home for us; we want to feel that the group cares for us and sustains our life. We want it to require of us courage, tested competence, a real fight put up for what it values. So do our children and youth, and if they cannot find this in the church they must find it in their own "free-wheeling" groups.

Where but in a group can we become aware of our responsibility for each other, and of the prodigal journeys that we rush off on from time to time? Unlike the thieves in the ancient story, in a group we cannot go off and leave our wounded man half dead— we have to keep meeting him time after time in most intimate quarters. Nor does the man stay wounded along the road, awaiting our beneficence. No, he is not lying on a hospital bed needing the gracious chaplain, nor is he a person in deep trouble turning to the trusted counselor. He is often a cantankerous adult whom we deeply resent; and he comes not to seek help, but to stab us in public.

In such situations is the battle for one's own very soul fought when we risk membership in a group. At such times, we cannot avoid asking, "What do I really intend with my life *right here and now?*" and out of our thinness of spirit, cry inwardly, "Oh, for some empowering from something beyond myself!" What can save us but the holy, the eternal One? And the lived experiences of the "saints who from their labors rest"? And some in this very group who are a presence to us?

A Christian Group Has Vocation

A grasp of the church as a people of God also brings us a vocation—a calling—that puts structure and power and direction into our wandering energies. Without the call of a destiny, life has planlessness and "torn-to-pieces-hood." Without a sense of mission and head-on encounters with evil and a resistant world that requires transformation, without the agonizing of intellectual struggle, fellowship groups can become cliques of tenderized mediocrity, and little worlds of self-reference. People's need for acceptance is so great today, and we are still so weak and unskillful in extending it, that one hesitates to say that "acceptance is not enough." Acceptance there must be, but a Christian group must also go farther. There are evils to be fought, generations to be taught, ideas to be tested and thought, institutions and worlds to be created—enough for a whole generation of "collective genius."

My own guiding image as I participate in group life—wavering as is my hold on the vision—is this: that a Christian lives within the constant expectation of the coming of the Kingdom of God. He knows that there is a depth to every human relation; in that depth are hidden the potentialities of the Kingdom of God, and they will break forth in power if he can only sense their presence, and by his behavior invite their coming.

A Gift of Life

We return to the image with which we began—the image of a people of God. The idea that the members of a congregation are members one of another, and share in all the ministries of the church—is this not an idea whose fullness of time has come?

To the minister as well as to the people we will say: "Place yourself 'at one bound' *within* a people of God, not at the top; and see what graciousness happens to you." Instead of the church being a vertical "totem pole" up which people must struggle to reach top place, suppose it is a divine-human community? Suppose the minister is not the top divinity who showers blessings upon his sheep and rushes frantically to perform the ministry required of the whole congregation. Suppose the full range of ministry is a blessing we crave for all members, and that they are willing to become competent in the ministries of a people of God. Suppose the writer of the letter to the Ephesians really told the truth, and that this reality is a gift waiting to bring us to life.

Some Forces That Operate below the Surface

BY LELAND BRADFORD

The main reason for people coming together and forming a group is that there is a publicly stated, agreed-on task to be accomplished. This is the surface, or public agenda. It may be a program, a task, an objective. But below the surface there are quite apt to be hidden agendas which the group probably does not openly recognize.

Each agenda level affects the other. When a group is proceeding successfully on its surface agenda with a sense of accomplishment and group unity, it is evident that major hidden agendas have either been settled, are being handled as the surface agenda is being worked on, or have been temporarily put to sleep. Let the group reach a crisis on its surface agenda and run into difficulties, however, and somnolent hidden agendas come awake.

Groups can work hard on either or both agendas. A group frequently spends endless time getting nowhere on its surface agenda, seemingly running away from its task, and yet, at the end, gives the impression of a hard-working group. Often group members leave a meeting saying, "Well, we got somewhere at last." Yet, if asked where they got, they would have mentioned some relatively trivial decisions on the surface level. What they were really saying was that some very important hidden agendas had been solved.

A group may have been working hard without visible movement on its appointed task. Suddenly it starts to move efficiently on its

Leland Bradford, "The Hidden Agenda," *Understanding How Groups Work* (Chicago: Adult Education Association, 1955), pp. 33–40. Used by permission.

surface task and in a short time brings it to an adequate conclusion. The group had to clear its hidden agenda out of its way before it could go to work on its obvious job.

Hidden agendas are neither better nor worse than surface agendas. Rather they represent all of the individual and group problems that differ from the surface group job and therefore may get in the way of the orderly solving of the surface agenda. They may be conscious or unconscious for the member or for the group. They are not to be blamed or damned.

Burying them does little good. Pretending that they, like country cousins, are unrelated to the group is equally ineffective. They are important, because they concern the group, and something needs to be done about them. The answer may be to solve them or to shelve them.

Groups, fortunately, can work on both agenda levels at the same time. What is needed is improvement in effective ways of working on hidden agendas as well as on the surface agenda. The first step toward greater effectiveness is to recognize the kinds and sources of hidden agendas.

Hidden agendas can be held by:

Group Members
The Leader
The Group Itself

Each of these, in turn, can be divided in terms of the cause of the hidden agenda held and the person or group unit to which its actions are directed.

The Members

While the group may be struggling for an acceptable solution to its problem, some members may have brought answers in their hip-pockets. Obviously a hip-pocket answer is usually not acceptable to a group because it implies that one individual stands to gain, somehow, more than the rest, and because it implies that the individual, by himself, is much more competent than the group. So the individuals with hip-pocket answers wait until they judge the time is appropriate for them to have just thought of a good idea. If their minds are pretty well closed to any other solution but their own, and if they are intent on watching the group discussion to find the best time to enter their solution, they are probably not the best contributing members of the group. Their hidden agendas are definitely affecting the group.

In back of some group members stand invisible companions. They, with the particular group member, belong to some other group and they are present to make certain their representative fights for the special interest of their group. The fact that these invisible companions are present only in the mind of the group member makes them no less effective in controlling his behavior in the present group.

So some group members are torn by divided loyalties. They are members of two groups at the same time. So long as the groups follow the same path, there is no conflict. Let the paths divide and the individual must try to bring them together or be forced to choose between them. The individual may change from a flexible, cooperative group member to one who is more tense as he tries to push the group toward a point to which it doesn't particularly want to go. To the group which doesn't know of the hidden conflict of divided loyalties, the behavior of the individual may seem suddenly incomprehensible.

As a group moves toward the solution of its task, it may suddenly threaten some group member and make him fearful. Perhaps a staff group is about to make a decision that threatens to bring criticism to the job area of one individual. Perhaps a group is approaching a decision that makes one group member fear he will have difficulty in defending his colleagues in another group. Perhaps the class discussion, in high school or college, is approaching the point beyond which the group member has studied. Perhaps the group discussion of intellectual ideas is beginning to challenge certain long-held beliefs of a group member—beliefs he doesn't want to re-examine. For differing reasons these individuals would hesitate to state their fears. Nevertheless, these fears are going to become dominant hidden forces causing members to try to change the group's direction, irrespective of the logic or desirability of the path the group is taking.

The Individual and the Leader

Each individual possibly has a special set of hidden agendas concerning the leader.

He may compete with the leader for influence on the group. Obviously he cannot state his purpose—he may not even be aware of it. He would have to make denial if it were brought up. But his hidden agenda comes through in a variety of indirect ways. He may challenge what the leader has said at some point. (There is a definite but not always easily recognizable difference between the legitimate member challenge of a mistake by the leader, and the challenge that has for its purpose the destruction of the leader.) Usually the competing member waits until he senses the group is reluctant to follow the leader, and so his challenge is more likely to gain group support. By directing questions at various other group members, he may try to direct discussion back to himself, and so, for a while, control the group. By suggesting acceptable solutions to group impasses, or by making procedural suggestions, he may try to prove himself more important to the group than is the leader. He is usually content that the designated leader retain the title so long as the group is largely influenced and controlled by him.

He may, as another type of hidden agenda, feel generally hostile to all leaders. This hostility, usually unconscious, probably has grown out of childhood experiences with his father, school teachers, church leaders, etc. One difference between attack on leadership growing out of such hostility toward leadership and attack growing out of desire to take over leadership is that hostility to leadership does not always lead the individual to desire to dominate the group himself. He may be more concerned with attacking leadership wherever found.

On the other hand, childhood experiences lead some individuals generally to seek to be dependent on leadership. For these people there is greater satisfaction when they can find and cling to a person who assumes leadership responsibilities. Their hidden agenda is to maintain the comfortable state of dependence and their group contributions are affected by the degree of attack upon the leader and the extent of group acceptance of the leader.

On the conscious level, individuals may have certain hidden agendas in relation to the leader. If he is seen as likely to make possible the acceptance of a solution favorable to them, they will support him. He may equally well be rejected if the individuals feel he endangers the solution desired by them.

Most people have no great hostility toward leadership or overwhelming need to compete for leadership. Furthermore, the hidden agendas toward leadership are seldom clear cut. A number may be present, to greater or lesser degrees, in any one individual.

Also group members rightly need to criticize and endeavor to change the leadership in its direction because of the mistakes of omission or commission the leader may be making. Since criticisms do not necessarily indicate indulging hostility toward the leader this article would be failing of its purpose if it made people feel guilty every time they differed from the group leader.

The Leader

Even the leader has his hidden agendas. One may be merely the desire, which he nobly or prudently inhibits, to cut the throat of an obstreperous individual. Another, and unfortunately too frequently present when the role of leader should be that of helping the group work out its decisions, may be a hip-pocket solution which he inserts when he thinks the group has reached an impasse and is ready to accept his solution.

On the deeper, and usually unconscious level, his hidden agenda may be that of maintaining his leadership at any cost. The position of influence and power is pleasing, and he will resist relin-

quishing it. One of the hardest tasks facing any leader of a continuing group is to allow it to grow up and to be less dependent
on him. In little ways, as so frequently parents do, he maintains
his control over the group.

On the other hand, other individuals may tend to want to give
away their leadership at the same time they seek it. Usually this
ambivalence grows out of a feeling of guilt about wanting to be
leader.

Of course, many leaders have neither hidden agenda. They may
be willing to accept leadership when the group requires it, be
pleased by their opportunity to serve and to have recognition, but
glad to release the leadership and pass it on. Where groups have
grown in ability and maturity to a point where every member is
playing a leader role in some way in the group, pressures toward
maintaining the leader role are greatly reduced.

The Group

Once a group has begun to form (when there is some expectation that it will meet more than once and when there is felt to be
some common concern of the group as a whole), it shows many
characteristics common to individuals. Its most fundamental trait
seems to be a will to survive. No matter how much at war parts
of the group may be with other parts, there is usually a movement of the group itself that can only be explained on the basis
of an urge for survival. A group under attack, either from a
source outside the group or from one of its own members, will
move to resist this attack, whether or not it is a logical criticism of
the group's operation. A group with absent members will show
signs of depression and worry. Somehow the fact that these members are absent seems an attack on the group—as if the members,
if they really valued the group, would find some way of attending.
When new members come into a group, there is a period in which
the group exudes a sense of tension until it knows whether the
new members will disrupt the group. When one member moves

too fast and too far, causing potential splits in the group, a quiet resistant movement grows within the group.

A group is fearful of conflict when the conflict promises to destroy the group, even though it permits and encourages conflict among members, against the leader, against an outside force, as a means of escape from its job. The difference lies in whether the conflict threatens the basic group being. Warfare is tolerated—is even fun—until it threatens the basic survival of the group.

The group may have hidden agendas about its task. If the task is seen as too difficult; if it suggests consequences that might be harmful to the group; if it has been pressed on the group by some outside group or individual that is disliked by the group; if it is solely the leader's task, the group's hidden agenda may be to slow down on the task. While this is never brought out on the surface, the group has many ways of running away from its job. One pattern of flight may be that of endless discussion over unimportant details, another the flight through listing on the blackboard endless lists that could better be done by one person later. Escape into discussion of principles, or into esoteric arguments is very common. Anecdotal periods that delay work are found in many groups.

Groups develop hidden agendas about a given group member or leader. Where some one has been overly aggressive, the group may center its hostility upon that individual. Under tension from sources that cannot be adequately attacked, a group may scapegoat one of its own members. Thus groups distort the pattern of work on the task level to fit the many hidden agendas present.

Groups can readily develop hidden agendas concerning the leader. If he is too dominant, the hidden agenda reaction may take the form of passive resistance. If he takes sides on crucial issues or leaves the group with no security about his fairness, active revolt may take place. Frequently a group is obviously following the leadership of one of its members, while it permits the designated leader to go through the empty forms of leadership.

What to Do about Hidden Agendas

The problem of handling hidden agendas in such a way that they do not block group productivity or lead to group failure and disintegration faces every leader.

Pretending these agendas are not present, ruling the group with an iron hand, and forcing it to stay on the beam have been relatively unsuccessful. Usually a leader who acts in this way comes out with an apathetic endorsement of his own plan, with no responsibility upon the parts of the members to carry it out, with much conflict and aggression in the group, or with many efforts of the group to run away from its job.

Effective leadership, however, can do much to help the group bring together its work on both its surface and hidden levels. The leader who recognizes that his function is basically to help the group at its points of need, rather than to direct the group or pull it along, reluctantly, after him, can do much with the problem of hidden agendas. His approach of service to the group should tend to make him more sensitive to group needs and more diagnostic about group problems.

Such a leader can observe the following suggestive points:

1. Look for hidden agendas that are present. Recognition of the possibility of hidden agendas on individual and group level is the first step in diagnosis of group difficulty. Diagnosis is the necessary first step before intelligent action can be taken.

2. Remember that the group is continuously working on two levels at once. Consequently it may not move as fast on the surface task as the leader might wish.

3. Sometimes the leader can make it easier for a group to bring its hidden agenda to the surface. The leader may say, for example: "I wonder if we have said all we feel about the issue. Maybe we should take time to go around the table so that any further thoughts can be opened up."

4. When hidden agendas can be laid on the table and talked about, they are easier to handle. *But many hidden agendas would*

hurt the group more if they were talked about openly. A leader or group member needs to be sensitive to this point and should try to recognize what a group can and cannot face at a given point.

5. Don't scold or pressure the group because it has hidden agendas. They are present and legitimate and need to be worked on as much as the surface task.

6. Help the group to remove feelings of guilt about hidden agendas. As groups are aided to bring out into the open some of the hidden agendas and treat them legitimately, there will be a lessening of feelings of guilt about them and a tendency to lay more of them on the table. The leader might say: "We certainly could expect that each of us might see things somewhat differently and we certainly shouldn't feel guilty about wanting different things accomplished. That is all part of the many differences that make up a group."

7. Help the group work out methods of solving their hidden agendas just as they develop methods of handling their surface agenda. Such methods may vary, but basically they call for opening up the problem, collecting as much relevant data as possible, and seeking a solution based on such data. Obviously, data relating to the individual's feelings and problems are as important as more logical data. In the last analysis, problem solving methods are needed for solving hidden agendas.

8. Help the group evaluate its progress in handling hidden agendas. Each experience should indicate better ways of more openly handling future hidden agendas. As groups grow in maturity and strength, the number of hidden agendas that remain hidden is definitely reduced. Short evaluation sessions, either the last fifteen minutes of a group meeting, or one meeting out of a series of meetings, can be very profitable to a group. In such sessions a group can look back to see how many more problems it was able to talk freely about and how much more confidence the group had in its members.

Toward Better Group Work in the Church

BY GORDON LIPPITT

Some helpful suggestions for better group work have grown out of the research in Group Dynamics. The following principles suggest ways in which Church workers can go about improving their group work:

- Help the group *decide clearly what its purposes are in coming together*. It is important at the beginning of any group's life that it have a clear understanding of the goals it wants to reach.
- Help the group to *become conscious of its own process*. This relates to the realization that if a group is going to improve its operational efficiency, it must see the desirability of looking at its own procedures. Then the group will learn to take some responsibility as to how they operate and realize that by improving the process of the group they can improve their problem-solving ability.
- The group should be helped to *become aware of talents, skills, and other resources alive within its own membership*. In some of the quiet members of the group, there are potential sources for help on the matters being discussed.
- Develop the *group methods of evaluation* so that the group can have ways of improving its process. This evaluation helps the leader and group members to become aware of how the others are feeling.

Gordon Lippitt, "Suggested Principles for Improved Group Work," *Religious Education*, November–December, 1952, pp. 375–376. Published by The Religious Education Association, New York. Used by permission.

- It is important to learn to *accept new ideas and new members* into the group without irreparable conflict, to learn to *accept discipline in working toward long-range objectives,* and to learn to *profit from failure.* Often we can take advantage of a poor meeting as a way of seeing how frustration can lead to a group of newly motivated members, instead of its being a symbol of defeat.
- Help a group to *create new jobs or committees* as needed and to *learn to terminate them* or the group itself when it is wise to do so.

These few suggestions and additional skills are the responsibility of any good group to develop as they proceed to make more effective decisions in both a democratic and a Christian way.

This section does not permit elaboration of some of the techniques and skills that have been developed within the past few years to aid groups in solving problems. Such skills as the group observer, role playing, post-meeting reaction sheets, and so forth, are not to be confused with the term "Group Dynamics." These techniques have been found helpful in improving group effectiveness. Their usefulness for training and leadership have emerged from the early research in the field of Group Dynamics. *They are, however, group techniques and not Group Dynamics.* The dynamics of groups, then, has been a field for scientific analysis, study and understanding. Coming out of this study is an educational method related to effective group functioning that is meaningful to the church. If the essence of Christianity is maturity in relationship to the adjustment to one's environment, the study of Group Dynamics gives us much to be sensitive to in the development of our group work in the Church.

8. HOW PLAN TO TEACH?

ASSUMING THAT a capable, consecrated teacher has been chosen, success or failure in teaching depends more on advance preparation than on any other single factor. This planning must be of two kinds. One is long-range planning that looks ahead for a quarter or a year or more, and that aims at all-round Christian nurture of the class or group. The other is session planning that cares for the details of a particular session, so that the session will fulfill its part in the long-range plan. Both types of planning are necessary.

The general procedures in planning are much the same for teachers of all ages, and for group leaders (such as youth fellowship advisers) who do not ordinarily think of themselves as "teachers." Obviously, the content of the plan differs from age to age and from group to group.

The readings that follow deal with both kinds of planning, and they represent the whole range of age groups. The first recalls the basic truth, mentioned in chapter 3, that leader and group are a team. It describes ways in which this principle may be implemented. The next three readings deal primarily with long-range planning. The last three deal with session planning. It is suggested that the reader begin with the article or articles related to the age with which he is working, for these will speak most directly to him. Then he should proceed to the other articles, noting how their suggestions may need to be adapted to the particular age or group involved.

All writers agree that planning must begin with the spiritual preparation of the leader himself.

How to Teach in Groups

BY PAUL B. MAVES

Whenever a church takes seriously what is now known about the dynamics of group life, it seeks to establish the conditions in which communication can take place most effectively. Whenever a church really believes it is a community of grace and seeks to act that way, it gives careful attention to establishing groups which truly reflect Christ's love and in which Christian growth can take place.

The Whole Church Teaches

First of all, such a church becomes aware that it is the character of the whole life of the congregation that is the chief influence upon our pupils of the church school and other members. This means that we cannot talk about one thing in classes and in the pulpit and practice another thing in our relations to each other.

There can be no feeling of the church school or a church group being an organization separate from the church. The whole congregation is responsible for the educational aspect of its life, as well as of its evangelistic, devotional, and service program. Parents and teachers find ways to consult with each other and work together on mutually accepted goals. Workers' conferences and teachers' meetings become working fellowships involving worship, personal enrichment, and mutual planning rather than routine assemblies for announcements or endless discussion of trivial details.

Paul B. Maves, *International Journal of Religious Education*, May, 1957, pp. 18, 19, 24. Used by permission.

Teach in Teams

One of the best places to start is with the teachers themselves—by having them teach in teams. There is discipline in teaching in relationship with one or more other teachers in a cooperative enterprise. Teaching teams help to maintain creative relationships with the pupils. They help to provide, at the outset, an atmosphere of shared responsibility.

Sometimes teams are comprised of good friends who work together, others of a teacher and an observer. Sometimes a husband and wife work together, provided both are acceptable as teachers and equally concerned. Some teams consist of a head teacher and several assistants. In some adult groups, the teaching is done by a committee of several persons who lead the group through an entire unit of study, another team taking the next unit. In this way every member of the class serves on a teaching team and takes some responsibility for planning the program. In each case planning, teaching, and evaluating are done cooperatively. Usually it is much easier to get two teachers for a class than one. It is sound planning to be training new teachers and leaders by having them serve as apprentices on such a team.

Use Natural Groups if Possible

In developing relationships through which communication can take place, it is well, when possible, to use natural, primary groups, especially with children, and interest groups with adults. For example, teaching a children's class which is also a neighborhood play group can be more effective than working with a group of children brought together on Sunday but who hardly know each other, who go to different schools, and do not see each other except in church school.

A class made up of the Protestant members from a single grade class in public school presents real advantages. Unfortunately competitive denominationalism often makes such a possibility remote except for weekday or vacation schools.

Vital communication can take place among adults best when there is a variety of groups meeting at convenient times to fit the needs and interests of their members instead of one large adult class at nine-thirty on Sunday morning into which everyone is jammed. Occupational groups, interest groups, block and neighborhood organizations often make good functioning units.

Most important of all, we must see the family as the primary unit for religious education, and arrange our programs and schedules for families to be together in programs, as well as helping families to be more Christian in the home itself.

Where we do not work with natural, primary groups special attention needs to be given to helping classes and groups grow into cohesive units. One way to do this is to help them to find a common interest or bond that can weld them together and to work on common projects which are meaningful to all. Another way is to meet often for a variety of activities filling a wide range of needs.

It is essential, too, that members come to know each other as persons and assume some responsibility for helping each other achieve individual goals. This means that groups must be kept small enough so this can happen. Where large numbers are involved, small subgroups must be formed. A high school fellowship with sixty or a hundred members might be divided into four grade units. Any large program will be most meaningful to the persons involved if it is broken into interest groups so that there is opportunity for full participation in intimate fellowship units.

One advantage of groups gathered from many backgrounds, on the other hand, is that in them barriers of class, neighborhood, and cliques can be transcended and groups can be deliberately made diverse and more stimulating.

Help Groups to Grow

Communication can take place best when people who work well together are in the same group. Instead of trying to break up friendship groups and to disrupt cliques in order to have everyone in "one big, happy family" it is better to encourage them to grow in their friendship so they will feel secure enough to open their group, to widen their fellowship, and even to spawn and start new fellowships.

In one class of fourth-graders each member was asked to write on a card the names of two or three persons in the class he would like to work with and the names of any of the class he would prefer not to work with. Only the teachers saw the cards and the preferences were kept confidential. It was discovered that there was one child in the group who was actually rejected by nine-tenths of the class. When project groups were set up he was put with the one group of more mature youngsters who had not rejected him, even though they had not selected him. At the same time an effort was made to help him develop his strengths so he could become a valuable group member and learn to relate to others better. When the device was used again a few months later, it was seen that this child was actually selected by a number of others and rejected by only a few. The attitude toward him had been changed and his attitude toward himself was much more wholesome.

An exclusive church or a closed church school class which admits only those who are mirror images of the present members is not Christ's church or class. Quite often the person who needs love the most is the hardest to love, and is the first to be rejected by classmates and ejected from the class.

Meet Individual Needs

Teachers need to become much more conscious than many are of their relationship to individual members of the class. The teacher's primary responsibility is for what is happening to the members of the group rather than with covering lessons. He can communicate a Christian faith only when he can accept each person as he is without condition and can love him without strings attached.

A rough, rude, boisterous, noisy youngster was warmly received and welcomed by his teachers, although firmly held to class standards. He was helped to see himself as he was and to modify his behavior out of consideration for others. However, the teacher who was able to accept this obstreperous child was not able to relate warmly to another child who was sullen and hostile, and feels she did little for him. The more we know about the importance of interpersonal relationships as a means for communicating the gospel, the more we see the need for mature, balanced, warmly accepting teachers.

Teachers who understand the importance of such relationships try to understand each pupil—his needs, his interests, his purposes, his hungers, and his hurts. They try to get acquainted with each pupil as a person by visiting in the home, by talking with parents and with other teachers who know him. They try to help each pupil at the point of his deepest need, using activities, projects, the study of the Bible and church history, and their own understanding of the Christian gospel as resources for meeting that need. Class sessions become for them occasions for helping persons grow; lessons are resources for working with persons in meeting their needs so that, in relationship, those persons experience God's love as it was manifested in Christ.

In a class where one boy was scornful and aloof, a spontaneous dramatization was planned so he would be drawn into the group. In another class a shy girl with a low estimate of herself was chosen for the part of Mary in the nativity pageant, instead of the prettiest and most popular girl.

Help Pupils Learn from Each Other

It is important that teachers be conscious of the relationship of the members of the group to each other. A boy who is being rejected by his classmates is not learning much about the love of God. The child who feels worthless and whose sense of inferiority is heightened by unfavorable comparison within the class is not likely to understand Christ's love for him. Aware of this, teachers can help each person to win a place for himself in the group and can help the group to accept each person. In one class a mentally retarded child was given responsibility for passing the offering plates, laying out the hymnals, and such routine tasks as were within his ability. Brighter class members then helped him to make a scrapbook of pictures of Jesus' life.

Frequently the teacher must interpret the unusual child to the class and help them to know how to accept him. A first-grade teacher prepared her class for the reception of a hard-of-hearing child by saying she needed their assistance in helping him. When he came, wearing a hearing aid, time was spent in understanding what it did and why it worked. As a result there was no teasing, ridicule, or uneasiness, but only a friendly acceptance by all the children, and pride in the boy's accomplishments.

Teachers have a responsibility for setting standards, developing an atmosphere, and establishing patterns of relations between all the members of the class or group which would be increasingly consistent with the Christian spirit of love. Their purpose is not only to bring individuals, but also groups to Christ's way, and to guide groups in becoming responsible for redeeming others. The class can be a laboratory for the testing of Christian ways and an outpost in the Kingdom of God, in which the members are being redeemed themselves at the same time they are reaching out to redeem others.

Share the Responsibility

Communication takes place best when the pupils share in the teaching and the teachers share in the learning; when members of the group participate to the best of their ability and assume as much responsibility as they can for the direction and outcomes of the group.

In the younger groups the teachers must be alert to pick up suggestions from the class members in informal conversation and from spontaneous and casual remarks. Whenever possible they will have the children themselves take responsibility—for praying, for telling a story, for sharing an experience, for bringing in a report, for arranging the room.

In older groups planning committees and steering committees

can be used, with the entire group membership being encouraged to participate in the plans by acting on committee suggestions. Standards of behavior and rules are most effective when developed by the group, not imposed by the teacher or laid down by a small group of directors.

Our teaching will have power when we learn how to live and to work in true community and partnership according to the will of God as we know it in the life and teachings of Jesus. The scientific study of group life is helping us to understand better the meaning of these teachings, and to open the way for the Holy Spirit.

The Nursery Program and How to Plan for It

BY PHOEBE M. ANDERSON

A Look at the Program

Recalling some of the experiences of Alice Todd on Sunday morning (see the article "What Three-Year-Olds Are Like," chapter 2) will give us a pretty clear picture of how a morning program runs. At the beginning of the church school year there is no total group activity as such for three-year-olds. Most activities run along at the same time, engaged in by two or three or even four children who may or may not be playing together. Most likely the children will be playing beside each other. The teachers may decide that the total group will go for a walk, or plant crocuses in the churchyard. But if the children have a choice, very likely there will be some who will prefer to play with clay or work puzzles. Later, when the children are four, or approaching this age, the total group may voluntarily gather on the rug for a story and song and conversation time, and the children will be able to participate in the experience together for five or seven minutes before they become too restless. But this is not likely to occur in the fall and winter when the children are younger and still adjusting to one another, to their new adult friend, and to an environment that offers unlimited possibilities for creative and imaginative play.

The exact order of the morning's activities will change from time to time as the children become acquainted with their nursery room and as they grow older. Generally speaking, it suits the child best to have the room set up when the hour begins and, therefore, this is the best way for teacher and child to become acquainted. Each child chooses what he wants to do as he enters the room, and he is free to move from one activity to another all during the free play period which probably should last for forty-five to fifty minutes of the hour. Going to the bathroom and getting a drink can be done by each child as he feels the need to do these things. Toward the end of the hour, the teachers can help the children draw their activities to a close and put away the toys until next Sunday.

One teacher should be sitting at the edge of the rug reading stories, telling stories, singing, or doing finger plays so that, as the children finish what they are doing, they can join the group on the rug and look at books themselves or participate with the others in whatever activity is taking place. This *may* be the time when a prayer follows a particularly good story. It will not always be. The real prayer of the morning may have been said when some of the children held a little brown crocus bulb and looked at a picture of the flower which the teacher told them their bulb would grow to be. The prayer may be voiced by a child as he relates a particularly significant event in his life, and then it is his prayer. Some Sundays there may not be a spoken prayer, but it would be quite clear to the wise observer that the quality of the living that went on in the room was both prayer and praise.

The teachers work together in the nursery group according to a previously agreed-upon plan. Each one knows which part of the room she will have as her "station": who will greet the children; who will supervise the bathroom; who will conduct the quiet activity on the rug, and so forth. The teachers may take turns by Sundays with these responsibilities, or they may decide to stay with one sphere of activity for some time. It does not matter how this is arranged so long as each teacher is having an opportunity to share in the planning and the execution of the program.

The nursery home visitor—if she is not also a teacher—should be present on most Sunday mornings to greet the families as they arrive and to keep her relationship with them alive. If she can also visit the three-year-old group frequently enough to get to know the children and for them to know her, she will find home visiting more rewarding both to the family and to herself.

Adults Must Plan Together for Youth Work

BY CLARICE M. BOWMAN

In a very small church, there may be just one teacher of the younger youth, and possibly one for the older ones. They with their minister should plan together, and invite one or more parents to meet with them, to bring in the point of view of the home.

In larger churches, workers with young people may be more numerous and may serve in more varied capacities. Whatever their title, they are all "teachers" in the deepest sense. These may include: youth division superintendents, counselors for age-group departments, teachers in the Sunday morning sessions, leaders in expanded or additional sessions, counselors for evening meetings, advisers to committees or commissions, pianists, record-keepers, club leaders (Scouts, Camp Fire Girls, etc.), representative parents, pastor, general church-school superintendent.

All workers with young people in *any* church should meet often together to "see the program whole," as it is affecting the lives of the young persons to whom they are attempting to minister. Does this imply that *adults* are urged to meet and plan? Would that not rob youth of "participation"? No! Clear thinking will suggest that this over-all survey and general planning by adult workers in no wise overlaps youth's own areas for planning. There are some things youth cannot do! Likewise, there are some things—those within the experience range and abilities of the age level of youth involved—adults should not rob them of their chance to do. But short-sighted "letting youth do it all" may mean failure on the

Clarice M. Bowman, *Ways Youth Learn* (New York: Harper & Brothers, 1952), pp. 37–40. Used by permission.

part of adult workers to attain a level of youth work worthy of a Christian church!

Of concern for all "teachers" of youth in any church are these imperatives:

- To study the needs, problems, and interests of the young people of their church; to read or hear book reviews and learn of other helpful materials to guide them in their relationships with their youth; to hear from experts who have studied youth of the different ages; to confer with parents, club leaders, and schoolteachers working with these same young folk.
- To study what should be the general goals of all church work with young people, and with each age level; to receive guidance from qualified leaders about theology, and renew their own awareness of the basic beliefs of the Christian faith; to consider these beliefs in relation to the curriculum used, their methods and their Christian example.
- To consider principles and policies for youth work in their church that should be talked over with the young people for their viewpoints, and recommended to the church official body responsible for the total program of Christian education.
- To study what their church is now doing with each age level with a view to making the best possible use of time schedule, room space, and equipment, printed materials, and organization.
- To study the curriculum materials provided by their denomination for the Sunday school, evening meetings, weekday sessions, vacation school, camp, story papers, and the like. To make recommendations to the youth officers and to the church board of education so that orders for proper materials for each age level may be sent in sufficiently early for workers and young people to have sufficient time to prepare their units well in advance.
- To study the available room space and equipment, to determine ways for making the most effective use possible of what

is available and for suggesting recommendations for improvement.

• To plan for the next forthcoming units of study and worship *together*—that is, workers in the Sunday school and workers in the evening meeting going over materials for both sessions and helping each other plan, so that for the young people themselves their work may be a "living whole" instead of two wholly unrelated parts sometimes overlapping and sometimes leaving out important areas.

• To evaluate methods used in teaching and counseling, with a view to conserving the values of earlier training the young people have had through the children's division; and with a view to preparing them for experiences they will face as adults.

• To plan for ways of celebrating great days and seasons of the church year, so as to open for the young people doorways into highly meaningful experiences.

• To give consideration to any personal or special needs arising among individuals; and to seek to meet problem situations in such a way as to make them steppingstones forward.

• To co-operate with the pastor in preparing young people for church membership, and in helping them find places for active service in the church.

• To study community and other influences impinging upon young lives; to seek counsel with leaders of youth in other agencies and to work out means for co-operation in eradicating community evils and promoting character growth in the youth of the community.

• To co-operate with other age-group departments of the church school and with all-church enterprises. To seek to help youth extend their interests and loyalties to the work of the whole church, and not alone of their youth fellowship.

• To encourage one another as workers with youth to take advantage of all possible opportunities for growth: leadership courses in schools and through correspondence, informal meetings and conferences with persons who can help; recommended reading; films; etc.

• To keep in touch with connectional workers of the denomination who may give helpful advice through correspondence or visits.

• To hear reports of committees, commissions, interest groups, or individuals who have taken special responsibilities.

• To give attention to the financial program with youth, and to consider whether Christian beliefs and habits of stewardship of money are being fostered.

• To clear dates on the all-church calendar.

• Etc.

Pupils of All Ages Can Help Plan

BY GLADYS M. JACKSON

Much of the success of any undertaking depends on planning. Some teachers determine their method of procedure, but find it difficult and sometimes impossible to communicate their plans to the pupils. The best teachers draw the pupils into the planning because if they are involved in it they are already beginning to learn.

Every teacher knows that pupils learn readily after their interest has been caught. Having them help with the planning is one of the best ways of catching that interest. Everyone likes being "in on" things from the beginning. He begins to feel it's *his* activity, *his* room, *his* project. This proprietary interest determines much of his enthusiasm.

Before a junior high department moved into a new room the teacher asked the pupils for suggestions about furnishings. They made a serious study of sacred art which resulted in selection of appropriate pictures. The experience was meaningful because they had done the planning.

A young adult group had just completed a study of Acts. The teacher felt that a study of Romans would be the next logical step. However, they were using an elective type curriculum and she asked the group to consider the matter. They suggested various books, but finally agreed that since they had been studying about Paul and the final part of Acts referred to his preaching in Rome, Romans would be the best choice. The class was more ready for

Gladys M. Jackson, "Let the Pupils Help Plan," *International Journal of Religious Education*, May, 1954, p. 12. Used by permission.

the study of Romans than if the teacher had announced, "We will follow Acts with a study of Romans."

One reason learning is sometimes slow is that the pupils have no sense of direction, no feeling of looking for anything in particular, no understanding of why certain things are done. Sharing in the planning helps them achieve a sense of purpose.

Arrangements were made, following suggestions in the printed materials, for the seniors to visit a synagogue. Their leader suggested that they list the questions about the Jewish faith they would like to have answered. They made out a list and gave it to the rabbi. When they visited the synagogue they didn't waste time collecting their thoughts. They knew what they were there for.

One teacher felt that pupils were not experiencing real worship in Sunday school. She began a system of asking four pupils to meet with her during the week to help plan worship for the next Sunday. Out of that experience came a new appreciation for worship. Within a few months everyone had helped at least once. More meaningful worship resulted because pupils helped plan it.

Some pupils were considering the question, "How can we build a deeper Christian fellowship in our group?" They turned the hour into a planning session, dividing into small groups for discussion. When reports were made, lists of suggestions were compiled to be considered further by the adult leaders and by the officers.

The kind of planning done may range from small children's choosing the prayer they use to adults' choices regarding curriculum. Pupils should be encouraged to share in decisions as much as possible, consistently, unit by unit, rather than spasmodically.

Planning with pupils creates a partnership. More is accomplished as time and energy are invested in this way. Learning of content is not the only result. Important by-products are derived: appreciation for necessary work and detail and a sense of values in human relationships. Problems of attendance and discipline fade as the teacher lets the pupils be partners in a common undertaking.

Principles in Planning a Unit—*Written for Junior Teachers but Adaptable to Any Age*

BY DOROTHY LA CROIX HILL

1. Begin your preparation by asking not what "you are going to present," or "put across," but what it is that you and the juniors will find out together. This you may discover by skimming the entire unit, both pupils' and teacher's material. If you still feel unenthusiastic about the subject and about trying to teach it, read one of the books listed under "Resource Materials for the Teacher." It may open up the subject for you and make these weeks of teaching a thrilling experience for you as well as the juniors.

2. Think about the unit in the light of your pupils' past learning experiences in church and at home. Which of these can they put together with experiences of this unit to make new learnings, deeper insights, keener appreciations? What special needs of your boys and girls can this unit help meet? What skills have they which can be utilized in this unit with value and with satisfaction?

3. When you have read the whole unit, and thought about your pupils' experiences, needs, and skills in relation to it, try to state in your own words the purposes of your work for the coming weeks. Remember that there are always three kinds of goals—to help juniors discover certain facts, to help them feel in certain ways, and to help them respond in desirable ways because of what they have discovered and the ways they feel.

4. Thinking of what you hope to accomplish, review in your

Dorothy LaCroix Hill, *Working with Juniors at Church* (Nashville: Abingdon Press, 1955), pp. 71–76. Used by permission.

mind the different kinds of teaching materials used in the unit. Do certain ones seem to be "key materials," to have in a special way the "idea" of the unit, as you have discovered it? Perhaps this "key material" is a Bible passage, or one certain hymn, or a group of stories or pictures used in a particular way for a particular purpose. Jot these down for special study on your part. Plan to use them not only for study in the class, but for worship when they have become familiar and meaningful to the boys and girls. In a small church or in a junior department your juniors may share these materials with other classes during the period when all join in worship.

5. Now try to decide what special ways of learning will be most useful in this unit. Perhaps directed study of the Bible will be one of the very important teaching methods used in the coming weeks. You will want to think of ways to make the juniors eager to study these passages; of ways to make this part of each session move smoothly and quickly; of interesting interpretations which will help the boys and girls to understand and enjoy the Bible material.

Opportunities for worship must always be included in planning. Worship can lift learning to the high plane of spiritual experience and deepen, strengthen, and enrich it.

Plans in the teacher's manual will probably suggest that helping the boys and girls to do one particular thing is extremely valuable *for the purposes of this unit*. Perhaps they are to make a visit to the synagogue, or bring an offering for work among migrants, or plan a gift of books which will help primary children to understand how people lived in Bible days. There will usually be some one large activity or experience like this in which the whole class will share. To make it meaningful requires careful thought and planning. You must contact the rabbi well in advance of your trip to the synagogue, write for materials about work among migrants, or find out what books on Bible background are recommended for primary children. True, the juniors themselves must make as many of these plans and preparations as possible; but the teacher must be ready to help them to plan successfully.

6. Along with this large and important "thing to do" will be other activities for individuals, interest groups, and committees. Because boys and girls are all different, because they have different interests and different skills, each will do his own best learning in his own way. Juniors learn in many active ways. Some of these will be the best ways of learning for the unit you are planning.

If you do not have a helping teacher, you may need to enlist a mother, a father, a schoolteacher, a young employed person, to work with one group on a certain kind of activity while you give guidance to another. It will be necessary to meet with this person, to acquaint him in a general way with the unit, to suggest sections which he needs to read, and to provide him with materials which will help him to do good work and have a satisfying experience with the juniors.

7. The first session of a unit confronts us with what is probably the most difficult of our teaching tasks—to help boys and girls who have no idea about what they want to learn in this area of religion to find some definite purposes which are important to them. These will give momentum to their study for the next few weeks. To some degree we keep on doing this throughout the unit, with boys and girls who have been absent, with new pupils, with those who easily lose sight of their goals, with the whole group when interest lags or when the interval between sessions makes new motivation necessary .

As teachers we must remember that all boys and girls want to learn. They are made that way. Discovering how to channel their interest toward desired Christian ends is a teaching skill which comes through experimentation, through trial and error, through experience. Suggestions in our lesson materials can help us to get started on this highly creative, highly satisfying part of teaching.

At this point in the preparation of a unit you will give careful study to all suggestions for helping the juniors to become interested in the unit and in each session's discoveries. What materials in your room need to be put away so that interest will not be scattered, but will be channeled toward this unit? What materials are to be displayed, and how are they to be used to arouse curiosity, questions, and discussion? Is the room to be arranged for directed study; for conversation, with a blackboard ready to record important ideas; for individual investigation? How will the teacher proceed so that children will begin to wonder, to guess, to ask, to seek information, to think, to worship? How can anticipation be built up for what is to be found out or done in the coming session?

The purpose of this first session is always to create a desire to begin learning in this area of religion, to give the boys and girls an exciting taste of what lies ahead in the unit. At the very beginning they must experience the satisfaction of discovering something new which, put together with their past knowledge and experiences, makes for new and different understandings and relationships in their Christian experience. What happens in the first session must be interesting enough to bring the juniors back for the next session.

8. Plan to make creative use of your materials. A creative cook probably uses the same ingredients as other cooks, with a dash of something that is peculiarly his own idea or a special way of putting the ingredients together so that the result is recognized as superior. So as you give close attention to the Bible passages, the suggested conversation, the story to tell, and the other activities in which the class will engage, you will be thinking about that additional something from your own experience and about exactly how and when to use each piece of material, each kind of activity, each guiding thought, so that in combination with the thinking and doing of the boys and girls who make up the class, these may be productive of the results stated in your aims for the session.

Write down this "creative thinking" which is your way of planning for the session. At first this session plan may be quite full as you "live through in imagination" the ways in which you will guide your class of juniors. In many particulars it will be like the plan in your teacher's text, but in other ways it will be peculiarly your own.

Next review your teaching plan and make a list of everything you will need to use in the session—the Bibles, the pictures, pupils' books, pencils and paper, markers to put in the copies of the Bible, chalk, chalk board. Note everything you will need to do in order to be ready for the juniors. How will you make the room say something about the unit or the purposes of the session? How will you arrange chairs, tables, and other equipment in the light of what the group will be doing today? When will you do these things so that, as the children arrive, you will have time for fellowship?

Study the materials you will use until each has a message for you. If the group is to read in unison, you can help to make the reading meaningful and beautiful by the way you lead. Decide how you hope the juniors will feel because they have heard or read these Bible passages or a certain story. Practice the story or reading aloud until you are sure that you can help the juniors to feel that way. Be clear about the meaning of each Bible passage or hymn stanza.

Perhaps a song in the pupil's book will interpret the experience of persons you are studying about or will help the boys and girls to put into words what you hope they are feeling. Take time to learn the song thoroughly through the week, humming the melody, thinking the words, singing them together, until you do not need a piano. Now you have made the song a piece of teaching material, like a story, a Bible passage, or a picture.

9. Rethink your plan. How does one activity or piece of material lead into what follows? If you know, then you will have little difficulty in remembering what comes first, then next, and next. Your boys and girls will move along smoothly through the session, because there is always a purpose for what they are doing. At what points in the plan do you see possibilities for worship—after the story, when you have made plans? Will one of the Bible

passages have special meaning for the class right then? What thoughts might make a meaningful prayer?

Through such preparation the teacher visualizes in advance the experience of the class session. When he begins to look forward eagerly to the class hour, he is really *ready to teach.*

Planning the Session—Written for Primary Teachers but Speaks to Others Also

BY HAZEL A. LEWIS

The wise leader will sit down as soon as possible after one session of the department and begin to think about the next one. While the experiences of the day are fresh in her mind, she will make notes concerning needs that were revealed and that could not immediately be met, conduct problems that were evident, things the children said about what they would like to do, or something they would like to find out, the general atmosphere of the department. For example, perhaps certain children in the group are dominating the situation to such an extent that other less aggressive children are not having an opportunity for their share in the planning and activity of the department. Or, perhaps interest in some undertaking has become so intense that the purpose of getting it done satisfactorily has caused some unhappiness and the good will and joyousness of fellowship have suffered. Perhaps some child who is a bit of a bungler but nevertheless loves to help, has been made very unhappy. In other words, good will is being sacrificed for thoroughness. The leader faces the problem, in planning the next session, of choosing activities and program materials that will supply these interests, meet these needs, correct the undesirable attitudes.

Hazel A. Lewis, *The Primary Church School* (St. Louis: Bethany Press, 1951), pp. 79–83. Used by permission.

Seasonal Interests

There are seasonal experiences of the children to be taken into account, interests which loom large in the children's lives, or others which are important and might be overlooked. A wise leader will make note of these interests and make them an avenue of enriching the religious experiences of the child.

Group Activities

There are activities which are going on in the smaller groups. In the department plan of organization these are class groups. In the single grade or department unit plan, they are interest groups. It is not necessary to coordinate all of these with department activities, nor to coordinate the program of the department with all of the group activities, but there are certain of them which involve intergroup activities or which are more effective when they can be shared with the other children of the department. There is a need for the interweaving of interest and activities between the groups.

Emergencies

There are also emergency situations which must be taken into account. Perhaps these can scarcely be considered as part of a plan made in advance, because frequently they occur too late to be planned for. But when there has been a community disaster during the week or radio and headlines tell of war or other disasters, it is reasonably certain that the primary children will be excited about it and also frequently true that they will have overheard adult conversations which give a religious implication to the event. The wise leader will plan a session or a series of sessions that will help the children think more clearly about how God works in the world, what he expects of us at such times, and to feel secure in his love, even though neither they nor the adults in their world can always feel physically safe.

The Children's Interests

The children themselves will have a large share in determining the direction the session will take, if their initiative has been encouraged and allowed to find expression in the activities of the group. For example, a department superintendent who had planned to tell a story might find herself involved instead in a discussion, launched by the children and growing out of some activity. She would be very unwise indeed, if the discussion is a profitable one, to insist upon interrupting it in order to tell the story she had planned. Perhaps she had brought a picture which she had expected would serve as an approach to a new song, but instead she found the interest in the picture itself so great that an interpretation of that seemed the most desirable thing and the most fruitful, so that a picture appreciation took the place of learning a new song for that particular session.

All of this makes it necessary to face the problem of how any plan can be made for a session in advance. Yet the leader who has no plan is at a serious disadvantage and usually gives evidence of it in the uncertainty of her leadership. No matter how good her educational background may be, how sound her educational theory, or how rich her resources, it is necessary to make certain plans if her leadership is to be effective.

The Plan

But of what will the leader's plan consist? Would it be a program of songs, prayer, picture verses, stories, and other materials? Certainly these would be included and the plan would also contain alternative materials. If the leader profits by past experience and cultivates her imagination a little, and if she knows her group of children, she will be able to have some general idea of what will probably occur, although she may not know the exact trend that it will take. Perhaps the thing she plans to do one Sunday will fit another occasion even if it had to be abandoned on the day for which she planned it. She will also be very wise if she makes notes on her plans, after the session, indicating how the plan was modified or changed, and why.

Sequence in a Session

A primary leader who is sensitive to the interests of children and the factors mentioned above, will probably not know the exact sequence in which the program will develop. When the department is organized on the single grade or departmental plan the experiences of the session may follow the needs and interests of the children. Even then the work of different interest groups must be considered. When different grades and classes are using the same room, or are joining in the same assembly for worship and fellowship, there must be a certain schedule so that the teachers, as well as the departmental leader, can be ready to guide the work in the group for which they are responsible. But it is doubtful if it is necessary, even then, to have a rigid time schedule. Certainly the plan of having children assemble on the click of the clock for fifteen minutes of worship, followed by a fellowship period of ten minutes, a march to classes at a certain time, and a return for dismissal, does not permit a very natural or spontaneous religious experience on the part of the children. Custom and the limitations of rooms and equipment may seem to make such a rigid program necessary, but it is usually possible to secure greater flexibility when there is a desire on the part of leaders and teachers to provide the children with the best opportunity for work and worship.

For example, in one department which was organized on the department basis, with smaller class groups, and which had only the limited one-hour schedule, all too meager at best, the leader made out a tentative schedule for each morning. A copy of this she placed on a bulletin board above the secretary's desk. The teachers read it as they came in. Perhaps it would read something like this, "Work (interest or class groups) 9:15 to 9:45." (The formal time of opening the school was 9:30. Thus work began fifteen minutes before the regular time of opening the session and extended beyond that time fifteen minutes.) Under the heading of this period were listed the various activities that would probably be going on. Some of these were class groups who had work under way. Other children would be arranging and caring for the room and there was a group project in which the entire department was interested. The library table was also listed as one of the activities. Thus there were five kinds of probable activities listed under the first heading.

The next item on the tentative schedule was, "9:45 to 10:00. Worship and Fellowship." Under this were listed some of the materials (songs, Scripture, story and other things) that would probably be used and the particular problem around which the period had been planned by the leader and which had grown out of something that had taken place the week before. Perhaps it would seem that this fifteen minutes is entirely too brief a period for worship and fellowship, but it must be remembered that there would certainly be fellowship and sometimes worship connected with the work of the smaller groups. The next item on the tentative program was "10:00 to 10:30, Class Groups." The groups did not reassemble for dismissal, but each teacher planned for this in her own class.

It was quite definitely understood by the superintendent and the teachers that perhaps this sequence would not be followed. Especially if a number of the class groups were engaged in activities in the work period, it might be very much better to have the class groups immediately follow the work period and have the worship and fellowship at the close. Or perhaps the time for work at the beginning would be shorter, depending upon what there was to be done. There might be a brief period of fellowship which emerged from the work period and took place wherever the activities were being carried on, without taking the time to assemble and thereby losing the timeliness of the situation. After this, the children might go to their class groups and return for a period of worship at the close.

Changes in the plan or schedule will be made on the basis of the leader's observation of what is going on in the smaller groups, upon suggestions and requests which come from teachers and children, and upon evidences of needs or interests. She will make sure that it does not seriously affect the work of any group. If a change is to be made, the leader will quietly let the teachers and leaders of the smaller groups know what change is being made. This can be done without interrupting the work of any group, even when they are meeting in separate rooms. Quietness and ease of manner, as well as alertness, are essential for the leader of an informal session.

If the department had been organized on the single grade plan or the department unit, the leader would have maintained similar relations with the assistant teachers. Even though the initiative would have rested to a greater extent with the leader and the program would have been even more flexible, it is still important that the assistants shall know what materials and procedures will probably be used.

Slavishly following a pattern for a session, administered according to a bell which is rung in some central place in the church building, is unnecessary in nearly every instance. Flexibility can be secured when the leaders desire it.

Questions about Planning—For Teachers of Adults, and Others Too

1. *Have I made adequate personal preparation?* Have I studied and meditated on the various Bible passages recommended? Have I read carefully the lesson material for both students and teacher? Am I familiar with the entire unit? Have I been on the watch for helpful resource material?

2. *What is my exact aim for this session* (in relation to the general purpose of the quarter or unit)? Do I want the members of my group to be changed in some specific way; for example, *to know* the facts of Paul's life, or *to feel* differently toward another social group, or *to take* some definite action?

3. *Am I keeping in mind the immediate needs and interests of my group?* Of all the things we might talk about or do in this study, what will appeal to the members most? If let absolutely to themselves, what would they pick out in this area of study as most interesting?

4. *Have I arranged for all the materials I shall need in the class period?* Bibles, student quarterlies, statistics or other data, a blackboard, map, charts, newspaper clippings, audio-visual resources?

5. *How shall I get started?* How shall I get the interest of the students? Shall I tell an unusual personal experience, review a current problem, tie in with the previous lesson, show a picture, ask a question?

"How to Plan a Lesson," *Good Ways to Lead Adults* (Richmond: John Knox Press, 1951), pp. 28, 29. Used by permission.

6. *What shall I do next, step by step?* What methods shall I use: telling, asking, showing, guiding discussion, developing activities? What does my guidance material say? What adaptations shall I make? Exactly what questions shall I ask? What illustrations shall I use? How can I make the discussion grow out of the needs of the people? How much time shall I plan to give to each part of the lesson?

7. *How shall I conclude?* How can I "drive home" the truth effectively? By an appropriate picture, a suitable poem, a story, a worship experience? How can I "clinch" the point of a discussion? How can I achieve the goal for this lesson?

8. *What shall I do toward building up the next session?* How can I best use the last five minutes? How can I encourage independent study? Shall I have books available for members to take home with them? Shall I ask certain persons or committees to report on specific areas of interest? Shall I encourage members to participate in a forum, a panel, a project, buzz groups, the use of audio-visuals, a field trip?

9. *How can I improve?* After the session I should ask myself such questions as: How did I achieve the purpose of this lesson? What did I do right and why? What did I do wrong and why? Did I keep the parts of the lesson in proper perspective? Did I meet the needs of the group, and make the members feel the session was really "theirs"?

9. WHAT MATERIALS SHALL A LEADER USE?

CURRICULUM INCLUDES far more than the basic pupil's book and teacher's guide for the church school, or the kit or program guide for the youth or adult group. Properly understood, curriculum includes all of the resources that leader and group utilize in their work. An awareness of the varieties of material that are available and of the ways in which these materials may be taken into account in planning is important.

Some church group leaders, especially in the church school, have little opportunity to select basic curriculum materials, for the church is committed to a particular series. There are important occasions, however, when a decision must be made as to the basic curriculum material to be used in a school, department, or class. This happens frequently in the church school that permits its older youth and adult groups to work on an elective basis, choosing materials that deal with their needs and concerns. It is important that sound criteria underlie these selections.

Materials a Teacher Needs and How He May Plan to Use Them

The snow was working up to a blizzard. It slapped hard against the windows as Joe Davis pulled up a couple of chairs, sat down in one, put his feet in the other, loosened the collar of his blue denim shirt, and reached over to a bookcase nearby. He took out a large, worn Bible, a book in maroon binding, and a well thumbed, paper-backed pamphlet. Opening the pamphlet, he read *The Story of the Hebrew People,* January 27: "Joseph, A Young Man Who Remembered God."

Joe smiled with relief. Now that's the kind of lesson I like, he thought, something I know something about. One of those old Bible stories makes me feel good. I'll just read it in the Bible first—let's see now, where is it? Near the beginning. Well, here's the reference in the quarterly: Genesis 37. Joe picked up his Bible, found the right place and began to read. The snow was piling white along the window sill now and the comforting whir of the cream separator sounded from the kitchen.

Say, this thing is really long. Didn't know there was so much to it. Kind of awkward to read, too, not like I remembered. I'll see where it stops. Well, what do you know? Thirteen chapters! Wonder what the quarterly says about it—and where's that other magazine? Joe found what he was looking for and turned to January 27 in *Leaders of Youth.* Now that's what I want. These references

"Joe's Kids," *A Guide for Curriculum in Christian Education* (New York: National Council of Churches, 1955), pp. 15–18. Used by permission.

have selected the main points of the story and made it into something you can handle.

Maybe this other version will be easier—the way our literature says it is. Joe reached for the book in the maroon binding and glanced at the shiny gold lettering: *Holy Bible—Revised Standard Version.* Finding the references, he began reading again. The pages turned more quickly now and there was an eager concentration in the tilt of Joe's shoulders against the chairback—"Then Joseph took an oath of the sons of Israel, saying, 'God will visit you, and you shall carry up my bones from here.' So Joseph died, being a hundred and ten years old; and they embalmed him, and he was put in a coffin in Egypt." (Genesis 50:25–26, RSV)

Say, that's quite a story—*A Man Who Remembered God.* He sure did, even if it was a long time ago. Wonder what my kids at the church will think of it? My kids—the corners of Joe's mouth quirked up and he hunched himself lower in the chair. Thirteen-year-old Kenneth—can't be still a minute. Best natured kid but always up to something. Lena, now there's a pretty child—could be she's too pretty now she's turned fifteen—must think of something big for her to do to take her mind off herself. Polly—she'll really go for this story. She's such a reader, but I don't know about Orin—he's kind of dull, somehow. His father makes him work too hard. No sense in tying a kid to a tractor all the time. Maybe I can do something about that.

I'd like mighty well for them to see Joseph as a real man thinking of God's plan for people and trying to do what God wanted. I'll see what their lesson quarterly says.

Fifteen minutes later he was calling: "Martha, isn't there a pencil around here some place?"

"On the shelf behind the clock," shouted a voice from the kitchen over the noise of splashing water in the sink. Presently Martha came into the front room wiping her hands on her apron.

"You know what?" said Joe. "I'll bet those kids of mine would like to do a television show."

"What?"

"Not a real one, of course, but a good imitation, and do the story of Joseph in the Bible. It's just what they need—something sort of hard but interesting. I've been jotting down here some of the things about Joseph that I think would appeal to youngsters today. They can put those in the play, just as it says here in the lesson."

"But Joe, you don't know anything about putting on a play."

"No, but I'll bet that new teacher at the County Consolidated School does. She doesn't go anywhere to church, I've noticed, and we might as well give her a good reason to start coming to ours."

"I've been thinking we ought to have her to dinner some day. What about next Sunday?" Martha didn't wait for an answer but started toward the back door. Joe made more notations in his teacher's book and shouted again to Martha.

"What did the preacher say those new pictures cost that go with these lessons?"

"Two dollars a set. But Mr. Simpkins said there wasn't any money left for that."

Joe frowned and studied what he had written. "I was thinking," continued Martha, "that we could take that much out of the cream money."

Joe stood up and stretched. The kids can do that play, he decided, right in the choir alcove where we have our class. He followed Martha who had opened the back door a crack.

"It's stopped snowing and must be getting cold. If it doesn't snow any more, the roads should still be open Sunday."

Here is a class of young people in a one-room church in the open country who can look forward to their church school with zest because of the resourceful way their teacher uses the curriculum. Joe had to start with only his Bible and the pupil's quarterly plus his own teacher's book. But even before our story opened he had begun to supplement these materials with a second Bible, one using the best modern English, printed readably, and bound for easy handling. To these he planned to add some flat pictures in color so "his kids" would be encouraged to visualize Joseph and his story.

The affection with which he thinks of "his kids" shows that he knows and understands them. The lesson is not a body of subject matter to be got over to them, no matter how important, but religious truth and resource with which to inform their minds, catch their imaginations, nourish their spirits, and foster them in Christian action. In planning for his class session he not only reads the Bible and reflects upon its meaning but keeps these individual boys and girls also in the center of his thinking—their desires, qualities of personality, their personal needs, and family situations. Their growth to ever brighter aspirations, ever wider concerns, ever deeper commitments is his purpose. Such growth he knows comes because of the goodness and love of God, made plain in the pages of the Bible.

Joe realized that such growth is more certain if the young people read the Bible with purpose and if *together* they discover its meaning. Therefore he plans when introducing the story of Joseph as dramatically as he can, to propose a group activity, well within their ability, but one that will call forth all their powers of imagination, inventiveness, curiosity, and dedication. In this fellowship of work and study Kenneth will have outlets for his energy, Orin will have needed fun and lift of spirit in association with other young people, Lena will have a chance to grow out of certain young vanities in preoccupation beyond herself.

It is likely that Joe, for all his concern for "his kids," would have felt much more helpless without the ever-present resources of the curriculum materials, especially that part provided by his denomination. He found rather quickly that thirteen consecutive chapters of Genesis, even on a subject with which he was at ease and familiar, were hard going. With the pupil's and teacher's texts to select, analyze, and emphasize the formidable body of Scripture, Joe found the long and complicated story falling into a dramatic pattern, its points of significance standing out strongly and clearly.

Joe is an experienced and secure teacher, understanding that he does not need to possess in himself all the necessary information and skills. So he is ready to call upon the new school teacher, and doubtless other people also before this "television show" goes on the air. We need not be surprised if he works Orin's father into the project before it is concluded.

Varieties of Material Available for Use

In order that the materials may not be thought of in a limited sense as a prescribed body of knowledge to be mastered or even memorized, the following listings of some types of resources have been made.

Printed Materials

> Teacher's guides
> Pupil's books or study sheets
> Home reading books
> Resource books
> Special courses
> Story papers
> Religious periodicals
> Activity sheets
> Leader's magazines
> Parent's materials
> Creative activity materials

Audio-Visuals

> Flat pictures
> Maps and globes
> Charts
> Slides

"Resource Materials Available," *A Guide for Curriculum in Christian Education* (New York: National Council of Churches, 1955), pp. 67–68. Used by permission.

Filmstrips
Recordings
Sound films
The room and its equipment
Costumes, curios, etc.
Recall of radio and television programs

Additional Resources

Kits
Packets
Workers' library
The total resources of the church and community and outdoor world
Trained resource persons
Denominational helps and personnel

Factors to Remember in Choosing Curriculum Materials

BY PAUL H. VIETH

It has been emphasized that to a large extent curriculum must be "home-made." However, lay workers do not have the time or the training and experience required to create their own teaching matcrials. They must depend on some form of published curriculum materials as a starting point for their own creative efforts.

The study of curriculum which we have suggested will therefore need to include an evaluation of the materials in use. If this leads to a conclusion that a change is desirable, a further study must be made to determine what materials might be selected better to serve the purpose.

Criteria for Selection

The basic question to be answered in evaluating the material in use, or other materials considered for adoption, is whether this series is the best that the church can use to achieve its purpose. This may require an examination of several series. Publishers will send a prospectus and sample materials on request. The committee making this study should seek answers to the following questions as a basis for reaching its conclusion:

1. Is this series basically Christian in nature, and will it help us have the kind of Christian education that we need?

2. Does it provide a comprehensive coverage of what is most

Paul H. Vieth, "Choosing Curriculum Materials," *The Church School* (Philadelphia: Christian Education Press, 1957), pp. 86–90. Used by permission.

important in Christian education, and are the several elements of content properly balanced so as to put emphasis on those things which are most vital?

3. Is the treatment of the Bible—in amount of biblical material included, portions selected, and method of use—such as we want?

4. Is the plan of grading (i.e., group or closely grading) such that we can best use it in our situation?

5. Does it provide sufficiently for relation to the church so that we can make our Christian education a real part of the total church program?

6. Does it include worship materials for the several departments, properly related to the teaching material?

7. Does it take sufficient account of the abilities, interests and needs of pupils so that it will be a satisfying experience for them?

8. Does it make provision for home relationships, in a way that is practical for us?

9. Can our teachers handle these materials? Are they written so as to be easily understood? Are they helpful in biblical and theological interpretation? Are the methods suggested such as our teachers can use, or learn to use?

10. Does it provide adequate and attractive materials for pupils, such as text-books, reading books, workbooks, activity materials?

11. Is the material attractive as to type size, page format, illustrations, use of color, binding?

12. Is the cost of this series within the financial ability of our church to meet?

The last question, concerning cost, should not be allowed to weigh too heavily. The best quality materials are never the cheapest. Most churches do not spend enough rather than too much for curriculum materials. A yearly expenditure of $3.00 to $4.00 per pupil should be considered a good investment. If this is beyond the present budget, it is time to increase the budget rather than to settle for cheap material.

Probably no system of curriculum materials will ever meet all these tests to the full satisfaction of any church. Considering the thousands of churches they must serve, it would be too much to expect denominational curriculum committees to produce materials which exactly please everybody. The nature of curriculum is such that printed materials must always be creatively adapted in actual use. If more workers realized this, there would be less complaint about lesson materials.

Shall We Use a Single Lesson Series?

Our discussion thus far has assumed that a church will select a series of curriculum materials and use it throughout the church school. This is the most common practice. In most cases it is the wisest practice. A series is a unified whole, it "hangs together," with common objectives throughout, uniform theological and educational outlook, and builds in each age group on what has gone before. To mix up different series may lead to duplication and confusion. If effort is put on using a series effectively rather than on "shopping around" for something to substitute at one point or another, the results are likely to be better.

There may be occasional unusual circumstances which make it wise to substitute another course in a given class or department, because everything considered this will better meet the abilities or the needs of pupils. In such cases, care should be taken that the substitution does not duplicate what is provided in the series before or after the point where the substitution is made, that it does not exclude something essential from the series, and that what is substituted is of a quality as high as or higher than what is replaced. A practice not to be encouraged is for individual teachers to select their own material to satisfy a peculiar interest or whim of their own.

Some churches with unusual educational leadership find it best to make their own curriculum by deciding first what they want to accomplish at each age and then selecting material from any source which will best serve their purpose. This involves problems which are beyond the purpose of this book.

Why Use Denominational Materials?

Theoretically, a church is free to choose any system of lesson materials which best suits its needs, no matter who publishes it. But there are important reasons why first consideration should be given to the publications of its own denomination.

1. These materials are prepared with the needs of the churches of that denomination in mind, by people who are within the traditions of the denomination, and responsible to the whole church for what they do.

2. They are written from the viewpoint of the theology, history, church organization, and program of the denomination.

3. They include the missionary and benevolent emphases of the denomination, and these are the local church's responsibility.

4. As a member of the denomination, each church has an interest in what is done by its board of Christian education, and the board in turn has a right to expect the church's loyal support. Such support includes the duty of constructive criticism and suggestions for improvement.

5. The problem of selecting curriculum material is greatly simplified if only the series of a church's denomination need to be considered. It is then only a matter of choosing one of these series which best fits its needs. In most cases this should be the group graded or closely graded series.

In view of these considerations, it is strongly recommended that a church select its curriculum materials from the publications of its own denomination and concentrate its efforts on using them as effectively as possible. If a church finds it necessary to go outside its denomination, this should be done in the full knowledge of the disadvantages incurred, and with the expectation that such material will be supplemented with denominational materials for denominational emphases.

10. HOW CAN CHURCH AND HOME WORK TOGETHER?

WE HAVE BEEN slowly recognizing that the family is the most effective teacher of religion. Theoretically, this is not a new idea at all, for we have long known the effectiveness of the family as teacher (cf. Deut. 6:6–9; II Tim. 1:5). Functionally, however, this family emphasis is new. It is within recent years that curriculum materials and program guides prepared by national agencies have given real place to the family. Even now, it is the rare local church that enlists its families in real partnership in Christian nurture.

There is need to find more ways in which home and church may develop a relationship in which the family is truly the senior partner. There is greater need to use consecrated imagination in trying out these partnership activities in individual churches. National agencies and their materials can help, but only the parents and church group leaders working together in a Christian congregation can truly know and truly demonstrate what may be accomplished through the partnership of home and church in Christian nurture.

The Case for Church-Home Partnership

BY WESNER FALLAW

In this coming together on the part of lay or professional teachers of the church and that other group of lay or professional teachers, parents in the home—who are also within the church—there will be modification of the church school program by the considered desires and purposes of the Christian home and a qualification of the home by Christian standards and objectives expounded in the church. Unified work, and especially the success of this kind of effort, can only come about as the home and church explore together their common problems and unite in guiding the religious growth of children. But in the midst of guidance given the young by the combined efforts of parents and other adult religious teachers in the church, the adults themselves will be involved in their own educational and religious growth. The teacher who says he himself learns a great deal—perhaps more than his pupils—needs to have a counterpart in the home—a parent—who says the religious education program jointly conducted by home and church is teaching him a great deal. Only so can the parent be a worthy teacher. Only so can the young have adequate religious guidance.

There must be basic agreement, or at least informed respect, between church school teachers and parents—the teachers in the home. Home teachers and church teachers need to know wherein their ethical, social and biblical interpretations fail to harmonize

Wesner Fallaw, *The Modern Parent and the Teaching Church* (New York: The Macmillan Company, copyright, 1946), pp. 204–207. Used by permission.

and then come together and modify their conflicting beliefs by that which they find to be the interpretation closest to the cardinal Christian principles. Religious attitudes, values and loyalties concern both the home and the church. In this area the teaching of the home stands first in importance. Biblical knowledge and information about the history and meaning of Christendom are also the concern of the home and church. But in this area we shall have to rely first on the importance of the church's teaching—though this should become less true as parents make religious teaching increasingly effective in the life of the individual and of society.

In any given community a union of parents and church school teachers might well begin around the problems which the home faces with respect to the growth of children. While primary responsibility for the religious guidance of the young rests upon the home, primary responsibility for helping the avowedly Christian home rests upon the church. The school of the church, therefore, must give direction, authoritative and clear, to the religious growth of adults seeking help for their children—and for themselves. The authority of the church must be like that of the Teacher of Nazareth—an inner, spiritual authority; never an external, coercive one. For that is the only kind of authority which falls within the framework either of education or of the Christian religion viewed from the Protestant standpoint.

This program of church-family education lays exacting demands on adults, who are probably busier today than ever before. But if there is genuine concern that falsity and secularism shall give place to truth inhering in Jesus Christ, then fathers and mothers will have to give their time and themselves to the task of guiding their children in religious knowledge and religious living. Only so will there be adequate growth of youth and adults. Admittedly, before this can take place, a program of Christian education will provide adult education as a by-product of child education. Or better, inversely, we must educate the child as a by-product of adult education. It would seem that educators, teachers and ministers, along with thoughtful laymen, recognize that the crucial problem of religious education lies in educating the whole family, not merely the individual child. This work belongs to the church.

But before a church is ready to take hold of a full measure of work with the home, its responsible organizations, and congregation as a whole, need to get a fresh perspective with which to examine the implications for church-family education. In sum, a fresh perspective might indicate the following points:

1. Biblical knowledge is essential to, but by no means all of, a program of religious education.

2. Belief in God, loyalty to Christ, right thinking, right conduct, while in part dependent upon knowledge and understanding of the Bible, are not thereby guaranteed.

3. Basic to religious faith and right living on the part of the growing child is, more times than not, parental example which is clearly Christian. The child is not apt to become genuinely religious unless he enjoys consistent Christian nurture *in the home*— the sort of home wherein the real meaning of the Christian church and the truth personified by Jesus are woven into the chief values and aspirations of mother and father.

4. Most homes of the modern community, and many homes of professing Christians, fail to live up to the standards in point 3 above. These homes can better actualize these ideals if they will confer regularly at the church and rely on the church for guidance; and if mothers and fathers will become *purposefully* and systematically active as teachers of religion in the home.

5. Actually, the home is more important as religious teacher than the church. Despite this, modern society has left almost the whole of the religious task to the church. The extent of this error is now being understood and is evident in the emphasis upon wider and more effective religious education in America.

6. Week-day religious education alone, conducted in churches or public schools, is not adequate; extended Sunday morning teaching periods alone are not adequate. These may benefit chil-

dren and improve society. But Christian nurture is safely achieved only as homes, fathers and mothers, parents and children together examine and share by repeated testing the terms of Christian thought and act.

7. Parents, as religious teachers in the home, and other adults, as teachers of religion in the church, *can* unite for common and clear effort to teach children—if a church provides leadership and incentive.

8. The home has the right to expect of its Christian fellowship—the church—helpful and devoted teaching, teaching which is done regularly, with desire, by persons expressing themselves out of deep faith.

9. The church has the right to expect of its chief constituent unit—the home—diligent and faithful teaching, teaching which is done systematically, as well as indirectly, by mothers and fathers who refuse to make their child religiously underprivileged because of parental inertia, indecision or preoccupation with things of lesser value.

10. *The local church should purpose, therefore, to guide the religious living of the family as a whole.* This guidance is best effected by an educational procedure. This procedure necessitates a program. This book outlines a program.

Parents Must Be Active Partners

BY LILLIAN RICHTER REYNOLDS

A church in a southern city began its Sunday school several years ago by requiring that parents enroll as they enrolled their children. It is still a nine-day wonder, but this church school has grown to be one of the largest in its city, despite all predictions to the contrary. All church leaders were sure parents would not accept such a requirement. They were wrong. Parents do respond to the church's efforts to enlist them in a program of good Christian training for their children.

Most church schools would feel that this particular approach to the problem of enlisting parents is a little drastic and perhaps not absolutely necessary. For them there are other ways of enlisting parents in the joint task of Christian education. Since all church educators recognize that parents are the real teachers of religion and freely admit that little is done for a child unless the church and home work together, this matter of enlisting parents is not optional.

Any church that wants to see more parents taking an active part in the church's Christian nurture program can make definite progress by following a few methods that have worked in other churches.

But first, the church must be sure its attitude toward parents and their training of their children is right. Parents often make mistakes; they sometimes fail to do the best things for their chil-

Lillian Richter Reynolds, "The Church Must Enlist Parents," *Christian Home,* April, 1956, pp. 22–24. Used by permission.

dren; they, in our day, may depend too much on church and school and community to meet their children's needs.

Nonetheless, nothing is calculated to arouse the ire of parents faster than the assumption on the part of any group that they, and not parents, have first claim on the children. If the church wants parents to take the first responsibility for the religious education of their children, then the church must be sure that she understands her role as being one of helping the parents. She must cease talking about parents "co-operating with the church" and speak more often of "working with the home."

Church-school teachers must understand that the aim of home instruction is not to prepare the child's lesson for his Sunday-school class, but that the Sunday-school class can serve the purpose of strengthening the teaching and practice of the Christian faith that takes place at home.

When a church understands clearly and speaks intelligently concerning its role as one of the factors in the spiritual growth of children, with parents always having the prior responsibility before God, then parents can be shown that they need to work with the church-school program if they want the best for their children.

This does not at all relegate the church to a less important role. It puts the church in much the same position as the family doctor who co-operates with the home in keeping all members well and healthy. He cannot see that all his families get a balanced diet, enough rest and exercise, prescribed medicines when they need them, and so forth. He can only, out of his expert knowledge, advise parents on these things, help when problems arise, take over in crisis situations. Such must also be the role of the church as she ministers to the spiritual health of her families.

And that is perhaps the second thing the church ought to consider—ministering to the spiritual health of her families. After the attitudes are right on the part of the church leaders, then if the church would truly enlist parents they must offer some genuine help to families in their home program of Christian education. It is not enough to say read the Bible to your children. And families are not hearing something new when someone tells them they ought to have family prayers. Likewise to be admonished to attend the public worship of the church with their children is not necessarily helpful.

Parents, especially young parents or those young in the faith, need some concrete help. They need a book that will help them know how to read the Bible to children. They need some counseling help from their minister or other leader as to how to begin having family prayers. They perhaps need to think together with other parents about how to make church worship more meaningful to their children. When a church offers concrete help to parents through a library, counseling services, classes, and discussion groups, then parents begin to believe that this matter of teaching religion to their children is an important part of their responsibility and they begin to want to enter more fully into the church-school program.

And finally, and maybe most definitely, parents must be given opportunities actually to do things in the church program. Unenlisted parents probably ought to start with some short-term jobs. A church that had always employed a summer youth worker decided one summer that such an expenditure was impossible. Before giving up the youth recreation nights they called meetings of parents and asked for volunteers to provide the necessary adult leadership. They were not sure they would have enough parents to keep the program going all summer. They found that they had more volunteers than they could use!

And young people and children welcome having their parents, especially when they come to do something. A group of junior high boys and girls always protested when parents were asked to come to parties as chaperons. The problem was solved when one teen-ager and his parents were asked each week to be responsible for the fun time following their program. After the group had enjoyed singing led by some families, good games planned by others, magician shows by one, and various other talents, they welcomed their parents at any of their parties.

A three-year-old nursery group enlisted parents by inviting one mother or father to come in each Sunday as visiting helper. Each parent understood better than ever before why this group of very small children needed good play equipment and how they were taught through play. Many of them found they were interested in teaching and enrolled in classes to help them learn to teach. All of them felt more able to discuss problems with their children's church-school leaders. From henceforth whenever the nursery teachers wanted help from parents, they had only to ask.

Actually, asking is almost all any church has to do. The trouble sometimes is that a church does not ask for specific help; parents do not know how to offer help; so each plods along without the other. An excellent way to prevent this sort of impasse is the use of parent-sponsors. Many churches find this plan indispensable to their program. Each department or grade group appoints parent-sponsors for a period of time—about six months being the most popular.

These parents are asked to do some definite things which probably ought to include visiting the teaching session at least once. They ought also to call all parents to talk with them about the current plans and unit of study. They can plan for parties at frequent intervals, enlisting the help of other parents in the planning and in providing refreshments. They surely must attend the planning meetings of the teachers to offer suggestions (it is surprising sometimes what parents can know about children) and to learn from the teachers what their aims and purposes are and what materials and activities they plan to use to carry out these goals.

When these parent-sponsors have served their term they will never be disinterested again. Usually they can recommend the next parent-sponsors on the basis of what they have discovered about the interest of particular families through their recent contacts.

Out of this sort of approach can grow many other good things. Out of it has grown requests for classes on how to teach religion to children. In one church parent-sponsors called teen-age parents together to discuss common rules for dating, allowances, and other such things that plague parents of teen-agers. Churches using the parent-sponsor plan usually find it pays large dividends in teachers enlisted in their leadership education program. Sometimes these working parents can refer special needs of families to their minister for further help.

The church school can never do its best work if it is compartmentalized in the church building and is not working with the home. When both home and church face their common task together then there is no need to ask how to enlist the co-operation of parents. They are enlisted because the church-school program is theirs, being designed to help them teach their children, and they want to be a part of it. One parent summed it up like this: "I used to think it was the church's job to teach my child about God, and I wondered why they didn't do a better job of it. Now I know it is my responsibility to teach my child the things of our faith, and I am amazed at how much the church school does to help me." She was an enlisted parent.

What May Church and Home Do Together?

BY W. NEILL HART

Organized Study Clubs

While a class organized on a temporary basis will be helpful, many churches are feeling the need for a regular study club with a permanent organization. This need is especially apparent for parents.

How can I get my child to eat a balanced meal? Why will junior tease his little sister? How can we stop Jimmy's prevarications? To punish or not to punish—that is the question. What shall I tell Mamie when she asks where babies come from? How can prayer be made real and meaningful to my child? Does family worship still have a place in modern life? Can it be made rich and meaningful?

What parent has not faced these or similar questions over and over again! Where can one find practical help for the many problems mothers and fathers inevitably encounter in the all-important task of rearing a child?

As has been stated, more and more parents are finding practical guidance and continuous help through permanent study groups in the local church. The experience of one church will illustrate the possibilities here.

A pastor and his wife, having small children of their own and realizing their need of help, discussed their problems with the nursery and kindergarten department superintendents, both charming women with rich experience in child guidance. These discus-

W. Neill Hart, *Home and Church Working Together* (Nashville: Abingdon Press, 1951), pp. 59–63, 72–74, 78–82. Used by permission.

sions were so mutually helpful that the four decided to invite others to share their experiences. Accordingly, the minister and his wife invited a group of mothers with preschool children to meet on a certain afternoon at the parsonage. They knew that this personal invitation would bring out most of the group.

After a short social visit, the pastor reviewed briefly a good book of interest to parents, then led a lively discussion on the practical problems that parents face today. Quickly these problems began to come to light, and soon the group saw that solutions might be found in discussion, study, and shared experiences. Consequently, a motion was passed to have another meeting for the purpose of organizing a permanent parent study club.

Details of organization were discussed. A nominating committee was selected to name prospective officers to be elected at the next meeting. As this was a neighborhood church, the group decided to meet monthly in the homes of the members and to combine a social hour with the study.

A program committee was selected, composed of a departmental superintendent, a teacher, and three others. A yearbook was made outlining the programs, selecting the speakers and designating the places of meeting. *The Christian Home, Parents' Magazine, National Parent-Teacher,* and many books and articles were carefully studied and tabulated. The committee spent many hours gathering and sorting material so that every speaker would have ample resources for each message. Book reviews and outside speakers were interspersed to give variety to the meetings. These programs, carefully planned, proved to be interesting and helpful, so that the group quickly grew in numbers and enthusiasm.

In order to foster a closer relationship between the church and home, the nursery and kindergarten workers were included in the organization. Throughout the year they brought to the club detailed explanations of the purposes and activities of the church school, and made suggestions for home co-operation. In turn, the mothers took the two departments and their needs as a club project.

A list of books of interest to parents of preschool children was passed around at one of the meetings and each member checked off a book she would be willing to give to the club. Thus a fine library was secured, and each member had access to some of the latest and best books in this field. The library was kept in the kindergarten department, and the books checked out by the superintendent. Through the year the superintendent of the children's division gave members of the club leaflets on pertinent topics.

When it was found that some of the mothers could not provide for their children adequately during the time of meeting, a competent nurse was employed to keep the children while the club was in session. At least one program each year was given at night so the fathers could attend. Occasionally there was a picnic or an outing for the entire family of the members.

At the end of the first year the study club for parents of preschool children was well organized and functioning smoothly. So the pastor and his wife turned their attention to the mothers of the grade school children. Several of these were already in the preschool study group. With these mothers as a nucleus, it was a simple matter to organize a study club to consider the problems peculiar to primary and junior children.

At the end of the second year, when both groups were well organized and successful, attention was given to the organization of the mothers who were facing the many complicated problems of adolescence. Care was given to get each club well organized and functioning before attention was given to the next group. Thus all clubs continued to do good work after they had been started.

When a church is not large enough to support three study clubs, two or even one group can be used. However, since there are problems peculiar to each age, greater interest can be sustained if full attention can be given to a smaller range of problems.

When two or three study clubs have been organized in the local church, one over-all organization may be perfected. In one large city church where the members are scattered, these groups assemble at the church for a combined meeting with a good speaker, book review, or some other program of interest to all parents; then they divide into smaller groups to consider topics of particular interest to each age group.

This larger organization is strong enough to bring to the city outstanding speakers in the field of the home. These leaders are sometimes secured for a period of several days, speaking in the daytime to the club and at night to a larger meeting in which fathers and general public participate. Usually these leaders are available for conferences.

This larger organization, because of its size, is a strong factor in opposing social evils and facing problems affecting childhood and youth.

All together these clubs offer rich possibilities for parents for continuous study and help. No one plan is imperative. Local conditions will govern the time and place of meeting, nature of program, and details of organization. Many different combinations have been beneficial.

In a small suburban church the leader of a standard training course on the home talked to the class at its last class session about organizing a permanent study club. He had in mind a Mothers' Club, meeting in the afternoon, but one of the men remonstrated, saying, "If you have the meeting in the afternoon, the men can't attend; and we need it as much as the women." Accordingly, the group agreed to have a Parent Study Club, meeting at night so the men could attend. A young married woman, however, objected, saying, "Some of us don't have any children yet, but we are as interested in the home as people who have children. What are you going to do about us?" With this in mind a Home Study Club was organized with a man as the president and another man as vice-president.

Four years later the club was still meeting regularly with the men participating as actively as the women. In speaking about the work of the study club, the pastor referred to it as being the "backbone of our church."

Any interested person—pastor, superintendent, teacher, or parent—can take the lead and get others interested in organizing a permanent study club; and any church, regardless of size, will find such an organization of great value to both church and home.

A departmental superintendent testified about one of the clubs: "The parent study group in our church has greatly improved the quality of work being done in our primary department. Attendance has been better, the interest greater, and the co-operation of parents has improved 100 per cent."

A pastor added his testimony: "Our parent study clubs have not only been of great benefit to the parents and materially improved the quality of work in the church school, but they have been a valuable 'feeder' for the whole church. Many people, not active before, have become interested in our parent study groups, and have later joined church school classes, W.S.C.S. circles, and the church. Many of our most loyal workers have been discovered in this way."

Visits in the Home

Systematic visiting offers one of the most fruitful sources of co-operation between the church school and the home.

Who?

There are many people in the church who will find visiting profitable: the minister, the home visitor, the nursery home visitor, church school officials, teachers, class parents, and special visitors. Especially will visiting be helpful to the teacher in taking over a new class. In fact, if her teaching is to be effective, it will be almost imperative that she make one or more calls in the homes of her pupils every quarter.

Purpose

There are many lasting values that will come from regular systematic visiting in the home.

1. One of the most important purposes of a visit is to understand the home situation. Since children are the products of their

family life, it is necessary to know the home environment to understand the pupil.

A teacher who was concerned because a child had an inordinate desire for attention visited in his home. When she learned that the little boy had an afflicted sister who took so much of the parents' time that he was not able to get the care and attention that he craved, she understood her pupil for the first time. No longer was Ralph a "problem"; he became her joy, one she could mother and give attention to.

A teacher visiting in the home of her pupils discovered Betty was living "across the tracks" and embarrassed because she could not dress like the other little girls. Charles lived with his grandparents because his mother was dead and his father married again. Mary's mother was ill most of the time and therefore cross, irritable, and out of patience with the daughter's exuberance. Theodore was an only child with doting parents. Raymond, whose parents were divorced, was torn between two loyalties, as he loved both his mother and his father. Knowing the home life of her pupils, this teacher was able to understand their needs and minister helpfully to each one.

2. Since parents often do not know the teachers of their children, and the teachers do not know the parents, one of the chief purposes of visiting is to get acquainted and to establish a feeling of being *en rapport*. As a salesman knows that he must establish a "we" feeling with his customers if he is to be successful, so the teacher will be far more effective if a strong bond of friendship has been established between her and the parents.

3. Through visiting in the home, many needs will be discovered not only of the pupil, but also of the home. Some of these conditions will be beyond the power of the teacher to change; but for others practical help may be available. Sometimes the aid of the minister may be enlisted, sometimes the help of a class or other interested groups may be obtained.

Tommy was very irregular in attendance because his parents usually slept too late on Sunday morning to get him to church school. When the assistance of the Men's Bible Class was secured and the father enlisted as an interested member of the class, Tommy was usually in his place on time.

4. Through visits in the home, opportunities will be given to explain the work of the class or department for the coming quarter, and to secure active co-operation. Too many times parents do not know what is being attempted at the church school, hence they may not only fail to give co-operation, but may even hinder. Through visiting, the teacher will have an opportunity to see whether or not her efforts are understood. The parents will also have a chance to ask questions and discuss the lesson material with the teacher.

5. Often the teacher making a visit will want to share pamphlets, leaflets, booklets, or some other resource material with parents.

6. When a teacher is sympathetic, friendly, and understanding, often counsel will be solicited by the parents. If a teacher is distressed over a problem in the class, quite often parents are concerned over the same problem at home.

Even when counsel is not solicited, a tactful teacher may get favorable results by asking the advice of the parents, using such questions as, "What do you think about this?" "Could this be done?" She may then plant in the mind of the parents the suggestion she wishes them to have.

Open House at Church

More and more churches are holding annually—or quarterly— open house at church. Parents are invited to visit the department, division, or church school in which their children are pupils.

Many values are to be gained by this method. The parents not only get to meet the teachers, superintendent, and officers, but they also get to know each other. A fellowship period can be enjoyed—with or without refreshments. The work of the department can be explained by superintendents or teachers, thus the co-operation of the parents secured. Some churches use this opportunity to have a display of current curriculum materials and activity projects. Often a teacher has for parents' help mimeographed outlines of the unit being studied. This material could also serve as a basis for group discussion.

This meeting should be held at a time when parents and teachers can attend most conveniently. Sunday afternoon is often used, or a week night may be preferred. Sunday evening just before the preaching service is also a favorable time, especially if there is to be a special sermon of interest to the family and the church school officers and teachers.

Care should be taken that necessary plans are made to assure a good attendance. Often superintendents and teachers have made elaborate preparation, only to have a very few parents attend because inadequate means of securing attendance had been used. Letters, cards, and telephone calls will be helpful but may not be sufficient. Better results will be obtained when pupils assume responsibility for bringing their parents, or have personally written an invitation during the church school hour. Sometimes Johnny's definite part in making the written invitation and the responsibility of delivering it bring Mr. and Mrs. Johnny and the whole family.

Often a committee of parents assists in the planning and assumes the major responsibility for attendance. Frequently arrangements can be made whereby people who do not have adequate transportation are brought by neighboring families who have cars and are willing to render this service.

Parent-Teacher Meetings

A Joint Meeting of Workers' Conference and Parents

Such a meeting can often obtain favorable results. The parents and teachers get to know each other better. The work of the church school can be explained with perhaps the entire group breaking up into smaller units when found advisable. Common problems may be faced and plans worked out together for the improvement of the church school.

Using a blackboard, one minister led a helpful discussion at a joint meeting of the workers' conference and large group of parents. First parents talked on the subject, "What a Parent Has a Right to Expect of a Church School Teacher." After about fifteen minutes given to this topic, the teachers spoke on the subject, "What a Teacher Has a Right to Expect of Parents." The group entered heartily into the discussion.

The workers discovered that parents expect of a teacher:

- A genuine interest in the welfare of the pupil.
- Promptness and regularity in attendance.
- An interesting, prepared lesson each week.
- A familiarity with the whole program of the church.
- A willingness to visit the parents and give essential information about the program of the church school.
- Sympathetic counsel and advice, if requested.
- Understanding of the characteristics of the age group.
- A knowledge of each particular child and his needs.
- Skill in the guidance of the pupils' religious experiences.
- An example of real Christian conduct and attitude.

Teachers heartily and readily agreed. Since many of the teachers were parents, they helped formulate the standard.

The expectation from parents listed by teachers included the following musts:

- Help the pupil to be regular and prompt in attendance.
- Encourage him to study outside the class session.
- Provide a Bible and other needed materials.
- Help maintain a friendly attitude toward the teacher.
- Co-operation in carrying forward the regular and special projects of the class or department.
- A genuine interest in the religious development of the child.
- An environment in the home that is conducive to Christlike growth.

Through the tactful leadership and comments of the pastor, a fine spirit of comradeship was developed; and parents and teachers left the meeting understanding more clearly the need of co-operation and the ways in which they could help each other.

Class or Department Projects

Projects will enable parents to have fellowship together with the pupils. The Intermediate Department of one church school plans each quarter some activity in which the parents meet with the pupils. In this way the parents have not only become well acquainted with the officers and teachers and with each other, but they know intimately all the pupils. A fine spirit of comradeship has been developed in the group involving teachers, pupils, and parents.

Class Parents

As another method for bringing home and church school into closer contacts, some church schools are using to advantage class parents who will be responsible for the school-home relationship. Just as the Parent-Teacher Association has been using room sponsors for a long time, so church schools are now using the same plan. The parents of some pupils are carefully selected for each class, either by the Board of Education, or by the pupils. The teacher will then have these parents as counselors and friends with whom he can work and from whom he can receive active help. Whenever practicable, it will be found desirable to have both mother and father act as class parents.

There are many ways in which these class parents can make a valuable contribution to the group and the church school. Whenever there is a class activity in which the teacher needs the cooperation of the parents, these helpers will be the ones she can call on for assistance. The class parents will be responsible for promoting good fellowship. They will perhaps invite all the other parents to their home, having the teacher as honor guest. Thus the group will have a chance to share experiences and to get acquainted with the teacher and with each other. When problems arise, the teacher will have persons who understand to whom she can go for counsel and assistance. If desired, one of the class parents may act as substitute teacher for the class.

Parents in the Youth Fellowship

BY HENRY A. TANI

To provide an opportunity for better understanding between teenagers and their parents, the three-phase parent-youth series is recommended.

1. *A fellowship evening constitutes the first phase of this series.* On a Sunday, the young people and their parents come together for a late afternoon vesper service. Leadership in the worship service may be shared by parents and young people. The service is followed by an informal buffet supper, with food brought by each family. There may be a few skits, some fellowship singing, and a funny story or two at the table.

A general discussion period in another room follows. The topic can be any of the following: dating practices, hours to come home, use of the car, purchase of clothes, family chores, allowances, drinking, vocational preparation, or some other parent-youth concern. Any of these subjects can be discussed in a friendly, objective manner. which in a home situation may be emotionally upsetting.

To present the subject-matter, try role-playing or the use of some film or filmstrip. It is also possible to divide the parents and young people into buzz-groups, to identify the most pressing parent-youth problems. When all buzz-groups have reported, agree on the two or three items most frequently mentioned, for general discussion. The minister may be called on to make some concluding remarks, setting the problem in the light of the Christian message.

Henry A. Tani, "Parent-Youth Series," *Ventures in Youth Work* (Philadelphia: Christian Education Press, 1957), pp. 121–123. Used by permission.

Move next into a period of group recreation. One of the parents or a parent-youth team may lead the group through some active and quiet games, ending with a friendship circle.

2. *A work-night is the second part of this series.* There may be a major task in a general spring-cleaning of the church, some landscaping around the buildings, painting and repairing furniture, or other such jobs. Whether on a Saturday or an evening during the week, parents and young people are called together to join in this fellowship of work. There is no pretense at worship, or eating, or playing. The project needs to be cleared with the proper authorities, and adequate leadership should be provided.

3. *The last of the three-phase series is a study night.* The recommended procedure is to divide the young people and their parents into clusters of four or five families, on the basis of geography, or of the age or school-grade of the young people. These family clusters meet simultaneously, preferably in homes, to study some specific area of Christian faith. For study material, the minister may preach a special sermon on a Sunday morning, and provide discussion guides for each cluster. Perhaps some church school lesson may be reviewed and discussed. A chapter or two from a book, an article in some church magazine, or other sources may be used. One solid hour of intensive study on some aspect of Christian faith will be helpful to both parents and young people. An alternative to meeting in homes is for the whole group to meet at the church, see a film, or hear a presentation, and then meet in cluster groups in the church building, coming together again for review and evaluation of the discussion.

This is not a general family-night event, but limited to teenagers and their parents. Thus grandparents and kid brothers and sisters are not invited. All three parts ought to be done within a four-week period. To attempt to do all three in one week is ambitious. Advance notice of these dates should be announced so that parents may clear their calendars. While some parents may not be regular church-goers, their participation is nevertheless encouraged. Try the parent-youth series. It's dynamite.

What Should Be Reported?

BY JOHN L. LOBINGIER

Some time ago the Research Department of the International Council of Religious Education (now the Division of Christian Education of the National Council of Churches) made a study of this whole question of report cards and found that they had their widest use in junior departments and are less extensively used in junior high and primary departments. Of greater significance was their finding that the items on which reports are usually made are these, and in the following order: (1) attendance, (2) punctuality, (3) offering, (4) church attendance, (5) lesson study, (6) lesson recitation, (7) memory work, (8) bringing a Bible. This is well enough as far as it goes, but unfortunately it appears that very few who have sent reports to the home have given attention to such points as the attitudes of pupils, their spirit of co-operation, their participation in worth-while causes, growth in Christian character, advancement in knowledge of the course of study. Do not these represent our real aims even more than some of the eight points above? Even though some of the eight are more easily measured, they are still means to an end rather than the desired ends themselves. Some of these eight items should be included, but not to the exclusion of points that deal with growing reverence, Christian attitudes, co-operation, religious knowledge, Christian service, Christian character growth.

What is included in any kind of report indicates what leaders regard as important; and surely that is something more than at-

John L. Lobingier, *The Better Church School* (Boston: The Pilgrim Press, copyright, 1952), p. 86. Used by permission.

tendance! One report form includes (1) attendance, (2) punctuality, (3) the teacher's name, (4) the nature of the course of study, (5) a statement as to the general attitude of the pupil, (6) an estimate as to the quality of his work, and (7) something as to his spirit of co-operation.

The Report Form One Church Used

Winnetka Congregational Church School
Winnetka, Illinois

PUPIL PROGRESS SHEET

Date _____

For (name of child) _____

Days absent _____ Days tardy_____

To Parents:

On this sheet we give you something of your child's progress in the Church School. Your attendance at monthly conferences provides an opportunity for discussion with the teacher—discussion of curriculum and other problems. Your co-operation is necessary if we are to guide children in Christian living.

The Record	Most times	Sometimes	Seldom
1. Prepares lesson			
2. Is co-operative			
3. Enters activities program			
4. Accepts responsibility			
5. Evidences Christian growth *			

* This item, clearly, is difficult to check. If the teacher leaves it blank the parent will understand that not enough is known about the child's spiritual development.

Wesner Fallaw, *The Modern Parent and the Teaching Church* (New York: The Macmillan Company, copyright, 1946), p. 224. Used by permission.

An Experiment in Home and Church Cooperation

BY EDWARD D. STAPLES

Over a period of four years sixty-nine Methodist churches have been experimenting with a plan for encouraging closer co-operation between the homes and the church school. Interest in this experimentation arose at about the same time in Michigan and in Northeastern Ohio. There were twenty-six churches in this territory which agreed to work together under the guidance of the executive secretaries of Christian education in these states. Other churches began the second year. The General Board of Education agreed to work with them.

Plans for the project were made in a five-day seminar at Albion College. Each participating church sent four representatives to share in the planning. When completed, the plan had no essentially new features but brought together the best of many tested ways of helping parents understand themselves and their children and of relating the teaching of the church to the much more extensive teaching going on in the home.

The churches working in this experiment from the beginning met twice each year for further planning. This fellowship and sense of sharing in a common task was felt to be extremely valuable. Groups of churches coming into the plan later in California, Wisconsin, Pennsylvania and New York met only once a year and expressed a need for more frequent evaluation. These groups took the materials planned in Michigan and Ohio and used them without essential change.

Before the plan was launched in a church, a study was made of

Edward D. Staples, *International Journal of Religious Education*, March, 1955, pp. 11, 12. Used by permission.

its present church school organization, using an eight-page questionnaire or rating scale. This revealed many weaknesses. In one church, no teacher had ever taken a course in leadership education. Few churches were helping parents by providing appropriate literature. Many of these weaknesses were corrected before the plan was launched.

The Plan Is Interpreted

Every available means for interpreting what was expected of parents and teachers was used. Ministers preached upon the values of working together in home and church; publicity articles were prepared for the local papers; every family with children in the church school was visited and enrolled.

Both parents were invited to sign their half of the agreement card, which contained these promises:

—to participate in the total program of the church.
—to attend church school regularly.
—to follow suggestions in the Parents' Guides.
—to attend Parents' Study Groups.
—to confer with church school teachers quarterly.
—to report regularly to teachers, using printed guides.
—to read *The Christian Home.*

There was strong agreement among the participating churches that the more the church school leaders expect of parents the more they will respond.

Parents Get Printed Helps

The Methodist church school curriculum carries many helps for parents. It was felt necessary, however, to focus attention upon these, so a quarterly guide for parents was prepared for every piece of Methodist material used by the pupils, both closely graded and group graded lessons. Most of these helps have now been incorporated in *The Christian Home,* a magazine for parents. This worked well the last year of the experimental period. Many churches sent *The Christian Home* to all the enrolled parents, paying for it out of the literature budget. Other churches asked parents to subscribe, but these reached only about half the homes with the magazine.

It was found that a personal letter from teacher to parent, to call attention to the units being studied, was most helpful. In one primary department, the child takes home a suitcase with a book for the child and a copy of *The Christian Home* for the parents, and sometimes a leaflet or two. Then the following Sunday, a different child takes home the suitcase for a week.

Each church provided a few good books for parents. These included books on child care, psychology of adolescence, parent relationship, teaching religion in the home, and the Christian faith. Book reviews in adult classes created interest and the books were placed where readily available. Several public libraries assisted with book displays and talks.

Parents Study Together

As each parent was asked to participate in a parents' group in the church, the church had responsibility for scheduling these groups. Larger churches divided the parents into three groups; smaller churches were content with one. Some churches found Sunday morning the best time for meeting; others found it more convenient to meet on a week-night.

These groups studied the discussion guide in *The Christian Home* or elective units selected on the basis of their interests as revealed through a check list. It was discovered that parents are concerned about problems of child psychology but do not want to spend all of their time on these problems. After a few months of study of home difficulties they asked for units on the Bible, the Christian faith and social issues. They frequently approached these basic enrichment units from the angle of how to answer children's questions.

Special activities were planned frequently, such as family nights at the church, at-home-nights, picnics, hobby groups, etc. One church had a summer "splash party." After the families had been swimming together they came back to the church for refreshments.

Parents Meet with Teachers

Church school teachers were encouraged to visit in the home. When new teachers were enlisted they were told that visitation was expected. Teachers of large classes used class visitors to help. The churches agreed that quarterly was not too often to visit, but it was discovered that many teachers were not willing to visit so frequently. It was then decided to ask for one or two visits to the home each year and to make other contacts with the home at least quarterly.

The value of such visits was illustrated in the case of George, who was constantly causing trouble in class. The teacher looked upon him as a spoiled brat and did not seem to be able to find any contact of friendship with him. The report card indicated that the mother was having difficulty at home also. A visit revealed that George lived in a broken home. His mother and grandmother were often sharp with him and he needed a different kind of affection. When the church school teacher understood his family background, she was able to be more patient with George, to get him into a Boy Scout Troup, where he found male companionship, and to help him feel wanted in the group.

Parent-teacher interviews were also found most effective. Parents were invited to meet the teacher at the church at a specific time. By scheduling interviews fifteen minutes apart, the teacher could see most of the parents of his class in one Sunday afternoon.

Group meetings, teas, an open house in the church school room, or parents' day at Sunday school offered opportunities for teachers and parents to talk over the objectives of their program, but were not quite as effective as the personal interview or visitation. Telephone calls were helpful for reaching parents if other means failed. One church invited two parents each Sunday to observe in the church school and talk with the teacher afterward.

Report cards were sent each quarter to the parents, interpreting the progress the child was making at church school. Parents were asked to fill in the form on the back of the card and return it to the church. The reports showed evidence of initiative in class work, encouraging signs of progress, and evidence of Christian growth. Parents were asked to indicate home progress and areas in which they needed help.

Response from the parents to the card varied from fifty per cent to ninety per cent. The reports of progress were favorably received though some parents thought they should be more specific regarding the quantity of material learned. Most of the teachers preferred the more general type of report of progress.

Evaluation of the Experiment

Every church taking part in this project showed a higher average attendance in proportion to its enrollment than at the beginning of the plan. In one community, the average attendance in church school jumped from fifty to seventy-eight per cent of the church's enrollment and the church school had to take over a lodge hall across the street for classes.

It was the new insights into teaching which seemed to be one of the greatest values of the experiment. The fact came out in one evaluation session that teachers were no longer "teaching the lesson" but were teaching the children. Most churches reported that teaching improved and that teachers were now better prepared. One parent reported that she had never before realized the importance of a rain-drop going down a window pane. It had never occurred to her to use a simple fact of nature in teaching religion in her home, as was suggested in her church school materials.

Expanded sessions resulted in some churches so that parents could attend the regular church services and their children could learn at the same time.

All were agreed that it was not a multiplied number of activities which created a family-centered church, but it was an attitude which undergirded all of their planning of the church's program.

Adopting this plan will not perform miracles. It requires hard work and expects much of those who would teach in home and church. It should be entered into prayerfully and hopefully, with a determination that a closer relationship between home and church can be brought about if people care enough.

PART III

WAYS

OF

WORKING

WITH

CHURCH

GROUPS

11. GUIDE GROUP THINKING

GROUP DISCUSSION is more than random talking or "pooling our ignorance," as some cynics have intimated. It is purposeful group conversation about a subject or problem of common interest, aimed at finding solutions, determining procedures to be followed, or arriving at common understanding. Effective group discussion, therefore, must be based on sound group thinking, and the function of the leader is to guide this process of group thinking.

Discussion is one of the most widely used procedures in church work. It has long been recognized as an important part of the work of the church school class and of the youth or adult group. It is also involved in most of the committees or commissions through which the program of a church is carried forward.

Good leadership plays a large part in effective discussion. To help church workers develop their ability to guide group thinking, the readings which follow have much to say about the preparation which the leader should make and the techniques which he should employ. More important than the leader's technique, however, is the spirit or attitude which he has. By "spirit" we mean more than the basic Christian commitment which every church worker should have. We mean the trust which a leader must have in the group. Assuming that they know the subject and that they have examined the factors which are involved in it, he must trust them to arrive at sound conclusions. He must be willing to abide by these conclusions, even though he may not entirely agree with them. This does not mean that the leader abdicates. Rather, it means that he places real responsibility on the group. True, there is risk involved. They may take a long time to reach a conclusion. They may reach a poorer conclusion than the leader has reached by himself. It is also possible that the group's conclusion may be better than the leader's conclusion! Most important of all, it is the group's conclusion, and the members are committed to it as they would not be committed if the leader had merely given them the results of his own thinking.

How the Leader Prepares for Group Discussion

BY J. JEFFERY AUER AND HENRY LEE EWBANK

Study the Group

We tend to talk more easily and less formally with those we know. It will help the members of the group, then, as well as the leader, if he can get to know them before the meeting. In this preliminary contact his primary purpose should be to discover their points of view on the topic to be discussed; incidentally he may learn much about their common interests, vocabulary level, and general knowledge.

Study the Topic

The leader should develop a general familiarity with the topic and the main lines of thought it may set off. The more he knows about it the easier it will be for him to follow the leads of the members of the group and to anticipate what may develop in the discussion. Selected materials useful for discussion can be gathered in any good library. The best kind of study, of course, will start with available source material, progress from general background information toward the more specific, and be selective enough to encompass all points of view.

Prepare Introductory Remarks

A discussion group is seldom equipped with a self-starter; the leader will need to get it going with at least a few brief comments.

J. Jeffery Auer and Henry Lee Ewbank, "Preparing for the Group Discussion Meeting," *Handbook for Discussion Leaders* (New York: Harper & Brothers, 1947), pp. 52–56. Used by permission.

A statement of the topic, with a word about its importance, is a minimum. In some cases the leader may feel it necessary to sketch the general background of the topic, point out significant questions, and bring it to a sharp focus before the group takes over. The length of this introduction will vary with the leader's estimate of the interest, experience, and previous knowledge of the group; in a discussion scheduled to last an hour it might take only five minutes, but seldom as many as fifteen. Experience has shown that leaders are more apt to talk too long at this point than too briefly. If the group is unfamiliar with the discussion method, it may be wise for the leader to comment on general objectives and procedures, as well as to suggest that discussion is concerned with ideas, not personalities, and that any contribution will be welcomed so long as it bears upon the topic. He may also wish to invite people to take part and to feel free to speak up as in any informal conversation, raising such points or questions as occur to them; at the same time he will ask them to be fairly brief and to the point and to keep within the rules of common courtesy. In order to become familiar with what he plans to say and to say it well and within a limited time, the leader should practice his introductory remarks. Some leaders make use of assistants, often to give the introduction to the topic; because it tends to shift the group's focus and disrupt continuity, however, it is not a recommended policy. Occasionally the introduction may be built around an unusually effective visual aid such as a map, graph, or picture.

Prepare a Discussion Outline

Although the informal group discussion proceeds with a minimum of organization, the leader should have an outline for use in guiding the conversation. The leader's outline should not be a strait-jacket but a guide; if he occasionally wishes to announce its three or four main topics in advance, the group should feel free to suggest changes, but the chances are that any well-prepared outline will be accepted, even though the discussion may depart from it widely. The typical outline for an informal and impromptu discussion consists of a series of questions which the leader can throw out to stimulate the thought of the group and to direct it along somewhat logical lines. Knowing that some of the questions will not impress the group the leader will usually prepare more of them than can be fully considered. He will also realize that the discussion, once started, may take an unexpected turn, compelling him to make up a new outline as he goes along. Even should this happen, some plan will have been better than none at all.

Most discussions will focus not only on a specific problem but also on one particular phase of it. It is possible, however, to set up a general outline that can be adapted to various problems. Such an outline, based on the normal steps in thinking through a problem, is given below. It is unlikely that any single discussion can cover all these points.

General Discussion Outline

I. *What is the nature and extent of the problem?*

    A. What background information is necessary to an understanding of the problem?

    B. What is the specific question to be decided?

    C. How serious is the problem?

    D. What factors must be considered in deciding on a solution?

II. *What solutions are proposed?*

    A. What are the advantages of each proposed solution?

    B. What are the disadvantages?

III. *What is the group's initial reaction?*

    A. On what points does the group substantially agree?

    B. What are the chief differences?

        1. On matters of fact?

        2. On matters of opinion?

    C. How fundamental are these differences?

IV. *Which solution, or combination of solutions, seems best?*

    A. Can a compromise be reached that will meet with general approval?

    B. If not, which solution, after debate, is favored by a majority?

V. *How may the chosen solution be made effective?*

    A. What can this group do?

    B. What can I do?

Here is a sample outline on "What can we do about death on the highway?" It was prepared for a group already familiar with the nature and extent of the problem; it began, therefore, at the the stage of examining possible solutions. The leader phrased it in questions which he could throw out to the group. He was prepared to break the outline down into even smaller units or to omit some parts if they failed to interest the group.

Sample Discussion Outline

I. *Nature and extent of the problem.*

    A. Two-minute summary of information gained at previous meeting.

    B. Can anyone add anything to this?

II. *Where can we begin to tackle this problem?*

    A. How about teaching safe driving in our high schools?

    B. How can we approach our adult drivers? What about men's luncheon clubs and women's organizations?

    C. What about our local traffic laws? Are they adequate?

    D. Are we getting proper enforcement of our local traffic laws?

    E. Can anyone suggest still other ways of reducing traffic accidents?

III. *What steps should be taken?*

    A. Can we agree on what ought to be done to meet this problem? What seems the best place to begin?

    B. What can this group do?

    C. What can we do as individuals?

Planning for Group Participation

If the group is familiar with the discussion method, the leader will need to do little in advance to assure participation. But if members of the group are not sure what to do in a discussion they may do nothing rather than take a chance on revealing their ignorance by doing the wrong thing. It is primarily for use in this awkward opening pause, when everyone waits for the next fellow to get going, that some leaders make sure that preliminary and authoritative information is at hand by providing certain members with books, pamphlets, or clippings dealing with the topic. Another common device is to distribute ahead of time brief items of information and have them read at the beginning of the meeting. People who have lived or traveled in certain areas, those with special experience or contacts in particular fields of interest, or others with special knowledge pertaining to the topic will naturally provide a pool of information. They may be contacted before the discussion and invited to make specific contributions. Once the ball starts rolling in the meeting and members are convinced that their ideas are wanted, group participation is assured.

Some Suggestions for Improving Group Discussion

BY SARA LITTLE

Conversation is often mistakenly called discussion. Real group discussion presupposes preparation on the part of the members, who are aware of the need for disciplined and purposeful thinking, and who are willing to work to improve their skills in co-operative efforts to solve some problem, to arrive at some decision, or to come to some understanding.

No two discussions are alike, and there is no rigid pattern to be followed, but it may be helpful to look at three steps which are frequently found in a discussion.

The Statement of the Subject to be Discussed

Many times people do not address their remarks to the subject because they are not sure what they are discussing. After giving a brief background or explanation, or an introduction designed to arouse immediate interest, the leader may wish to state in *one sentence or one question* exactly what is to be discussed. It may need to be modified. Its limitations may need to be stated. But people can work better when they know what they are discussing —and when the subject is one suitable to be approached through the discussion method (as many subjects are not).

The Discussion Proper

A good leader would work out a discussion pattern in advance, but would be willing and able to modify it. He would have some

Sara Little, "Group Discussion," *Learning Together in the Christian Fellowship* (Richmond: John Knox Press, 1956), pp. 40–46. Used by permission.
328

plan for getting the discussion started, and some idea of the pattern of development it might follow. For example, to aid in orderly movement, he might wish to list questions on a chalkboard, and then follow the listing; or he might wish to list major areas—as "issues involved," "available facts," "possible solutions," "obstacles"—to serve as a guide. Always listening to people and respecting them, seeking to make it possible for all to contribute and none to monopolize, he would sometimes rephrase questions, sometimes stop for a brief summary and restatement of the goal.

Summary and Conclusion

If it is possible to do so, it is well to state the conclusion at which the group seems to have arrived, in a way satisfactory to them. But often no real agreement has been reached, and there will be a summary of progress and a statement of unsolved issues. Many times this final statement is unnecessary. A small group where members have met and worked together for a long time might find a verbalized statement an objectionable rehashing of what they knew. A sensitive leader, however, will know when to summarize and state conclusions, or when to end a session in some other way.

A general discussion often includes many types of discussion within one session—buzz groups, panels, question and answer periods—or combines with other types of study procedures. This means that a good discussion leader is not only flexible, but is a person of great resourcefulness. Such qualifications would reveal themselves in at least two ways: the leader would be familiar with and skilled in the use of many aids to discussion, and he would be sensitive to individuals within the group.

There are innumerable aids to discussion which are especially valuable in getting started, or in stimulating new interest when attention seems to lag. The use of a brief unfinished story, or a dramatization or a tape recording, or a case study—any of these can prove of value. One study guide suggests two other ideas. The first is that of using a problem census.

Before the group adjourns, do a problem census. Distribute 3" x 5" cards to each person. Ask each member to write on one side of the card his answer to this question:

Of the many social problems presented in the Report on "The Responsible Society," what problem do you believe is of greatest concern to Christians in this community?

On the other side of the card, each group member answers this question:

As a responsible Christian and a member of this church, what would you want the church to do about this problem?

Collect the cards and tabulate the answers on a blackboard. Many of them can be grouped for similarity.[1]

A second idea is that of using an opinionnaire.

In each question or statement, check the phrase that seems to describe *most accurately your opinion* or understanding of the issue.

1. Apathy to social issues is due principally to:
 .....a. inadequate instruction in the Bible and Christian theology.
 .....b. lack of information and understanding of public issues.
 .....c. belief that religion and politics do not mix.
 .....d. sense of hopelessness and futility of individual efforts.

2. Christians can work *most effectively* for a responsible society by:
 .....a. concentrating on the salvation of souls.
 .....b. conscientious study of present-day issues and urging their public officials to take these issues seriously.
 .....c. working faithfully in the political party of their choice.[2]

Use of both the problem census and the multiple-choice opinionnaire or questionnaire will help stimulate interest and raise issues that need consideration. Another idea that may help if a group is stymied, or contributions seem to be pious or prosaic, or

[1] *Every Church and Evanston* (New York: National Council of Churches, 1955), p. 29.
[2] *Ibid.*, pp. 27–28.

members tend to sit in judgment on each other, is "brainstorming,"
a term coined by Alex Osborn in *Your Creative Power*.

Its procedure is simple. Rules of judgment are suspended, if
only temporarily. A problem is posed. For a period of ten or fifteen minutes the members of the committee or audience are urged
to put forward their most ridiculous ideas. These are recorded
without comment and without criticism. Criticism is reserved. . . .
And the practice of letting the creative imagination run riot without the usual shushing restraints tends to loosen up the group, to
encourage suggestions, and to foster a spirit that cannot possibly
develop in any other way.[3]

Business has used the idea to improve insurance policies and to
manufacture new erasers. Program planning groups have dealt
with subjects for meetings, titles for speeches, publicity plans. We
are advised that "brainstorming works best when it is applied to
really difficult problems," [4] and that it provides a means of getting to the spontaneous ideas on people's minds.

Sometimes students have real questions about doctrinal beliefs,
or interpretations of Bible incidents, and think the questions are
too absurd to be mentioned. Freed from the possibility of being
criticized, they may bring out into the open vital questions or new
insights. What is not good can be discarded when the group gets
back to a more reasoned discussion—and members will have enjoyed the experience.

No matter what plan is followed to aid in the movement of a
discussion, it is doomed to failure unless the leader knows how to
use carefully worded questions. There are ways of helping persons to be specific and clear in their thinking. There are ways of
helping a whole group to see where it stands and to work together
with maximum effectiveness. There would be questions like
"Why?" and "How?" and "Such as . . . ?" Or, "Is this what
you're saying?" and "It seems to you that . . ." And there would
be "Is this what we've said so far?" or "What is our next step?"

---

[3] *New Hope for Audiences* (Chicago: National Congress of Parents and
Teachers, 1954), p. 12.
[4] *Ibid.*, p. 12.

A casual observer, looking in on a group where a good discussion leader is at work, hearing only his brief questions and comments, would doubtless be entirely unaware of the concentrated effort demanded, a labor that is mentally exhausting, but that enables him to know when questions are needed to bring forth more information, or indicate relation of facts, or to stimulate deeper inquiry into issues involved.

The need for the leader to be sensitive to individuals within the group has already been mentioned. One person, having heard that wide participation was desirable, said to a shy member, "Mary, you haven't said anything today. Do you know the answer to this question?" It was a factual question, and Mary did not know the answer. The leader had violated Mary's right *not* to speak, and had embarrassed her. Had the leader felt that Mary *wanted* to speak, and only needed a slight encouragement, he might have said, "Yesterday we were talking about . . . Your idea comes in right at this point, Mary. Want to tell the group about it?" He might use some other plan. Usually, it is better to address questions, especially factual ones, to the group as a whole, rather than to individuals. When a member begins talking too much, the leader can summarize what he has said, and ask for someone else's opinion, or he can say, "I see . . . I believe we have an idea over here." Only rarely would he deliberately say, "Bill, why don't you give somebody else a chance to talk?" Of course it is impossible to say what words or expressions to use and what not to use, because the tone of one's voice often determines what is really communicated. The leader whose genuine interest in people springs from his basic Christian motivation will know what to say and do; there are no rules to follow, but there is an attitude which finds a way of expressing itself.

Discussion, as Used with Children

BY FLORENCE B. LEE

Conversation is used with primary children to help them share experiences and information and to develop self-confidence and self-control through listening and taking turns in speaking. It may stimulate creative thinking. If we are to be successful in the use of this method with primary children, we must respect each child as an individual and have regard for the contributions which he makes. A feeling of friendly sharing, seeking answers, and exploring interesting subjects should permeate the conversation period. The teacher will listen to what the children have to say and show evidence of real interest in it.

Informal conversation is not a question-and-answer period in which the teacher asks a question of each child in turn and receives answers. Something of interest to all is introduced by a child or teacher, and the group talks about it informally, each one making his contributions, asking questions and exchanging ideas as interest leads. The teacher guides skillfully so that the conversation is purposeful and worth while.

The teacher should help each child to respect the contributions of the other children. She is alert to help every child participate and to see that no child monopolizes the time and attention. Questions should be stated directly and simply. Questions that can be answered with "yes" or "no," or which suggest the answer, do not stimulate thinking. The best teaching helps children think. Conversation can do this.

Florence B. Lee, "Conversation," *Teaching Primary Children* (Philadelphia: Judson Press, 1951), pp. 80–81. Used by permission.

Informal conversation is especially valuable as the children arrive, for then they will be eager to share with the teacher interesting things that happen during the week. These may give the teacher insight into the children's thoughts and feelings and help her discover their needs. Conversation may be used in the class session for review, making plans or evaluating work done. The children may be called together in the midst of an activity to talk over further plans or solve some difficulty which has arisen and clarify plans and responsibilities. Children enjoy talking about pictures and songs. They can talk about trips before they go and when they return.

Where there is understanding and wholesome respect for each other and for each other's ideas, freedom of conversation will abound, and teacher and children will have through it many joyous learning experiences together.

Clues to Successful Discussion Leadership

BY GORDON LIPPITT

Getting Ready

- Arrange group in circle, so each person can see every other person.
- Provide table space, if convenient, for leader and entire group.
- Let all stay seated during discussion, including leader. Keep it informal.
- Start by making everybody comfortable. Check ventilation and lighting.
- See that everybody knows everybody else.
- Learn names of all as soon as you can.
- Have blackboard, chalk, and eraser ready for use in case of need. Appoint a "blackboard secretary" if the subject-matter and occasion make it desirable.
- Start on time, and close at prearranged time. If you have an observer's report, be sure to allow time for it.
- In opening, emphasize: *Everyone* is encouraged to take part. If one member's view fails to get out in the open, the discussion falls short in its permissiveness.
- Toward this, emphasize: No speeches, by leader or group member. No monopoly.

Carrying On

- Help the group to clarify its objective so that the purpose of the meeting is clear. Let the group build the agenda out of its

Gordon Lippitt, "Suggestions for Group Discussion Leaders," *Religious Education,* November–December, 1952, pp. 376, 377. Published by the Religious Education Association, New York. Used by permission.

own needs, but keep it limited to the task upon which it is working.

- Aim at the outset to get a sharply defined question before the group. Have three or four alternatives put on board if you think this will help: "Which do you want to start with?" "Is this question clear?"

- In general, don't put questions to particular group-members, unless you see that an idea is trying to find words there anyway: "Mrs. Brown, you were about to say something." Otherwise: "Let's have some discussion of this question . . ." "What do some of the rest of you think about this?" "We've been hearing from the men. Now how do you women feel about this?" "What's been the experience of you folks up in the northern part of the State in this connection?" Etc.

- Interrupt the "speech maker" as tactfully as possible: "While we're on this point, let's hear from some of the others. Can we save your other point till later?"

- Keep discussion on the track; keep it always directed, but let the group lay its own track to a large extent. Don't groove it narrowly yourself.

- Remember: The leader's opinion does count in the discussion, but keep your own view out of it as much as possible. Your job is to get the ideas of others out for an airing.

- If you see that some important angle is being neglected, point it out: "Bill Jones was telling me last week that he thinks . . . What do you think of that?"

- Keep the spirits high. Encourage ease, informality, good humor. Let everybody have a good time. Foster friendly disagreement if it occurs. Listen with respect and appreciation to all ideas, but stress what is important, and turn discussion away from what is not.

- Take time every ten minutes or so to draw the loose ends together: "Let's see where we've been going." Be as fair and accurate in summary as possible. Close discussion with summary—your own, the secretary's, or the observer's.

• Call attention to unanswered questions for future study or for reference back to speakers. Nourish a desire in group members for continuing study and discussion through skillful closing summary.

12. GUIDE GROUP ACTIVITY

IF PERSONS LEARN through their own active participation (see chapter 5), it follows that the church group leader should draw the members of the group into active participation in some form of Christian enterprise and should guide them in that participation. There is a profound truth here which group leaders have been slow to take into account.

For the teacher of a class, this truth has a number of implications:

1. The focus shifts from the teacher to the pupil, for it is the pupil who does the learning.

2. Real teaching takes place only when learning takes place, which means that what is taught becomes part of the life and thought of the pupil.

3. Activity, and participation in activity, must have a purpose. Otherwise it is mere "busy-ness" and is of little value to pupil or teacher or church.

This truth applies not only to teaching but to group leadership of all kinds. The effective group leader does not do the work of the group himself. Rather, he guides the members while they do the work. He knows that only when the members of a group be-

338

come personally involved in its work will they become dedicated to the purposes for which the group exists. We have followed this principle more effectively in our work with children than in work with other ages. It is just as true, however, for the adult in his committee as for the small child in his class.

Boys and Girls Learn through Guided Activity

BY DOROTHY LA CROIX HILL

In this chapter read first the section "From a Teacher's Notebook." Then study "Principles in Guiding Active Learning." Compare the numbered paragraphs in each section.

From a Teacher's Notebook

1. *After the second session.* Our minister was wonderful today. He read and translated for us from the first chapter of Mark. I asked him to copy Mark 1:1 on a large sheet of paper and teach us to read the Greek. The boys and girls loved that. Languages are exciting to juniors.

When he had gone away, we turned our chairs to face a group of pictures illustrating Mark 1:32–38 and above them the picture of someone writing on a scroll. Just turning their chairs rested the boys and girls. Looking attentively at the picture, I said, "I am thinking about that man who nearly two thousand years ago took his reed pen and his ink of soot and gum and wrote on the right-hand column of a new papyrus scroll, 'The beginning of the gospel of Jesus Christ.' Where did the man live? Why did he want to write a book? How did he know what to put in it? Get a Bible from the shelf, take three paper markers from the box on the table, and find these three references in Mark which I am writing on the blackboard. Then you will be ready to help me tell the story."

So I told that story just as thrillingly as I could. I had put time

Dorothy LaCroix Hill, "Guiding the Active Ways of Learning," *Working with Juniors at Church* (Nashville: Abingdon Press, 1955), pp. 83–99. Used by permission.

and study into preparing it, reading it over and over from the pupil's book, adding some details from the articles in the *Interpreter's Bible,* actually memorizing the way to begin and end it. I told it to myself after I went to bed and sometimes when I woke in the morning. A lot depended on that story. It might prove the springboard for our planning of activities. I wanted to make those dangerous days for the Christians in Rome seem real. I hoped some juniors would identify themselves with that company and feel glad when one of their number decided to write a story of Jesus designed to give them new faith in their heroic leader and courage to face death for his sake if need be. In unison, with Mrs. Rilling leading, the boys and girls read their parts of the story which were the verses from Mark.

Everyone was so still at the close of the story that we bowed our heads and used as a prayer the stanza about the Gospels from the hymn "For Man's Unceasing Quest for God."

2. "Let's see," I said, pondering. "What do we know now about the writing of the Gospels?"

The answers showed that the juniors were thinking and learning. I wrote them on the blackboard—how the books looked, the language in which they were written, the materials used; how, where, and why scholars think Mark was written; "and how that language—*Koine*—looks and sounds," quiet Anne reminded us.

I looked at the list. "We really ought to find some interesting ways to tell what we are discovering," I said.

"Give a play," suggested Esther.

"With a big fight in it between the Christians and Nero's soldiers!" proposed Steven. Instantly half the boys were fencing with imaginary swords, and the girls were saying, "No!"

I said mildly that the play committee would have to decide about that, because fights are very hard to do in a play. People usually get too excited; then the whole thing looks silly when it is supposed to be very serious. But the play certainly ought to tell in some way about the trouble Nero was making for the Christians in Rome.

Steven looked pleased and stopped fencing.

"We could make peep shows," said Robert. I asked Mrs. Rilling to tell about another kind of "picture in the box," called a diorama. Often two or three people work together on one. I do hope Robert gets into some kind of group activity in this unit.

"We could write stories," Anne suggested shyly, "and put them in a notebook."

Some of the boys made very impolite sounds at the word "notebook." Anne flushed and said that she would help with the play. She must write her stories, too.

3. I printed the three suggestions—giving a play, making peep shows or dioramas, and writing stories—on the blackboard. Anne's name went up next to the play and the story writing. In a very short time everyone's name was beside one of the three kinds of activities. It took Kathie longer than the rest to decide, but by the time a committee for the play and one for peep shows and dioramas had been formed, Kathie had chosen the latter. She needs a good teammate, one who would not think too fast and would let Kathie do some of the planning. Mary Ann would be good. I must telephone to find out why she was absent today.

Sam has been sick. I must take a pupil's book to him. He is always so regular and such a worker that he will feel lost to come back into the middle of a unit. Why not ask him to report on ways that the American Bible Society is telling the good news of Jesus today, and how we might help? I will lend him my teacher's book. Having something important to do will make him a part of the class experience next Sunday.

4. Coming back to last Sunday, once our committees were formed, Mrs. Rilling joined the peep-show and diorama group, and I sat in with the boys and girls who want to make a play.

The story about how Mark was written had dramatic appeal evidently, for that is the play committee's choice of a subject. I put an outline on the chalk board to get them started:

Our Play: What is happening?
To whom is it happening?

Who is making it happen?
Where is it happening?
When is it happening?

Lots of ideas came out. Both groups were still busy when it was time to close.

Mrs. Rilling reported that, after they had consulted "what-to-do" and "how-to-do-it" books, and had discussed a variety of ways to make "pictures in a box," Robert was still planning a peep show. Billy and Tim had decided on a diorama, and Kathie rather indecisively thought she would try one if someone would help her. They had made a list of materials they would need and knew who would bring what. Mrs. Rilling will send them postcard reminders. No one was sure of a subject for his picture, although Robert was thinking of a man writing on a scroll, as in the teaching picture on the wall. Mrs. Rilling suggested that they take their study books home as usual and that they read the stories about Matthew and Luke with their families. That might help them to find some interesting and important idea to make into a diorama.

We both told Anne that we hoped she would write a story. "After the class has enjoyed it, you might mount it on construction paper and put it on the bulletin board," I suggested. "Then anyone who comes into our room could read it and learn something about the writing of the Gospels. If you should choose to tell about the writing of Matthew, you could read your story to us next Sunday instead of our hearing the one in the pupil's book."

Well, next Sunday will surely be a work session. That means some special kinds of preparation if we are all to have a good time and get well along with our activities.

5. *After the third session.* The room was ready for work because I set it up on Saturday. That takes time, but it does pay off when boys and girls come in, find things ready, and go to work.

The diorama committee had two long tables at right angles. That was to encourage fellowship and interest in one another's work. Back of the piano I arranged a small table with two scrolls, a low bench, two stools, a small chestlike box. I hoped that these articles would help the play committee put themselves at once into the setting of their dramatization. The hymn "We Would See Jesus," lettered on a long sheet of white wrapping paper, I hung above a table. On the table I laid a pile of pictures which could be used to illustrate the hymn stanzas. I made a friendly corner, with study books and pictures, in which to meet the pupils who have been absent, to help them find their way into the unit. Mrs. Rilling had made a poster record of our plans. Its title was wordy, but exact: "Ways to Share With Other People What We Are Learning About the Writing of the Gospels." She left blanks for titles of stories and dioramas, for the "idea" of the play, and for the names of new committee members who might come today.

The diorama committee. Robert came early and started his peep show of paper and cardboard before the others arrived. They held a meeting and added this information to the record poster:

Robert—peep show of man writing on scroll (for Mark).

Kathie, Mary Ann, Susan, Joan—diorama of teacher instructing group of new Christians from a scroll (for Matthew).

Billy and Tim (Robert offered to help them make sheep)— diorama of Luke talking to an old shepherd at Bethlehem (for Luke).

6. *The play committee.* These juniors did some remarkable work. In trying to analyze why this was so, I believe it was because Steven completely identified himself with the early Christians of Rome. That put the other children into the play more fully than anything else could have done. As soon as I had briefed the five who had been absent in earlier sessions—Sam had read the pupil's book and was a great help—and they had chosen activities, I pulled up a chair with the group behind the piano.

"What is happening here in Rome?" I inquired.

"Terrible things!" they told me. "Christians are being put in prison and even killed."

"Why?" I asked innocently.

"Because Nero burned Rome, and now he is blaming the Christians. Haven't you heard about that?"

"Is anyone we know in prison?" I asked.

"Peter!" they cried in a chorus.

"Listen," Steven said urgently, "you are a stranger, like in that first story in our books. We have to tell you what is happening in Rome. All the Christians are here at my house."

"Why?" asked one of the girls.

Steven pondered; then his face lit up. "We could be having a party, with real things to eat!" he exclaimed joyfully.

The rest of the committee looked steadily and hopefully at me. Somehow it didn't sound just right, their eyes said, but, oh, if it could only be that way! How juniors do love to eat!

"Well," I said slowly, "you have told me such terrible things that I don't believe I feel much like a party. I'm not even sure I could eat anything."

Steven looked sober. "I guess we wouldn't be having a party," he agreed; then his face brightened a little. "But we might be eating to keep up our strength."

I love those youngsters—so earnest, but so truly children. I'll take homemade cookies to Saturday's rehearsal, but it probably won't turn the play into a party.

"Being in Rome is dangerous!" I was frightened.

"What are we ever going to do?" anxiously queried Anne.

"We could run away!"

"Or hide!"

"Maybe we should stop being Christians."

"We might pretend not to be Christians, but really worship Jesus in our hearts," suggested Anne thoughtfully.

"Do those sound like good ideas?" I asked Steven.

"No, we must not do things like that," he declared. "We should be Christians even if it is dangerous, even if we *die* for it!"

There was a long pause. Uncertainty filled the air.

"You may be that brave," I finally said, "but the rest of us don't seem to be. If Peter should be put to death, that would probably take away our last bit of courage."

And that's the way it turned out. A Christian who had been watching near the prison brought us that terrible news. Everyone fled to his own home, afraid to be found in a Christian gathering. Only Steven—who by now had become the man who would write the Gospel of Mark—and the messenger remained. Steven's head was sunk on his arms. His whole attitude was one of despair.

"What are you thinking about?" I murmured from off stage. "Are you wishing that Peter were here, because he would know what to say to these frightened Christians?"

And Steven took it from there.

"Bring me a roll of fresh papyrus," he ordered the messenger. "Go to the market—"

"That would take too long," said Esther, the practical one.

"That little box," Anne pointed. "It's like the one where Luke kept his notes and little scrolls."

"From the chest," amended Steven. "My ink and reed pen can be right here. I'll write down everything Peter told us about Jesus—especially about how brave he was and how he had enemies, too. That will make them brave again."

"You could be saying out loud what you are writing," Anne suggested, "you know, the first verse of Mark, 'the beginning of the gospel of Jesus Christ.' Couldn't that be the end of the play?"

It could be, and it is.

We'll work it through again on Saturday. I had hastily jotted down on a pad most of the dialogue, chiefly because it was too good to lose. The juniors helped me get it straight, each one remembering what he had said.

This is a different kind of play than I have ever seen juniors work out, and I think it is the best kind of all. Each person created his own lines and therefore his own part. There just isn't any question about who will be who. And they know the lines because they made them up. Well, we certainly do live and learn when we live with juniors and let them be our teachers.

7. *We worshiped.* First we reported our progress and filled in the blanks on the planning chart. It made us feel good to see our work so well organized. I purposely left the work Sam had done during the session for the last report. He had chosen pictures to illustrate each stanza of the hymn "We Would See Jesus." I had suggested that he do this when he seemed to be listening in on the play from the picture table, but did not want to take part in it. It is a little hard for Sam to co-operate in something he has not thought up himself. We must look for opportunities to help him over this problem in his Christian growing.

Well, when I mentioned that Sam had selected pictures to illustrate "We Would See Jesus," it was only natural that we should all sing the stanzas as Sam showed the pictures. That led us into worship. Anne read us her story about the way that Matthew probably came to be written. I suggested that we use the Bible to find out if Matthew is still a good teaching book. We found three passages telling how to pray, how to treat enemies, and about serving the "least of these" in the name and the spirit of Jesus. We read these in unison and decided that Christians still need these lessons. So we sang our stanza of thanksgiving for the Gospels. I said "thank you" for the Gospel according to Matthew in a simply worded prayer, ending with thanksgiving for the prayer Jesus taught his disciples, in which we all joined.

8. I introduced Sam's report as a possible way for us really to show our thankfulness for the story of Jesus. Quite on his own, inspired by pictures in the pupil's book, he had made a fine poster showing some of the people to whom the Bible Society ministers. Sam is one of the juniors who occasionally does something like this at home. Of course the poster added interest to his report. He was sincere and earnest as he told about the work of the Bible Society, and of course the juniors were eager to follow his suggestion that we plan a gift.

It would be possible, Sam said, for us to provide some copies of the New Testament for Indian children in reservation schools or copies in other languages for foreign-speaking Americans, or to use our offering toward the cost of a Bible in braille for the blind. On our reading table were samples of all these, even the cards with a verse in braille. After much discussion and many questions which Sam and I answered together, the boys and girls voted to bring an offering for making the Gospels available to some blind person. From their experience in another unit the juniors decided to bring just one offering in the last session of our unit and appointed a committee to write post-card reminders.

There was a strong group feeling in everything we did today. Even Sam, who had been absent for several Sundays, finally found himself caught up in it when the others accepted his report and suggestions for sharing with genuine appreciation and enthusiasm. This was one of those wonderful, occasional days when teaching juniors seems about the most worth-while thing you do.

Principles in Guiding Active Learning

"We cannot use activities in our teaching. We do not have the space or the time." Teachers who say this understand only a part of what is meant by learning through activity.

Boys and girls are learning in active ways whenever they are reaching out for information, when they are stretching their minds to make new associations of ideas, when they are enjoying and appreciating Scripture or a picture which expresses what they are thinking and feeling. A girl's sigh of content, the long stretch of a restless boy at the close of an engrossing story, tell that they were living the story, that for them it was an active experience. Juniors who twist, squirm, poke, and talk while a teacher stumbles through the reading of a story or urges them to pay attention and think what the Bible verses mean, are saying by their behavior that this, too, is an experience—an experience in boredom.

1. Making every step of the class session an active, enjoyable experience is especially important in early sessions of a unit when boys and girls are acquiring the background they must have before undertaking so-called "creative activities." Later on in the unit the good use of materials is still important, for through them

developing ideas, attitudes, and resolves are fed and nourished, and learning is deepened and strengthened.

2. When the first session has stimulated active interest in the unit, when through the good use of materials the boys and girls have a reasonable amount of background in this area of religion, the teacher may help them to set up some purposes for their learning. Often these purposes come to light as the group tries to decide what they will do with the discoveries they are making.

However, it is important to remember that this may be attempted too soon, with the result that chosen activities die quickly from lack of nourishing ideas. In the first session of the unit, for example, the only activity the class might think of would be to draw a picture, probably of a man writing on a scroll since today they have discovered that the first Gospel books were scrolls. A little later, as they find that Matthew was written to instruct new Christians, that Luke seems to have sought out people who knew Jesus, that Mark may represent much that Peter remembered of Jesus, many choices of subject matter for pictures, for dioramas, for plays, for storytelling and story writing, present themselves. Now the boys and girls must judge and compare, sort out ideas and make choices. They must search for details, verify their discoveries through Bible study. As they do all these things, they will be learning richly and deeply.

For the richest learning the boys and girls need to participate fully in every step from the first suggestions of activities and the initial planning to the final evaluation of what the group and its members have been doing. The teacher may make suggestions, too, for in a good fellowship of learners he is as much a member of the group as are the pupils. However, his suggestions—like theirs—may be accepted or rejected by the class. Always he will try to help the juniors recognize the worth of each individual and the value of each one's contribution to the planning of the group. This is not only the democratic way to guide boys and girls, but the Christian way as well.

3. Activities must provide for choice, because everyone learns

best when he is working out purposes that are important to him. If a group is not too large, juniors sometimes agree on one plan, such as giving a play or a program for parents and friends. Both of these are large experiences, with opportunities for many kinds of work and activity.

Often, however, the class is not so unified in purpose. Individuals differ in interests, background, and abilities. Some lack confidence in their ability to work acceptably on a group enterprise. Others need help in finding co-operative activities satisfying. This kind of readiness cannot be forced, but the wise teacher finds ways to make what each one is doing contribute to the purpose of the group. Gradually he will guide these boys and girls into satisfying group experiences.

A helping teacher makes it possible to guide more than one kind of activity and is always a steadying influence in the group. Moreover, the experience of juniors is enriched by working and learning with more than one adult. In your church there is probably at least one person waiting to be asked, one who wants to help.

4. Once the boys and girls have decided upon activities, the teacher guides so that each child may participate fully in what he has chosen to do. The extent of a junior's learning and growing will depend upon the degree to which he feels himself a part of the experience, upon how deeply he gives to it his interest and attention, his feelings, and his energies.

By questions and comments the teacher indicates that activities the boys and girls have chosen are important and worth doing. By records on the chalk board or newsprint he helps each one to be clear about his responsibilities, and helps the group to accomplish its goals. Through leading questions and guided discussion he encourages the juniors to do efficient, purposeful thinking.

The teacher guides by introducing new materials and suggesting new points of view. He helps the juniors to obtain information they need in order to move ahead in their activity. His teaching rises to a high point of effectiveness when he helps one child, or the group, to discover from a Christian viewpoint, meanings and relationships between past experiences and what they are doing and learning now. He guides when he finds good ways to use discoveries or accomplishments of individuals or committees for the richer learning of the whole class.

The teacher gives especially good guidance whenever he stimulates juniors to work or study at home. However, boys and girls need to be sure that this at-home preparation will be put to good use in the coming session. Like adults they are busy people, but like adults they find time to do the things which seem important and worth while to them. Juniors are often eager to take assignments if this will help their own purposes or plans to move forward, or if it will prove an important, appreciated contribution to the class learning or goals. Again like adults they usually need a reminder in the form of post card or telephone call.

5. The teacher guides in a most important way, but unobtrusively, through room arrangement; the materials displayed; pictures and objects; books with markers at certain pages; the open Bible; study or work directions on the chalk board; records of class purposes and plans where they will be constant reminders; the hymn, Scripture, and poems for memorizing neatly printed on posters.

In preparing for each session, the teacher needs to rethink the purposes of the unit and how these are being realized through the purposes and activities set up by the juniors. He tries to picture how far the class may move ahead in the unit today and checks progress against the unit goals. He sees that, because certain things happened in the last session, there are natural next steps to be taken today.

As he prepares, the teacher tries to see each child in relation to the unit. What will John, Mary, and Sandra be discovering today? What will they be doing and contributing to the group experience? Are special materials needed for individual pupils if they are to keep learning and growing as Christians in the unit?

In each session interest must be reawakened, and group plans must again become uppermost in importance. It is easy and quick to say, "Class, last Sunday we decided to make dioramas. Now let's get to work!" But such a summons does not mean that the juniors will be ready to do so. It is better to say, "John, just before we went home last Sunday, you had a wonderful idea about using clay for the wall in your diorama. Do you think that would work for the house that Esther and Jean want to put in theirs? Or would a salt and flour mixture over cardboard be better?"

6. We will judge the worth of any activity not by the perfection of the finished product, but by the depth and quality of the children's experience. Has something good for his growing happened to each one who worked on the frieze or took part in the dramatization? This is the matter of true importance. We guide an activity always with the hope that whatever we say or do, whatever help we give, may make the experience more vivid, real, and satisfying to the boys and girls. For this reason we try to help juniors plan their frieze carefully. They will be dissatisfied and unhappy about it if the result is not pleasing to the eye. We try to help them remember their lines in the play and speak them with feeling so that they will be the person they represent, thinking his thoughts, sharing his experiences. Flashes of insight, of real learning, come to boys and girls when their interest and feelings are deeply engaged by the carefully chosen, carefully guided experiences of a unit.

When the play described in "From a Teacher's Notebook" was to be given for parents and friends, Steven arrived wearing without a trace of self-consciousness a most realistic corn-silk beard. While the teacher helped him into his costume, he said wonderingly, "I'll bet the man who wrote Mark never thought we would be giving a play about him or that people would read his book two thousand years after he wrote it."

"No," the teacher agreed, "but his good news was so wonderful that people still want it and need it. That is what makes the whole Bible different and lasting."

A sixth-grade girl tried to tell in verse how she thought the people of Jesus' own day felt about him. Out of her past experiences and new learnings she wrote:

> He lived like God
> For men to see!

In occasional flashes like these we are privileged to see what is happening to boys and girls. Usually these wonderful, revealing moments come in the midst of the activity, suggesting that in doing, in creating, juniors have their finest experiences of growing and learning.

But there are values in sharing with other groups in the church school, with parents and with friends, what the boys and girls have done in a unit. The interest of others helps juniors to feel that their work has been worth while. As they try to put together materials and activities of the unit in ways that will be interesting and helpful to an audience, they may find new meanings and relationships, new insights, in the experience.

"Will our program be helpful to the parents and friends who see our plays about the lost coin, the lost sheep, and the lost son?" asked a teacher.

The juniors pondered a moment, then:

"They will know that God is loving and forgiving."

"Maybe someone will come who should ask God to forgive him for something. After he sees our play about the lost son, he might do it."

"Have we learned any hymns or Scripture which might help our program to do those two important things?" asked the teacher.

Suddenly the boys and girls realized that the hymn "There's a Wideness in God's Mercy" could help. They had studied its meaning and learned to sing it well. Now they sang it with a purpose that was important. They added a prayer written by one of the group and a choral reading of the hymn "Brother of All the World." [1] Their sharing program became a genuine experience of worship for both juniors and their guests.

---

[1] *Hymns for Junior Worship.*

In guiding activities, how much help does the teacher give to individuals or to groups? There can be no definite rule. Certainly the teacher will never take over an activity and "run" it, nor will he deal out advice in wholesale lots. Instead he is "available" when help is needed and boys and girls ask for it. Never will he take the brush or pencil from a young artist's hand and add telling strokes to the child's picture, nor will he add words to a young writer's masterpiece. When the junior is dissatisfied with his efforts, on another piece of paper the teacher may indicate what would help. It is unforgivable to destroy a child's sense of "ownness" in his work.

Yet it is not good leadership to meet requests for advice or help with constant urging to "think it through yourself." Should an adult ask what we would do or what we think, we would respond honestly and freely, but always leave wide open the right to accept or reject our counsel. Juniors respond best to the same courteous, friendly treatment we give to older people.

7. In every session it is important to help the boys and girls have a sense of achievement. We must round up the experience and lead on into new avenues of discovery and planning. When the class has worked on activities, groups and individuals must have a chance to show or to tell what has been done. If this is not included in their reporting, the teacher will indicate how the work contributes to the larger plans and purposes of the group.

Throughout the session as juniors and their teachers work and study and plan together, a sense of oneness should be developing. This unity makes the group ready for good worship experiences, as they seldom are at the beginning of the hour. In the small class or large grade, in the one-room church or the big junior department, teachers must plan to lift each session into a high moment when juniors sense that all has been done "to the glory of God."

8. By the methods of teaching we sometimes employ, it is possible to defeat our purposes for living in Christian brotherhood. When the adult leader singles out individual children to participate because they read exceptionally well, learn the lines of a play

quickly and speak them loudly, or sing beautifully, quite unchristian attitudes may be taking root in these juniors and in their classmates. To pass these privileges around is not the solution, for the boys and girls will still be vying for the favor of the teacher. They will be ruled by a spirit of rivalry and competition which will inevitably destroy their Christian fellowship. In a group where the cry frequently arises, "Let me! Let me! I'll do it! I'll do it!" the teacher needs to examine his teaching procedures. Such a spirit indicates that juniors do not have opportunity to plan their own activities or to enjoy rich, rewarding experiences in their units of study.

A sense of "togetherness" comes when we work in groups and make most of our contributions as groups. Group singing, choral or unison reading, dramatizations with a part for everyone, are better methods than solo work. In these all may share, even the child who does not carry a tune and the most self-conscious, stumbling reader.

When individuals do contribute—and at some time every child should do so—this should be a sharing of their own creative work. The teacher accepts the excellent report, the well-written or well-told story, the fine poster, not with praise for the ability of the child, but with appreciation for the way it contributes to the group's purposes. Once this spirit takes hold, juniors often express sincere appreciation for one another's work. Every session with juniors should be an experience of "dwelling together in unity." When each child feels himself loved, accepted, and valued, he will be able to do his best and to be his best. He will be experiencing the spirit of Christ in the fellowship of juniors.

The Small Child Learns through Play

The young child is most typically himself when he is happily at play. He tries new things: he plans, decides, fails, tries again. He makes friends; he shares; he wonders; he loves! The child is growing according to God's plan!

Yet the concerned kindergarten teacher wonders, "In one short hour, can I afford to let children play? Shouldn't they learn ideas here, and play about them at home?" She must decide whether a child learns only by spoken words and ideas, sometimes not understood, sometimes forgotten, or whether he learns better by discovering these ideas for himself in guided play experiences. Of course the teacher will work with the parents. Both parent and teacher observe and interpret free play experiences. From this observation adults learn much about the children and their problems; and they help the children learn by interpreting what they see. Free play in the church school enhances home experiences by providing a selected age group under the eye of a teacher who is especially interested in those situations which contribute most to Christian growth. The teacher cannot enter every home and teach each child a table grace as he sits down to his food. But as he shares an imaginary breakfast in the church school with his playmates and hears a prayer of thanks, perhaps he too can experience the joy of being thankful.

"Earnest Play—A Child's Labor," *Church and Kindergarten Child* (portfolio) (Philadelphia: Board of Christian Education and Publication, Department of Children's Work, Evangelical and Reformed Church). Used by permission.

Four-year-old Jimmy's worried mother had already spoken to his teacher about the child's jealousy of the new baby. One morning the teacher was about to go to the rescue of the rubber baby doll into which Jimmy was gleefully thrusting a pin again and again. The five-year-old mother in the play house darted past her and snatched the doll away.

"Stop it," she shrieked. "You're mean! I won't let you hurt the dolly."

"It's mine," Jimmy protested. "You have the big doll. You can't have them both."

"I can too! I'm their mother and you can't be our daddy unless you're nice to all the dolls!"

The teacher stood by speechless. In that small scene Nancy was saying more than the teacher could have said in hundreds of words. Then Nancy relinquished both dolls and sailed back into the house; Jimmy burst into tears as he hugged both dollies to him.

In planning for our church school hour, therefore, we must hold clearly in mind the advantages that free play offers to the children.

Toys, The Child's Tools for Learning

If play is the child's work, then toys are his tools. The best toys for the small child are those that can be used for many purposes so as to allow free rein to his creative ideas; that is, large smooth blocks in various sizes and shapes are better than small plastic bricks with ready-made doors and windows. The latter may build a more realistic house, but will use less of the child's planning and imagination in it.

A group of four-year-olds built a swimming pool in the kindergarten by making a rim of large blocks on the floor. When Bobby's mother came to take him home the children were busy "diving" and "splashing" and "swimming" in it.

"One more dive!" he called to his mother as he hurried around to the end of a line of five or six children.

"Why don't you dive in once more from this side," his mother asked, impatient to be on her way.

"We can't! We have to dive off the board or we might hurt someone! Besides, this is the deep end." So the mother waited.

Imagination at work, taking turns, following rules, concern for the welfare of others—all these were a part of this experience with ordinary building blocks.

The two interest centers in the kindergarten that allow the most variety of activity and stimulate the greatest imagination are the block-center and the home-center. A few pieces of kitchen and bedroom equipment, a laundry, and dolls, will keep a group of children busy for hours. The child's home is the center of his world. To it comes the milkman, mailman, baker, delivery man, doctor, friends. It is his security: it is also the place where he meets many of his problems in living. In the play situation he can work through many of these problems, removed from the pressure of reality.

Of great value also are the transportation toys. A kindergarten rarely has enough trucks, planes, boats, trains, cars. We live in an age of travel, with mechanical wonders very close to the child. There should be small cars he can hold in his hand and carry around the room or put in a block garage. There should be large sturdy trucks to carry loads of block "vegetables," "coal," or "packages." Such versatile items are more valuable than expensive mechanically assembled toys such as the gasoline station or train round house where the toy itself does the planning and the work, and the child only presses a button and watches. Wooden animals and people are also very useful in the block center.

Some children will not move readily into large group activity. For these there should be a supply of individual toys—here again, flexible ones, capable of many uses. Balls, punching toys, and movable teeterboards are among these because the child may welcome a playmate to catch his ball or balance his board. The individual peg board of the nursery will give way to the larger peg table where four or five children can plan peg villages of houses, streets, and trees.

For the thoughtful child, or one who needs to withdraw from the group excitement for a moment there will be wooden puzzles, books, and pictures; and the "wonder table" with objects he can see, smell, and feel.

Noise-making toys—drums, horns, whistles—are conspicuous by their absence. There will be rhythm instruments ready for the children's use under the teacher's leadership, but the children should not be encouraged to make noise for its own sake.

Dramatic Play

The play-work in the kindergarten with fours and fives is not the same as the general "busy-ness" of the three-year-old. The four-year-old is not so completely centered in himself. He is aware of the larger world and can imitate and wonder about the people in it. He will co-operate with the five-year-old in planned play. Together they will play a sequence of events, or plan and build different kinds of buildings and talk about them. Their pictures are of special things. They tell stories.

Because the four- and five-year-olds can think and plan, they can work with the teacher in guided play. If she sees the children playing aimlessly with the blocks she may simply say, "Why don't you build a store, Jimmy, and think of all the helpers who bring things to it." Or more specifically, during the group conversation she may say, "Let's play a story about how the flowers grow!" The children can decide who will be flowers, who will be the sun, the rain, and the gardener. In the home center he dramatizes family life. Such play is creative drama at its best for the kindergarten —translating ideas, words and feelings into actions.

The kindergarten child loves to dramatize a familiar story. No costumes or properties are needed, though simple ones may give pleasure. The children enjoy doing the same story over and over. They will "share" it with parents on visitor's day—not as a performance with rehearsals and standards of perfection, but as a simple, natural classroom activity. If space to move around is not available, similar results can be achieved with hand puppets. Balls of cotton covered by muslin mits, with penciled faces, are good for table dramatization. Some children may enjoy adding crayon hair and clothes, but realism is not important. The same puppet can be many characters in many stories. They can also use wooden figures.

Sometimes the imaginary becomes so real that the small child cannot distinguish between them. For such children, dramatic play is a helpful corrective outlet for the imaginative mind.

> A child rushes into the room saying "I saw a big bear in the play yard chasing Timothy! I really did!"
> "You did, Johnny!" says the wise teacher excitedly, taking him by the hand, playing his game. "Brown, or black or a polar bear? Let's go see it!"
> Then after a moment she will gently lead him back into the real world by saying, "Isn't it fun to *pretend* we are chased by bears?"

In selecting and planning a story drama, the teacher should keep in mind what she hopes to accomplish. The children play the story not so much to learn the events in sequence, but rather to help them *feel* the story by identifying with the characters. They need to experience the adoration and hope of the shepherds approaching the manger in Bethlehem. They can feel concern for the lost sheep, or the joy of the children, going to see Jesus, in the story of Jesus and the children. They can also identify with inanimate things as they dramatize them—feeling strong and fun-loving like the wind; or warm and secure like sleeping seeds in winter. The teacher will tell her story with this purpose in mind, encouraging children to talk about their feelings as they plan to play the story, and as they experiment.

These emotional aspects of a story are not separate from the ideas—rather they are a deeper level of meaning. It is at this deeper level that meaning can be most richly communicated. When a child hears a story about "Davey" being selfish with the cookies the day guests came, he says to himself, "That was Davey. *He* was very unfriendly." But if he *is* Davey in the play—feels and does as Davey did; sees how sorry Mother is; regrets his actions as Davey did—he can learn as much from the play-story as he could from a genuine experience without the guilt feelings that accompany such situations in real life.

Projects Can Help Young People Develop

BY OLIVER DE WOLF CUMMINGS

Time and Energy May be Saved by Wise Choice

Careful consideration must be given to the selection of projects, to the time requirements and to the relative values for educational growth and accomplishment. Many projects require a great deal of time without proportionate spiritual outcomes. Time and energy may be saved, if good judgment is shown in picking the right projects. It is essential that the young people themselves manifest real interest in the projects chosen and that these develop from meaningful study. It often is true of youth that they become overly enthusiastic on a sudden whim and will need tactful guidance in bringing their ideas down to earth. The leader should be aware of the spiritual needs of the group and possess resourcefulness in suggesting suitable projects.

Materials and Tools Needed Should be Anticipated

It often is not expedient to tackle certain enticing projects because of inadequate equipment and materials. When a definite project is decided upon, it is necessary to determine what tools and materials will be required and to have them ready for use. For example, if a redecorating project is to be undertaken, paint and brushes, ladders, drapes and curtains and other necessary materials must be provided. If a relief map is to be constructed or a

Oliver DeWolf Cummings, "Projects Need Careful Planning and Guidance," *Guiding Youth in Christian Growth* (Philadelphia: Judson Press, 1954), pp. 123–125. Used by permission.

Palestinian village re-created, the necessary framework, paper pulp, clay for models, and other materials must be at hand.

The Right Steps to Be Taken Should Be Understood

It is necessary also to map our goals to be reached, problems to be solved and logical steps to be taken. Many a hastily conceived and poorly organized project has justified the counsel of Jesus, "For which of you, desiring to build a tower, does not first sit down and count the cost, whether he has enough to complete it?" Certain questions need answers: How, where and when shall we begin? How much time will be required? What are we proposing to accomplish? What will it take to achieve these results— in money, in materials, in effort? Who shall have which assignments? What about incidental or secondary outcomes? How and when shall we check up on progress?

Appraisal and Follow-Through Are Desirable

Many projects are of such a nature that it is easy to be satisfied with a measure of physical accomplishment without sufficient consideration of the educational results. Often the by-products are of great value. For example, in a seminary course in religious education, the construction of a Palestinian village was undertaken as an example of a suitable project for an intermediate age class. The focus at first was upon the physical tasks to be performed, the topography, the construction of the houses, the sheepfold, the wine-press, the synagogue. Soon it was necessary to examine the Old and New Testaments for data and incidents revealing facts about village life. There were lessons concerning the vineyard— "I am the vine, you are the branches"; the sheep—"the ninety and nine"; the fields—"a sower went forth to sow"; the synagogue— "he entered into the synagogue and taught"; and Palestinian houses—the story of the four men who tore a hole in the roof and lowered their sick friend into the presence of Jesus. Thus, much insight was furnished; there were summarized evaluations and provisions for follow-through on subprojects.

The Role of Activities in Adult Groups

BY RICHARD E. LENTZ

"That is the most active class I have ever seen. Something is going on every minute." This description of a certain local church women's class was spoken by a visitor who attended several sessions.

Most people assume that it is good for church adult groups to be "active." One prominent church leader said recently that he equated "activities" with "program" in his thinking about adult groups. However, it can be said of individuals that activity is sometimes an indication of ill health. People who are never still are sometimes ill. Also there are certain activities which are unwholesome for persons or groups of persons. Perhaps we should examine the role of activity in the program of an adult class. It may be that groups can be "too active," or active in unwholesome ways.

Study is itself an activity. Usually even the leaders of adult classes think of the study program apart from the activity program. Activity of any sort by a group establishes a learning situation. In this respect and for this reason all activities of a class, whatever may have been their intended purpose, actually become a part of the informal teaching of the group.

Three Case Illustrations

Groups engage in many kinds of activities. Some activity is necessary to maintain the group itself. An example of this sort is the

Richard E. Lentz, "The Role of Activities," *Making the Adult Class Vital* (St. Louis: Bethany Press, 1954), pp. 76–82. Used by permission.

preparation of the upper room by the group of Jesus' disciples (Matt. 26:17–19). In order that the whole group might have the experience of eating supper with the Master, someone had to secure and arrange the place. Food had to be procured and prepared. Finally, the basin and towel were required.

Every group—including the adult classes of the church—has many necessary "preparations" which are required to maintain the group itself.

The account of Jesus' feeding of the five thousand hungry people illustrates another type of group activity (Mark 6:39–44). While there were certain necessary preparations to make, the main purpose involved persons outside of the group of the disciples. Some call this activity the "service projects" of a class. "Project" is a good word for them: they are "projectiles of good will." Through them an adult class projects itself, its influence or spirit, into the community.

It is a question whether an adult class can thrive without expressing in practical ways the essential love that constitutes the gospel.

A third sort of group activity is demonstrated in the sending forth of the seventy disciples to herald the coming of Christ (Luke 10:1–20). The "project" had its service aspects—the heralds were preparing people to hear Christ—but the main reason for their being sent out seems to have been their own development through the experience.

Adult class activities help to develop the personality of the "actors."

A Catalog of Activities

The following list of activities found in adult class programs is not intended to be exhaustive. The classification obviously is open to question, for every activity has the elements of all three types. Also there is no feeling that those who engage in Type I are "less spiritual" than those who share in Type II. If there are certain necessary chores to be performed, those who do them contribute to the whole program of the class.

Type I. Group Maintenance Activities

Preparation of the classroom, chairs, hymnbooks for the session.

Greeting of strangers, visitors, and members.

Keeping class records of attendance, offerings, meetings.

Taking the offering.

Arranging transportation for homebound members or for field trips of the class.

Making name tags, cards.

Sending out letters, notices of meeting.

Maintaining membership, mailing, committee lists.

Telephoning to stimulate attendance, special offerings.

Writing advertising, publicity or news releases for class events.

Checking books in and out of class library.

Ordering and distributing supplies and literature.

Developing class budget.

Maintaining class "archives."

Operating projector and record player for audio-visuals.

Type II. Service Projects—Activities "for Others"

Sharing in a wide variety of specific missionary work through financial aid, supporting a living link, or conducting a single project such as collecting clothing.

Sponsoring organizations for a younger group of persons such as Boy or Girl Scout troops, Teen Canteen, boys' clubs.

Providing eyeglasses or hearing aids for the needy.

Sending CARE packages to famine areas.

Conducting or sharing in civic drives or campaigns of many kinds.

Arranging a Bible story hour.

Sponsoring religious broadcasts or TV programs.

Cooperating in the activities promoted by the local Council of Churches.

Arranging a picnic or excursion for older people of the parish.

Arranging a picnic or excursion for children of the church, a local settlement house or sanitarium.

Helping other adult classes without leadership by supplying substitute teachers.

Sharing in the vacation church school program as sponsors, leaders, assistants.

Securing and distributing information on social conditions, issues, problems of the community.

Assisting in the church program of evangelism, stewardship, worship by recruiting leaders, distributing literature, making surveys.

Sponsoring community forums on important social issues such as race relations, labor problems, delinquency.

Helping recruit leaders for the children's and young people's programs of the church.

Providing an employment or counseling service to members.

Scheduling "baby sitters" for church couples.

Rendering special services to the homebound: reading, visiting, shopping, recording church services.

Conducting class parties, socials.

Type III. Activities for the Participants' Development

Promoting activities such as parties, talent nights.

Providing special hobby or interest groups such as public speaking class, photography club.

Arranging for group discussion leaders coaching or intern-training.

Encouraging members to serve on boards and committees of community agencies (for the training value of the experience as well as the service value).

Providing scholarships for class members to denominational assemblies, summer conferences, training classes.

Supplying scholarships to interdenominational conferences, conventions or schools.

Cooperating with the high school or college in "vocation days."

Maintaining a speakers' bureau for service to community groups, including panels and book reviews.

Joining in the sponsorship, leadership, or promotion of community activities with the Council of Churches or area denominational organization.

Some Guiding Principles

Every group will decide upon the principles of selection which it will use in determining its program. Some suggestions are made here to stimulate the thinking of local groups.

An adult class cannot support all of the good endeavors of the community. Leaders of an adult class, therefore, will need to develop some guiding principles to aid them in selecting worthy activities for their group and in locating program weaknesses where activities need to be provided.

- An activity must be consistent with the Christian convictions and commitment of the class; otherwise its educational significance will be negative or destructive.
- An activity must be within the resources of the class. It must not place too heavy a drain on either leadership or finances.
- An activity should include only a wholesome emphasis upon competition, never a "win-at-any-price" psychology.
- An activity should be supplementary to the purposes of the class as an educational group, helping persons to learn and to develop.
- An activity should provide opportunity for as wide a group participation as possible, utilizing a diversity of abilities and giving the satisfaction of achievement to the whole group.
- An activity should contribute to good public relations for the class in the community or denomination.
- An activity should be planned and carried out by the regular class organization in so far as possible.
- An activity should contribute to class harmony and unity.
- An activity should reflect the class's respect for persons in all phases of its development.
- An activity should be related to the full program of the class and the local church.

13. USE AUDIO-VISUAL RESOURCES

AUDIO-VISUALS are past the experimental stage. Their value has been demonstrated, and it is assumed that alert church group leaders will use them. Production has reached the stage where good materials may be secured on almost any subject in the church program. In most instances there is sufficient variety so that the leader may select the particular audio-visual that appears best suited to the age of the group and the purpose of the particular program.

It is better to speak of audio-visual resources than to speak of audio-visual method. Audio-visual materials are resources which a group uses in its work. They are aids, to be used along with other materials. Some kind of group process, involving one or more methods, almost always precedes use of an audio-visual. Some kind of group process follows the audio-visual, as the group discusses, evaluates, plans.

As the fourth reading will make clear, "audio-visual" is a broad term. It includes materials that are to be seen (visual), materials that are to be heard (audio), and materials that are to be both seen and heard (audio-visual). It includes not only materials that are to be projected but a considerable variety of nonprojected materials. It includes materials which have been commercially produced and which the user either rents or purchases. It also includes materials which the user makes or collects, even the highly individualized use he may make of a chalkboard.

Little is said about particular types of equipment or sources of materials. So much depends on the reader's background, on his geographical location, and on the resources of the church and community. Furthermore, these sources are constantly changing. It is best for the leader to make his own selection of equipment and sources of supply, utilizing the best advice he can get at the time when decisions are to be made.

How Does the Teacher Plan?

BY MARY PHYLLIS YOUNG

Denominations now understand the value of audio-visuals in teaching and realize they must help teachers. They vary in their progress toward their goal of integration and of giving help to the teachers. Some are actually "building them in" and providing help in the lesson materials. Others simply list audio-visual materials, mentioning specific films, filmstrips, and slides that would fit into a lesson. Some give instructions for use; some do not. Others have not even begun reference to these materials.

It is important for the teacher to remember, however, that he is the key to good use. The finest material and the best suggestions will be useless unless the teacher "tailors" the filmstrip, slide, or film to fit his purpose and his class. He need not follow the script word for word. It would be far better for him to *ad lib* it and use the script only for information. He can stop a filmstrip, ask questions, have a child give a report, use a map. Then it is "his" teaching tool. It is not meant to do the teaching itself. Only the teacher can relate it to what the class learned last week or know what he intends to have them do in relation to its content a few minutes after it has been presented.

The integrated use of audio-visual materials requires care in planning the unit of lessons, the individual lesson, and the use of the particular audio-visual selected. The teacher should study all of the quarter's materials as soon as the church receives them. Taking notes on ideas for a variety of ways to provide class par-

Mary Phyllis Young, *International Journal of Religious Education*, November, 1957, p. 9. Used by permission.

ticipation will be valuable later. Teachers in a department should meet to plan cooperatively for use of audio-visual materials as they preview and plan the lessons. There may be duplicate requests for ordering films or filmstrips which must be considered. Also cooperation in taking turns in using equipment will be needed. The department superintendent and audio-visual counselor should attend, as they can see the department's requests in relation to requests by other departments.

After the advance planning has been completed and the time for the use of the audio-visual comes near (two to three weeks ahead), the teacher should go over his plan carefully, deciding just how he will use the audio-visual material. When possible, members of the class should share in the planning.

If the lesson suggests an interview, the group may want to record it on tape and plan to use all or part of it in the class at the proper time to present the point of view, or to give facts. What was learned in the interview or on a field trip may be shared through posters, charts, simple drawings on the chalkboard or a timeline, perhaps with a three-D effect to arouse their interest.

Such tools in no way minimize the importance of study of the printed page. The audio-visual materials should not be over-used. When used correctly with participation and in a variety of methods, such resources will encourage study, preparation, and thinking, as well as playing a part in meeting the other important needs of people, such as sharing in group work, learning tolerance, and acquiring an ability to think critically and to express one's thoughts.

Steps to Effective Use of Audio-Visuals

The effectiveness of the audio-visual method depends on using the right material in the right way. The following are steps to effective use:

1. Determination of Purpose

What is to be accomplished in the light of the purposes of the program of the church? How may this be done? How will audio-visuals help?

2. Selection of Medium

What type of audio-visuals can best help achieve the specific purpose? Should a motion picture be used or a filmstrip or record or other type? Is it feasible to use it in the given project? Some situations do not lend themselves to using the medium best suited to the purpose so the next best may have to be used.

3. Selection of Specific Materials

What is available? Where can a reliable evaluation be secured?

4. Booking of Material

Reserve material and equipment for the desired date. Do it early—three to six months ahead.

5. Leader's Preparation

Preview the material. Study how it may be most effectively

"How Best Use Audio-Visuals?" *Using Audio-Visuals in the Church* (New York: National Council of Churches, 1950). Used by permission.

used. Plan the session (time schedule, before and after discussion, tests of effectiveness to be applied, follow up, are all important).

6. Room Preparation

Everything should be in readiness, with the group properly seated. For maximum smoothness of program, prepare the room early.

7. Group Preparation

Since these eye and ear tools are used to a purpose, care must be taken that they get the right setting with the group. Always this requires some statement of purpose. Sometimes it requires discussion before the showing, or presenting a number of questions to sharpen up observation. This preparation may be at the preceding session of the group, and, more often, just before the material is used.

8. Presentation

Presentation of the audio-visual should be in connection with the unit of learning.

9. Follow Through

Make sure the purpose is achieved and the learning related properly to the pupil's experience. Educational use of audio-visuals is not the same as entertainment uses. The materials should be interesting, but the question "How did you *enjoy* the picture?" (or record) is never in order.

10. Testing

Provision should be made for some sort of formal or informal tests to discover change of attitudes, and habits.

Does not all this make for more work than simple oral teaching? Of course! But it also makes for *less* work. It makes the presentation easier and more explicit, leads to more effective learning and is always worth the effort.

Common Pitfalls to Be Avoided

1. Over-Emphasis on Audio-Visuals

The *use* of projected pictures should not determine the program, but should be considered only as an aid for more effectively carrying out the church's program of Christian education. Enthusiastic interest in audio-visuals may cause an over-emphasis upon this method in teaching. Such an emphasis may reduce the effectiveness of well-planned and prepared curriculum materials provided by the Christian education agencies of the denominations.

2. Poor Selection

The subject content of audio-visuals must help in achieving the planned purposes, goals, and objectives of Christian education. The use of technically excellent or colorful materials simply because they are interesting and easily available should be avoided. In no case should a piece of material be used just to fill in time.

The use of an unsuitable motion picture can be a waste of both time and material and give a bad impression or produce an adverse result. A well-selected recording or projected still picture or group discussion may be more effective in a particular situation than a motion picture.

3. Failure to Preview

Embarrassment, presentation of highly undesirable material, or loss of opportune learning experience will result if audio-visuals

Using Audio-Visuals in the Church (New York: National Council of Churches, 1950). Used by permission.

are not *pre*viewed. The leader must know the content of material before it is used with a group. Always preview all materials.

4. Bad Timing

The integration of audio-visuals calls for careful scheduling as it is used. Good teaching procedure will be violated if not enough time is allowed for needed discussion, action, or follow-through. If a piece of audio-visual material requires a running time longer than the period available for a given unit of study, some other type of material must be shown.

5. Equipment Bungling

The bungling use of equipment and the disrupting of a satisfying learning experience will occur if there is no rehearsal. Good timing, proper order and handy location of materials will make for an effective presentation.

Failure to have a spare lamp on hand may result in the complete inability to use an effective piece of projected audio-visual material.

6. Faulty Ventilation

Lack of good ventilation in the room will decrease the effectiveness of all audio-visuals. If the room must be darkened with heavy drapes, mount the drapes a foot or more from the windows and leave the windows open for ventilation by circulation through the space at the top and bottom of the drapes. If darkening blinds must be used, provide some form of a light-trap ventilator for several windows. Whatever means are used for darkening the room, provide some form of ventilation.

What Types Can Be Used?

BY JOHN W. BACHMAN

After deciding that a particular audio-visual experience is desirable for your group, you will want to consider which type of material can best provide the experience. Should you use a chalkboard or a filmstrip? A tape recording or a motion picture? A feltboard or a flat picture? You can take advantage of the wealth of audio-visual resources only if you know the possibilities and limitations of each type.

Audio Materials

The term "audio" is sometimes swallowed in "audio-visual" and almost overlooked, except in a supporting role as sound for motion pictures and television. As someone quipped, "You cannot whistle an algebraic formula." But neither can some whistles be reduced to equations! Both the auditory and visual stimuli have distinctive functions.

Listening experiences provided by radio and recordings offer these advantages:

- The voice is frequently the most revealing expression of human personality.
- Music is essentially a listening experience.
- Necessary scenery, properties, costumes, and weather conditions may be suggested by the imagination, stimulated by inexpensive sound effects, narration, and dialogue.

John W. Bachman, *How to Use Audio-Visual Materials* (New York: Association Press, 1956), pp. 10–32 (portions). Used by permission.

- The mental pictures thus conceived may vary with the individual. This is especially convenient in dealing with biblical themes, where many people have strong preconceptions.
- Unnecessary scenic details may be omitted, allowing the sound to concentrate on fundamental principles.

Disadvantages are these:

- With nothing to watch, listeners are more subject to distractions, thus limiting their attention-span.
- Listeners are likely to imagine only those visual elements which they have already seen; it is difficult to suggest new visual experiences through the ears alone.
- Some concepts may be portrayed more clearly in visual than in auditory terms. Maps, for example, make clear at a glance relationships which would be difficult, if not impossible, to describe orally.

Radio and disc recordings, whether 78, 45, or 33⅓ rpm, differ in these respects:

Radio	*Records*
Offers resources beyond any record collection	*but* Can be scheduled whenever desired, not just when broadcast
Is less expensive than record collection	*but* Can be played many times
Its immediacy is attractive	*but* Can be studied in advance

The tape recorder combines most of the advantages of both radio and records, along with some of its own:

- Broadcasts can be recorded and filed to be played when convenient, so long as they are not used for commercial purposes.
- Since the tape can be played many times, then perhaps erased and re-used, the process is comparatively inexpensive.
- Tapes can be played in advance, interrupted, and replayed—thus making up for the loss of immediacy suffered by a few programs such as news and special events.

• Tape makes possible a satisfactory quality of local recording at less cost than was possible with disc recorders.
• Splicing and editing are simple tasks.

The tape recorder has become recognized as one of the most useful and versatile of instructional materials. Along with radio and records, it is being used for the following purposes:

• To bring from a distance, or even from the past, speakers who would be unable to address your local group in person. Some of these resources are available in tape and record libraries, others may be taken off the air, still others may be secured by individual request.
• To enrich the local program with nationally produced dramas and documentaries.
• To collect broadcast commercials, news, and other programs for propaganda analysis, thus contributing to the development of discriminating listening.
• To bring national panels, forums, and town meetings into the local group to stimulate discussion.
• To preserve local discussions for later analysis by leader and participants.
• To exchange local programs with other groups.
• To file a spare program or sermon as protection against sudden illness of a leader.
• To maintain oral contact with group members away or ill.
• To preserve meetings, conventions, and worship services for shut-ins and other absentees to hear later. (Tapes of business meetings are also useful to a secretary in compiling minutes.)
• To provide music for worship, for social functions, or for study. The wide choice of commercial discs or tapes, along with developments in "high-fidelity" and binaural (two-ear) recording, stimulates this use.
• To preserve events such as dedications and anniversaries for archives.

- To prepare attractive annual reports, using selected segments of tape used during the year.
- To preserve a wedding ceremony. The playback can be a moving experience for a couple who probably heard little of the original service!
- To provide an exact record of counseling sessions for private, analytical use by the counselor. As psychiatrists have noted, the pitch, tempo, volume, and inflection of the voice may be as significant as words.
- To allow speakers and singers to hear themselves as others hear them, making possible critical group or private analysis.
- To assist in language training, especially for drill in pronunciation, partially substituting for the conversational experience essential to acquiring a speaking knowledge of a language.
- To record dramatic rehearsals and performances for interpretative analysis.
- To provide sound effects for drama and interpretative readings.
- To record sound track for filmstrips, slide-sets and films, thus producing a combination audio-visual material, which will be discussed in the following section.

With some experimentation you will be able to add to the list above.

If you do not have the necessary equipment for such projects, you will wonder how to decide which machine to purchase. In general, select a reputable dealer who will be able to make repairs when they become necessary. Specifically, each type of equipment has certain features which should be evaluated in relation to your intended uses. In a *tape recorder,* for example, you will consider these factors:

—quality of reproduction. How closely do the recordings resemble the original sounds? The quality is likely to be roughly proportional to the cost—and also to the weight!

—recording speeds in inches per second: 1⅞, 3¾, 7½, 15. The slower the speed, the longer a recording can be made on a reel of tape. The faster the speed, the better the quality. For music or even for careful study of the speaking voice, any speed below 7½ generally is unsatisfactory. Two-speed machines give you greater flexibility.

—single or dual track. A dual-track machine (recording on only half the width of the tape in one direction, then reversing and using the other half) saves tape, but makes splicing and editing difficult or impossible.

—speedy forward and rewind action, desirable for all purposes.

—constant speed of motor and dependable brakes. You will have to depend on your dealer at this point, or on the analysis of mechanically competent friends.

—ease of operation, especially important if many different persons are to operate the mechanism.

—an index counter, which is helpful for editing or "spotting" sections.

—a playback system which operates when the reels are moved manually across the head. This is most helpful in editing.

—a monitor system which can be operated during recording. This is necessary only if you plan to undertake complicated productions without the facilities of a control room.

Nonprojected Visual Materials

Nonprojected materials offer a "do it yourself" approach to program enrichment. Materials which you make or mount will probably not have the slickness and scope of a film produced in Hollywood, but this is often overbalanced by the following advantages:

• When you create, or at least collect, your own materials they are almost certain to be related directly to your goals. There will be little danger of your regarding them as a substitute for preparation or as an independent form of entertainment.

• They can be adapted specifically to the local situation.

• When members of your group make or handle materials, their participation will stimulate learning.

• A nonprojected material can usually deal briefly and directly with a single concept. Thus a single picture or a simple flannelboard presentation may be more appropriate than a film for the attention-span and comprehension of a small child. A combination of various nonprojected materials may be used to express different aspects of a more complex frame.

• They are less expensive to use than most projected materials.

There is such a variety of nonprojected materials, with lengthy booklets available concerning almost every type, that we shall confine ourselves to listing a few practical suggestions concerning some of the common forms.

Chalkboards

Modern chalkboards are usually green, rather than black, thus contributing to the attractiveness and eye-comfort of the room. Most leaders use them, but few have thought seriously about their possibilities.

The chalkboard is more than a place to write words and other symbols for all to see simultaneously. Even this is an important function and calls for a clean, uncluttered board with symbols legible and large enough to be visible to the entire room. Beyond this, however, chalkboards may be used to visualize many concepts and relationships through such forms as outlines, diagrams, and maps.

For example, in studying biblical history and geography one member of your group may sketch on the chalkboard his version of a map of Palestine in relation to other lands. Other members may suggest and make revisions, then perhaps use colored chalk to indicate boundaries and divisions at different periods of history. The result can be compared with printed maps.

Flat Pictures

Flat or still pictures are among the most accessible and least expensive of all audio-visual materials. Usable illustrations can be found in most periodicals and others are available from commercial and educational distributors. They can be passed around a group and examined carefully by individuals. Children especially enjoy drawing or painting their own pictures, sometimes in such terms as "stained-glass" windows, and when they do, the value of the experience is increased both for the child, because of participation, and for the leader who can thus learn about the child from his creation.

Flat pictures can provide variety which helps to prevent stereotyping. Series of biblical films, featuring the same casts, are likely to standardize the impression of a character, especially because the motion picture lends more finality to characterization than do the still arts. It may not matter whether or not a generation grows up in the belief that Don Ameche invented the telephone but it may matter a great deal what impression children get of the personality of Jesus, especially if it is a saccharine, spineless portrayal. A committee of the Division of Christian Education of the National Council of Churches, appointed to study the problems of visualizing Bible characters and Bible teachings, reported, "In art the differing presentations of Jesus make for a wholesome balance as no single one is taken too realistically. In the motion picture medium the very realism may at times be a hindrance; especially children may be influenced adversely by a one-sided presentation of Christ. . . The frequent use of flat pictures is recommended to counteract and balance the impressions gained by the film." [1]

When you want all your group to see the same small picture simultaneously, opaque projection is the obvious solution.

Which pictures are worth showing to your group? To a great extent this is a matter of taste, of course, but there are certain generally accepted standards for selection:

- A picture should present a single, clear center of interest related to your purpose. The main idea visualized should be apparent immediately, and this should be an idea which is

---

[1] Adapted from "Visualization of Bible Characters and Bible Teachings." Copyright 1954 by the National Council of Churches. Used by permission.

relevant to your study theme. The picture should not be cluttered up with distracting or irrelevant details.

- The picture should be truthful. For newspapers, picture selection may still be dominated by the "man bites dog" theme but you will generally want to present scenes which are typical, rather than unique or startling. To portray South Africa exclusively through pictures of witch doctors is to deceive, rather than to clarify.

- High technical and artistic quality should characterize each picture. Photography, composition, and color should be attractive.

- In most cases the picture should stimulate the imagination, either through suggestion of new experiences or re-creation of previous ones. This may be accomplished by implied action, or "human interest," or, in the case of more sophisticated groups, by various forms of symbolism.

- A picture should be suitable to the age and background of your group. This is most important, of course, when a symbolic approach is used.

Other Flat Visual Symbols

Here we shall refer briefly to diagrams, charts, graphs, maps, posters, and cartoons, all of which are symbolic representations or explanations, rather than pictorial reproductions.

Diagrams and charts are condensed visual summaries of facts and ideas, clarifying relationships. Charts are primarily orderly arrangements of words and figures, but diagrams feature lines and symbols. Both usually require some background to be understood. The schematic diagram of your television receiver will not enable you to repair the set unless you have a knowledge of electronics. Generally, then, charts and diagrams are more useful in summary and review than in introduction of material. However, when your group begins with a body of common knowledge and your only purpose is to study relationships, charts and diagrams are appropriate. If, for example, questions arise concerning apparently overlapping responsibilities of various officers and committees with whom all are familiar, then a diagram will visualize the problem with its possible solutions for all to analyze.

So-called *turnover charts* often include not only charts and diagrams but pictures, graphs, and whatever else may be helpful for the presentation. These are mounted or printed on large sheets which are shown in sequence by flipping them over the top, where they are bound and supported in some fashion. Annual reports of group activities or proposed budgets may be presented in this way.

In making a chart or diagram (1) concentrate on key ideas and dispense with nonessentials, (2) use symbols large enough to be seen easily, (3) make it attractive through use of contrast, space, and perhaps color.

These same principles apply to *graphs,* which are a form of diagram but represent numerical data. They include (1) line graphs, probably the most accurate of all graphs and useful in plotting trends, growth, or frequency; (2) bar graphs, good for visualizing comparisons; (3) circle or pie graphs, useful for teaching the relationship of individual items to a whole; (4) pictorial graphs, using figures of varying sizes to represent large numbers. Thus, a man six inches tall may represent a population of a million; a man three inches tall or half a man six inches tall may represent a population of five hundred thousand. These are easily understood at a glance but are not precise.

Maps are another form of diagram visualizing geographical relationships. Many maps are available commercially, but homemade maps may focus on a particular area under study. One form of production is to utilize inexpensive or used light-colored window shades, painting the map with India ink or Tintex dyes.

The *cartoon* is another graphic form of representing ideas, situations, and relationships; and it also depends upon unity, clarity, and attractiveness. Distinctively, however, the cartoon features exaggeration and humor. Its appeal is demonstrated daily in the newspapers where most readers will look for the cartoon but neglect the editorials usually found on the same page and dealing with the same issue.

This situation also illustrates a weakness of the cartoon. It is usually an oversimplification, if not an outright distortion, and may tend to establish and perpetuate stereotypes. Realizing this, however, you may use cartoons to stimulate interest but supplement them with qualifications and additional information on which to base more mature judgments. In this process you may help to develop more discriminating viewers of cartoons.

From the cartoon has developed the amazingly popular, admittedly powerful form of communication, the *comic strip* and comic book. To many critics the comic book is a form of "Seduction of the Innocents," encouraging escapism, violence, and illiteracy. Some educators, on the other hand, defend the comic book as an art form and use it in the teaching of language, science, history, the social studies, and even religion. It is claimed that the comics personalize instruction and thereby stimulate interest in subject matter and in reading generally.

Somewhere between these extremes may be found a sensible view of this controversial medium.

Many current commercial comics obviously cater to low ethical standards and even lower esthetic tastes. Even some of the strips which profess to have constructive purposes seem to be influenced by the prevailing patterns; some of the religious series, for example, are characterized by poor art and specialize in sensationalism. The comic magazine has associations, at present, which make it difficult for discriminating viewers to regard it as a worthy form for presentation of significant ideas. Nevertheless, cartoon strips, merely as sequences of related drawings, have definite possibilities as teaching tools, especially with children and persons whose reading abilities are limited. They may be used to create interest conducive to learning, after which the skillful leader will be certain to introduce supplementary materials.

The *feltboard,* or flannelboard, or flannelgraph, takes advantage of the fact that wool and cotton felt will adhere to like surfaces. On a board covered with felt, various picture symbols are placed. When these symbols are made from felt or backed with felt or sandpaper, they will stay in place even when the board is in a vertical position. A presentation can be built up piece by piece, dismantled, and reassembled for review. Children especially enjoy placing the pieces on the board as a story is told. Words of quotations may be placed on the board in scrambled order for study and rearrangement. Alternative orders may also be considered—for example: "God is love" versus "Love is God."

The figure below shows a feltboard sequence used by a group of young people to focus their thinking on the relationship of their Christian faith to their occupational plans.

Many industrial organizations are using feltboards in sales work and personnel training, and the armed services have found them very effective in their "Character Education Program." At least one university professor believes that the feltboard is uniquely adaptable to the teaching of logic because it can so conveniently and effectively portray spatial designs which clarify relations between concepts. Both board and materials can be made at relatively little expense.

Three-Dimensional Materials

Some materials add a third dimension to visual images. Their realism offers a supplementary appeal to the sense of touch. Common three-dimensional materials are objects, models, and mock-ups, globes, terrain or relief maps, and dioramas.

Objects are simply the real things, usually taken from their natural setting to be used by your group. Objects of art from other civilizations may contribute to intercultural understanding.

Globes and relief or *terrain maps* are really forms of models. They visualize geographical relationships and may be used for such varying purposes as explaining principles of soil conservation, studying highway problems, or planning a trip. Many visitors to Chautauqua Institution, New York, have gained a new

Factors influencing oc-
cupational choice in-
clude income, prestige,
opportunities for ad-
vancement, leisure time,
family provisions. What
is missing?

When Christian commit-
ment is considered, is it
simply added to other
factors?

Should it, instead, re-
place some factors, such
as income, family con-
siderations?

Or does it become cen-
tral to all other factors?
Can you suggest a more
appropriate arrangement
of symbols to portray the
desired relationship?

understanding of the geography of the Holy Land by walking
around the acre-sized scale model of Palestine there.

The *diorama,* or three-dimensional picture, is another form of
model. From the Globe theater to television stage sets, dramatic
students have been using dioramas for many years. Students of

religious education have constructed many models of "typical Palestinian homes."

You will want to use three-dimensional materials when the addition of depth or substance will contribute to understanding; when it will help to see or touch an additional dimension. When you do use them, be certain they can be perceived in whatever way they are distinctive; this may mean seeing them at close range, or handling them, or operating them, as in the case of mock-ups. To be unable to do so is simply frustrating.

Nonprojected Audio-Visual Materials

Field trips and drama combine sight and sound without projection.

The possibilities in *field trips* are so affected by the location of your group that there is no point in devoting much space to a general discussion. Museums, art galleries, parks, farms, industries, utilities, courtrooms, and legislative chambers are only a few possible destinations of trips. Exchange visits with other groups, particularly with those from different social, economic, or religious backgrounds, may be revealing and stimulating. Field trips make it possible to observe and occasionally participate in firsthand experiences, but they are less selective than more contrived materials and demand an unusual amount of advance planning and careful follow-up. Your group will have to decide in each case whether or not a proposed trip will be worth the time required.

Projected Visual Materials

Desirable characteristics of projected materials include these elements:

—attractiveness. An image, projected by brilliant light onto a white screen in a darkened room, almost compels attention. Distractions are minimized and viewers are peculiarly receptive to personal influence in the privacy of the darkness.

—group visibility. The image is large enough for all to see simultaneously, small enough to be seen from a single vantage point.

Various lenses can make this true, regardless of the size of the original object or activity.

Other characteristics are not so desirable:

—Most projected visual materials are more expensive than audio or nonprojected materials.

—A rather high level of skill is required for their effective use.

In addition to these general characteristics, each type of projected material has its own distinctive features. Before proceeding to the familiar slides, filmstrips, and motion pictures, let us consider an instrument which serves as a link between projected and nonprojected materials.

The *opaque projector* enlarges to screen-size nontransparent materials such as flat pictures, maps, and diagrams. It will project outlines, clippings, sheets of typing, and music, all of which would be difficult to transfer to the chalkboard. Collections of pictures may be mounted, perhaps joined by masking tape and fed successively into the machine in an organized sequence. Potentially, therefore, opaque projection is extremely valuable.

You may have been discouraged by the big, clumsy machines which must usually be operated comparatively near the screen. Since reflected light is used, all possible outside light must be kept from the screen, and the image is still likely to be less brilliant than in the case of transparencies. The materials projected, especially books, sometimes become overheated when held on the screen for more than a short period of time.

Despite these limitations, however, the opaque projector is such a versatile instrument and will allow you to make use of such a wealth of illustrative material at little or no cost that it will be worth your time and effort to experiment with it. In purchasing an instrument, select one which will accommodate material up to 10″ x 10″ in size, which uses a 1,000 watt lamp and has an efficient cooling system. You will want one which reflects the most possible light with the least possible heat on the projected material.

At least one manufacturer offers an adapter which will convert slide-filmstrip projectors into small opaque projectors. The effective area projected, of course, is only as large as a 2″ x 2″ slide, but even this allows the user to create many inexpensive materials.

Slides and Filmstrips

Like the opaque projector, slide and filmstrip projectors make use of still pictures and other flat visual materials, but only after they have been converted into transparencies. Thus, production of materials for a single user is more complicated than in opaque projection, but duplication in quantity is made possible and projection is simplified.

Most modern slides are 2″ x 2″, the size popularized by the 35 mm. camera, although the older 3¼″ x 4″ size is still used occasionally, especially when slides are made by hand.

A filmstrip resembles a series of slides; it is a related sequence of still pictures or images on a single strip of 35 mm. film. Filmstrips are also available in two sizes, single or double-frame. Most projectors accommodate both types, but almost all commercially produced filmstrips are single-frame, making each transparency about half the size of a 2″ x 2″ slide.

Slides and filmstrips can be compared thus:

Slides	*Filmstrips*
1. Less expensive to produce *singly* than motion pictures or filmstrips.	1. Less expensive to produce *in quantity* than motion pictures or slides.
2. So easily produced and such a variety available that individual slides may be woven directly into local unit of work.	2. Can be moved quickly and simply through projector, especially desirable when accompanied by disc or tape.
3. Sequence of slides can be revised for various showings; time can be allowed during showing for discussion.	3. When script is presented live, rather than recorded, time can be allowed for discussion.

Both slides and filmstrips are limited by their inability to portray motion. Photographers and artists often suggest action, but their products remain essentially *still* pictures, and not motion pictures. A slide-set or filmstrip is not a cheap movie; it is comparable to a news column, or an editorial, or a nonfiction book rather than a short story or novel; it will often approach the function of a documentary but seldom that of the drama. Slides and filmstrips are less likely than motion pictures to involve emotions and influence attitudes, but they are often at least as effective as motion pictures in conveying information and stimulating discussion.

Since most groups will be using both slides and filmstrips, a combination slide-filmstrip projector will be most economical. In selecting one, look for these features:

—at least a 300 watt lamp—more wattage if your showings are to be seen by more than about one hundred people or if almost all extraneous light cannot be removed.
—efficient cooling system.
—appropriate lens. Most such projectors are equipped with a 5" projector lens, which is satisfactory for moderate-sized rooms, but if you expect to use the machine in a large auditorium also, it will be wise to purchase an additional longer lens, perhaps 7".
—efficiency of the lens system. You can compare the light output of various projectors with an ordinary light meter.
—slide carriage: ease in changing.
—filmstrip mechanism: it should support projected frames firmly enough to prevent them from going out of focus when heated.

Some projectors are equipped with automatic feed, remote-control frame change, or filmstrip-tape synchronization. Each feature could be desirable under some circumstances, but for most groups they are all unnecessary luxuries.

A variation of the slide projector is the *overhead transparency projector,* which is operated from the front of a room, rather than the back. The leader faces the group and writes or indicates important points on a plastic transparency which is projected on a mirror, which in turn reflects the image on a screen placed behind or in front of him. Writing on a plastic surface is done with a china-marking pencil and is wiped off with cleansing tissue. Most of these machines can be supplied with an adapter making possible the use of both 2" x 2" and 3¼" x 4" slides.

Motion Pictures

Motion pictures, commonly called simply "films," can be more realistic and more attention getting than other projected materials, but they are also likely to be less flexible and more expensive.

The illusion of motion, added to sight and usually sound, provides an element of *reality* which compels attention and involves emotions. The driver who has once had a serious auto accident may push the accelerator with careless vigor years later and statistics of traffic fatalities are not likely to lessen the pressure, but the film of an accident will probably revive his memory and influence his foot, at least temporarily.

Films not only portray actions but subject them to careful analysis by speeding them up or slowing them down. A flower may be seen to grow in seconds instead of in weeks; the reaction of a driver applying his foot to the brake pedal of a car may be observed in reference to the distance traveled during the process; centuries may be telescoped into minutes. These techniques, of course, may be confusing instead of helpful; a child's sense of historical time relationships is particularly subject to twisting when these techniques are employed. It is up to the leader to be aware of impressions received and to carify them when necessary.

The movement which adds reality and attractiveness to films also makes them *less flexible* for study purposes; it establishes a tempo, especially in dramatic productions, which cannot be interrupted without annoying observers. Unlike slides and filmstrips, films can seldom be stopped for discussion, nor can they be shown at varying speeds to suit the background of the viewers. To overcome this drawback many instructional films are being produced with accompanying filmstrips to be used at a more leisurely pace in follow-up sessions; a few are produced with unresolved endings to stimulate discussion. You may also wish to show a film a second time, substituting for the original sound track your own commentary or observations from your group.

Television

Television offers resources even beyond the range of motion pictures, featuring greater immediacy and less expense. Like radio, however, television confronts the leader with scheduling problems. In rare cases you may be able to show your group desired programs after they have been telecast by arranging with the station to borrow a kinescope, which can be shown on an ordinary 16 mm. sound projector. Magnetic tape recordings of both the sound and picture of telecasts, to be played back through a television receiver, should eventually simplify such delayed use of programs. Meanwhile, however, your group may find great value in viewing selected "live" programs and then discussing them. The "selected" programs need not always be those produced for educational or religious purposes; there are cultural implications in all the output of the mass media, and your group can profit from discriminating analysis of every type of program.

14. USE STORIES WITH A PURPOSE

"LET ME TELL THE STORIES, and I care not who writes the textbooks," said a teacher of history who was fond of stories and who used them to good purpose in his own teaching. Two of the Gospel writers summarize a portion of the ministry of Jesus by showing his use of stories. "All this Jesus said to the crowds in parables; indeed he said nothing to them without a parable" (Matt. 13:34, RSV). Think of the meetings where an important point was made clear or a significant decision assured by a good story aptly told. Small wonder, then, that stories are so widely used in church groups.

It should not be assumed, of course, that a leader will always resort to stories. Let him use a story when it appears that storytelling will serve his purpose better than any other method. The use of the story is good for such purposes as these:

- To motivate, as in a worship service.
- To introduce a new subject or curriculum unit.
- To introduce a problem or situation for discussion.
- To make a situation concrete.
- To help members of a group identify themselves with a character, cause, or situation.

394

Often the writer of program materials or of curriculum will suggest an appropriate story for a particular occasion. Often, however, the leader is left with a problem of selecting his own story. A good story has these qualities:

- Is in harmony with Christian faith and life.
- Is appropriate to the subject and the purpose of the session.
- Is suited to the interests and understanding of the group.
- Has good literary quality.
- Can be used effectively in the location and time schedule of the meeting.
- Is suited to the understanding and ability of the storyteller.

Though stories are used most frequently with children, they can be used to good effect with groups of any age.

Purpose and Basic Procedures in Storytelling

BY MARY ALICE JONES

It cannot be said too often that it is not the purpose of the church school to tell stories, not even to tell Bible stories. It is the purpose of the church school to guide children in Christian growth. In this purpose it often finds telling stories a very useful method.

Yet it is easy to expect too much of storytelling. Because a child listens to a story does not guarantee that he is learning from it what the teacher wishes him to learn. If he is told a story of Daniel refusing the king's meat, with the purpose of helping him to learn to stand for the right in hard places, it does not always follow that this is what he learns. There will be transfer from the story to the child's own life to the extent that the elements in the story are familiar. Now, present-day American children are not in the situation in which Daniel found himself; so the elements are not very similar.

To help the child "make connection," and yet avoid the offensive "pointing of a moral," the teacher may consider before the story is told the situations in the child's life in which the same quality of courage is required as that shown by Daniel. When the children have their own problem in mind, the teacher may say, "There is a story in the Bible of a boy who was in just such a jam. Of course, what he had to decide was not the same question you have to decide, because he lived long ago in a very different country. But what he did may suggest something to you."

After the story is underway, to interrupt it is to ruin it, for the

---

Mary Alice Jones, "Storytelling," *Guiding Children in Christian Growth* (Nashville: Abingdon Press, 1949), pp. 88–90. Used by permission.

396

story is a work of art. It is a unity, a whole, just as is a piece of statuary or a beautiful building. If the story is to have an opportunity to appeal to the children it must be handled as a work of art, as a whole, without interruptions and without the interjections of any comments of the teller. Let the story speak for itself. It will if it is a good story. The children will live with the characters, actually sharing their experiences.

If a story is to be well told, it must have a structure. First, it must have a beginning. This beginning must set the scene and introduce the characters. Then the characters must be in that setting, must be consistently themselves, and must take over the situation. To interpolate, "And then I think Joseph must have . . ." is to get Joseph off the stage and put the storyteller on. "And then, children, what do you think Joseph did?" brings the children back to themselves. Let Joseph do his own thinking and speaking and acting in his own character. Keep him on the stage.

After the character is introduced and the scene set, something must happen right away. The character must purpose, plan, carry out his plan, meet other characters, react to them, face problems, find solutions to them. The action must move from one incident to the next without tedious detours or unnecessary explanations. And each incident must grow out of those that have gone on before, so that the child understands why events come to pass as they do.

The incidents, however interesting in themselves, must get somewhere. They must not be just one incident after another. They must bring the characters to the place where they are able to solve their problem. This is the climax. After the climax is reached, the conclusion should follow quickly. The ends must be tied up neatly and the story concluded. And when it is ended, let it stand in its own right. If it has been a worthy story, well-told, it will win response on its own merit.

Most of the lesson materials contain stories written out for the teacher to tell. And most of them are well written. But no teacher can tell effectively a story someone has written without getting inside it herself and making it her own. She will not memorize it as it is written in the book, but she will live with it until she knows it. She will tell it aloud to herself or to some willing relative several times before she tells it to her class. When she knows it and when she appreciates it, she is likely to tell it well.

The parent and teacher will wish to select other stories for telling to their boys and girls, stories to meet special needs that arise, stories to supplement those provided in the lesson materials, stories for special days, stories for use in worship, stories for parties and recreation.

Preparing to Tell the Story

BY JEANETTE PERKINS BROWN

Become Thoroughly Familiar with It

You have found the climax. Read the story again and note how each item contributes to it. Eliminate any which seem irrevelant. Read again for the beginning and ending.

Visualize Your Characters

What do they look like? What are their names? What are their respective traits? Even if you are not going to describe them they must be clear in your own mind, so their actions and conversation will describe them. See them in one scene after another. One storyteller used to say she pictured in her imagination the scenes as in framed pictures on a wall. But they must have been "stills." Some would prefer visualizing motion pictures, to remind them how one bit of action leads to another or prevents another.

Make an Outline

Write out an outline that will include:

- Introduction: names, setting, situation, with indication of the hope or problem;
- Action: the sequence of events which show progress towards the climax and obstacles as they are met;
- Climax (be sure it is an answer to the curiosity and anticipation aroused in the introduction);

Jeanette Perkins Brown, *The Storyteller in Religious Education* (Boston: The Pilgrim Press, copyright, 1951), pp. 53, 56. Used by permission.

• Conclusion, which winds everything up quickly and satisfyingly.

After a while you will be able to do this outlining in your mind, but even experienced storytellers often jot down these items. They aid memory and provide brief notes which can be filed to recall the story at a future time.

Tell the Story to Yourself

You'll probably have forgotten some item. Go back to the book, refresh your memory, but do not concentrate on memorizing the story word for word. That would be restricting; what you are after is to impress a picture or a sequence on your mind.

Tell the story again—as often as possible—to anyone who will listen, adding conversation and details which you feel enrich the story for your particular audience.

The story is now yours. You are ready to share it appreciatively as you would an interesting or challenging experience.

Techniques in Storytelling

BY JEANETTE PERKINS BROWN

Telling versus Reading

As a storyteller you have the advantage over the one who reads a
story. There is nothing between you and your listeners. You look
directly into their faces. There is a rapport established between
you not possible when you are following the printed page. You
are not bound by the phrasing of the author, but are telling his
story in your own words. You are communicating something worth
while. Your coming upon it was a delightful (enlightening, worshipful) experience for you; you want to share it. That others
may share it fully, you study the ways of making your story effective.

Comfort

You take care that your listeners are comfortable. They can all
see your face, so continual scraping of chairs or craning of necks
will not be necessary. They can all hear your voice, for you speak
to the back row, not the front. The ventilation must be good, or
at the end of what you consider a successful effort, you may look
at faces flushed with heat rather than interest, and the only comment you will hear will be like Freddie's "I'm thweat'n'."

You are comfortable yourself. Your collar is not too tight, your

Jeanette Perkins Brown, "Telling the Story," *The Storyteller in Religious
Education* (Boston: The Pilgrim Press, copyright, 1951), pp. 61–65, 68–71.
Used by permission.

belt needs no adjustment. You know your story; every character is clear to you, every scene is a picture in your mind, every act is a part of a sequence leading to a climax. Your own mastery of the situation arouses confidence in your listeners that you know where you are going.

Naturalness

If standing, do not strike an unusual attitude, but stand in a natural position (natural for good posture, of course, with feet together and hands at ease). If sitting, your manner is intimate and conversational. If it is natural for you to use gestures with hands or body, use them, but do not force or overdo them for what you think is dramatic effect. You are telling a story, not acting. Anything which comes between the story and the listener is bad. Your desire to make your story dramatic might mean that you are spotlighting your own ego, instead of the story.

Do not use meaningless gestures. Leave beads and buttons alone; keep hands quiet, or they, too, may divert attention. You remember the story of the judge whose idle tearing of paper into bits throughout the defense testimony so distracted the jury that they hardly heard it and brought in a verdict that won the case for the prosecuting attorney.

Voice

Speak in a natural tone of voice, but project it. Do not keep it caged in the roof of your mouth or back in your throat. Breathe deeply, from the diaphragm, and your voice will project itself more surely.

Avoid honeyed accents. Cultivate variety of tone; children loathe monotony. "How would you like it," a junior girl once asked a leader, "if your teacher just went 'oooooooooooo' all the time? I like people to go 'oo-oo-oo-oo-oo-oo-oo.'"

In telling stories to children, imitate sounds indicated in your story, winds blowing, thunder rumbling, dogs barking. Part of the attraction of *The Little Engine That Could* lies in the variety of sounds the engines make. Change your voice to suit the age and character of the one speaking. One can hardly imagine the Three Bears all using the same voice as they go through their house after Goldilocks has been there.

Hurry when swift action is indicated. Let your voice reflect wonder, strength, joy, as called for. Use pauses for impressiveness or to increase suspense.

Never let your voice get flat; you will see interest waver. Remember you are communicating something, not reciting.

Look at Audience

Speak directly to the audience as in a conversation, looking at them instead of over their heads into space. Avoid, however, fixing your glance on one victim until he squirms. Take in the whole audience as you talk, so there will be no danger of a child on the outskirts begging, at the close, "Now tell it to *me!*"

Tell the Story Creatively

Use your imagination in the telling, and your listeners will use theirs. Someone has said, "A story is not what you say, but what you see; it is not what a child hears, but what he sees."

Though storytelling is not acting, the unfolding of a story is like the unfolding of a drama. But a play has scenery and characters and off-stage devices to help create realism. The storyteller must, single-handed, supply sights and sounds and actions of the drama. She must make each character come alive, every scene clear and vivid. If you are a beginner, keep your outline in your hand so you will not wander off the path of sequence.

Make the Characters Come Alive

They will not come to life merely by your talking about them; for example: "Jesus was always helping people"; "David was a brave boy"; "The disciples learned a great many lessons about helping people." The storyteller may *say* that a person is thus and so, but that does not convince us. We want to see the person in action, we need to hear him speak; then we can judge for ourselves. We must in our imagination *see* Jesus in the act of causing a sick man to rise from his bed and walk. Let us *see* David killing that lion that threatened his flock. We want to be in the room where Jesus got water and a towel, and *see* him act out a lesson.

Keep Your Characters Moving

Let them describe themselves. Note, in the following excerpt, how much is told about these characters entirely by what they do and say.

> Now it so happened one day that a man came to Chihua who was rich and big and drove a motor car, and he knew beautiful things when he saw them.
>
> "Aaaah, ooooh," sang the singing potter, rolling his pushcart down the road, "Aaah, ooooh."
>
> "How much?" called a woman, stopping the cart and shifting her baby on her hip.
>
> "Five cents. A bowl to keep rice and beans for a whole family. . . ."
>
> "Hé!" cried the woman, "five cents is a great sum for a bowl."
>
> "But not for a singing potter's bowl. Happiness—"
>
> "Say four cents."
>
> "Happiness goes with it. Joy—"
>
> "Wait," cried the big rich man, getting out of his car. "Wait; I'll give you fifty cents for that bowl."
>
> Now in all the history of Chihua no one had ever said such a thing as this. But the potter stood firm.
>
> "Five cents," he said, looking at the woman.
>
> "Here," she replied, slipping the coin into the potter's hand.
>
> "A dollar," shouted the big rich man.
>
> "Ah, señor, it is sold." [1]

The author has depended for her effect much more on verbs

---

[1] From "The Singing Potter" by Dorothy F. McConnell, in *Sugar Is Sweet* by M. E. Forsyth and D. F. McConnell. Quoted in *Missionary Stories to Tell*, The Friendship Press. Used by permission.

than on adjectives, and on the speech of the characters themselves, rather than any observations about them.

Use Direct Discourse

Nothing makes a character come alive more than the use of direct discourse: "And he said unto them"—Jesus' voice is almost heard in what follows. The stories would sound quite different if the narrator had used indirect discourse: "He told them that—" "He reminded them that—"; or "He asked him what the law said and the lawyer told him that it said to love God with all one's heart and all one's soul and all one's strength and all one's mind, and one's neighbor as oneself. Jesus told him he had answered correctly and if he did that he would live."

Supposing the author of "The Singing Potter" had written:

> The rich man got out of his car and went towards the potter. He could not persuade him to sell the bowls. He told him he would be famous and rich, but when the potter still refused, he went back to his car, thinking the potter was stupid, while the potter thought him just as stupid.

That was not the way Dorothy McConnell told the story. She makes us see pictures, and hear speech, and feel personalities.

> "Come, come!" cried the big rich man impatiently. "I will buy all your pottery, . . . and I will pay you much, much money to make bowls and jugs and pots like these."
>
> "But then," objected the potter, "what would the people of Chihua do for their pots and bowls and jugs?" . . .
>
> "You would become famous if you worked for me. And certainly you would be rich."
>
> "Señor," and the potter shook his head and looked troubled, "I know nothing about all that. It sounds very strange to me. I make my wares for Chihua." And he shrugged his shoulders politely. . . .
>
> "Oh, these stupid natives," said the big rich man to himself as he drove his car down the road. "They will not do what is for their own good."
>
> "Ah, these stupid foreigners," said the singing potter to himself as he trundled his cart up the hill. "They think that money is everything." . . .

"Aaah, oooh," came the sound of the singing potter's voice from the road beyond Chihua. "Honk! Honk!" went the big rich man's motor horn.[2]

Direct discourse here is even carried to the motor horn, to make the final picture vivid, leaving the listener to make his own appraisal of the characters and their viewpoints.

Use "Action" Verbs

In conversations in your story, choose verbs that in themselves describe a character's appearance or mood. It is the movement in the verb that makes the character come to life, and incidentally avoids wordiness.

"Well," he grumbled, "I'll do it this once."

We see him. He is living, breathing, scowling. You know how he feels. That one verb "grumbled" tells as much as if a paragraph were used to describe him.

Compare the following two ways of showing a reaction. Which is more alive? Which makes you feel more awe?

1. "Not *really?*" she gasped.
2. Marcia couldn't believe it.

So also, "she sighed," "he bellowed," "she wavered," "she panted," picture living, breathing persons. Verbs are alive. Her eyes *blazed*. His fists *tightened*. Her dimples *twinkled*. His steps *lagged*. Her gaze *wandered*.

Making Scenes Vivid

In drama there are lights, color, and properties to create the proper atmosphere and give realism. The story must supply this atmosphere. It is like a game, trying to find words which will immediately conjure up settings and give the desired impression. Study Anne Lindbergh's *North to the Orient* to see what words can do to make you see and feel; or the Cratchits' Christmas dinner in Dickens' *Christmas Carol,* to make you smell and taste! This is fun. Put your creative imagination to work—or play.

---

[2] From "The Singing Potter."

There is a point in your story where it is quiet. How quiet? Make your listeners almost stop breathing for fear they will disturb it. "It was so still you could have heard the new grass growing."

It is a hot day. How will your audience know? Can you make them realize it through every sense until they *hear* it with the midsummer insects buzzing at their ears, and *feel* it in the torrid breeze, and *taste* it in the dry dust, and *smell* it in the heavy scents from the garden, and *see* it in the dripping brows, until the audience's tongues are hanging out, and they're reaching for fans?

That sense appeal is important. To make an impression clear ask yourself, What would it look like, feel like, sound like? Did it have a taste, an odor? What were they like?

In Frances Weld Danielson's book, *The Practice Storytelling Class,* the teacher says, "Describe a giant so I shall see him."

READY-TO-TRY: Once there was a big, tall man.

LEADER: I don't see him.

READY-TO-TRY: He was very tall.

LEADER: I don't care.

QUICK-AS-A-FLASH: Don't you care if he was as tall as the moon?

LEADER: Yes, I do. Now you've done it. You've given me something with which to measure my giant. Can somebody do this without exaggeration?

READY-TO-TRY: A giant is at least a foot taller than a tall man.

LEADER: You forget that I'm posing as a small child, and that to me a foot means only the foot on the end of a leg."

SLUGGARD: A giant is taller than the tallest man you ever saw. Once a giant stood beside a man and he put his elbow on the man's head.

QUICK-AS-A-FLASH: Once there was a giant, and he was as tall as this (*raising her hand high above her head*).

CYNIC: There was a giant who was so tall that when he lay down he had to put his feet out of the window.

LEADER: Splendid! Do you know what you three have done? You've used comparison and gesture and action, to make me see your giant. All of them are good storytelling methods.[3]

Creating Suspense

We know how important the suspense element is in story, motion picture, or drama. Remember the story lacks "punch" without it. A boy wants something. As you tell the story, make him want it terribly. Make your listeners feel with him that life just won't be worth living if he can't have it. He has thought of it, dreamed of it, saved for it for weeks. Don't let him get it too easily! Put plausible obstacles in his path, even if they are imaginary obstacles which occur to you, one after another. They will be real to him, likewise to your listeners. Make the realization of his dream a tremendous relief because of the uncertainties you have emphasized.

If you are telling a biographical story you will be working towards a climax, whether the story is to be told as a whole or serially. If serially, each chapter, though a step towards the grand climax, should have its own high point, which is reached through difficulty. Make the difficulty the point of struggle towards accomplishment of that one step.

Gentle Student, if the story you have chosen—from fiction, biography, or text—lacks the dramatic element to make it "come alive," bring it to life yourself by your own creative imagination, supplying it with vitamins of direct discourse, action verbs, vivid picturing, comparisons and contrasts—and suspense.

Questions and Interruptions

The children's storyteller who asks a rhetorical question in the midst of her story must expect anything but a rhetorical answer.

---

[3] From *The Practice Storytelling Class*, Frances W. Danielson. The Pilgrim Press. Used by permission.

We think the lady in California who interrupted the story of the Flood to ask of a child more engrossed in showing off her new dress, "Anna-Marie, what would you say if it rained forty days and forty nights without stopping?" deserved the response, "I'd say it was very unusual."

But when the questions come from the children, they are often contributions and indicate interest and attention. Children's comments are usually not interruptions. Sometimes they show how much they are identifying themselves with the story—of a boy named John, for instance: "My brother's name is John"; or of Chinese children playing jackstones: "I play that game."

Sometimes their questions are for clarification. "What does that word mean?" "Miss——, you use such big words my head goes round and round." Welcome such "interruptions" and learn from them not to soar above their spinning heads.

Two Don'ts

In telling your story, if you suddenly discover you've left out an important point, *don't* try to correct yourself with, "Oh, I forgot to say. . . ." You confuse and may lose your audience. Bring in the item as naturally as you can wherever it best fits into the sequence, as if you'd meant it to be there all along.

And *don't* tack on a moral to your tale!

Suggestions for Using the Story with Youth

BY CLARICE M. BOWMAN

All the world loves a story! The worker with young people can improve his skills in the fine art of storytelling, and can encourage young people themselves to do so. Children's workers make abundant use of stories; perhaps fuller use may be made with intermediates, seniors, and older youth. Too often, when used, they are not used wisely and well!

For example, in some churches, apparently the use of stories is thought of in connection with "devotionals"—yet, upon analysis, this devotional or worship period should instead be God-centered rather than instructional. The function of the story is to impart information and to bid for vicarious identification; when used as a part of a learning process when the thoughts thus gathered can be discussed and further evaluated, the story proves tremendously useful. But in average Sunday school "devotionals"—aside from a vague moralistic tone—the long and sometimes highly symbolic stories tend to focus minds upon a subject other than that which will be discussed later in the lesson units, and to take up time needlessly both from the God-centered worship experience and from the lesson following.

In a class group or youth fellowship, in the ongoing unit, one or several little stories may be needed. Let the atmosphere be created, either by the setting around the group, or by the very spirit of the storyteller. At a campfire out-of-doors, it may be

Clarice M. Bowman, "Meaningful Use of Carefully Selected Stories," *Ways Youth Learn* (New York: Harper & Brothers, 1952), pp. 103–104. Used by permission.

easier for a group to transport themselves in imagination to the campfires of Hebrew nomads as they moved from one watering place to another, and paused at nightfall for the oldest member of the tribe to recount the ever-thrilling story of Jehovah's dealings with His people . . . episodes of epic grandeur imparting a sense of security and infinite worth to the individual and to the group. Or perhaps the young people are having a unit on devastation wrought by war and pathways to peace and they have a refugee campfire, imagining how homeless peoples must feel; perhaps a sacrificial meal can be partaken around the fire, with offering for relief. In their meeting room in the evening, the lights may be shaded for a folk-story hour; or in candlelight, the biography of a giant of the Christian faith may walk into their very midst, thrilling them with the possibilities in human personality when the living God works through someone. Music or pictures used along with stories may help enhance the meanings.

Stories may also be used to startle. At the beginning of a unit opening up a raw problem in human relationships, a story may be launched right into—with no attempt to build atmosphere first. The impact of the facts will speak for themselves. Committees of young people, assisting the adult worker in planning for their units for Sunday school and evening meeting, may find and prepare such "openers." Excerpts from the best works of modern fiction and drama may help bring problems before the youth. The relating of recent incidents in community life may point up the stark need for doing something about the evils thus felt. With such situations, a leader may leave a story unfinished, challenging the group to decide what the ending should be.

15. USE DRAMA IN ITS DIFFERENT FORMS

DRAMA HAS LONG BEEN USED in the work of the church, and it has appeared in many different forms. Traditionally, drama involved performance before an audience, and the work of preparation was done for the sake of a high-quality performance. It was often discovered, however, that the finest values were the understanding and maturity gained by the characters themselves in the process of their preparation. One who is concerned about Christian nurture would say, therefore, that the process was more significant than the performance.

In more recent years drama has taken on varied forms. There is informal dramatization, entirely without audience. There is playreading, often with little rehearsal. There are psychodrama and sociodrama, now becoming popularized in the form of role playing. The following readings seek to interpret these various forms of drama and to show their place and values for church groups.

The Place and Value of Drama in the Church

BY HAROLD EHRENSPERGER

The church is rediscovering the arts. That is, the church is finding again that even the most profound thought ceases to hold attention unless it is put into artistic expression. To put a thought form into words, on a canvas, in the action of drama, in glass, stone and steel, through the creative imagination, is to make it arresting as well as significant in a unique way.

Drama is one of the major art forms to be a part of this renaissance in the church. It is the form that brings characters to life at crisis moments through dialogue and action. All art has attempted to capture the highest and purest revelation of the spirit. In drama this spirit is seen in action at conflict moments which produce a crisis. Religious drama may be judged by how much the creative spirit is shown to work constructively in crises to overcome the disintegrating forces of this world.

Christian drama finds its origins and its continuing illustration in the life of Jesus. His life is "the" Christian drama because it unfolds the spirit of God taking on flesh and living in the world creatively against the forces that sought to kill it.

Christian drama begins with the birth of Jesus as the evidence of a divine-human force free to work constructively in the world— to overcome the world. It continues as this force meets the temptations of the world, refuses to yield to them, gathers strength through followers and seeks to establish in man and through man

Harold Ehrensperger, "Drama Is at Home in the Church," *International Journal of Religious Education*, June, 1956, pp. 17, 18, 34. Used by permission.

a kingdom of the spirit. The drama is heightened as it progresses in the life of Jesus to what seems the great tragic moment of the betrayal and crucifixion. The resurrection is the overcoming moment which turns the drama from tragedy to what might be called the "divine comedy."

To a degree, all Christian life follows the same pattern. It rises to noble heights as each man masters and overcomes the negative forces of his own person and those of the world. When it is temporarily overcome by these forces, it produces tragedy. When the spirit is triumphant, man achieves a Christ-like character. This is seen in the lives of martyrs and saints, in the men and women whose long shadows have made Christian history a glorious chronicle, and even in us, today, as Christ's spirit becomes flesh in us and our action reveals for the moment, for the present, this "now," the living Word.

Drama is the only art form which uses life as its material. Painters use canvas; writers, words; sculptors use stone, metal and wood as materials—the dramatist uses living people who act out for a present moment the life situation he has created. Drama is not complete until it is finally alive, until even the words of the script, the dialogue, become flesh; that is, until it is acted. Its appeal, its reality for both actors and congregations—both participants—is in terms of life.

Through drama names become people, stories become situations and even great literature takes on added values when its words become alive in people. This gives drama an immediacy, an importance for the moment that is unique in the arts. In its expression it is experienced only once. However, it comes a part of experience through memory.

It is a face to face confrontation of life for the moment when it is alive in the play.

Creative Drama with Children

Drama uses techniques which are natural to man. This is evident, for instance, in the play of children. This play is dramatic because it is the expression of their imagination, their ideas, as these take form and come alive. The child first creates situations that are simple; he imagines himself a man, a woman, an animal or a machine. He plays being these. His first dramatic experience is in making these come alive.

As he grows older the child combines with these "live" characters situations in which they can play a part—a home, a school, a city, a farm, or whatever frame of reference he is familiar with. Still later he begins to create stories or to make stories come alive. In these there are opposing forces, good and bad, and he generally continues the action until the good force has triumphed. As he acts the parts, he feels an immediacy in relation to the story and the "role" that is drama's most effective educational value.

Play loses its dramatic value for children when it ceases to be creative expression and is organized and imposed upon a person or group. It then becomes production of a drama created by someone else and the creative act is confined to acting and production.

The dramatic method may be used with children to bring to life religious values such as love and sharing, or to make biblical characters become real. The primary and junior teacher has always used the dramatic method to interest children in content material or to help them see how principles of living can be carried out in action. Role playing is as natural as any play the child experiences.

Older children are genuinely interested in role playing. Sometimes this can take the form of acting out in their own way a Bible story which has relevance to their own experiences. What a real experience the Good Samaritan story becomes when, with the group, the boy or girl creates the characters of the Priest, the Levite, or the Good Samaritan! It is much more than a story told in an ancient book by a person named Jesus. It is a present day situation related to ideas in Scouting, to the best conduct he has heard about. It is an experience in education as real as life itself.

He will want to play the role of Jesus, too, and with imagination he can construct stories about the choosing of the disciples,

Jesus' relation to his family, to the people who sought to stop his teaching, and to the little group of followers who were to go with him throughout his ministry.

Drama with Junior Highs and Young People

Junior highs are genuinely interested in role playing, created by themselves to illumine problems they themselves face in life. They will also like to act out stories from the lives of the saints, from episodes in the lives of figures in church history, including those who in our own day are making Christianity a realized life pattern.

As they grow older, young people will want to use printed plays. Those dealing with seasons of the church year are valuable. Interesting celebrations for the great days of the year can become a recognized part of the church program.

Young people need to learn the difference between the theatrical, which should not be brought into the church, and the dramatic. The theatrical expression is always external, something put on. The dramatic is always genuinely felt, arises in the inner self and moves outward.

There are problems in the use of drama in the church school that are not easy to solve. One of these is the time element. If the creative method is used with the junior high age, the church school period ought to be extended if any consistent work is done. At least a full hour is needed to tell a story, select the boys and girls who are to play it, create the play action and then discuss what has been done, replay the action with another group, perhaps, and finally make judgments as to the group accomplishment.

The creative method is valuable through the junior high school age. For senior high and older groups, simple plays can be used if there is sufficient time for rehearsal. Formal plays to be presented before audiences or pageant-plays to be done for the church necessitate organization and rehearsal of a much longer time. The value of group participation, or co-operative endeavor, as well as personal values that have to do with personality development, are all assets inherent in the use of drama.

Drama with Adults

Older groups can use plays for readings if there is careful planning and direction. Plays built on subjects where religious values are brought to bear on the situation and where religious living is demonstrated can be "brought to life" as they are read by the group. This necessitates a loan or purchase of sufficient copies for the principal characters, but the books can be kept for further use for succeeding groups in the same age group. The use of this method has not been sufficiently explored by older young people and adults.

Sociodrama has become a recent vogue and it has a valuable contribution to make to the educational work of the church. It is adult creative drama. Examples of this form are found in the plays of Nora Sterling written for the Mental Health Association.

Any situation that raises social problems, that calls for ethical and moral decisions, can come alive in the creative adventure of playing the role. A typical life situation can be selected, a "plot" created to show the conflict or struggle with the resultant solution or with the question left to the individual to decide. The actors create the roles, making up the lines after they have thought through the action and have decided on the outcome. Naturally this form can be used only for the participating group and is not judged on the basis of a play that is performed. Its purpose is to allow people to play a role or to set forth a situation so that it is made real and convincing.

Interest in drama is life-long. It may begin with play, continue through creative drama, reach its most appealing form in the formal playing of older young people, and be interesting and stimulating as acting or as reading for any adult. Since drama is action that makes a story live in the "now," it can come alive for any age group at any time in any place. It can be as simple or as complex as the group wishes. It is always arresting and valuable because it gives a perspective to life as seen through the action of persons at crisis moments.

How to Dramatize a Story

BY ARMILDA KEISER

Here's Why

The "acting out" of incidents, characters, and ideas of worth helps children not only to remember the story but to gain insight into the way characters in the story feel and better to understand their own feelings about the decisions, choices, and behavior of people in the story. It helps to create a friendly feeling for the character dramatized. There's a fancy word for it, if that helps—identification. "Children need to identify," say the mental hygiene experts.

Here's How

Know well the story to be dramatized.

Tell the story to the children. Use conversation more than description. As the characters begin to "come alive," the children will identify themselves with the people in the story.

Help the children to decide upon the main point of the story. They will have good ideas about this. A question such as "What is it we want our play to tell?" will start them thinking. Guide the children in choosing the scenes to play. Write a list of scenes on the board.

Now for the characters! Use only those that will help make the main point clear.

The story again, please! After the group have done all this thinking and discussing, they will need to hear the story again to

Armilda Keiser, "Dramatize a Story," *Here's How and When* (New York: Friendship Press, 1952), pp. 15–17. Used by permission.
418

be sure that they don't wander too far from it. Some changes may be called for.

What should the characters say? The children will help with suggestions and from them will come ideas for dialogue. The exact wording of the story will often be used, but encourage the children to use their own phrases also.

Who will be who? Children have pretty good ideas about which person will be suitable for a certain part. Questions such as "Who will be Little Plum Blossom (or Sita or Rosita)? Who will be Little Brother?" will help. It is a good idea to let different children take turns at playing the parts. This is better than the tryout, which is too competitive.

What shall we use? The props may be as simple as desired or as complicated. A simple story calls for simple props. The children's imagination can supply a lot. Again questions may be used to bring forth ideas: "What shall we use for a kite? What can we have for a hospital bed?"

If it is planned to present a story to a group of visitors, scenery and costumes may be wanted. A backdrop may be painted on large sheets of paper and tacked to a wall to give atmosphere.

Consult books and pictures for information about trees, flowers, and whatever details will prove helpful to those painting scenery or arranging a stage set.

Dress up if possible. A scarf, a ribbon, or a shawl can work wonders. You can arrange them to look like the clothes of the boys and girls in the pictures you consult.

A play being given for parents and friends may have programs and ushers, if desired. But the play should be given chiefly for the enjoyment of the class.

The play is NOT so important as the children. Annie may be a too-fat princess, but she'll stand taller and feel less like the little tub she is if she has a chance to play the part of somebody "elegant."

In the Sunday-Morning Class

BY MARY ALICE DOUTY

Many a teacher has said, "I can't use drama in the Sunday school . . . I haven't a room for my class. Other classes are all around us. How could I let my class act out a play?"

But teachers in similar situations have used the dramatic method in teaching. The essential of drama is getting into the character of another person. For this no props, no scenery, no costumes are necessary. Action even can be dispensed with.

We are not speaking here of "putting on a play." Rather we speak of living the mind of the character in the play.

A group of intermediates questioned the story of the feeding of the multitude. They had read the account of the boy who offered his lunch to the Master and saw it distributed to feed thousands.

"How could he do it?" said one boy flatly. "I just don't think that's possible."

The teacher in preparation had thought through the same problem. She was aware of the difficulties involved in questioning a miracle. She knew the solution suggested by some that the boy's act of generosity had prompted others in the group until everyone shared and there was much left over. Would the boys and girls think that a suitable explanation? Was it better to say simply that there are some things we don't understand, but that with God all things are possible? Or was there perhaps a deeper lesson in the story for these questioning intermediates?

She thought there was, and she made ready to approach the

Mary Alice Douty, *How to Work with Church Groups* (Nashville: Abingdon Press, 1957), pp. 127–130. Used by permission.

matter through re-creating the boy in the minds of her students.

When the challenge came, the teacher waited. There were comments from the group about this and other miracles. Honest doubts and some fears were expressed. If you didn't believe the miracles, what could you believe?

At this point the teacher asked, "What is a miracle?"

That stumped the group momentarily. Then a girl said, "Well, it's something supernatural."

Another said, "It's something happening that you know couldn't happen."

"Suppose you took a radio to a primitive tribe of people and turned it on. Would they think that was a miracle?" asked the teacher.

The group agreed that they might. They decided that there might be cases where a miracle had some explanation which was unknown to those who saw it.

"We don't know everything," the teacher reminded them. "And I'm sure we don't know all the power of God. But I think there's another kind of miracle in the story we have read. Think about that boy and try to imagine his home and his day."

From what they knew of Palestine, the intermediates imagined the boy's home, his mother and father. Their teacher led them to wonder how it happened that this boy was in the crowd at Jesus' feet. They developed conversation that might have taken place in the boy's home that morning. They called the boy David, and the conversation ran something like this:

DAVID: Mother! Joel says that the Teacher is in our village. He says that everyone is going to listen to him on the hill outside the town. Joel's going. Mother, may I go? Can't you and Father go too?

FATHER: What teacher? What are you talking about, boy?

DAVID: His name is Jesus. And already there are people leaving town to hear him. Joel heard him once and he says that there is no one like him. Can't we go, please?

FATHER: I have work to do. Other people can sit around. I must get to the shop.

DAVID: Please, Mother. I want so much to hear him. Can't you and I go?

MOTHER: Not I, David. I have too much work to do. But you may go if it means so much to you. It's a good day to be outdoors. I'll pack a lunch for you.

That ended scene 1. The group was satisfied as to why the boy was in the crowd and alone. When they got into scene 2, they made two important discoveries. In all that crowd the boy was on the front line, close enough to hand his lunch to Jesus. Then they discovered something else, even more startling to intermediates. Apparently the boy had been with the crowd all day. It was now evening. And the boy hadn't touched his lunch! What was more, when lunch was mentioned, instead of feeling his hunger and eating, the boy gave his lunch to the Master.

"What a man he must have been!" said one boy, not irreverently.

They worked out a dialogue for the boy, the Master, and a disciple for scene 2. As they thought and as they talked, a new understanding of the personality of Jesus emerged. The physical miracle was unimportant to them now, so much greater was the impact of the man, not only on the boy of twenty centuries ago, but on themselves today.

Did this teacher need a private room for her class? Not at all. The crowded corner or the pew in the one-room church offers no barrier to creative dramatic thinking—unless the barrier be in the mind of the teacher.

In the Small Church

BY VIRGIL FOSTER

One of the most creative activities used in teaching is dramatization. One need only to watch children at play for a few minutes to see how real to the child is the imaginary hospital where he is the doctor. The play storekeeper is in business in a big way. The adventure story on television is not followed by a discussion—it calls forth stick daggers, imitation six-shooters, and bandanas knotted around the neck as the story is re-enacted by youthful cowboys or bandits.

The small church school too frequently rules out this method of teaching because of lack of space. But many Bible stories do not demand much space nor do they attract the attention of other classes if simple dramatizations are selected.

The story of the good Samaritan is a good story, but it is filled with words and images that do not always register with a child. Although he may repeat with the teacher the important words, "Which of these three, do you think, proved neighbor to the man who fell among robbers?" the repetition of words does not always mean realization of their meaning. On the other hand, if a group discusses the story and then acts out the scene simply, the process of living the characters for a few minutes makes them very real to the participants and adds interest for the spectators.

One sixth-grade class of boys had in its membership a noisy, unco-operative youngster, somewhat larger than the other boys. One class period centered on the story of Nehemiah and his work

Virgil Foster, *How a Small Church Can Have Good Christian Education* (New York: Harper & Brothers, 1956), pp. 29–31. Used by permission.

in rebuilding the walls of Jerusalem. The teacher told the story in words the children could understand but at the same time built the situation into a dramatic episode, ending with Nehemiah's lecture to the workers on the necessity of their working together to accomplish the seemingly impossible task they had undertaken. The story ended, the teacher suggested they might make a short play out of it. The incorrigible boy was selected to be Nehemiah, while the class became the men on the wall assembled to hear their leader. The space needed for dramatization was no more than the group was occupying for the class session. The youthful Nehemiah gave his classmates a scorching lecture on co-operation that even Nehemiah would have been glad to hear. It also corrected his tendency to be a troublemaker. He was committed before his classmates to greater co-operation.

Perhaps few adults would select the story of Moses and the burning bush as their choice to tell to third-grade children. But it was the required lesson for a mixed class. The teacher told the story exactly as the Bible recounts it. Then she asked if the children would like to play the story and suggested that one of the boys be thinking who would make a good Moses while the other children suggested the necessary props for the setting. They decided the only object needed would be something for a burning bush, whereupon a vase on a table near them was put onto the floor to be the bush. For Moses, the casting boy selected a beautiful curly-haired girl. The teacher suggested that each child find Exodus 3:12 and hold the Bible on his lap till the verse was needed. The acting began. Moses stood silently beside the bush while several seconds passed. Then she shook her head solemnly. "No, God, I can't do it." Another silence. "No, God, I'm not smart enough." A longer silence. "God, why don't you ask my brother, he can talk better than I can." Silence again. Then, "All right, God, if you will really go with me maybe I can do it. At least, I'll try." A signal from the teacher and the children read in whispers, "Certainly I will be with thee."

No space needed, no equipment required, no noise, no confusion. But a great experience in living with Moses and God for a few minutes. Not every story will lend itself to dramatic treatment but the good teacher looks for dramatic possibilities in situations that can be handled even in small quarters.

Playreading Has Many Uses

BY JAMES H. WARREN

"Say, I'd like to be in the church play, but I just haven't got the time." This is a familiar comment. Drama in the church is a fine thing to have, but only now and then, because it takes up too much time. And when one thinks of drama he thinks of actors, costumes, lights, scenery, and long periods of preparation. But good as all these things are, they are not absolutely essential. For the magic of audience and actor feeling together a great dramatic moment can be had without these things. Give a person or group of persons a script and have it read before an audience, and the conditions of drama are fulfilled.

Playreading for An Audience

"A playreading? But that sounds so dull. No scenery? No costumes? I don't call that very dramatic." This was the response of one youngster who had never seen an effective playreading. The truth is that effective play "readings" can create the same experience as that found in a fully produced play. The difference is that the emphasis is on the voice and acting, with the audience invited to imagine all the effects the stage hands would ordinarily create.

The actor reads his script with understanding and familiarity. He is free to look up at his fellow actors, to respond to them, to make his lines sound as if they were expressing what he really thought. At times he may gesture, lean forward, shift and move in his seat—all of this coming spontaneously out of genuine feel-

James H. Warren, *International Journal of Religious Education*, July-August, 1957, pp. 19–21. Used by permission.

ing. The audience often forgets where it is, is not even aware that there are no curtains and lights, and will often find itself caught up in an exalted experience of God. Thus we have religious drama presented without a stage or memorized lines.

Since actors and scripts are the only essentials, playreadings can be presented anywhere in the church building. A church school room, a banquet hall, a church lounge are a few possibilities. Playreadings can even be held in the room of a bedridden invalid.

Of course it is usually best to have a platform so that the actors can be seen, but this is not absolutely necessary. By spacing the chairs the audience can see the actors, and where there is no platform the actors may stand.

The arrangement of chairs is very important. The most important characters are seated in the center. Characters who have scenes together may sit next to each other. A semicircle is the best arrangement, since it opens the readers to the audience and also gives the readers a chance to face each other as they play their parts.

Actors should feel free to move around in their chairs as much as possible. In some cases they can pantomime bits of action as they remain seated. When they are "onstage" they should sit forward and face their fellow actors. When they are "offstage" they may sit back in the chair, lower their heads, and turn away from the group.

There are other kinds of arrangements. "Crowds" may sit or stand back of the actors. Sometimes several tiers of platforms are used and chairs are placed on these. At other times high stools are used instead of chairs. It is best that chairs have no arms, and that they be placed together as close as possible, still leaving the actors room to shift their positions from time to time.

Quite often chairs are not used at all, and actors stand for their reading. They may use lecterns or music stands for their scripts or may hold them. They may stand in still, "frozen" positions to one side and come forward, read a scene, and then go back to their

positions. They may stand on boxes draped with solid, dark material, and read their parts from these. This type of reading has
a tendency to be "stylized" and is usually, but not exclusively,
suited to plays that are fantasies. Sometimes areas may be spot-
lighted and actors may enter and exit from these areas, standing
and reading their parts.

Atmospheric music and sound may be woven into the reading.
One church recently did a reading of Gian Carlo Menotti's one-
act opera, *Amahl and the Night Visitors,* using the composer's
music, which has been recorded, in the background. Choirs, octets,
quartettes, trios, etc., may stand to one side and set the various
scenes with appropriate hymns or anthems. A speaking choir can
often be used to tie together scenes, reading appropriate scripture
or selections from literature that fit into the play being read. The
possibilities are limitless and groups should be creative and imaginative in their approach to playreadings.

Intriguing worship centers and symbols may be placed in the
center of the reading area or just above it. Bits of costuming may
be used, as was the case in a reading of Thelma Brown's *Joint
Owners in Spain* (Baker's) where shawls and period hats were
placed on the readers.

For a playreading before an audience a director will be needed.
A person with drama training is preferable. If such a person is
not available, a mature person may be found who can help the cast
analyze and feel their characters. This person should be in charge
of all arrangements for rehearsals and performers.

The director will want to find a place for rehearsals that is comfortable and conducive to discussion. After the group has read
through the script uninterrupted (except for help on pronunciation
of words, etc.) the director will be prepared to help the cast think
through the meaning of the play, the individual thoughts of the
lines, the interrelation of character with character, the way the
story develops, and what is the high point (or climax) of the play.
It is important that each actor not only know what his characters
think and feel, but how his part brings out the meaning of the

drama. Actors will try to find experiences in their own lives that throw light on the experiences of the character. If the cast is groping for a new experience they will need to find out what it is like, for they must understand what they are saying if they are to feel genuinely the emotions of the characters. After discussing the parts they will read straight through the play uninterrupted so that they can assimilate all that they have learned. In this type of rehearsal there should be a minimum of stress on "technique."

The next rehearsal will continue this emphasis on getting at the feelings of the characters. Toward the end of the rehearsal the director will want to help the actors "pick up their cues"—the art of not letting unnecessary time lapse between lines. Sometimes, of course, dramatic pauses may be deliberately planned, but it goes without saying that slow, spotty reading is deadly to any performance.

The final rehearsal should be held in the place where the play will be performed. Seating arrangements will be worked out. The director will caution the actors to speak loud enough to be heard. He will also help practice "entering" and "exiting" in character. He will let the actors be free to move in their chairs, and even to pantomime "properties," etc., if it does not slow down the reading.

A narrator should be chosen to describe the setting in an imaginative manner, tell the time of the play, and introduce the characters. Sometimes the narrator may be a member of the cast. His opening remarks must fit into the mood and feeling of the play. He should rehearse with the actors at least once.

Some groups have presented "cuttings" of novels, short stories, books of the Bible in the fashion of a playreading. One person reads the narration; others take the parts of the various characters, reading the dialogue as if it were a play script. Short scenes from great Christian literature can be used most effectively for worship services.

But, you say, doesn't this take just as much time as a regular play presentation? No. Much of the time spent in a fully produced play is used by actors in adjusting themselves to properties, costumes, etc., but in a playreading actors need to have only enough time to become familiar with the script and feel their characters. Three or four rehearsals are sufficient, and sometimes, with experienced groups, one or two rehearsals may be adequate. Longer plays, especially three-act plays, naturally need more preparation.

An extension of the playreading technique is the "walking rehearsal." Here the actors add movement to their parts, pantomiming all properties and scenery. A few chairs and tables will suggest a set. The proscenium or regular stage style (with the actors in front of the audience) is good, or the new "in-the-round" style (with the actors surrounded on all sides by the audience) can be used. Walking rehearsals require approximately twice as many rehearsals as playreadings.

How Playreadings May Be Used

One of the delights of the playreading is the variety of purposes it can serve. A Sunday evening fellowship could use playreadings. A group might present a thought-provoking playreading followed with discussion, or they might present a deeply inspiring play as a part of a worship service. Or some evening they might take their playreading team to visit other churches. They may want to share it with various church groups, like the ladies' group, the men's club, or present it on a family night occasion.

A Sunday morning class might be delighted and stimulated to hear a reading of a one-act play (or scene from a longer play) and to discuss it. Every three months or so an occasion of this kind would add variety to the teaching methods of church school classes. Of course the play should be integrated into the regular studies. A committee from the class might be looking ahead two or three months to such an occasion. Quite often denominational study guides will have suggestions about plays that might be done in conjunction with a study unit.

Before we pass on to other considerations may we say one word about the use of playreadings for discussion. First, the play itself must present issues that evoke thinking. Some plays inspire; some probe thoughts. Needless to say, a play that does not present sharp issues will not create much thought. Second, discussion is most natural and genuine if it is based on thinking about characters in the play. People get excited when they talk about people, and great statements of Christian belief become real when seen manifested in the lives of people.

Playreading Just for Fun

Some groups like the sheer fun of reading plays together with no thought or plan of giving it before another group. They enjoy the adventure of discovering different experiences of life through plays, and they like "trying on" different personalities as they read various parts.

When great literary masterpieces are being studied resource people may be brought in, such as college or high school teachers. They can share their knowledge of the play and the background of its time. They can lead the group in a stimulating discussion of the philosophy and attitudes of the author as revealed in his works. If resource people are not available, then members of the group may wish to do special study on plays that they plan to read. Over a period of time playreading groups develop a keen awareness of the best in religious drama and can offer suggestions for local church drama productions. Playreading groups may number as few as two or as many as thirty. The main point is that they be composed of people who really enjoy the fun of reading plays together.

Some playreading groups may relate their play selections to projects and activities of their church. When a special area of missions is being studied this group might read plays that deal with a particular country or section of the world. John Patrick's delightful play, *Teahouse of the August Moon,* would make a fascinating study of the ways of another culture. Or a fellowship group planning a service project in a slum area of a city might be enriched by reading and discussing Sidney Kingsley's *Dead End,* or Elmer Rice's *Street Scene,* excellent treatments of city slums.

Playreading groups might want to set up broad areas of study and then find plays illuminating these areas.

Selecting Plays for Reading

A small committee in the church might take responsibility for reading widely in the field of published plays and recommending those suitable for either private or public playreading. Many public libraries have collections of current plays as well as the classics. Lists of plays of special religious quality are given in church publications and occasionally in the *International Journal of Religious Education*.

If the plays decided upon are published in pamphlet form by play publishing houses, copies for each reader may be purchased at a cost not greater than for many lesson quarterlies. If the plays are in hard cover books which are too expensive for each person to own, extra copies might be borrowed from individuals within a community. Readers can double in roles, if necessary, and as many as three people can "share" one script.

Perhaps a warning should be given. It is illegal to copy plays, even for class use. The matter of paying royalty for production is not easy to state accurately, as there seem to be no standard procedures as far as publishers are concerned. Usually when playreading is used within a classroom situation there is no need to pay royalty. When a play is produced as a playreading before an audience, there may or may not be a royalty. The copy of the play will state whether a royalty is required. Some publishers make reductions for playreading. It is therefore important to clear with the publisher regarding these arrangements before giving a play before an audience.

What Is Role Playing?

BY ALAN F. KLEIN

Role playing is one of our newest tools for improving meetings, conferences, and leadership-training sessions. The idea is so natural and so simple that it is surprising that we had not thought of it before. Children have been role-playing for years. "Let's play house. You be the father and I'll be the mother and Jenny will be our daughter," or "Let's play store. You must come in to buy the food." And so on it goes, you be so-and-so, I'll be so-and-so, and we will play roles. It was not until Dr. J. L. Moreno of the Psychodramatic Institute in New York introduced methods which he called "psychodrama" and "sociodrama" that role playing for adults as a human relations training method came into its own.

Of course, even that is not strictly true. Industrial firms and department stores had been training salesmen, for example, by having their employees act out make-believe sales interviews with each other as a means of practice for their jobs. Such methods have been effective and successful. In recent years role playing has become popular in other fields.

When Moreno developed his techniques he was interested in therapy for certain kinds of personality disorders and this he called "psychodrama." His "sociodrama" was a method for testing ideas before putting them into actual use, as in the training of the

Alan F. Klein, "Using Role Playing in Your Meeting," *Role Playing in Leadership Training and Group Problem Solving* (New York: Association Press, 1956), pp. 17, 18. Used by permission.

salesmen we were talking about. It is this idea that has developed into role playing.

Role playing takes place when a group watches other members enact roles in a skit for the purpose of analyzing some real life situation in which it is interested. The performance is followed by discussion. The skit may present a situation so that the audience can be helped to understand what happens or happened in a given circumstance. The main point is that role playing is used to make a situation, problem, or incident real and thereby to make it possible for the group to understand it and to discuss or cope with it.

Helping the Group to Role-Play

BY ALAN F. KLEIN

Creating a Readiness for Role Playing

We shall assume now that our group is interested in human relations and in leadership training and that the problem upon which it is working is real, also that the problem would lend itself to role playing. The leader would explain what role playing is, if the group had not used it before. He might then discuss why it would be useful in dealing with the problem at hand. Even with a group that has role-played before, it is advantageous to explain why it would be a good method to use at the time. For example:

> I should like to suggest that we role-play this situation. Just talking about the problem does not seem to give us all that we need. If we could see it I am sure that it would become clearer.

In another context one might say:

> This question involves a matter of skill that can be acquired best by doing rather than talking. I suggest that we role-play it so that you can practice how to handle this kind of situation.

To reduce the feeling against acting in front of other people, start a group role-playing something familiar, simple, and nonthreatening. This can be done by having everyone role-play at the same time, with no audience, since everyone is acting. You could introduce role playing to your group by showing the film "Role Play-

Alan F. Klein, *Role Playing in Leadership Training and Group Problem Solving* (New York: Association Press, 1956), pp. 45–47, 49–52, 63–64, 67–70, 71, 79–81, 84–85, 103, 104, 105–107, 131–134. Used by permission.

ing" [1] or the films "Invisible Committees" [1] or "Meeting in Session." [2]

When introducing role playing, as much threat reduction as possible should be included. That is, you explain that no one will be ridiculed or judged, that those who participate will get the most out of it; that it is enjoyable and that everyone in the session is there to learn. One might say, also, that it is better to make mistakes here in a protected setting while making believe than to make them out in real life where you have "to play for keeps." Another protection is that no one is playing himself and since he is in a role he can experiment with how to act in the situation without any fears. It is well to focus any tension about role playing onto the problem, "We want to solve this problem pretty badly. Let's try to solve it. Let's role-play it."

The person doing the leading must be warm, relaxed, and easy. He must expect that the group will respond. He should make it easy for people to be themselves, to speak freely, to act as they would with friends, to be involved and participating.

Before we can enact our role play we must prepare for it. We do this by establishing the situation so that it is actable and so that the points to be learned will be brought out, by casting the characters, and by briefing and warming up the players.

Establishing the Situation

Let us examine these preliminary steps in some detail since successful role playing depends upon proper preparation. First of all, the situation needs to be considered.

To Work on a Problem Situation

If the purpose of the role playing is to work on a problem that is situation-centered, the roles of the actors should be defined,

---

[1] "Role Playing" and "Invisible Committees" can be secured from National Education Association, 1201 Sixteenth St., N.W., Washington 6, D.C.

[2] "Meeting in Session": Center for Improving Group Procedure, Teachers' College. Columbia University, New York, N. Y.

but the situation can be left open to allow the group freedom to explore it.

An example may make this clearer. If the group is discussing juvenile delinquency and its control, the problem may be centered on the subject and not primarily on the behavior of the role players. In this case, if the situation is too carefully structured the role players will have no scope in which to explore the problem or seek solutions. However, the players must be prepared to know just who they are and what their relation to each other is in order to be free to center their attention on the problem. For example:

In a middle-size midwestern city the delinquency rate has been rising. Some children have been put in jail, but it has not seemed to help. The children of better-class families have become involved in delinquent behavior, and the residents have become concerned. The police say that they cannot handle the problem without the help of the parents.

A committee has been called by the Council to consider the problem and to suggest solutions. Some facts are that 30 per cent of the adolescents have been in some trouble with the police in the last year. Fifteen per cent have been punished through some form of court action. Most of this 15 per cent come from broken homes or blighted areas. In these areas there is little play space and there is unemployment.

We are about to role-play the committee in order to explore the problem, and not to focus on the human relations behavior of the players.

We have given the framework of a situation, but there is leeway for the role players to explore the causes of delinquency, discuss possible solutions that they know have been tried, and go on to problem solving. The purpose here is to involve the group in the question of delinquency, to encourage maximum participation, and to stimulate discussion; therefore we define the roles carefully but do not structure the problem.

The committee consists of the following characters (note how the roles are set):

MRS. MCKEE—a laywoman of a fine family. She is interested, hard-working, willing, well informed.

JUDGE BROWN—Juvenile Court judge. He is old, steady, conservative, kindly, and worried about the problem.

JOE RUNNER—a representative of the Recreation Committee.

A. LEAF—the high school principal.

MISS KOTTER—case supervisor of the Department of Public Welfare.

AL LUND—the chairman. He believes in the democratic process but he also believes that problems have solutions; that if facts are put together in an orderly fashion the parts will match and the answer will be obvious.

We cast the kind of roles that are normal or usual in such a situation. We are not looking for conflict or special problems of resistance but just a discussion of the delinquency situation.

In such a situation we can look in addition at how the chairman approaches the chairmanship job, also how the member roles shape up, and how an ordinary group tackles a problem. With just the information we have revealed thus far, the group can role-play for the purposes stated.

How to Design Your Situations

In discussing the design for role playing we come into a most interesting and provocative area. Even with so new a method, different schools of thought have arisen with champions for each. In this book, we intend to present many approaches. You may take your choice.

The design of your role playing, like any other design, allows for your imagination, creative ability, and adjustment to the level of the group for which it is to be used. It will depend upon the skill that you acquire in using the tool appropriately.

It should be clear now that role playing may be a training device, or it may be a device to stimulate discussion and engage in problem solving. As a training device it may be used to learn a specific skill or to get insight into one's own or another's feelings. On the other hand it may coax out feelings which affect the members' and groups' behavior but which are not verbalized generally and may bring them before the group for examination. In other situations role playing is used to convey information, to communicate content, or to report. Here now are the basic fundamentals that determine design.

Should the role playing be completely unplanned or should the situations be prepared in advance of the conference, meeting, or training session? Which is preferable?

The way it is to be done will be dependent upon the outcome desired or needed by the group at the time. We have several alternatives. The role playing may be planned in advance by the leader or person responsible for the session; it may be planned by a committee which has assessed in some suitable way the needs and interests of the group; it may be planned by a subcommittee to fit into a conference theme; a member or the leader can suggest an actual incident to be played; or the group can make up the situation at the meeting right there and then.

Casting the Characters

Casting can be arranged for most readily by the person directing the role playing. The group lacks sufficient insight usually into the purposes of the experience, and the needs of the persons, to do the casting.

It seems best to ask people to assume the roles rather than to assign them. People find it hard to perform in a role with which they cannot identify. If they cannot do it the reality is gone, and the other actors are thrown off their stride. Assigning roles is an imposition unless, and this is a big *unless,* it is a training group and people have agreed to this procedure because they are relying on a trainer who they think knows what experiences will be productive. It is believed that no one should be forced or be overly urged to do a role.

It is surprising how people will catch on to their own needs if the atmosphere is not threatening and if the interpretation is good. We were called upon recently to present role playing to a group about to retire from work. The purpose was to develop some insights into the problems of retirement and to look at some solutions. The role players met at dinner to plan the situation. They selected as one situation the person who is a perpetual crank and grouch, and how others react to him; and then the same scene with a person who is pleasant, and how others react to him. When the casting was being done one man agreed to be the grouch, and then he added that it would be easy for him because he was that way naturally. Someone else commented that it would do him good to play the pleasant person. He laughed it off. Twenty minutes later he seized upon a pause in the discussion to ask if he could change his role, "To see how it feels to be a lot of fun."

With a new group or one not used to role playing it is a help to start easily with very simple roles and ones that are quite familiar to the players and that offer no threats or real challenges. As the group becomes more adept and more secure in the idea, roles can be cast that cause people to stretch themselves.

There are some disadvantages to using people in roles for which they volunteer if one is interested in skill training primarily:

- The easy and articulate people volunteer first and often need the experience least.
- The ones who need the practice may not volunteer.
- The volunteers may not choose roles that will help them most.
- It is difficult to get people to volunteer for unpopular roles or difficult ones, or where they may reveal themselves.

In small groups everyone may be drawn into a role eventually, and so the first and second disadvantages are not serious. In large groups this is not true. Also, by the method of reversing roles on the redoing, the third disadvantage may be avoided. The leader may do the unpopular roles himself or ask high status persons in the group to do them. Lastly, the members of the audience can get insight by watching the role playing even if the onlookers are not in the act. If a group is using role playing for training itself over a period of time, all the disadvantages disappear by themselves. If it is being used at a conference or once at a meeting, perhaps we cannot expect that the one shot will produce miracles. Even here by redoing, testing, and discussing, some results may be achieved. Surely within the broader objectives many excellent results are accomplished.

Casting should not use the players' own names. Persons should not play themselves or their own roles except under very special situations as for personal diagnosis, or in advanced human relations training courses to test and practice. Even here it is desirable to play roles when role playing. It is preferable not to enact the actual event as it occurred except for diagnosis and here only if the persons are willing to open themselves for criticism. It is very possible to hurt people this way, undermine self-confidence and, one might add, lose friends. In our club life it is not recommended, and in personnel training it may be useful only if it is conducted in well-controlled educational conditions with top-notch trainers. Not under any circumstances would one recommend therapy in unskilled hands. Giving people more self-awareness than they can handle, with no out such as that it was a make-believe role, can prove damaging.

In some circumstances it is useful to help people assume roles to which they aspire and hence give them practice in something they may soon do or hope to do.

Some persons prefer neither to assign roles nor to ask for volunteers. In their method they staple the instructions for each role together in any order and hand the packet to the group instructing them to take the top one off and pass the set. Each plays the part he gets by chance.

Briefing and Warming Up

Briefing may be oral or written. If the situation is quite simple the briefing may be done orally. The planner must decide how much he wants all or any of the parties to know. Again this depends upon the purpose of the role playing, what would be true to life, and how he sees the human relations aspect of the situation.

Warm-Up

The warm-up process is one of the most important steps in role playing and yet one that is often neglected. The actor is about to enact a role; he is going to be someone else. The briefing will, at best, give him a very sketchy picture of this person in most instances. Whether he knows the character he is portraying or not he does not know, generally, the relevant or pertinent facts. He needs a framework of agreed-upon background to guide him in being the character. How he will respond and interact with the other actors depends in part upon the background of information from which he can draw. If he has a picture of the role he can be consistent, remain in character, and not be left speechless when an unexpected comment is made.

Whether the warm-up is done publicly or privately depends, as in briefing, on how much you want the others, including the audience, to know. Some may be asked to leave the room while others are warmed up. The warm-up puts the actor into character and fixes in his mind and in the minds of the audience who and what he is in the story. The warm-up consists of helping him to create the character by asking a series of questions to which he responds "ad lib" to make the character his creation and thereby to insure a more natural scene, to make him comfortable with it, and to foster spontaneity. A question-and-answer session between leader, L, and actor, Mr. Hall, will illustrate what is meant:

L: Mr. Hall, you are the administrator of this hospital?
H: Yes, that is correct.
L: How long have you been administrator?
H: Going on six years. (*This is his own idea.*)
L: I see. You are a doctor?
H: No, I'm not a doctor but I am trained as a hospital administrator. (*The latter part is his own idea.*)
L: Does not being a doctor in any way make your job difficult?
H: No, not my job. It does make a difference to some of the medical staff. A few doctors are sticky about this.
L: How does it make you feel?

H: Oh, I don't mind—although I think those doctors are stuffed shirts. In a way I wish I were a doctor. I'd feel more secure. Mind you, I know my job and I run a good hospital—but I would feel easier.

L: I see. What is your biggest problem in running this hospital?

H: Budget. We never have enough money to do what has to be done. We need repairs, equipment, better salaries, more space, and heaven knows what else.

L: Do you mind if I ask your salary?

H: Not at all. I get $8,000.

L: Were you born here in this city?

H: Yes, I was—local boy makes good, you might say.

L: Does this make for any problems?

. . . And so on. Obviously you ask questions that you think will help develop some background and will be useful in the play. The warm-up is not just a chat. It is carefully thought out to supplement the briefing, to put the actor into his role, and to help the audience see the character more clearly. It should be short and be well paced, that is, not allowed to drag.

We do not use warm-up for every role-playing situation. In some there is no need for special role differentiation or for such background as we have shown here. When to have warm-up depends upon need and purpose.

Where the group has some experience with role playing and the actors have no hidden motives they can warm each other up out of the room. By asking each other questions to establish roles and to clarify who is who, the actors learn who each other is and what to expect. All this adds up to building the situation to approximate reality for everyone.

Acting

The actors in the story, problem, or social situation enactment should be asked to avoid long speeches and irrelevant material. They should be instructed to keep the pace up, the dialogue fast, and come to the important points quickly. Note, however, where the role playing deals with the problem-solving process, spontaneous behavior, and interaction for human relations experience, no such instructions should be given. You want people to act as they think real people in those roles would act.

Cutting

It is up to you not to let the role-playing scene last too long. Keep your purpose clearly in mind. You can defeat your purpose by letting it go on beyond its usefulness. Cut the action when in your opinion enough has been seen for an analysis of the problem, or for the actors and audience to have gained some insight, or when the skill has been practiced or tested. Cut it when the audience is stimulated and ready for discussion. If it is a problem story to be enacted, cut it when the group has seen enough to be able to finish the story.

Cut the action when an impasse has been reached and nothing more will happen. Cut when the players are merely redoing or re-saying the same things. Cut if you think an actor has had as much as he can take of psychological stretching or if tension has risen about as high as is good for anyone at that moment. Cut if you feel that the situation is approaching therapy. Obviously, cut when the situation has reached its natural end.

Involving the Audience

We are interested in role playing as a method in leadership training and group problem solving. Role playing is not a show for entertaining but a device for stimulating and training our groups. How do we affect the audience in order to achieve maximum results?

One of the advantages in the use of role playing is that it is possible to affect the audience as well as the actors. There are several principles to be mentioned here. We know that leadership and human relations training is more effective when the members participate in the program and are involved in the situations that are being studied. We know, also, that interest is maintained when the people are actively involved in what is going on in a meeting, conference, or course.

Simultaneous Learning Devices

There are several learning devices going on in the same role-playing session. Let us look at them more closely. The actors are experiencing the enactment and are getting the feel of it as well as the feelings of it. The audience is experiencing the enactment through dramatic impact. It is possible to increase this emotional reaction by helping the audience to see what is happening, to feel less like an audience and more a part of the experience. People tend to see more if they know for what they are looking, and if their perceptive organs are focused. There are several interesting techniques for this purpose in addition to the general introduction and briefing.

Listening Sections

For this method sections of the audience are asked to listen specifically for certain things such as assumptions, assessments, prejudices, preconceptions, hidden motives, voice changes, tempo, and the like. By concentrating attention people are helped to focus, the effort holds interest, and it produces more points for the discussion that will follow the role playing.

Watching Sections

In the same way as above, sections of the audience are asked to watch for body tension, facial expression, behavior change, gestures, and so on. Some may be asked to watch any one role player especially.

Explaining

Explaining to everyone what to look for, that is, asking everyone to look and listen for the things listed under *Listening* and *Watching Sections* or, perhaps, asking the group to notice when leadership behavior changes.

The Audience Consultants

Here the audience is asked to form buzz groups and discuss how a situation could have been handled more effectively. The actors are then advised by a reporter or a buzz group, and the scene is replayed. The more the audience is involved in the role playing, the more and better the participation, discussion, and the learning to follow.

Empathizers or Identifiers

Here certain people or sections receive the same role briefing as the actors but instead of taking the actual role they observe it and try to put themselves into the shoes of the particular actor as much as possible. They may be called upon later in the discussion to describe their reactions and feelings.

How Role Playing May Be Used

We have discussed the reasons for and the techniques of using role playing as a training device. Out of the material let us try to systematize the uses and draw out some general principles. Let us remember that our design must of necessity depend upon the purposes to which we are putting the role playing. The major uses for role playing are these:

- To stimulate discussion.
- To train in skills.
- To train in sensitivity and acquire insight so as to solve social and human relations problems.
- To deal effectively with certain emotional problems that block group productivity.

We shall examine one of these purposes in greater detail.

To Stimulate Discussion

It may happen that our group is not stirred up enough about a subject to be stimulated, and hence is slow to discuss; or perhaps it needs to be warmed up. To begin a discussion at the outset of a meeting tends to be difficult. We use speakers to start the ball rolling and hope that a good discussion leader through provocative questions will draw the group out. Maybe the group does not understand the subject well enough to risk discussion, or fails to see the subtle implications. More likely it may not feel the problem. By taking the group right into the situation through role playing every last member may be reached. Everyone has a chance to share in the group feeling in the same way as when one sees a moving play. The live presentation has more realism than even a motion picture. No matter how able a speaker may be, he cannot create this illusion of reality. No matter how well a written "case" may be presented for study, it needs people acting it out to make it live for the audience.

Because the enactment lives and transports actors and audience into the situation by virtue of the shared emotional experience, everyone is participating whether he speaks or not. The likelihood is that the reaction will prompt more people to speak spontaneously.

Take for example the following simple scene concerning a typical teen-age problem that might be discussed by a parents' group.

FATHER: I told you distinctly to be in by 11:30. Tomorrow is a school day. I cannot have you out on the street at all hours of the night. Here it is midnight and you are just wandering in.

DAUGHTER: But, Dad, it's only a half hour later. We missed the bus.

FATHER: Missed the bus. Every week it's a different excuse. Leave on time and you won't miss the bus. I told you what would happen, didn't I?

DAUGHTER: I'm the only one who has to be in so early. Everyone else can go out for a hamburger after the dance but me. I'm always the baby. They think I'm treated like a child.

FATHER: I don't care about them. I'm not *their* father. No daughter of mine can land in here at midnight on a week night. I won't have it, do you hear?

DAUGHTER: I'm so miserable. I could just leave here and never come back.

FATHER: That may be just what you'll have to do if you keep this up.

DAUGHTER: Are you threatening me?

FATHER: Just for that you can't go to the Prom Dance next week.

MOTHER (*enters hurriedly at that*) : But John, what is so terrible about a half hour? She could have missed the bus. She has a new dress and a date, and she can't break it now.

Even if you do not have this problem you cannot resist being stirred when it happens in front of you. Surely you want to tell John that he is getting nowhere fast. Or maybe you identify with the father and think our daughter should be in early on a week night. Whatever you think, of one thing you are certain—neither party is helping to solve the problem, and mother is just making it worse. How would you suggest it be handled? The discussion is on.

16. USE THE LANGUAGE OF MUSIC

MUSIC HAS A LANGUAGE of its own, and it speaks to the spirit of man. It is a language of feelings and appreciation. It speaks of mood and spirit rather than of precise meanings. It reaches to depths of feeling and of motive, as words can seldom do. It allows each to respond in his own way and according to his own feeling, as verbal communication seldom allows us to do. It uses the medium of the human voice, as well as the varieties of instrument that the genius of man can devise. It appeals to some of us to create music, to others to reproduce what the composer has created, and to still others to listen in appreciation. Music is a better medium than words to communicate many of the messages of God to man. Paul's suggestion may be addressed to us as aptly as to the Christians at Colossae: "Let the word of Christ dwell in you richly, as you teach and admonish one another in all wisdom, and as you sing psalms and hymns and spiritual songs with thankfulness in your hearts to God" (Col. 3:16, RSV). The use of music, then, is not an extra in Christian nurture, to be included if we have time or if the leader happens to "know music."

The final reading in the chapter deals with choral speaking. While choral speaking is not music, its effect, its method, and its procedures are closely related to music.

Music Experiences in the Age Groups of the Church School

BY VIVIAN SHARP MORSCH

Preschool

Singing Experiences

Small children are sensitive to the message and warmth of feeling in a teacher's singing voice. First attitudes toward the church are affected by the emotion reflected in the teacher's voice. The child gains satisfaction through his vocal response.

Songs are included at any time in the program and are related to any part or activity. They motivate, heighten, and enrich experiences, create attitudes and moods.

A few short, one-idea songs make up the repertoire of three-year-olds. As they grow into the kindergarten the repertoire increases in number and length of song.

Children learn by repetition of songs used in meaningful situations. They join in.

Many three-year-olds do not sing a tune. The pleasure is more important. Gradually experience helps them to improve. By five years they probably will have found their singing voices and the "head tone."

The voice range is limited to less than an octave from F (above middle C) to E above. The melody should not lie too close to either extreme.

Vivian Sharp Morsch, *The Use of Music in Christian Education* (Philadelphia: The Westminster Press, 1956. Copyright by W. L. Jenkins), pp. 93–99. Used by permission.

Playing Experiences

A music center is set up with a few percussion instruments, for free experimentation at times when it will not interfere with other people and other activities.

Nursery children experiment as individuals and sometimes come together in very small groups to play together, chiefly spontaneously.

Kindergarten children find playing together in groups more natural and satisfying.

Songs are accompanied, at times, with light, simple piano music. Many preschool teachers use a stringed chording instrument, such as a zither or autoharp. They are easy to play and children may "assist" the teacher with the accompaniment.

Rhythmic Experiences

Rhythmic experiences consist of dramatizations of simple action songs, singing games, and rhythmic use of the toy instruments.

Kindergarten children can also invent new stanzas to songs and dramatize each.

Listening Experiences

Children listen for the mood of the music, which creates the atmosphere of rest, worship, and play.

They listen to get a story from a song.

They begin to become familiar with hymns and they listen purely for enjoyment.

The piano, record player, and voice are used for listening examples.

Creative Experiences

Preschool children can invent conversational chants and songs, one-phrase melodies, and rhythmic patterns.

Kindergarten children make simple instruments, invent instrumentation to songs and pieces, and invent new stanzas for known songs.

Primary

Singing Experiences

Gradually the teacher can use songs that are longer and contain more ideas. One-stanza songs are best. Children enjoy singing many songs and hymns. Simple ones are best. They listen to good singing and imitate good tone.

Songs create atmosphere, attitudes, and moods, enrich the curriculum, make departmental worship meaningful, foster unity of the group, and awaken social consciousness.

Music interest groups may prepare songs for special occasions.

Children and teacher discuss the songs to be learned. The children listen several times to presentations, and learn quickly.

Primary children do not read music from hymnbooks. They learn by a simple rote method.

Songs should range between E flat (above middle C) to F in the next octave above. The high F should not be used frequently.

Playing Experiences

The music center includes a wider variety of instruments. Not too many are available at one time.

Instruments are used in real ensemble groups.

Instruments play with the piano or record player and may be used to enrich worship services and to illustrate curriculum materials (Hebrew temple music, the psalms, etc.).

Instruments may be used to accompany songs.

A piano or an autoharp, or both, may be used for light accompaniment to the children's singing.

Rhythmic Experiences

Song dramatizations.

Singing games. Instruments may be used.

Accompanying rhythmic movements with instruments.

Rhythmic experiences with piano and recordings, discerning the movement suggested by the music.

Processions dramatizing Hebrew festivals.

Listening Experiences

Listening to recordings in worship services—for atmosphere.

To create attitude and moods.

To illustrate lessons.

For enjoyment.

To present artistic performances.

To learn how to listen.

To learn a hymn or song.

Creative Experiences

Composing responses to prayer and Scripture.

Making new stanzas to known songs.

Composing tunes to Bible verses and poems.

Composing tunes to instrumental experiences.

Making instruments.

Junior

Singing Experiences

Songs are learned easily and the repertoire contains hymns, folk songs, and easy anthems.

Voices are flexible and clear.

Children like strong hymns that require emotional vitality to sing.

Folk songs are used to develop kindly attitudes toward other races and nationalities.

Hymns, responses, and anthems are sung with respectful reverence in worship services.

The children learn how to select appropriate music for worship through experience.

Songs are used to expand and enrich curriculum themes.

Special music interest groups may rehearse before the school session, or during the discovery period, in order to present music to the school groups.

Junior children may read from books while learning songs.

Some hymns and songs should be memorized.

Songs should range from middle C to F of the octave above. Because of the lowering of the voices of sixth-grade boys and the unison singing of the hymns, most of the songs should be no higher than E flat.

Playing Experiences

Discovery groups may explore the playing of instruments, to develop curriculum materials, to play in worship and for sheer enjoyment.

Many children play the piano or other instruments well enough to play for the entire group.

Some may learn to accompany hymns.

Rhythmic Experiences

Rhythmic experiences consist of song dramatizations, singing games, cumulative songs (weekday, vacation school, two-hour sessions) and hymn processionals.

Listening Experiences

Listening to recordings because of the relation of the music to a study theme, to create atmosphere of worship, to learn a hymn or song, to illustrate beauty of tone and artistic performance, for enjoyment, and to teach about people of other lands, races, and cultures.

Creative Experiences

Juniors can compose hymns—the words, tune, or both, and responses. Other creative experiences are furnished by improvised instrumental chord accompaniments for songs and instruments, and descants for hymns.

Instruments may be made and experimented with in discovery groups.

Youth

Singing Experiences

Hymns and other songs are selected for youths taking into account the changing voice and its accompanying self-consciousness.

Youth groups provide an opportunity for informal singing experiences which encourage participation. Folk and fun songs, especially with action, secure hearty participation.

From fun songs, the transition to serious songs such as spirituals and favorite hymns is an easy and natural consequence. Plenty of hearty fellowship singing makes a singing youth department.

Fellowship books usually contain spirituals and hymns that should never be sung in the mood of fun songs.

A good youth hymnal is an essential equipment item.

A good way to teach reverent participation in worship is to teach the service music, hymns, responses, canticles, orisons, calls to worship, to the youth division. They may sing a sanctuary service for their fellowship worship and participate more fully in the congregational worship service.

The youth division will be able to learn to sing in simple two-, three-, and some four-part harmony. Unison songs should be kept in a limited middle range D to D or C to C (in some cases). It is impossible to generalize.

Playing Experiences

Young people enjoy instrumental ensembles.

Bell ringing is an excellent activity for small groups.

Other combinations of instruments may be played together to prepare for participation in worship or fellowship events.

Young people should learn to accompany hymns. They may be used in their own age groups and in others.

Rhythmic Experiences

Song dramatizations of folk and fun songs.
Singing games.
Cumulative songs with motions.
Folk and square dancing in fellowship events.

Listening Experiences

Listening to recordings to study Church history, Bible stories (*Elijah, The Creation*), the life of Christ (*The Messiah, St. Matthew Passion*).
For worship services—listening for message.
To gain in sympathetic understanding of other people.
To learn the scope and significance of church music.

Listening to choirs, instruments, artists—to create interest in the profession of church music and perhaps to inspire some to choose the profession.

Creative Experiences

Invention of harmonized arrangements of song materials, experimenting with thirds and sixths, descants, and simple pattern bass, made up of I IV V chords or scalewise, tetrachord figures.
Invention of word stanzas.
Composition of vocal or instrumental music.
Experiences with making instruments in the musical laboratory or workshop.

Creative Music—By and for Children

BY ELIZABETH MC E. SHIELDS

Before we discuss the creative use of children's music, it will be wise for us to have a common understanding of the word "creative," for there are those who feel it almost sacrilegious to use the term in speaking of human beings—"Only God can create," they say.

One day after hearing an earnest Christian make this statement, I went to the dictionary for a definition of the word "create." Among those given I found: "To produce as a new construction out of existing materials." This satisfied me, for I knew that I could not "make something out of nothing," but that, working with God, I could shape some existing materials into forms that are new—at least they are new to *me,* and that is what is important. For example, I cannot create the notes of the birds or the laughter of brooks and children, but I can put *what they say to me* into a song—*my* song! My very own! Or I can listen to a song made by someone else and discover for myself a new meaning in it—new to *me.*

The Creative Teacher

It will be interesting to explore some of the opportunities a teacher may find for a creative use of music. Perhaps her ability will first show itself in the way in which, as she plans, she senses the appropriateness of a certain song for a given situation. "It just seems to take the message of the story into their everyday living," she

Elizabeth McE. Shields, "Creative Music," *Music in the Religious Growth of Children* (Nashville: Abingdon Press, 1943), pp. 71–77. Used by permisson.

thinks. "After their discussion, I believe this one will have real meaning—it will almost sing itself," she feels about another. Then she may soon acquire the sense of freedom which will enable her to change her plans when advisable—even in their execution— and use an appropriate song not in her program. It contributes to the experience of the children and becomes a part of "a new construction" of "existing materials" which is very satisfying.

Sometimes a leader will find a song that almost meets the needs of her children in a given situation. The change of a few words or the addition of a stanza will make it a proper vehicle of self-expression on the part of the children. For example, a Beginners' leader planned to make prominent the thought of God's gift of flowers and the distribution of seed by the wind. So after the children had enjoyed some interesting discoveries and conversation, she adapted the words of the following song:

A CHILD'S "THANK YOU"

Anonymous   ELDA FLETT BAKER

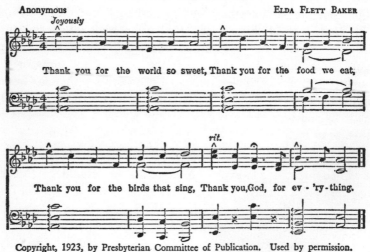

Thank you for the world so sweet, Thank you for the food we eat;
Thank you for the birds that sing, Thank you, God, for ev-'ry-thing.

Copyright, 1923, by Presbyterian Committee of Publication. Used by permission.

The words as she changed them to meet her needs were:

> Thank you for the flowers that grow,
> Thank you for the winds that blow,

Thank you for the birds that sing,
Thank you, God, for everything.

A creative teacher often adapts the words of a song when she feels that they may be puzzling and make a wrong impression. For example, the phrase *"Brooding us* ev'ry one" in Abbie Farwell Brown's beautiful song-poem "Overtones" is a most expressive phrase, which some of the older children may possibly appreciate; but it may be wise for most children to sing *"Caring for* ev'ry one."

Many teachers seem impelled to write song-poems and music for children. Consequently, the world is full of children's music— some worthy and some unworthy of the children for whom it is intended. The most successful song, from the standpoint of religious education, is written, not by one who merely feels the urge to write a song, but by one who senses the need of enriching a real experience of her children. There have been many of the latter type, and we owe a debt of gratitude to these understanding writers of children's music. May we make intelligent use of their contributions and follow in their train—in appreciation, at least!

Making Poems, Melodies, and Adaptations

In evaluating the creative work of children we must remember that all do not respond in the same way. An understanding teacher can do much to foster appreciation and a desire for musical expression, but she cannot force any child to give expression to something he does not feel and want to express. In my observation I have found that teachers who love music and express themselves readily and naturally through this medium are most likely to have responsive pupils. This is because the early singing of a little child is imitative, and love for music is caught rather than learned consciously. Or as someone has said, "Education is more a matter of infection than injection."

It has been a question through the years as to whether or not spoken words preceded what we might call musical sounds. At any rate, someone has suggested that if mothers would frequently communicate with their tiny children by singing instead of speaking, it would be as natural for children to sing as to talk. Thus, very early in life they would be singing their own melodies, and it would not be considered unusual for a child to make up a tune.

Teachers of very young children are beginning to realize the possibilities of this use of music—not overdoing it, of course. "Wake up," a teacher sings to her Nursery children who have been resting on their rugs. "Step very softly. Don't wake up the baby," she sings to a child who is inclined to "walk too hard" in the neighborhood of another who is putting dolly to sleep. Every now and then she finds little imitators of this method of conversing.

The creative efforts of a child in making music are likely to be of more value to him than to anyone else. In the first place, there is the satisfaction of expressing one's self through a beautiful medium—the joy that is felt by a poet or musician, even when there is no one near to hear his poem or his music. And if the contribution is received graciously by others, the self-respect and self-confidence of the young contributor begin to develop and he feels a sense of achievement.

Under wise guidance a creative child need not be an egotistical child—quite the reverse. He will take his poem or musical composition as much for granted as his spoken contribution to discussion or conversation.

While, as we have said, the musical compositions of a young child are likely to be of more value to him than to anyone else, we do not mean to minimize their value to the group of which he is a member. In many cases his contributions to group experience are of value in themselves.

I remember an interesting experience with Dr. Van Dyke's lovely poem:

> Every morning seems to say,
> "There's something happy on the way."

I had included the song in a new Beginner vacation-school course which was being used by a friend of mine before it was printed. As I was planning, I said to my sister, "I feel the need of a stanza to link up with what happens later in the morning, but I shall not presume to add a stanza of my own to Dr. Van Dyke's poem."

Little five-year-old children, however, are not respecters of persons, and a few days after the children in the kindergarten had begun to sing the "morning song"—as they called it—one of the little girls sang, happily and almost unconsciously, as she and the others were leaving for home at noon:

> Ev'ry noo-oon seems to say,
> "We've had a happy time today
> And God sends love to you!"

"Noontime" would have suited the meter better, but she had no difficulty in stretching "noon" into two syllables, and the children loved her song.

A contribution to the well-loved music of a group of Beginners was made by Marjory, who had been listening with the others to the story of the coming of the baby Jesus and the angels' song. When the story was ended, she said, "I feel like singing 'Glory to God in the Highest.' "

When her teacher encouraged her to sing, asking if she knew a tune to the words, she said "No, I don't." Then the teacher gave further encouragement by saying, "Perhaps you can make up a tune, and maybe I can play it on the piano."

Marjory was thoughtful for a minute or two, then said, "I have got one now," and sang the following:

Glo-ry to God in the high-est.

The leader went to the piano, and played the notes sung by the little girl—having her sing again and pass judgment on the correctness of the melody as played on the piano. Then she said, "That is a pretty tune. If you like, I shall write it down on paper so that we may all sing it when we want to."

After the notes had been written, Marjory suggested that all the children sing her song. There was a happy response, and then several children wanted to sing it by themselves.

The contributions of children are not always beautiful in themselves; but, just as to loving parents their babies are always beautiful, so these brain children are satisfying to those who bring them into being. However, many of the poems and songs created by children reach very high standards—even adult standards. To me the words and melody of "God's Trees" are very satisfying. They were composed by a little girl five years of age whose mother wrote the words and melody when Ann sang the song to her.

The little girl had been allowed on a summer day to take off her shoes and stockings and had been hopping up and down on the hot pavement as she told her mother when she reached the cool shade of a friendly tree. The shade was so welcome that her first thought was "God makes trees to give shade." Then she thought, "Not *just* for shade. Trees are pretty, and some give food." She remembered that at church school she and the others had talked about a verse in the Bible that spoke of trees as "pleasant to the sight, and good for food," so she found herself singing a little song. "I must have made it up, Mother, for I never have heard it before," she said.

The song follows on the next page.

The Book of Psalms has stimulated creative responses in many Junior children. They can be helped to visualize the temple service in which the material in this songbook of the Hebrew people was used, and many a child has written his own melodies to favorite verses or sentences chosen from the book.

"But how do you get them to want to do it?" someone asks. "It sounds all right, and I think if I could know just what a teacher says and does in a group of Juniors to start them off, I might be able to help my children. I do not seem to sense the happy medium between doing nothing and doing too much."

Perhaps the best answer will be to tell how one Junior leader proceeded with her group. They were midway in a unit of several

GOD'S TREES

A. McK.

Anne McKay

God mak-eth trees to be shad - y, God mak-eth trees to give food; God mak-eth trees to be pret - ty, God mak-eth us to be good.

This song was sung by five-year-old Anne McKay. The melody was transcribed by her mother and harmonized by Mrs. J. E. Purcell. Used by permission Presbyterian Committee of Religious Education.

weeks of study of the Bible as a book. When they began the discussion of the book of Hebrew songs and read one or two of the familiar psalms, they became interested in the fact that David wrote a great many of the songs. They knew that he was once a shepherd boy tending his sheep on the hills of Bethlehem, that he was sent to play on his harp and sing to King Saul, and that later he himself became King of Israel. And they spoke of these things, and of his probable early efforts at making tunes on his shepherd's pipe as he watched his sheep.

"When he was your age," the leader said, "he might not have been able to make up a long or difficult tune. Perhaps his first attempt was to play a birdcall or some other sound that he heard on the hillside. Then by and by beautiful words and music came to him, and later he came to be known as the Sweet Singer of Israel." Then she continued, "Some of you may enjoy finding a sentence or a verse from the Book of Psalms and making a tune for it, to be brought to church school next Sunday."

To the next session of the group, five out of the twenty Junior boys and girls brought original melodies to verses or sentences they had chosen.

They did their work in different ways. One had sung his tune to his mother and she had written the notes for him; three had written their own music; one arrived extra early and asked the pianist if she would let him sing his tune to her and write it for him before the other children came.

Criteria for the Selection of Songs

BY VIVIAN SHARP MORSCH

If music is to be related to all of a child's life, and continue to be so, as the child grows, then Christian educators must learn to make intelligent selections of music on the basis of:

- The goals of Christian education.
- The age level characteristics—mental, emotional, spiritual.
- The musical capacity of the age levels.
- The worth of the music.
- The ability of the music to communicate to the age level.

To like a piece of music is not sufficient reason in itself for its inclusion in a curriculum. Musical taste may have been immature when the liking was acquired. Enthusiasm for the song will be communicated to those who are taught. Perhaps the song is not worthy of perpetuation. On the other hand, the song may be excellent, but unsuited to the use to be made of it. The following standards will serve as criteria in the selection of songs:

1. The ideas in the songs should be in harmony with the total curriculum. Right ideas of God, Jesus, the Bible, the Church and social relationships must be embodied in the songs. Take, for example, the idea that one can pray at any time and anywhere, which is well expressed in the song "I Talk to God Wherever I May Be" (*Hymns for Primary Worship*, No. 38):

Vivian Sharp Morsch, *The Use of Music in Christian Education* (Philadelphia: The Westminster Press, 1956. Copyright by W. L. Jenkins), pp. 109–113. Used by permission.

I talk to God wherever I may be,
At school, at home, at church, or at my play;
He understands the thoughts I try to say—
He hears me! God hears me!

I talk to God when I am very glad
For lovely things that happen every day;
I tell Him "thank you" in my own small way—
He hears me! God hears me!

I talk to God when I am ill or sad;
I whisper to Him when I feel afraid;
He helps me to do right when I have prayed—
God hears me! God hears me!
                    —*Kathryn Blackburn Peck.*

2. The song-poem should be well-expressed and the phraseology suited to the age level for which it is intended. Sometimes simple ideas are expressed in phrases that need a great deal of explanation, and sometimes ideas phrased in simple words are too deep for children to comprehend. Although it is easier to explain words than ideas, it is well for both to have meaning for the singers. Symbolism is inappropriate to use with young children. For example, the poetic beauty of Psalm 104, paraphrased by Robert Grant in "O Worship the King," will be lost to children whose limited experience would prevent them from interpreting the word pictures with any real meaning. Even for junior children the poem is too heavily symbolic. The hymn becomes useful for juniors with careful editing. Three stanzas, the first, second, and third, set to the appropriate tune arranged from J. Michael Haydn, make this good hymn suitable to use with junior children.

"All Glory, Laud, and Honor" (Theodulph of Orleans), which is sung on Palm Sunday in all our churches, contains words like "laud," "Redeemer," "hosannas," which are not in the conversational vocabulary of primary children. Nevertheless, the concepts are easily grasped through simple explanation, and the song is given meaningful usage. The literary value is important. Eternal truths, God's laws for the universe and for our lives, should be spoken of in language of beauty and sincerity, the language of good poetry. Consider, as an example, this simple, direct song text from *Hymns for Primary Worship,* No. 15:

> O God, whose laws will never change,
> We thank You for these things we know:
> That after rain the sun will shine;
> That after darkness light appears;
> That winter always brings the spring;
> That after sleep we wake again;
> That life goes on, and love remains,
> And life and love can never die.
> *—Jeanette E. Perkins. Copyright, The*
> *Pilgrim Press. Used by permission.*

3. The rhythmic framework of the song should be strong. Rhythm furnishes the structural balance and proportion of music. All markedly rhythmic music is not necessarily in good rhythm. Clapping a rhythm will sometimes help to evaluate it. Monotonous repetition of a dotted eighth or sixteenth note figure tends to cheapen composition. Julia Ward Howe's "Battle Hymn of the Republic" has survived, in magnificent grandeur, in spite of the trite rhythm with which it has been associated. One has only to tap out the rhythm to see what the effect would be without the benefit of the beautiful words. One should beware of all "jingly" rhythms. Songs with repeated syncopations, the kind that affect the feet primarily, are not good for religious expression. For example, the accenting of the second pulse throughout will give this effect:

Contrast with that "limping" rhythm the strongly marked one of the "Adeste Fideles," which also employs a 4/4 framework, but has majesty and spirit in the distribution of accents:

4. Simple melodic lines are more apt to be good than over-elaborate ones. The tune should be singable and in the same spirit as the words. "Fairest Lord Jesus" is an excellent example of a well-formed tune. It lies almost entirely within an octave range, moves diatonically with few intervals larger than a third. The graceful dignity of the song-poem is repeated in the tune. Words and music communicate the same idea. The melody of a song becomes so completely linked with the words that it becomes difficult to disassociate them in one's thoughts. For this reason alone a good melody is of great importance.

"Melody streams from the heart flowing upon the joyous impulses of the soul in tune and in time with Infinite Cause.

"Melody is the charted movement of the feelings made glad by the soul's approval. In its harmonious embrace, brief as it may be, we feel related to something somewhere beyond ourselves" (*Beyond the Tonal Horizon of Music,* by Frederick Schlieder).

5. Harmonic value is difficult for the musically uneducated to judge. There are basic laws governing harmonization which, if followed, give a satisfactory effect. Harmony is inherent in the structure of a melody. It is also obvious when two or more parts appear simultaneously. Harmony enters into vocal music through the part song or by way of instrumental accompaniment to melody. For the purpose of accompanying children's voices, the harmonization should be simple, unobtrusive, and primary. Songs for the very young are effective without harmonization. In the youth and adult divisions of the church, two-, three-, and four-part music may be sung without difficulty. The hymns in their hymnals are usually written in harmonized form. Good harmonizations enrich the meaning of the texts. An example of a very good harmonization in a hymn is "St. Anne," by William Croft. Isaac Watts's words "Our God, Our Help in Ages Past" are at one with the strong harmony of the music.

Having said all of this in classes for many years, and having used examples both good and not so good, I am no longer surprised to have people come to me after a session concentrated on evaluation and selection, hand me a book of choruses or a book of gospel hymns, and ask seriously of specific hymns, "Isn't this good music?" Because our taste is something about which we are all more or less sensitive, it is difficult to discuss the subject and not tread on feelings. And the sensitivity is more acute when the experience association with the hymn is strong and important. The important factor is not that leaders should destroy experience memories, but that they must recognize the inadvisability of perpetuating unsuitable music with those to whom they teach music for its teaching value.

We do not necessarily recognize beauty because we have been told that it exists. The degree to which we discern beauty is, to some extent, determined by the experience that we have had with it, just as we cannot fully comprehend goodness until we have seen pure goodness in Jesus Christ. Mrs. Clarence Dickinson tells a story about an encounter that a Brooklyn librarian had with some young apartment house dwellers. Passing down a street paved with cement from one side to the other, she came upon a little group of children looking intently at something in the center of their closed circle. Recognizing some of the children, she asked what it was at which they were gazing. Whereupon, they faced her with glowing faces and pointed to a crack in the cement in which was growing a tiny patch of grass. "Look, Miss Brown," they cried, "it's a park." Souls starved for musical expression, and never having learned to discriminate between true beauty and its poor imitation, sometimes eagerly accept songs that have no more in common with true hymns than the patch of grass had with a real park.

Selecting Songs for the Kindergarten

BY EDITH LOVELL THOMAS

Some points to check in judging the fitness of songs for the kindergarten period:

Short and simple tunes—more of four lines than longer; more stepwise, than wider intervals; more straight quarter, eighth, and half notes than dotted notes.

Words easy to say and understand—more one and two syllable words than longer; more familiar vocabulary than new; more concrete than general ideas, attached to a child's everyday living, instead of doctrinal ideas or moralizing in adult language.

Natural feeling tone—spontaneous gladness, appreciation, hushed attitude, eagerness for a story, wanting to *do* something, like dramatic or rhythmic play.

Giving wings to imagination—including humor, looking through brightly colored glasses to find new friends and go places, missing no pleasures.

Sense of security—need to belong to family, church, God.

Right relations with people—friendly feeling for helpful action, thankful spirit.

Love of beautiful things—themes of good music, connected with the church, poetic verse, fine pictures associated with songs.

Questioning, wondering—exploring mystery, reaching out toward God. Source of all life.

Edith Lovell Thomas, *Music in Christian Education* (Nashville: Abingdon Press, 1953), pp. 89–90. Used by permission.

Listening to Music

BY VIVIAN SHARP MORSCH

Music is a tonal art which depends on aural sensitivity to transmit impressions to the mind, emotions, and body. Listening is the initial phase of every musical impression and a very necessary part of every musical expression.

A natural result of musical impression is some form of activity which involves either physical action or mental and emotional response, or both. These total responses to listening are highly desirable for children. They learn to listen more keenly when the impression is given immediate response through activity. By this process they learn how to respond to musical stimuli.

There must be some listening experiences, for people of all ages, in which the listener is quiet and allows the music to speak directly to the heart. This experience is closely akin to the religious experience of which the psalmist spoke, "Be still, and know that I am God" (Ps. 46:10). It is in outward quiet that the spirit of man apprehends God. It is when the body is inert and the mind and emotions are tuned to the sound of music that it possesses his being and he is truly aware of its meaning and significance. The experience of listening to music, in order to be possessed by its beauty, when joined to the suggestion of the psalmist makes a strong impact on the spirit. The discipline of listening to music (when so channeled) may well serve to strengthen the discipline of true worship.

Vivian Sharp Morsch, "Listening Experiences," *The Use of Music in Christian Education* (Philadelphia: The Westminster Press, 1956. Copyright by W. L. Jenkins), pp. 71–75. Used by permission.

Pure listening experiences may occur in the church school, the choir, the church worship services, the organizational meetings, and especially in the home.

A soloist, pianist, an organist, a group of singers or players, or a phonograph recording may furnish the music.

The Use of Phonograph Recordings

Phonograph recordings have many uses in a church program. Wherever Christian education is going on, recordings are invaluable—in the home, the Sunday church school, youth meetings, choir rehearsals, Women's Association meetings, vacation school, weekday classes, and Family Night gatherings. A creative teacher will discover, with joy, ways to enrich teaching experiences with recordings.

By using a record player and a few choice recordings, a person's musical horizon may be extended; higher levels of artistic taste may be developed; the joy and satisfaction of artistic performance, beyond one's own ability, may be vicariously experienced; a teacher is enabled to present teaching material with a degree of artistry to which he can never attain; learning experiences may be greatly enriched and heightened.

Recordings may be used for preludes, offertories, and interludes in worship services; moods and attitudes may be created; rhythmic activities and toy bands are made effective with recordings. Songs may be taught and lessons illustrated. The imagination may be stimulated and other creative activities motivated by the use of recordings. Besides all these uses, recordings may be used just for the pleasure of listening.

In choosing recordings for use with young children it is well to select predominantly melodic and rhythmic music. Especially suitable are those performed by solo instruments or voices, for young children "hear" solos better than ensembles. The span of attention in young children is short; hence, recordings for them should not be long. Small portions of long compositions may frequently be used effectively.

Selection of a Record Library

The church record library should be selected with great care. The best economy results when records are chosen that will have many possible uses. The selection of recordings is based on the same standards that govern the selection of good music in education. A basic library should be chosen to include some records for all age groups and to correlate with all areas of the program and curriculum. Children respond to and absorb only the music that they can make their own. Since many people own good private collections of records, it should be easy to borrow, from time to time, records for special purposes to augment the church collection. Parts of extended works that would not ordinarily be included in a church library, because of cost, are made available in this way. For example, some movements of symphonies and concertos are suitable for worship purposes, but are not available except in albums of the complete works. The second movement of the Brahms Violin Concerto and much of the Beethoven Ninth Symphony are uplifting and worshipful, but impossible to secure in part. A loan of the desired records will help to extend the library.

Preparation for a Lesson

In preparing for a lesson that will employ recordings, the teacher should plan carefully for their inclusion. He should:

- Be sure the recording will speak to the need in the "spot" in which it is to be used. (Is the purpose clear?)
- Familiarize himself with its language before presenting it to a class.
- Adjust the record player before the class period, for volume and tone.
- Be sure of the beginning and ending places if only a portion of the record is to be played.
- Plan the presentation and follow-up so that the record fits smoothly into the lesson.

Teacher's Attitude

The attitude of the teacher, while listening to music, will greatly affect the class's appreciation of the music. If he is attentive and thoughtful, so will the class be. If he starts the record player and then moves about the room, or focuses his attention on a book, looks out of the window, or in some other way distracts the attention, the class will be inattentive.

The Record Player

Record players are not necessarily expensive equipment. They may be purchased for as little as twenty-five dollars; however, it should be remembered that equipment gets hard use around an institution, and it is advisable to pay considerably more for a machine. The durability of the machine is therefore of more importance than the initial cost. It is also necessary that the record player be equipped to play records of different r.p.m. speeds. It is very desirable for each department to have its own record player. Preschool departments especially need their own, because in the very informal type of program, it is very difficult to know in advance when the machine will be most needed. It is possible, however, to so plan a schedule for the use of the equipment that one machine may be shared by the school. This does limit the use of the record library in any one department. It is wise to appoint a responsible person to care for the machine to make sure that the needle arm is fastened when it is being carried, that efficient performance is maintained, and adjustments and servicing arranged for.

Care of the Records

The records also represent a valuable investment, and adequate provision should be made for their storage. The library should be kept in one central spot, and one person should be in charge of cataloguing and loaning. A filing cabinet may be purchased or made. Records should be stored vertically and kept in a room that remains at fairly moderate temperatures at all times, to avoid warping. The record librarian should be contacted well in advance of the day on which a record is to be used in order that he may work out any conflicts in schedule that may occur.

A Long-Range List Should Be Made

The task of "digging out" a sufficient list of recorded music to meet the requirements of a church's education program is harder than it should be. The National Council of Churches, Division of Christian Education, has started creating record materials and lists, but until a great many more records with small bands have been placed on the market, it will be necessary to study carefully to get the greatest value for the number of records purchased. It may take time, research, and some money to build an adequate record library, but it is one of the most rewarding of educational projects.

A "dreamer's" list could be made up as a library "at the goal" and kept posted where all may see. Gifts of money and gifts of the desired records may reward you for your effort. Build your library gradually and carefully. Maybe you can buy only one or two records a year, but be sure that they will be the two most useful ones you can buy.

Relating Church School and Choir Musical Experiences—For Juniors and Teen-Agers Especially

BY EDITH LOVELL THOMAS

The sense of belonging is a deep need of every child as of every adult. As soon as one is old enough to sing in a group, he begins to draw satisfaction from the common heritage which is his as a member of society. The music that his spiritual fathers accumulated is a rich deposit and one of the most accessible of his possessions. The "perpetual hopes" of the great religious traditions are celebrated with peculiar power in poetry and music. These arts suggest the unseen and the real with compelling clarity.

The junior and teen-ager, being good "joiners" and keen about all lively and lovely things, are ready to enter with comrades into choir activities even though they have had no taste of them earlier. These express and cement for them more effectively, their relationship with the religious community. Through the choir their desire to belong can be fulfilled.

How a true ministry of music can be performed is hard to see without the educational training which an intelligent and systematic choir affords. In it are learned the best hymn resources of the ages and the art of singing them with understanding. Under its direction opportunity is granted to offer musical service in public worship, and the individual is initiated into the widest, most stimulating fellowship known to human beings—the Christian Church.

Edith Lovell Thomas, *Music in Christian Education* (Nashville: Abingdon Press, 1953), pp. 107–109, 109–110. Used by permission.

Worship, highest of all arts, demands long, diligent study and practice. Children and youth through choir auspices have opened to them tried disciplines where the art of worship is cultivated under competent teachers. Culture of the religious spirit in the impressionable young person is nurtured through the release of his finest emotions—love, joy, aspiration—on the wings of music. To deny him this outlet is to choke the very springs of his inner life at their source.[1]

Close correlation of the music taught in the choir with the curriculum the choristers are studying in their church school is an imperative commonly disregarded. Sometimes the two programs are rivals or even opposed to each other. How the singers function as live worshipers in both church and school is a responsibility that rests squarely on the shoulders of music leaders and teachers. Rewarding results come only from careful, co-operative planning. Without this boys and girls receive fragmentary impressions due to disparate efforts and unco-ordinated fare.

To get at the need for integration of materials, sharing of purposes, and working together for satisfying experiences firsthand information has been sought through personal correspondence. Recent reports, in printed or mimeographed form, of attempts to deal with the problem also are quoted to shed light on its solution.

Excerpts from replies to letters show concern over what is happening to junior and teen-age groups when blind guides are in charge, or because enlightened foresight is not present. This situation apparently has received slight attention. Now, however, anxiety over it is expressed and efforts to alter it are beginning to be made.

Music, a Meeting Place for Juniors and Adults

Here is an encouraging story from a teacher:

In a vacation school the juniors were using a unit on the church. In the course of our study we went to visit a Negro church. The

---

[1] Edith Lovell Thomas, "The Junior Choir," *Religious Education,* September–October, 1949.

minister of that church told us how the congregation had come to have their church and explained some of the symbols. He told us that his congregation loved to sing. We told him that we had learned to sing the Spiritual, "Lord, I want to be a Christian," at vacation school and asked if he would sing it with us. He replied that he usually depended on the choir and since some of the women were in the kitchen that morning, preparing a dinner, he would ask them to come in and sing with us. They came in quietly. Soon the church rang with the music of the Spiritual. It was beautiful. In talking over our visit the juniors agreed that the nicest part had been when they sang with the choir at the church.[2]

Beginnings of Integration

From a director of religious education:

What have I done in the musical ministry to integrate the activities and program of choirs and church school? My quick reply would be, "Only a beginning." The four youth choirs, numbering one hundred and twenty-five, are church school choirs. No one is a member who is not an active member in the church school. We have almost perfect attendance the year through, without any awards, prizes, etc. This is due largely to an approach through the medium of worship, building concepts of God on the various age levels, so that songs, hymns, and anthems have meaning for them. The groups all seem to have a deep sense of worship, both in the church and church school. For instance, we never have the problem of whispering. No adult ever sits with them. We study together not only the music, but the meaning of the words of the anthem, which results in vital, meaningful singing, and a real worship experience.

The former pastor of this church always worked with me on the worship service when the youth choirs sang—the third one of the month was their Sunday. The music of both senior and youth choirs was pertinent to the whole service.

As I work with the choirs I try to keep constantly in mind that it isn't how well they sing, though they do sing beautifully, but how fully they enter into the service of worship, and leave with a feeling of having shared as well as received.[3]

---

[2] Mrs. Fred V. McDonnell, Carlisle, Pennsylvania.

[3] Grace Mary Williams, Director of Religious Education (including music), Oak Park, Illinois.

Choir and School Working in Unison

A minister of music and education reports:

We have worked through the medium of a Saturday Choir School. The School is set up to enrich the regular Sunday Church School program and to give definite music training. In order to accomplish our purpose we have laid very careful plans. The leaders of each age group in the Sunday and Saturday Schools have met with both the Dean of the School and the Minister of Music and Education. Selection of material is made in order that each knows what the other is doing. The musical resource people, who were also at the initial meeting, then get together with the Minister of Music and Education and discuss the program of music, which, incidentally, includes choric reading material as well. All of this must correlate with the other materials being used.

Songs are selected for their melodic values and, of course, for the subject matter being taught. Scripture readings to be used in various corporate worship periods are worked out by the choric reading leaders and are taught to the children. Both the songs and the scripture selections are used in both the Sunday and the Saturday Schools.

Music is selected, for the most part, to meet the needs of the various age groups, but in cases where selections are to be used in corporate worship some suitable songs of each age level are taught to the children of all age levels. They therefore have some selections which they all know and can join in and sing together periodically.

It has been our experience that the children have responded magnificently to the program, learning very important basic philosophies set forth in the songs used. It is a startling fact that because materials to be used in corporate worship are known and understood by these children their participation in such services changes from, in some cases, chaos to dignified, meaningful worship for all participating—even in the situations where the children are sharing their worship experiences with adults in formal Sunday morning services.

Music has become among all these children a vital, living source of Christian character, I believe.[4]

---

[4] Nelle Gilmore, Minister of Music and Education, Old First Presbyterian Church, San Francisco, California.

Choral Speaking

BY MARY ALICE DOUTY

To one who cannot sing beautifully the discovery of choral speaking is an opening door. To anyone who loves great literature, the sound of words, and the noble expression of fine thought, choral speaking offers a new experience in understanding and enjoyment.

With the exception of melody choral speaking involves the use of every technique known to the singing choir, plus the additional freedom that comes from not being bound by the measures of printed music. There is opportunity for creative thinking about the passage to be interpreted chorally. Rich hidden meanings in the words come out as we try first one interpretation and then another.

A group of juniors was preparing the Christmas story for choral speaking as their part in a Christmas service. When they came to the verse, "And when they had opened their treasures, they presented unto him gifts," there was long discussion as to how the words should be said. Some felt that the word to be emphasized most was "him" since the gifts were being made to the Christ child. One boy said, "No, the important thing is the gifts." Other words in the line were suggested as being most important. Finally the sentence was spoken in every different way possible. When emphasis was put on the word "treasures," a new understanding came over the group. One of the children summed up

Mary Alice Douty, "Group Experience in Choral Speaking," *How to Work with Church Groups* (Nashville: Abingdon Press, 1957), pp. 141–153. Used by permission.

the feeling: "They didn't give him their leftovers or something they didn't want. They brought their treasures!" The group agreed that this was the way they understood the line and wanted to say it.

The important thing here is that the leader, while he had thought deeply about the passage, did not come to the group with a preconceived idea that it would go best with one particular emphasis. He had given the passage enough thought to be aware of many feelings and possibilities of interpretation. Yet he wanted primarily to involve the group in the passage to the extent that it would take on deeper meaning for them. The interpretation must be theirs, not his. As the group shared ideas, there was good thinking. The more people, the richer the interpretation.

Use choral speaking for a psalm or poem which your group has written. The piece will take on deeper meaning, even for those who shared in the writing. Speaking it chorally, the group will be able to share their thoughts with others in the beautiful setting that good words deserve. Some young people wrote a psalm of Thanksgiving, spending much time in thought about what gave them greatest cause for giving thanks. The psalm took the form of a litany. They named homes, country, friends, church, memories, learning, and the example of great leaders as the things for which they were most thankful. A sentence or two was written about each idea. After each idea a refrain followed, "We give thee thanks, O Lord." In sharing the litany with a larger group, half the young people spoke the idea. The whole group joined in on the response. On the next idea the other half spoke. Again the whole group joined in the response. So it went through the whole litany, giving variety and depth to the words.

Choral speaking also has the value of letting the shy person participate freely. Speaking with others, he loses the fright of his own voice. As he gains confidence, he finds a fullness in his voice that he had not known he possessed. He may even find himself expressing his ideas more easily alone. He has at least had the happy experience of contributing his voice to help make some expression more beautiful, more meaningful.

For junior-high-school people choral speaking is especially helpful in a practical way. It gives them the opportunity to try out the new, wider range of their voices without being subject to embarrassment. To speak as softly as possible, and then again with great volume, to speak in a voice as low deep down as a well, or again in a voice as light as a trembling summer breeze, helps a boy or girl to find new confidence in his voice and to develop its use. Choral-speaking youngsters do not grow up to become nasal-voiced adults. A pleasant and a powerful voice is a great asset. Practice, confidence, and enjoyment in the use of the voice contribute to this very practical goal.

A basic question about choral speaking is this: How does the untrained leader who wants to use this technique with his group begin? The answer is simply: *Think* and begin.

Start your group off with a well-known nursery rhyme. Adults have as much fun as children saying "Humpty-Dumpty sat on a wall." Start your group on the rhyme and then listen as they speak. Get some fun and laughter into the experience. Nothing frees and unites a group so quickly as laughter. Try another nursery rhyme, and this time mark the tempo with your hand, keeping the voices together. Take "Little Jack Horner." After the group has said the rhyme once, ask individuals to give some different inflections to the last line, "What a good boy am I." The boy can sound like anything from a prig to a clown depending on how the words are said.

To get a different experience, use the verse, "Pussy cat, pussy cat, where have you been?" Divide the group into two parts without any attempt at locating voices. Let one group ask the questions and the other group answer. Still keep the experience one of fun. No dull flat voices saying, "I've been to London to see the queen," but *"I've* been to London, to see the *queen."*

Then try "Jack Be Nimble." Let one group say the first line, the second part the next line, and the whole group the final line,

"Jack jump over the candlestick." Say the verse very fast without any break in the rhythm. It is not as easy as it sounds. If you are speaking with primary children, let them jump, still in rhythm, on the next beat after candlestick.

So you have begun. And what have you accomplished? You have led your group in having fun doing something together. Everyone has taken part. Each one has discovered and used his voice with the others. There has been a discipline within the group as each tries to stay with the rhythm. You have given them experience with unison and two-part speaking. And you have given them opportunity to try their own interpretations of the ways in which familiar words may be said. Also you have given yourself some experience, perhaps some pleasure and some confidence in choral-speaking leadership.

When you are ready for serious work with your group, you will want to arrange your speaking choir by voice. Speaking voices and singing voices do not always correspond. A woman may be able to sing notes very low on the scale and yet have what we call a "light" speaking voice. A little practice in listening will enable the leader to group the choir in many arrangements. For two-part work with adults there will usually be the men's voices in one group and the women's in another. But there will be exceptions. Some women's voices will be heavier than some men's. With very young children there will be little difference in the voices of most. It is hardest to group the junior- and senior-high-school ages. And there will be need for constant regrouping since the voices are developing and changing. Most choral work for this group, and indeed for older and younger groups as well, will fall easily into a three-part division: high, or light, voices; medium voices; and low, or dark, voices. There will occasionally be work in which you will want a cumulative effect, starting with a very few voices, adding a few more, then more and more until a climax is reached. This, added to volume control, can give a startling effect.

Rhythm is essential to effective speaking, but it can be a pitfall. All too often we have heard unskilled recitations of poetry in a sing-song manner. The beat of the poem has been strictly adhered to, but true rhythm is lacking. It is particularly necessary to help children to see the complete thought in a poem, never reading line by line. Here again the interpretation of meaning by the group helps to subdue the rhythm to its proper place of undercurrent.

In the matters of tone, volume, and breathing, little can be said that common sense will not readily support. Good posture, for example, leads to better speaking. Deep breathing produces a better tone of voice. A rounded mouth opening produces a rounder tone than a thin flat opening of the lips. Good diction involves the use of many muscles. Very loud and very soft speaking require additional attention to diction. And it is most important that loud speaking come from deep within the diaphragm.

In all of these matters nothing will take the place of thoughtful practice and experimentation. If your group is thinking and experimenting with you, together you will achieve skill in speaking and pleasure in using this method of interpreting and sharing fine writing.

Use choral speaking for a psalm and see how the words take on new meaning. An adult group studying the first psalm this way was delighted with the discovery of the word progression of "walk," "stand," and "sit." In changing from light to dark voices, they brought out the contrast between the good man and the wicked. Thinking about how the words should be spoken led to thinking about the meaning of the psalm.

Many of the psalms are meant to be used antiphonally or as litanies. They lend themselves so well to this treatment that one is tempted to speak them as they appear. Our purpose, however, is to stimulate thinking as well as to speak the passage beautifully. Without drawing out discussion too far, the leader must be sure that everyone has opportunity to suggest his interpretation of the piece. Then the emphasis which most people agree on is adopted and the interpretation is set.

The psalms are not the only portions of the Bible which can be used effectively in choral speaking, but they will help us to illustrate some of the wide variety which can be obtained through this medium.

A good example of antiphonal work is Psalm 24. The first two verses are a statement of creation and might be spoken in unison by all voices. Then come the questions and answers. Through several readings of the psalm, the group would have to decide whether the light voices or the dark voices should ask the questions. The group may feel that since there is more power of assertion in the answers, the dark voices should take this part. Another approach to this psalm would be to have a light group, a dark group, and a solo voice. In this case the light group and the dark group together could affirm the opening stanzas and the solo voice ask the questions. After the first question the light voices might answer alone. After the second question in vs. 7 the dark voices might answer alone. And after the final question both groups could join together in the strongest affirmation with which the psalm ends.

Psalm 46 is a good example of contrasts. It moves from the strength of God in the roaring earthquakes to the river of vs. 4, whose streams make glad the city of God. Then the psalm builds up again to a climax in vs. 7. Verses 8–10 introduce a mood of quiet and peace, ending with the line, "Be still, and know that I am God." This is a line which a group might want to whisper. The last two lines of the psalm would undoubtedly be spoken with all the strength of the combined voices of the group.

Psalm 136 offers the interesting possibility of an undercurrent refrain throughout the song. From vs. 2 to vs. 25 there is not one period or break in the psalm. Much of its beauty and movement is lost by the somewhat monotonous repetition of the refrain, "For his kindness is everlasting." If a group can feel the pulse of this refrain and put the opposing lines into that same rhythm, they can maintain a continuous speaking of both parts at the same time. Let the deep voices take the refrain and speak it softly but with definitely marked rhythm. The lighter voices take the first line of each verse, but after vs. 1 let them begin speaking immediately after "For his kindness." The dark voices maintain a continuous flow of the refrain, with the light voices speaking over them and always coming in at the same place. Finally at the conclusion of the psalm the dark voices have one full line of refrain after the light voices finish.

Psalm 148 is one which boys and girls like to speak chorally because of its closeness to Francis of Assisi's "Canticle of the Sun." And Psalm 150 offers an excellent opportunity for a study of the musical instruments of the Hebrews. Boys and girls like to make its "Hallelujah" ring and speak the first two and one-half verses with full strength. Usually they see a contrast coming in the line about the lyre and lute. They like to take this line softly and build gradually back to full strength for the crashing cymbals and the final "Hallelujah."

The Christmas story, with its angel's voice, Mary's song, and Simeon's prayer, gives ample opportunity for the use of solo voices. The Palm Sunday story with its "Hosannahs" is another of the passages which reads particularly well chorally. Throughout the Old Testament there are songs and poems which a group used to choral speaking would want to interpret. A class or department studying ideas of God in the Old Testament would find choral speaking of selected passages an excellent way to tie their study together and enrich it. And there are many passages in the words of Jesus and in the writings of Paul which ought to be in our possession. A sharp and living challenge to any group which prepares it for choral speaking is I Cor. 13.

The important thing always is that the thinking and the interpreting shall be done by the group. If the leader says, "Do it this way," the effect is much the same as putting on a play. If we are trying to make the Bible come alive, to get inside it, and to get it inside us, the thinking and the interpretation must grow within ourselves. We find help in sharing the thoughts of a group and the inspiration of a good teacher, but the thoughts we hold and live by must be our own.

A group of more than a hundred young adults at a conference had come together after a busy day of discussion and speeches for a time of relaxing and enjoying choral speaking. Few had ever participated in the art. The leader used "Humpty Dumpty" to break the ice and give the group a sense of togetherness. The ice was effectively broken when one of the group suggested the addition of the words "Poor Humpty" at the end of the rhyme.

Next a poem about the wind gave everyone a chance to blow off steam. The poem was done in two parts, one part speaking the poem while the other part gave a whistling, rustling undercurrent of wind effect. Of course the poem was done a second time with the parts changed so that everyone had a chance at being the wind! Someone suggested that the wind ought to begin blowing before the words began and that both should reach a peak of volume in the middle of the poem, then die away, with the sighing of the wind continuing for a second at the close of the poem. The effect was far different from anything the leader had anticipated. It was an immediate success. The group was functioning; it was creative; it was having a wonderful time.

James Weldon Johnson's sermon-poem, "The Creation," had been used at the conference earlier in the day. Parts of this were taken by the group and interpreted chorally. Small parts of it were used, so there was no need to have anything written. Papers or blackboard would have been artificial, and they would certainly have detracted from the air of relaxation.

One sentence that the deep-voiced men enjoyed especially was:

> Darkness covered everything,
> Blacker than a hundred midnights
> Down in a cypress swamp.[1]

---

[1] Used by permission of The Viking Press, New York.

No cypress swamp was ever further down than that one! The contrast of the next line was carried by the lightest voices: "Then God smiled."

A few lines of very fast-running words loosened any remaining tight muscle. When the hour was up, the group had three small parts of the poem interpreted and spoken to their satisfaction. They also had a refrain that fitted in after several sections of the poem. As a conclusion to the hour the leader spoke the poem, drawing the group in on the parts that had been practiced. It was obvious that the group had found relaxation and pleasure in an hour thus spent.

In another session the group turned to the majestic poem of creation found in Gen. 1. Parts of this were taken by the group and interpreted chorally. Small parts of it were used, so there was no need to have anything written. Only the leader and the solo voices had the words before them.

The rhythm of movement was appreciated as the group saw how the poem was divided into parts by the words, "Evening came and morning came, making the first day." They practiced this line to get just the right shading of pause and rest. They saw how each new day and act of creation began with the words, "And God said." One of the men who had a particularly good voice was chosen to speak the words attributed to God.

Following each of God's utterances the group saw the pattern of the words, "And it was so. . . . And God saw that it was good." They worked on these lines and selected an individual to read the detailed parts about each day's creation. When they came to vs. 27, where God created man in his own image, they decided to speak this verse in unison rather than solo because of its significance. Similarly, they all spoke the summarizing vs. 31, where God saw all that he had created. A solo voice read the next three verses which conclude the story.

At this point there was some dissatisfaction. Many in the group felt that there should be a concluding line spoken in unison, yet the last line of the poem did not quite meet the need they felt.

Several lines were suggested and tried, such as, "God created everything good," "God is the creator of all," and "In the beginning God created the heavens and the earth."

One young woman spoke excitedly after this last trial: "The point is that God is the beginning of everything. We don't all agree on the details of creation, but we do agree that God is the will and purpose and guide in the universe. So why not end the poem simply with the first four words, 'In the beginning God'?"

The group tried the phrase very slowly and quietly with a long pause before the last word. Agreement was unanimous. The choral speaking had ceased to be merely the beautiful rendering of a great poem. In those four words the group had found an affirmation and a conviction. They had found a kinship with the ancient writer. There might be questions among the scientific as to the details of creation, but a firm unity of fundamental belief filled the group.

That evening at vespers, sitting on the hillside and watching the glow of fading sunset, the group spoke the poem in worship. It was an act of reverent appreciation and dedication. An ancient truth had taken on new life.

Aside from its value for pleasure, its value for developing voices and confidence, and its value for reading more deeply into the meanings of great writing, choral speaking has its finest use in the service of worship. Think of the effect of having the psalms or some other poetic passage of scripture read chorally on a Sunday morning! Here also is an excellent way for the superintendent to bring in class participation in the departmental worship service. The Christmas story and litanies of Thanksgiving, as we have already seen, lend themselves very well to choral interpretation. Dramatic services of worship can also make effective use of the speaking choir.

A group of intermediates developed such a service at the conclusion of a study of the prophets. The service was extremely simple but powerful in its effect of drawing together the great thoughts of these men. The effect was similar to that of John Sargent's frieze. One after another the prophets appeared before the group in characteristic dress and pose. A spokesman gave a sentence or two about each one and his teaching. A choir speaking in the background then gave a verse or two that was most familiar from the prophet's writing. The dignity of the young people, the quality of their expression, left no doubt that their best thinking and planning had gone into this summary and sharing of their studies.

A final word about choral speaking and memorization. The juniors referred to earlier prepared the entire Christmas story, combined from Matthew and Luke, but with the genealogies and a few verses omitted. The story took one complete page, single spaced. When the papers were handed out at the first meeting, a cry of dismay arose from the group. "Do we have to memorize all this?"

The leader said, "No, you don't have to," and went on to the interpretation of the material. It was the juniors' interpretation that was used all the way through, just as we have seen with the word "treasures." There were six sessions spent in preparing the passage for the Christmas service. At the fourth session two of the girls announced, "We don't need our papers." The leader commended them and went on with the practice. She noticed that very few were using their papers. At the beginning of the fifth session one of the boys said, "Don't let's use papers. I think we do better without them."

Memorization? Yes! With understanding, appreciation, and use. Choral speaking gives all three with the additional values of fun and fellowship.

17. LET WORSHIP LIFT THE LEVEL

WORSHIP IS A NECESSARY PART of every Christian life. Otherwise our vision is too short, our challenges too small, our standards too low. Jesus, especially when he was under temptation or pressure, went into long periods of prayer. Typical of these prayer experiences was that in the Garden of Gethsemane, which enabled him to say, "not what I will, but what thou wilt" (Mark: 14:36, RSV). Small wonder that the disciples were moved to come to him with the request, "Lord, teach us to pray" (Luke: 11:1, RSV). Long years of experience in the church have shown that certain elements must always appear in the work of a Christian church. Worship is always at the head of the list.

The pattern of worship experience that most people accept as classic is that of the young Isaiah, reported in Isaiah 6:1–8. It contains the elements or steps that should be found in our experiences and services of worship. First, Isaiah was aware that he was in the presence of God. In the divine presence, he felt his own unworthiness. Then he had a sense of cleansing, or forgiveness, as one of the seraphim touched his mouth with a burning coal. After forgiveness, came a call to service. Then came self-dedication, as Isaiah answered the call by saying, "Here I am! Send me."

The real test of worship is the test of experience. Do the people who participate in a worship service have the types of experience that Isaiah reports? Do they receive calls to service, and do they respond in self-dedication? Worship takes place, if at all, within people.

The Purpose of Worship

BY ORENE MC ILWAIN

*At the heart of worship lies a fundamental human
need—the need of God.*—Powell.

Our deepest need in life is to know God and to respond worthily to His love. This response of the human heart to God, the Eternal, is worship. And it is this experience that the church and the church school seek to bring about in the hearts of little children, young people, and adults.

A minister summarized the purpose of worship in this way:

- To make God real—as real as a mother is to her child.
- To help persons feel strongly enough to DO what is right—not just to KNOW what is right.
- To inspire action.
- To bring peace to the heart—restoring peace and unity of spirit where it is lost, or creating it where it has never existed.

In a workers' conference a group of leaders once expressed the purpose of church school worship in this way:

- To help satisfy man's yearning for God.
- To help children, young people, and adults become *sensitive* to God's nearness, His holiness, His unfailing goodness, His forgiving love, His will and purpose for men and nations.
- To become aware of God's presence as a reality in human experience.

Orene McIlwain, *Worship God* (Richmond: John Knox Press, 1947), pp. 11, 13. Used by permission.

493

- To provide opportunities for worship for the three-, four-, and five-year-old child who seldom comes to church or who understands little of the service when he does come.
- To provide the content of worship at the level of the worshiper's understanding.
- To help the older child, the young person, and the adult understand better how to worship and how to participate in church worship.
- To lift the study of the lesson to a definitely religious level.
- To offer to all a chance to express praise and adoration worthily.

Worship and the Kindergarten Child

Worship for the little child does not occur when a clock says, "Time for worship!" Neither does it happen merely because Father or Mother says, "Fold your hands and bow your head," or because a teacher uses certain words, poems, songs, or Bible verses. Worship may be a reality anytime and anywhere. The small child's capacity for worship will be developed by all of his experiences at home and at church school; but spontaneous worship response may be nourished or blighted by a parent or teacher's own worship attitudes. Church school teachers and parents must work together if the child's worship is to become a meaningful part of his daily life.

A Vital Thread

The genuineness and depth of the child's worship moments in the church school will depend to a great extent upon the richness and effectiveness of the session as a whole. Worship should be a vital thread running through all the kindergarten hours. The child may feel the wonder akin to worship soon after he arrives, as he looks at a picture or an object of nature. His worship may be in a moment of reflection after the story, or in the joy of telling about something that happened that week. It might happen during a walk or while the group is playing and talking together.

It is the teacher's task to understand the child so well that she

Church and the Kindergarten Child (portfolio) (Philadelphia: Board of Christian Education and Publication, Department of Children's Work, Evangelical and Reformed Church). Used by permission.

will be able to recognize opportunities for worship and guide the child's expression. But worship in the kindergarten need not always be expressed in words. True worship is an attitude, a quickening of the emotions directed toward God. Quite often the rapt look on the face of the child, the light in his eyes or the smile is prayer enough.

Worship—Planned and Spontaneous

Whether or not there have been occasions of spontaneous worship, the teacher will plan a few worship moments, usually toward the end of the session, in which she will draw together the day's activities. There should be enough time to give a feeling of leisure, calm and quietness.

A simply arranged beauty center will help in producing an atmosphere in which the child will worship. A small table covered with an attractive cloth and holding a Bible and picture or objects in harmony with the session's theme and purpose can easily be arranged at the place where children and leaders gather for the planned worship. The teacher will watch for the children's readiness and her plans will be flexible; but the response of the children in these planned moments will depend to a large extent upon whether they sense from the teacher's attitude that the moments when we think about God are wonderful ones.

Growing in the Way of Prayer

The child's ability to pray—especially his ability to put his prayer into words—grows as his understanding grows. Because prayer needs to be genuine, parents and teachers must be sensitive to the level of development of a particular child or group of children and to give help when it is needed. Adults can do two things: point to times and situations in which prayer can be meaningful, and put the child's ideas into simple words for him, so that he learns the *way* of praying and can later pray for himself.

Five Stages of Growth

- The most elementary prayer situation is the sense of awe and reverence before beauty or goodness or complexity, and the sense that God is present in these things. There are no prayer words for these moments with the little child, but there will be the response of the spirit—the hush—the wonder—as the child "stands still before the wonders of God."

- Closely akin to such moments are the moments when the child feels directly benefitted by the good things around him. He can begin to form simple thank you prayers. "Thank you, God, for this good food." "Dear God, we are glad for the trees and flowers in spring. Amen." The table prayer of thanks is the easiest to teach because the situation is so common in the child's life. Usually Christian parents will co-operate with the church school in this if they are asked to do so. Many parents use a memorized prayer that is well worded, and is repeated regularly, but which has become routine and meaningless. The church school teacher will need to help the child understand that he can be glad and thankful to God for *any* good thing. Perhaps the parents will help by sitting down for a moment at bedtime, helping the child to think over all the good things that have happened during the day. The child can choose the nicest thing. Around it first the parent—later the child—can word a simple "thank you" sentence.

- As the child grows in his sense of God's presence in all things, his feeling of a personal relationship also grows, and he has feelings of adoration and love. God can become his friend. Spontaneous prayer about anything and everything is the natural result of this sense of companionship. The teacher can talk about God as being a close and interested friend, but here again she must enlist the parent's help. She can point out to them that the child who has learned to go to bed thinking about and talking to a loving God who is near, will not be afraid of the dark or of the bad dreams that begin to disturb

the late fours and fives. Here the child's inadequacy with
words need be no barrier. God understands even when the
child doesn't say it very well. We should put no limits on the
things he tells God—important or unimportant. We should
remember, too, that a child's life is not all "sweetness and
light." It is made up not only of things for which he wants to
say "thank you," but also of "bad days," when he needs sympathy and understanding. We should encourage him to share
these times also with God.

• When the five-year-old's world has widened sufficiently to include a vivid awareness of other persons and their needs, his
prayers should also include these persons. At first he will simply be talking about them as he talks about himself. Later he
will pray *for* them as he prays *for* himself. The vague and
impersonal "God bless Mommy and Daddy" can be made
more meaningful for the small child if we give it a little
thought. It might be "Love Mama and Daddy and be close to
them" or "Be their friend as you are my friend." Later perhaps it will be. "Take care of Mother and Daddy as you help
them to take care of me." These simple ideas, expressed first
by the teacher or parent, can be understood by the child. Later
he will choose his own words and say them himself.

• Finally, as the child thinks of himself as able to do right and
wrong, and becomes aware of his own mistakes and his own
unloving inward feelings, he can learn to pray for help. Too
often our church school language consists only of the positive
statements, "We love one another. We share. We don't hit, do
we Johnny?" But what if we do? Every child by virtue of the
fact that he is born into this present world in the usual self-
centered state, grows up with many unlovely feelings inside
him. He *doesn't* like everybody. He doesn't always want to
help, to share, to take turns. He may really love his baby
brother but he is also often very jealous of him. Sometimes he
does hate his mother and want to hit her. He *does* hit her.
The teacher who refuses to recognize this shuts herself away

from the child in the area where he most needs help. Jesus said he came to minister to the sick. Those who are well need no doctor. The Christian gospel is the good news of forgiveness, and there can be no forgiveness if we refuse to recognize our shortcomings. If a child feels close to God, and thinks of him as a loving friend, not as a punishing judge, he will be able to discuss his mistakes and his feelings freely and he will ask and receive help.

"I had a bad day today. Mother shouted at me when she called me for supper. I needed to finish my building. Mother made me knock it down with my foot when she came to get me and I hit her. Yes, I did! She made me knock down my building! I love my mother but why did she shout?"

These are his feelings. He may not put them into words; but he needs to feel that God loves him even though he has unpleasant feelings and makes mistakes. Then he is freed to work out his problems and do better. The church school teacher cannot sit beside him as he offers his bedtime prayers, but she can talk about his problems and show him how to pray about them. If parents and teachers work together a child will have the kind of help he needs.

Should Children Memorize Prayers?

The best prayers for the child are those he offers as a result of his own experience and needs. Our objective is to teach him to pray freely, not merely to "say prayers." The most helpful kind of prayers for the parent or teacher to offer are those which arise naturally out of activities or interest of the children. These should be very simply and carefully expressed in words the child understands. From one to four short sentences are usually enough. The teacher will teach the child some form prayers. These can be helpful, if they are good ones, because they supply a prayer vocabulary for the small child to whom words do not come easily. He will memorize them quickly if they are repeated a few times.

Memorized prayers and prayer songs may be helpful also in bringing the child's whole self into the presence of God when he might otherwise not be quite ready to pray. This is particularly true of bedtime prayer when the child is tired, and may be unhappy or cross or overstimulated. They may also make him familiar with different kinds of prayers. In teaching form prayers we must be careful not to develop a mere parrot-like repetition of words. The parent and teacher must be sure the child understands the words he learns as much as possible. He should be taught never to use prayers carelessly, and he needs to be reminded that the prayer is not his own unless he is thinking about God and about what he says. His prayers are directed to God, as Jesus taught us to pray. This will also help to clarify his ideas of God and Jesus that are often confused.

If a child is to use memorized prayers, therefore, he should learn several so that there is no one prayer that becomes routine. This will prepare him for making a variety of prayers of his own when he is able. Two good books of prayers about a child's everyday experiences are *Prayers for Little Children* and *First Prayers for Little Children,* by Mary Alice Jones. These can be used in the church school kindergarten or can be given as gifts or recommended for use in the home. Perhaps the teacher will want to help the children prepare their own booklets of prayers from those found in their church school materials. These also can be used in the home at bedtime or in the family circle. *Then I Think of God* by Niedermeyer and *Tell Me About God* by Jones, show how parents can guide a child's prayer thoughts.

Attitudes of Prayer

Children should not be taught that there is only one proper attitude for prayer—closed eyes, bowed head, folded hands. They should not always kneel at bedside. They should rather come to know that God is always present and ready to hear our prayers in any time or place or way. We close our eyes because we do not want to be distracted by things we see that are not related to our prayer: but when the sight of a lovely flower inspires the prayer the eyes will be open. We fold our hands to keep them out of mischief: but we do not fold them when we say thank you for a new gift we are holding. We bow our heads in a sense of humbleness before God's greatness: but if we are awed by the vastness of a starry sky then our heads will be up. Children need to know that it is what we think and feel that is important to God.

When Will Worship Occur?

BY HAZEL A. LEWIS

Planned Occasions

There will be occasions when definite provision is made for worship. That is, the leader in planning a session, or a series of sessions for a Primary Department or grade group, will plan the time and place and procedure for worship, although all of these may be, and probably will be, adjusted to meet the situation as it develops.

The plans for worship at these times will take into account the religious problems of children such as: What God is like, how he works in the world, how we work with him, how he cares for us, the meaning of prayer, all in the terms of a child's feeling and thought rather than adult theology. Sometimes these problems will be revealed to the leader by things the children say or do. They may be suggested by the teachers or assistants. But they may also come from the leader's knowledge of child life. Certainly we will not wait for children as a group or as individuals to raise great religious problems before we mention them. The risk would be too great. Children may be prepared to meet problems with right thinking and to grow spiritually by doing so.

Frequently those planned occasions will grow out of the experiences the children are having in their class or interest groups, and should always be related to them. The children may bring to the larger group discoveries they have made, problems they want to

Hazel A. Lewis, *The Primary Church School* (St. Louis: Bethany Press, 1951), pp. 93–96. Used by permission.

talk about (which will lead to worship) and things they wish to share, a hymn they have written or learned, a poem, a prayer, a picture. These will often be part of the course of study. In turn the teacher or leader of the smaller group will use the experiences of worship and fellowship in the larger group for the further development of the work in her group.

If a grade or group has a complete session in a separate room and the group is not large the time for worship will occur whenever the situation is most suitable.

In Relation to Activities

Worship may take place in connection with an informal group activity. Sometimes the joyousness of an experience out of doors or of looking at a lovely picture or of hearing a story about someone who has done something fine or great, or hearing of the needs of children elsewhere, will lead children to desire to talk to God about it. Just as it is natural for children to be eager to tell mother or father about anything, good or bad, that has happened or about which they have heard, so is it natural for children to whom God is a real friend and loving Father, to want to tell him about the things they enjoy or the things that are hard for them.

A group of children were at work on some gifts they were sending to a home for crippled children. They had chosen the particular things they were making and had entered upon the work with great enthusiasm. But it proved to be a little more difficult than they had anticipated and to call for a great deal of patience and perseverance. There was a sense of failure developing in the group and a little irritability. As the end of the work period was drawing near one Sunday, the leader voiced the feeling that the children evidently had and said, "Is this too hard for us? Do you think we had better give it up?" The children were very unhappy at the thought and they all sat down together and analyzed their difficulty. They discovered the things that were too hard for them to do and decided to ask a boy in the Intermediate Department to come in and help them the next week. They also found the places in which they were not being careful enough. Then plans for going ahead with the undertaking were made.

The leader could feel that the children were not entirely satisfied, that there was something lacking and so she said quite naturally and simply, "Shall we talk to God about it?" Most of the children nodded and only a few looked the least bit self-conscious. One very practical boy said, "Well, he is counting on us to do this and we'd better tell him how it is." So the leader led in a very simple prayer, "God, our Father, we came to a hard place in our work. Some of it we were not doing very well and we are sorry. Some of it is too hard for us and we are going to ask someone to help us. Help us to do the very best we can and to make the crippled children happy. We are glad that we have straight legs and strong arms. Amen." The joyousness of the children after the discussion and prayer made it evident that both had been necessary. Prayer as a means of discipline would be unthinkable. But prayer as a means of getting new courage and determination is a vitalizing Christian experience.

Sometimes the sense of companionship with God does not become so articulate. A group of children were having a happy experience working together and one of them said, "I'll bet He's glad we are having such a good time." Everyone seemed to know who the child had meant and they all joined quite spontaneously in the song, "There's work in the world for children to do." They had been aware of fellowship with God and felt sure he knew they were happy.

In the Small Group

Worship will also enter into the experiences of a class or interest group. Even if a group does not have a separate room or any seclusion, it is still possible for the children to have moments of worship together when these come as the result of a real need or desire felt by the children. There may be certain times, more than others, according to the lesson materials or activities that are being carried on in the group, when worship will be a natural part of what they are doing.

Personal Worship

Of course the child will have worship experiences when he is alone and when he is at home. Some of these will be at appointed times, such as his prayer at night or in the morning, the grace at the table, and other times when the family worships together. It is to be regretted that these occasions are not more frequent and that when they do occur they are not more childlike and natural. The child's experiences in the church school will help to make these times of worship outside the school more meaningful. They should help him to discover occasions and ways of speaking to God. They will help to make worship seem natural and real, as well as satisfying. Church school workers can be helpful by suggesting books of devotional material for use with children at home.[1]

---

[1] *Then I Think of God,* by Mabel A. Niedermeyer; *Tell Me About God,* by Mary Alice Jones; *God's Wonder World,* by Bernice Bryant.

What Forms and Materials Will Children Use in Worship?

BY HAZEL A. LEWIS

The Child's Spontaneous Expression

Another form of the question above may be: To what extent shall children use forms and materials in worship? Certainly not to the exclusion of their own spontaneous expressions. To substitute even a really good prayer-poem for something a group of children want to say to God, their Father and Friend, would hinder worship rather than enrich the experience.

The function of any worship material should be threefold and enable the worshiper to say what he feels but is unable to express adequately; to enrich and give deeper meaning to his ideas and feelings; to lead to greater freedom in spontaneous expression. These three functions may be applied as tests in the selection of worship material.

One answer to the original question is that they will use the forms and materials to which they are introduced, and this places upon the leaders in the church school the responsibility of making available to children materials which they can use and of guiding them into the discovery of forms of worship which are satisfying to them.

Material and form should be varied enough that the children may choose those which best meet their need. An evaluation of worship materials would include such questions as, Does it em-

Hazel A. Lewis, *The Primary Church School* (St. Louis: Bethany Press, 1951), pp. 96–97. Used by permission.

body the right idea of God? Are all the ideas that it contains consistent with a Christian attitude toward life? Is it worth while from the standpoint of literary and artistic merit? Is it within the vocabulary and the emotional capacity of primary children? It is evident, of course, that the leader who is to use these standards in the selection of material must herself have a Christian experience and philosophy of life that will enable her to decide the first two questions, she must have discriminating taste that will enable her to answer the third, and she must have a knowledge of primary children that will make it possible for her to judge its suitability as implied in the fourth question.

Evaluating Materials for Worship

BY VESTA TOWNER

In choosing materials for worship, we can test them by three simple questions. First, *Will this material be an aid to worship?* It should help children think about God with understanding and with reverence, and should help give the girls and boys a consciousness of God. Second, *Is it of high quality?* Nothing cheap, trivial, or superficial should be used in worship. Let us choose good music, good poems, good pictures for children's worship. Third, *Will it meet the interests and understanding of this particular group of children?* Will it have meaning for them *now,* not when they are older? Is it within their experience? Will they enjoy it? Understanding depends not upon vocabulary alone, but also upon ideas. Translating an adult story into words of one syllable will never make it a primary story. It will be merely an adult story dressed in words of one syllable.

Vesta Towner, *Guiding Children in Worship* (Nashville: Abingdon Press, 1946), pp. 69-70. Used by permission.

Planning a Service of Worship

BY VESTA TOWNER

"Formal worship" is a relative term by which we describe worship conducted in a regular order. With children, worship should never be entirely formal; it should always have a natural, informal quality. It should, however, be most carefully planned.

It should be developed around one central emphasis so that it will have unity. All materials used—song, scripture, story, picture, or poem—should express the same thought, emphasize the same idea. Miscellaneous items chosen without regard to unity of thought can never make a unified impression. Instead of selecting an abstract theme for the service which may be unrelated to the experience of the group, the leader will emphasize some idea about which the children have been studying and thinking in a current unit of lessons or will lift up and interpret some recent experience of the group, or perhaps the plans will be for a seasonal emphasis.

Since worship should be an outgrowth of the units being studied by the children and closely related to their present experiences, it is unwise for the leader to depend upon printed collections of ready-made plans for worship services. These are valuable for suggestions and as resource material from which to choose, but should seldom be used in their entirety. The leader who depends upon them is likely to have a series of programs rather than worship.

In planning a service of worship, the leader will remember that we do not expect children to follow an adult pattern. Usually chil-

Vesta Towner, *Guiding Children in Worship* (Nashville: Abingdon Press, 1946), pp. 105–107. Used by permission.

dren do not assemble with the conscious purpose of worshiping God. Their span of attention is very brief. In the space of a few moments, the leader must direct their thoughts toward God, help them feel his nearness, stimulate their thinking, and guide them toward a conscious response to God. A simple plan may be prepared in terms of the leader's purpose.

The Beginning, or Approach

Purpose: To secure reverent attention, to induce a mood of worship, and to introduce the thought or idea which will be emphasized in the service.

The beginning may include a musical prelude to create an atmosphere of quiet and reverent thoughtfulness, perhaps a call to worship either spoken or sung, an opening hymn, or an opening prayer. The beginning should not always be the same.

The Development of the Idea

Purpose: To guide the thinking of the group; to help them understand God's purposes in the world and feel their relationship to him; to present a challenge or arouse a desire.

This main portion of the service may include various types of materials, such as poems, scripture, hymns, stories, incidents, conversation, and pictures. Not all of these materials will be used in any one service. There need not always be a story. The leader will choose according to the purpose for the day, and will keep the service brief. It is highly important that the service be interesting. To sustain interest and attention, the leader will vary the service from week to week and will use a variety of materials.

The Climax, the High Point of the Service

Purpose: To bring the group to a moment of conscious response to God. This may be expressed in a prayer hymn, a spoken prayer, or sometimes in an offering. There are occasions when juniors might repeat the pledge of allegiance to the Christian Flag as a very real act of dedication. But if this were done every Sunday, it would become mere routine.

The Closing

The service of worship should be quickly brought to a close after the climax without announcements or other distractions. There may be a closing hymn or some form of benediction. If the climax has included a hymn, no additional closing hymn may be needed.

The Youth Fellowship at Worship

BY OLIVER DE WOLF CUMMINGS

Check Sheet for Evaluating Worship

1. Is it directed Godward?
2. Does it involve surrender to God and response to him?
3. Is it genuine and real, vitally related to the needs of youth?
4. Does it make effective use of the various elements of worship?
5. Does it have unity—a clear aim and central theme?
6. Does it reach a spiritual high point?
7. Does it make fresh appeal while expressing familiar experiences?
8. Are the physical surroundings such as to create reverence and reality?
9. Are appropriate aids used to produce a worshipful mood and a vital experience?

Elements of Worship

The Call to Worship

The call—"come worship"—is a summons away from the noisy, hectic confusion of a secular world into the union of thought and spirit of the group, a bringing of minds and hearts into focus upon God. Its purpose is to set a tone or mood, and to open a gateway into the life of the spirit. Scripture verses, particularly those from the Book of Psalms, help in accomplishing

Oliver DeWolf Cummings, *The Youth Fellowship* (Philadelphia: Judson Press, 1956), pp. 115–123. Used by permission.

512

this purpose. Sometimes a hymn, a poetic phrase or verse, or a meaningful quotation may be used. Using the familiar has value, but there is merit at times in acquainting young people with new passages of Scripture and fresh poetry. Here are two examples of calls to worship: "Be still, and know that I am God. . . . I am exalted in the earth!" (Ps. 46:10); "O come, let us worship and bow down, let us kneel before the Lord, our Maker!" (Ps. 95:6). In an evening Fellowship meeting, the leader may quote from a hymn such as "Day is Dying in the West." Then the entire group may respond, singing words of the chorus, "Holy, holy, holy, Lord God of hosts." Psalm 24:1–5 is appropriate as a call to worship when read antiphonally or by a verse-speaking choir.

Hymns

Of inestimable value, in the worship experiences of youth, are hymns. Through the wedding of good music to fine poetry, and group expression of high thoughts, noble aspirations, and deep feelings, the entire personality of each individual may be lifted toward God, and the entire group may achieve a solidarity of fellowship and dedication. Good hymns have important functions. They promote understanding of Christian truth; increase conviction in the Christian faith; develop appreciation of Christian ideals and attitudes; provide opportunity for Christian fellowship; encourage awareness of God and receptivity to his will; become a means for confession of guilt and failure, of expression of joy and thankfulness; stimulate right Christian choices, and sound and sustained Christian action.

In the planning of worship services, much skill is required in the selection of the best hymns for youth, for the specific theme, and for the particular place and purpose of the service. If it be true that second only to the Bible in the Christian education of youth is the hymnbook, then it is of utmost importance that the best possible choice of a regular youth hymnbook be made and of the hymns which are to find their way into the life experience of growing adolescents.

Among the tests of good hymns for youth are these: (1) Does the poetry express meaningful ideas in language which is beautiful, dignified, and effective? (2) Is the imagery appropriate for worship, and true to the Christian heritage? (3) Is the theology in accord with basic Christian teachings? (4) Are the ideas expressed relevant to the problems and needs of youth—junior highs, seniors, older youth? (5) Are they expressed in language which has meaning for them? (6) Is the music appropriate for the worship of God—does it have beauty, dignity, and strength? (7) Is it singable? (8) Does it possess enduring worth? (9) Do the music and the words say the same thing—that is, in its spirit and feeling, is the music religious?

Special Music

Vocal and instrumental music add greatly to the beauty and effectiveness of worship experiences, and afford a way to enlist the talents of young people who have acquired these special skills. Participants should be encouraged to prepare well, and to make their parts not performances but acts of worship. Through atmosphere music during the service (the prelude, postlude, offering, silent prayer, and so forth), the rich heritage of great religious music may become a factor in the experience of all who worship.

Prayer

At the heart of all worship experience, essential to individual growth and fellowship that is truly Christian, is prayer. This highest of all relationships—between finite human beings and infinite God—should not be approached carelessly or insincerely. Various forms of prayer may provide for meaningful participation: silent prayer, directed prayer (with suggested thoughts from the leader), musical accompaniment to the reading of a prayer poem, sentence prayers, reading of a written prayer, extempore prayer, prayer hymn, litany of dedication or of praise.

Scripture

Worship provides an opportunity to relive and re-experience the joy, gratitude, penitence, hope, and consecration of those who have sought and found God, have heard his voice, and have seen with clear insight deeply into the nature of man and the problems of existence, as revealed supremely in the Scriptures. Through worship, the living message of the Bible becomes a vital force in the present-day experience of youth. Many of the most appealing passages—from the Book of Psalms, for example—may best be brought to youth through worship, and may be used in a variety of ways in services. The Bible is often taken for granted through familiarity. It should be read clearly, with smoothness, intelligence, and color. Using it in different ways, from time to time, will make it more effective. Among such ways are: a musical setting, a dialogue, a dramatic background or setting, a verse-speaking choir, or the use of costume. Usually a Scripture passage holds the key to the central thought of the chosen theme. In addition, there may often be other ways of using the Bible, such as litanies, responsive readings, calls to worship and to service, scriptural sentences of affirmation.

The Spoken Word or Special Presentation

The talk or meditation, the story or dramatic episode, the audio-visual, or other presentation should be related to the theme and appropriate to the age-group level and experience. This presentation needs to be well prepared, sincere, and a genuine act of worship. The meditation is very effective, even though brief, in making explicit the implications of the theme. It has value because it directs thought, increases understanding, and stimulates feeling. Stories, dramas, picture interpretations, or audio-visuals, have the advantage of making personal involvement easier through appeal to the emotions. These procedures, going beyond the realm of the purely factual or logical into the realm of the feelings, change attitudes and conduct.

Young people may creatively develop various means of drama-worship—simple costumes, brief episodes, dialogues, dramatic incidents with appropriate background and properties. They may adopt some of the newer techniques of drama-worship—verse-speaking choir, rhythm choir, "readers," "voices," "spokesmen," "questioners," or "interpreters," without the necessity of costumes and exact memorization of lines. Sometimes participants are placed in the audience or at unusual positions in the room. Inspirational colored slide sets or motion pictures are used effectively, sometimes with the help of wire or tape recorder, or record player.

An effective drama-worship service was produced by young people in the author's church on the theme "Right or Wrong?" Many of the participants appeared in dramatic episodes. Others, placed at different points in the audience, at one point broke in, each in turn, with the words, "Is it I?"

The Reponse through Group Participation

The call to worship assumes a real and vital response to the living God, not merely disinterested observation or passive listening. Without the surrender of mind and heart to God, there can be no worship. The response may come in a number of ways—through unspoken prayer and commitment, through singing, through unison prayer, responsive reading of Scripture and litanies. There may be provided sentences of dedication, and also acts of commitment—especially an offering.

Principles of Effectiveness in Worship

The Necessity for Relevance—Meaning, Reality

Worship, if it is to be more than form, must be relevant to the lives and the problems of those who live in our contemporary world. Part of its value lies in its ability to lift them above their surroundings and, in the presence of God, gain perspective, poise, and power.

The Place of Unity—Value of an Aim, a Theme

The great advantage of having a clear aim and a well-stated theme is that they contribute to the achievement of a single, unified effect. Each worship service should seek to accomplish something definite—a new awareness of some aspect or purpose of God, a change of attitude toward people or things, a prompting to serve or to share.

The Need for Order—Progression, Balance, Climax

Every good worship service has a plan—not merely a series of worship elements stuck together, but the various parts arranged in a logical order. A study of good worship experience reveals a progression; for example, from reverent adoration and praise to confession, and thence to petition and dedication. In most worship services it is essential to maintain a balance between the various elements, and quite desirable for the progression to reach a high point or climax. Often this climax involves some act of surrender, or affirmation, or response, in which all may share—audibly or silently.

The Value of the Familiar, the Novel

In effective worship a good balance is maintained between the new and the old, the novel or unusual and the familiar. Great care is exercised to avoid, on the one hand, the repetition of familiar forms until they become dull and ineffective, and on the other hand, the use of the unfamiliar in such form that it distracts from the mood of worship, or the novel in such a way as to attract undue attention to itself. Often there is great merit in using a familiar order of service to increase a sense of reality and to reduce the amount of concentration required upon the forms. Again, there is great value in the forcefulness and the reality which come from that which is fresh, compelling new attention and response.

The Importance of Suitable Physical Conditions

God is a God of order and of beauty. His worship should be conducted in an orderly manner and in a setting which suggests his presence. Everything possible should be done to remove distraction, eliminate disturbances and interruptions, decrease bodily discomfort (through air, temperature, light and seating), and to create surroundings of beauty and meaning. Much is being done to provide rooms for worship and Christian teaching which are well arranged as to lighting, heating, seating, and attractive in their color schemes and equipment. Many churches can redecorate old rooms, and solve awkward problems by special draperies, panels, and furnishings. Of great importance is an adequate worship center, preferably one which is subject to change and variety.

Aids in Worship

Worship Centers

The increasing use of the worship center in the less ritualistic denominations is an indication of the value of the eye appeal in worship. Such a center is not a shrine. It is a place of beauty and order which directs and focuses thought and attention, helping to create the mood of worship. Psychologically, it acts as a unifying and centralizing factor for individuals who come to worship from all kinds of circumstances. The starting point is usually a wall upon which or against which may be set, permanently or temporarily, panels, cloth or other hangings or drapes, or other furnishings. Ideally, with young people the worship center should be such that it may be completely or partially changed from time to time during the church year. It can create specialized atmosphere appropriate to varied themes.

For most services, simplicity is an asset—one large candle, or perhaps three with an evergreen spray; an open Bible with a bouquet of flowers; the cross in one of its many forms; a globe with a cross; a beautiful religious painting appropriately mounted or framed. For special themes and occasions, young people with resourcefulness may supply or arrange meaningful and symbolic objects—a stained-glass window; a lighthouse; an altar of stones such as Abraham erected; Easter lilies; a bundle of wheat; fall vegetables and fruits; a Christmas crèche; a new year's bell; a madonna; a beautiful ceramic; a loaf of bread; a picture of hands —at toil, in prayer, outstretched, or clasped; a map with streamers to a church spire or a cross; a model church.

Hymnbooks

In recent years the different denominations have produced excellent hymnbooks appropriate for young people. These books contain the great hymns of the church, the rightful heritage of every Christian, plus the hymns which have special meaning for youth. Hymn appreciation, both of the new and of the familiar, should be a regular experience in all youth groups. Each group should collect good hymnbooks, both those for youth and those for general purposes, and make wide use of the poetry, music, responsive readings, litanies, calls to worship, and benedictions which they contain.

Picture File

A picture file and folio should be in each youth department, or at least available to all. The mounting size should be uniform but permit pictures of various sizes. The larger pictures may be placed in the folio for protection. A standard picture frame the size of the mounting can be fitted with a removable back so that pictures can be readily changed. Current and back issues of national magazines should be scanned for reproductions of suitable pictures, and catalogues secured from publishers and distributors. Guy Rowe's contemporary set, *Portraits of Old Testament Characters,* and Albert E. Bailey's set, *Christ in Recent Art,* are highly stimulating to youth. At least one good picture, in large size, framed, should be on a wall of each department and classroom. Good examples are Zimmerman's *Christ and the Fishermen;* Burnand's *Go Preach;* Taylor's *Christ in Gethsemane;* Sallman's *Head of Christ;* Hofmann's *The Rich Young Ruler* and *Christ in Gethsemane.*

Poetry, Quotation, and Story File

Poetry, stories, and pointed quotations are so effective in worship experience that they should be used frequently. A great convenience is a file, on standard-size cards, containing a wide assortment of devotional and inspirational materials. Beautiful, meaningful poetry, stories, illustrations, and quotations may be found in the daily newspapers, magazines, religious periodicals, and books. Get the clipping habit; save everything worth saving, classify it, and *use it.*

The Worship Bookshelf

Like tools to the carpenter are books and other resource materials to the leader of youth. For inexperienced young people and adult leaders, several fine books exist which contain services carefully worked out. As skill is developed, these and other books containing religious poetry, stories, prayers, and biographical incidents may be used as resource material. To these may be added several good hymnbooks, collections of daily devotions, inspirational books on the Bible and on the Christian life, books on how to prepare worship services, and a file of magazines containing worship programs.

18. USE SMALL GROUPS

RESEARCH AND EXPERIMENT in group dynamics (see chapter 7) have shown that certain very definite advantages may come to members of small groups. In a small group the individual counts, participation becomes relatively easy, and indifference becomes relatively hard. The implication is that every person should have some experience in a small group. A church would do well, therefore, to encourage the development of small groups for such purposes as Bible study, research, service, and social action.

This is not to say, however, that a person should have *only* small-group experiences or that a church should have *only* small groups. The large group has values too. The large group can often fulfill its purposes best and serve its people best if it will divide into small units for part of its work. It is in this way that the small group idea will probably be of greatest value to most churches. For this reason, all but the first of the following readings deal with the use of small groups within the ongoing work and purpose of large groups. The church that would provide Christian nurture for its people should have a program of group work which is flexible enough to give *all* its people the benefits of both large-group and small-group experience.

The Effect of the Small Group on Its Members

BY HERBERT A. THELEN

The central assumption of the principle of individual challenge in the least-sized group is that the quality of performance
depends on how one is motivated to perform, and that it is possible to compose groups in such a way that motivation is high.
Such groups are the *"smallest groups in which it is possible to
have represented at a functional level all the social and achievement skills required for the particular required activity."* [1]
In general, the way to increase motivation is to help people
find a wider range of "rewards" for working. This is done by de-
fining roles in such a way that each person is, and feels he is,
necessary to the group; each person has opportunity to grow on
the job; each person feels secure and able to do his job.

1. All too often people know that if they just "sit tight," someone else will do their job. The way to avoid this is to avoid overlapping of functions and duplications of roles.

2. All too often people find it hard to break into a discussion,
and so they withdraw. Thus they miss out on the testing of ideas
so essential to learning. The solution to this is to have the group
as small as possible, so that each person can have more of the
group's time.

Herbert A. Thelen, "The Principle of Individual Challenge in the Least-
Sized Group," *Dynamics of Groups at Work* (Chicago: University of Chi-
cago Press. Copyright, 1954, by the University of Chicago), pp. 187–188.
Used by permission.

[1] H. A. Thelen, "Group Dynamics in Instruction: The Principle of Least
Group Size," *School Review* (March, 1949), p. 142.

3. A small group also makes the nonparticipant more visible, and may lead him, when he does not know what the problem is, to inquire of the others so that he can see how to break in.

4. In a small group each person tends to feel a greater share of the responsibility for meeting the demand. This means that he also expects a greater percentage of whatever approval or punishment follows from the group effort.

5. A small group also can operate at a level of greater intimacy, and this means greater involvement of the members in the process of the group, and a wider range of possible need-meeting, extending into the personal domain.

6. A small group can work more informally because it does not have to make all rules and purposes explicit: people communicate more easily. This means greater relaxation, greater tolerance of individual effort, better morale, and more freedom to experiment.

7. The small group, as a subdivision of a larger group, also is likely to help its members adapt to the larger group. This is the place for tussling with the problems that cannot be discussed in the larger group; and such discussion should do much to help the larger group.

In general, if groups are composed in such a way that each person can have a larger "place" he will tend to try to move into this place. In effect, he accepts the challenge. The administrative and leadership problem is to see how to compose groups in such a way that the "place" people need is also the "place" people will have if they accept the work challenge.

The Buzz Session Insures Wide Participation

BY MARGARET E. KUHN

The buzz session is a practical way to get each member in the group to participate and contribute his ideas. It is applicable to many group situations. Although it may not be needed in small groups where full, free participation is possible for all members, it will greatly improve and enliven meetings of very large groups. If the buzz question is specific and thoughtfully worded, each member will respond with interest.

Here we need to distinguish between buzz sessions and work groups, and remember the value of both in encouraging full participation. Shy people who would never speak in large gatherings readily take part in small groups. They will even challenge the highly articulate participators and make them realize that they should give others a chance.

In both buzz sessions and work groups there is a minimum of organization, and a maximum of quick, spontaneous response. Buzz sessions meet very briefly and are most often used as a socialization technique to speed up interaction. Leaders from within the group steer the brief discussion, as described below.

Work groups frequently use resource persons who have extra insight and experience to share. They continue for much longer periods, and the length of the sessions is determined by the purposes of the group and the problem it attempts to solve.

Here are the procedures usually followed in conducting buzz sessions.

Margaret E. Kuhn, *You Can't Be Human Alone* (New York: National Council of Churches, 1956), pp. 23–25. Used by permission.

- The general group is divided into subgroups of no more than five or six persons. Even when the group is meeting in a church, the first three persons in one pew can turn in their seats to talk with the three persons immediately back of them, who lean forward to form a circle. In a less formal meeting place, the group leader should suggest that each buzz group move chairs to form a small circle.

- Each buzz group should quickly select a chairman or convener who keeps the discussion moving on the proposed question and sees that each member has a chance to speak, and a secretary-reporter who records what is said and reports *briefly* at the close of the buzz session to the main group.

Word of Warning: Do not let the buzz groups waste time quibbling over leadership. Make the method of choosing the chairman and secretary-reporter as simple as possible. It can be a kind of game or get-acquainted device. The person whose last name begins with the letter nearest the letter "A" of the alphabet is the chairman, and the person whose last name is nearest the letter "Z" of the alphabet is the secretary-reporter. Or the man with the bow tie is the chairman and the woman with a pencil in her hand is the secretary-reporter.

- The group leaders begin with the same carefully worded question, which may also be written on a blackboard. Each buzz group discusses this question at the same time.

- The discussion should be very short, *seldom more than five or six minutes*. Simple questions can be fruitfully explored in two or three minutes. The group leader should stop the buzzing promptly at the end of the appointed time, when presumably interest has reached a high point.

- The buzz groups merge into general group, and each secretary-reporter states in a sentence or two the most significant ideas from his buzz group. The convener of the buzz group may help the secretary-reporter to choose the points for general presentation.

• Reports are limited to a sentence or two and recorded on a blackboard as presented. General discussion of these and other points follows and should proceed at a lively pace. After buzzing, people are much more ready to talk in the larger group.

The size of the group and the purpose of the meeting will determine how this method is to be used with other group procedures. For example, a buzz session may follow or precede role playing, a panel presentation, or lecture. If the group is too large for reports from each buzz group, three or four conveners from the small buzz groups may form a panel to talk over findings and reactions.

Buzz sessions can be used most helpfully to locate a group's major interests and needs, problems, and questions to be studied, also to help the leader to summarize points of discussion, and to evaluate results of group study and action. They are particularly useful at the end of conference or workshop to suggest follow-up action back home. In leadership education buzz sessions give new leaders some experience in leading discussions.

Brainstorms for Creative Thinking

BY MARGARET E. KUHN

Brainstorming is a variation of the buzz session, making use of the principle of free association of ideas. It is particularly effective when a group is looking for new ideas and fresh approaches to old or new problems, and is coming to be widely used in science, business, and industry. Church boards and committees, as well as church organizations, have the same need for new ideas and creative ways to involve their members in policy making and program planning. Often, however, they do not know how to draw upon the ideas of the members. A brainstorm session operates in small groups, or in large ones which can be divided quickly into small working groups. These general "ground" rules are carefully put down before the brainstorming begins:

- Everyone present is asked to turn his attention to the same specific problem (i.e. how to get parent co-operation in the church school; how to make church officers aware of the church's mission to migrants) and say the first idea that comes to mind.

- Nobody in the group is allowed to criticize any idea even though it may be completely wild. Make clear that wild ideas are wanted—the more extreme the better, because these extreme ideas lead people to think of others that may be more practical. Some brainstorm leaders ring a bell or put a red mark on the blackboard when anyone in the group attempts to discourage an idea or to pass judgment on it.

Margaret E. Kuhn, *You Can't Be Human Alone* (New York: National Council of Churches, 1956), pp. 25–26. Used by permission.

Aim to get out all the ideas possible within a twenty-to-forty minute period. It may help to set a quota and say, "In a half hour let's have fifty ideas." Then write all the ideas on a blackboard, or large scratch pad, as fast as they come.

When the group has reached the time limit or the number they have set as a goal, they may decide to go on and get more ideas, or to begin to evaluate the ones that have come out.

Take time for evaluating and sorting ideas. Each idea may be copied on a 3 x 5 card. Several people can sort the cards and group the ideas. As they work over the cards still further ideas will come. If the problem requires an important decision, the evaluation and careful weighing of ideas might occur in the next meeting, with adequate time to test possible decisions and study the outcome. Develop a wild idea file to use in long-range program planning.

In using the brainstorm method it is important to bring together the people who are immediately concerned with the problems under consideration, or who have some general experience to contribute. Brainstorming has had some dramatic results. A group of scientists at M.I.T. solved a complicated problem in nuclear physics by brainstorming in small groups. They came up with a solution that had defied the experts working in their isolated laboratories.

The Dream Session

BY HENRY A. TANI

Try a "dream session" at this point. The total group is divided into small units of six to eight persons. Each group is asked to consider the same question, for example, "How can we improve the youth program at our church?" Give them one hour, and list these rules:

- Let the suggestions come at random, out of the sky, in complete freedom.
- Don't be restrained in any manner. Everything is possible. Let no one say it's been tried before, or that there is no money for such activities.
- Build on the idea of another. Go hitch-hiking or piggy-back on suggestions already made. Really go wild.
- Make a long list. Be profuse and generous. Twenty to thirty new suggestions should come out of such a session.
- Then begin to pick from the list those ideas which can be used now. Select five or six of the "immediately possibles" and submit these to the total group.
- List on the chalkboard, or on the turnover chart, the "immediately possibles" from each group, and put them in priority order of attention.

Henry A. Tani, *Ventures in Youth Work* (Philadelphia: Christian Education Press, 1957), p. 126. Used by permission.

The Cube Group Plan

BY HENRY A. TANI

A local church reported that it had thirty persons who regularly attended the Sunday church school in the senior high department. The department included a large number of the ninth and tenth grade, and a few of the eleventh and twelfth grade. One teacher taught this large group, and found it difficult to maintain attention and to secure adequate discussion.

This church had an evening youth fellowship, but only fifteen or sixteen active members. The officers who planned and conducted the meetings were usually the older eleventh and twelfth graders. The ninth and tenth graders dominated the attendance, yet found the meetings unexciting to them. A careful survey indicated that a total of fifty-five persons of this age were actually related to the church membership.

The cube group plan was recommended and adopted. The name "cube" was applied to the small-group units, since the cube is a three-dimensional figure, indicating the concept of a relationship between persons within the group and also of the presence of God in their midst. This is the plan.

1. *The active members are divided into units of about seven or eight persons, based first upon school grade and age, then on geography or interest.* If the persons live in a wide area, those from the north side would be in one cube, those from the east side in another, and so on. If the young people attend different

Henry A. Tani, *Ventures in Youth Work* (Philadelphia: Christian Education Press, 1957), pp. 170–176. Used by permission.

high schools, those from the same schools would be placed in the same cube. If there is a basketball team, an established clique, a group with very definite interests, they would be formed into a cube. Boys and girls would normally be mixed in the cubes.

2. *To each group is assigned a counselor, a person slightly older than the members in the group.* An older youth, young adult, young married couple, or some such person who is from five to ten years older than the group would be desirable. In all activities of the cube, the counselor is involved.

3. *To each group are assigned two inactive persons who normally would be related to the youth program.* For every function, meeting, activity, and class session of the cube, special effort is made to seek out and invite these two inactive persons. As soon as they become active, two additional inactive persons are assigned to the cube. Thus the cube is always reaching out to one or two inactive persons.

4. *The division into cube membership can best be made by a small committee of adult leaders, church school teachers, and' youth leaders.* Full consideration should be given to personality traits, interests, and other peculiarities of the young people which would tend to knit the members into a workable group. One should not hesitate to separate girl-girl and boy-girl combinations, as long as the base of division is maintained.

5. *The memberships in the several cubes are reviewed and reshuffled twice each year,* to take into account the loss and gain in membership. Always, the best workable unit is from six to ten young persons and one counselor.

6. *The counselors are responsible to a youth director who coordinates the activities of the whole youth program in the church.* The counselor is committed for the six-month period during which a cube is maintained, and he may be excused or re-assigned depending upon his availability and interest. The youth director, or adult adviser, has a long-term responsibility to provide continuity.

7. *Each cube is a Sunday morning church school class.* A mem-

ber of the cube prepares the lesson of the day, and conducts the discussion. The counselor will also be prepared, but his role is that of resource person, not that of teacher. Each Sunday a new cube member presents and conducts the class period. Opportunities for free inquiry and search are encouraged. Additional resource persons may be brought in upon invitation of the young person whose turn it is to lead.

8. *The cube meets in one of the homes of its members on Sunday evening.* Thus there are as many simultaneous meetings as there are cubes. These cube meetings in private homes are held on alternate meeting nights, and different homes are used for every meeting. Such a cube meeting has the elements of worship, study, and recreation, just as any other youth fellowship meeting.

9. *On the other alternate meeting nights, the total youth fellowship group of all the cubes meets at the church.* The program for that evening is conducted by one of the cubes.

This is the basic pattern for the operation of the cube group plan. But let us explore the other possibilities.

10. *Each cube is encouraged to choose one of the five commissions or program areas for its own specialty.* They may find that several meetings are required to survey the possibilities before they can agree on their choice. Several cubes may choose the same commission or program area. Within each commission and program area are several items which can be seriously pursued and studied.

11. *Each cube is urged to specialize in some activity,* such as recreational leadership, fellowship singing, drama, choral speech, puppetry, parlor games, folk games, crafts, mission study, Bible study, service project, and any other. One or two of the cube members may have a flair for one of these, and will introduce the activity to the rest. The cube might make itself proficient in the field, and then share this interest with the total youth fellowship group.

12. *Each cube must prepare a youth fellowship meeting pro-*

gram. On a schedule agreed upon, and perhaps on a topic assigned to them, or on one which the members choose out of their specialized interest, they will plan and present a complete youth fellowship program of worship, topic, and recreation.

13. *Each cube is encouraged to go on outings, picnics, swims, excursions, skating parties, and other suitable and appropriate functions of their own choosing.* Of course, in each instance, the counselor goes along. Such activities must be cleared with the youth director to see that they do not conflict with the over-all program.

14. *Each cube ought to undertake one major service project on its own during the half-year of its existence.* This should be apart from any major service project which the whole youth fellowship may do.

15. *The cube meeting in different private homes exposes the young people to the parents of those homes.* Their hospitality and refreshments are graciously received. The period of socializing should not include watching television, listening to records, or dancing in the rumpus room downstairs. The cube meeting itself should be quite orderly, punctual, and disciplined. One hour might be adequate for a cube meeting in a home. At a cube meeting, plans and assignments can be worked out. Every effort should be made to discuss subjects and topics of concern to cube members, who take turns in presenting the topic discussion of the evening. All the resources recommended for youth fellowship meetings should be available for this purpose.

16. *It is possible that some isssue or project which one cube has explored, needs support and participation by all young people of the total youth fellowship.* Some survey or inquiry, a work project or youth evangelism program, or other possibilities may be introduced.

17. *There are no officers within the cube group except for a rotating chairman in charge of the cube meeting.* The total youth fellowship maintains its usual organization, with officers and relationships to the congregation and denomination. There is no trans-

action of funds within the cubes. Any expenditure would be for the total group.

While these items suggest the essence and structure of the cube group plan, the following factors make it especially attractive for adaptation in our churches.

Evaluation of the Plan

Under the cube group plan, every person immediately belongs, and is expected to share in all the cube activities. He has a share in its decisions, planning and execution of the class session, cube meeting, and other functions. He is accepted for what he is, with all his peculiar strength and weakness.

The cube group plan protects the older teenagers from being overwhelmed by the younger teenagers. To keep the eleventh and twelfth grade persons in a cube for their age means to maintain a normal social level and to assure intellectual capacity for pertinent and interesting discussion.

When a large group of junior highs enter the youth fellowship, they will have a program more adapted to their understanding if they are kept in small cube groups of their age mates.

In a large church which has fifty or more senior highs, the cube group is sure to hold attendance and interest. There will be no fringe or occasional members. Either every person is actively related in a cube, or is an inactive person who is being pursued continually by the cube to which he belongs.

When a friend or a newcomer drops in, he can be included temporarily in a cube appropriate to him and later be assigned permanently. There is always the effort to reach out to the unchurched, the inactive, the fringe group.

In the more intimate cube group, the problems and concerns which face the individual members can be more honestly shared and discussed. After a period of time, they will know each other so well that they can give strength to each other.

The particular strength of the cube system lies in the experience that a definite group of persons has in a continuous program of study, worship, work, and play, in different settings and situations, over a long period of time. This is the redemptive society: a group whose members become concerned for each other's welfare, and which is affected and changed by this love and feeling of each for the other.

While we might assume that most teenagers enjoy a normal boy-girl social life, for those who fail to achieve friendship and dates the cube provides ample opportunity to share in co-ed experiences.

There is the danger that we are making several social clubs which can become cliques. The necessity for constant inquiry and activity, for sharing and reaching out, for facing personal dilemmas and problems in an atmosphere of Christian concern, makes it more likely that the group will arrive at new and higher motives in life.

The key to the cube group is the counselor. This kind of person may seem elusive and hard to find. The counselor may not understand his role in the cube. He may not know enough of the youth program, of group discipline, of conducting discussions. The church may look to its older youth and young adult members as prospective counselors.

Though no mention has been made of the Sunday morning worship service, it is assumed that regular attendance at church service is fundamental to good Christian living.

Parents of teenagers come into the picture quite naturally, as cube meetings are held in the homes of its members.

There is really no conflict with the commission or program area plan. The cube system provides the vehicle through which the substance and content of the program areas are conveyed.

This then is the breadth and depth of the total strategy of using the small-group technique, involving every active and potential young person in the life of the church.

PART IV

ADMINISTERING

THE

EDUCATIONAL

PROGRAM

19. EDUCATIONAL ORGANIZATION AND ADMINISTRATION

ORGANIZATION AND ADMINISTRATION are concerned with many matters which transcend a particular group and its work. Two reasons, however, prompt their inclusion in this book. One reason is that the administrator can do much to aid or hinder Christian nurture. He determines the ways in which the boards and committees of the church do their work. Therefore he helps set the conditions in which the whole church program operates. The basic ideas about teaching and learning that were considered earlier, especially in chapters 3 and 5, apply also to administration.

A second reason is that every group leader should be concerned about organization and administration. He is responsible for the organization of his particular group and for the administration of its work. He should see the way his group relates to other organizations and to the church as a whole. Therefore he needs to understand organization and administration.

No attempt is made here to suggest the form of organization that a church group should adopt. The polity of a denomination affects the way in which churches of that denomination are organized. The background of a particular congregation also affects the way it is organized. What is right for one church, therefore,

539

is not necessarily right for another. A particular church will do well to start with its own congregational and denominational practice, and make such adaptations as are suggested by the basic principles that follow and by its own needs and purposes.

The first three readings show basic principles of organization and administration. The fourth shows how the insights of Christian nurture may work out when they are applied to administration.

Principles of Organization

BY LEE J. GABLE

Organization exists to help the church in its work of developing Christian persons and a Christian society

If any agency begins to serve its own purposes rather than those of the church, it is time to ask whether that agency has a right to exist.

Final responsibility for Christian nurture should be vested in the official body of a church

We have in mind the body variously called official board, consistory, session, vestry, church council. This principle recognizes that the congregation as a whole is responsible for the Christian nurture of its people. Therefore the official body is responsible to see to it that an effective program of Christian nurture is provided.

Planning of educational policy and general supervision of educational program should be assigned to a board or a committee which is responsible to the official body of the church.

It is too much to expect that one elected church board will give detailed consideration to the work of all of the programs and agencies of that church. This is especially true of the large church, but it is also true of the small church. There is need for a particular group to oversee the educational work of the church. In most denominations this group is known as the commission, com-

Lee J. Gable, *Christian Nurture through the Church* (New York: National Council of Churches, 1955), pp. 31–33. Used by permission.

mittee, or board of Christian education. In others it bears such a title as program board or program committee.

Organization should bring about unity of program in the church

A good organizational structure requires that each group in the church be clearly related to the church as a whole, through the responsible board or committee. Each group should also be related to the other groups in such a way that they will supplement each other rather than waste effort through duplication.

Organization should secure the fullest participation by individual members of the church, including all age groups

Every member of a church should have the feeling that this is "our church" and that he is an essential part of it. Every time a person thinks of his church as "their church," there is a danger signal. Organization can go a long way toward assuring individual participation. It can see to it that every group is represented in the meetings where policies are made. Each member of the group may have a share in policy-making by giving suggestions to his representative in advance. Each member may be informed about policy through report and discussion afterwards.

When the organizational pattern of a church is charted, it should be possible to follow a line from any member of a church group through to the official body of the church. Information and suggestions should flow *both ways* so each person may feel himself a responsible part of the church.

Organizational structure should be as simple as possible

There should be as many organizations as are needed to get the work of the church done effectively, and no more. There should be as many offices and committees as are needed by the church and its organizations, and no more. Organizations, offices, and committees should continue as long as there is significant work for them to do. If the need no longer exists, let the organization go out of existence. One good rule is to appoint as few standing committees as possible. They tend to perpetuate themselves. Rather, appoint special committees which serve only until they have done their work.

The church can help simplify its organization by arranging for a statement of function for each organization and committee. Such statements of function will clear away a great deal of confusion, and will help church groups to work to advantage. They will also show which organizations have a real place in the life of the church and which serve no real purpose. The church may discover that some important work is not being done and that a new organization is needed or that an existing one should undertake a new purpose.

Functions of the Board of Christian Education

Such planning is best done by a carefully chosen, consecrated, informed group of people representing the total church life. This group is known as the Board or Committee of Christian Education.

First of all, the Board must define goals for the *total* program of Christian education—what must be done in the church to lead persons of all ages into a deepened Christian experience.

In the second place, the Board is responsible for developing a comprehensive program of Christian education. To do so requires thorough study and understanding.

The Board must continually try to arouse the interest and concern of the whole church in these goals and programs. An alert Board makes use of sermons, addresses, leaflets, exhibits, posters, and so on.

In the fourth place, the Board must provide for curriculum, which means not only selecting the materials used in the church school, but also guiding their use.

The Board must also work to increase enrollment and attendance. It has many methods for doing the job: home visitation, follow-up of absentees, and above all, a program to meet the needs and invite the participation of every individual.

The Board must coordinate the whole educational program of

Utilization Guide for filmstrip, "PLAN for Christian Education," *Church School Administration Audio-Visuals* (New York: National Council of Churches, 1955), p. 15. Used by permission.

the church: youth activities, Sunday church school, vacation school, week-day religious education classes, camping, etc.

It is the Board's responsibility to schedule the church's educational events so as to avoid conflict, encourage attendance and protect scheduled meetings. A long-range church calendar encourages a balanced educational program and makes each activity more significant.

The Board must find and train workers and teachers. Nominations for leadership positions may be made by others, but final responsibility belongs to the Board.

It must—to the best of its ability—provide rooms and equipment, assign classroom space and supplies.

The Board must take initiative in drawing parents into partnership with teachers and leaders—provide resources for use in homes.

It must cooperate with and promote significant inter-church educational activities.

And finally the Board must evaluate the total program and report to the whole church. Such a twelve point program is essential if a church is adequately to plan for Christian Education.

Functions of Administration

BY LEE J. GABLE

These functions form a cycle through which every effective group must go. We will list seven such functions. Failures in church groups can usually be traced to poor work in one or more of these seven functions.

Planning

This involves formulating purposes and arriving at means by which these purposes may be achieved. Church groups are often weak at this point, for we assume that everybody knows the purpose of the church and its organizations. But not everybody knows the purpose of every organization in the church. It is difficult for a group to plan the way it will achieve a purpose if that purpose is a hazy blur in the minds of its people.

Knowing that this is so, some administrators do the planning themselves. The results may look good on paper, but they are seldom good in individual and group experience. Let planning be a shared experience.

Organizing

Be sure that the organization needed to carry out the plans is provided. So far as possible use the organization that already exists. Where it is lacking or inadequate, take steps to change it. Responsibility for organization includes responsibility for providing the

Lee J. Gable, "Administration Performs a Series of Functions," *Christian Nurture through the Church* (New York: National Council of Churches, 1955), pp. 36–38. Used by permission.

necessary personnel, equipment, and finances. Delegation of responsibility is essential here. The good administrator does not try to do it all himself.

Executing

See that the plans are actually carried out. This must be done thoroughly, so the work is completed rather than allowed to dangle indefinitely in a half-finished condition. It must be done effectively, so people feel they are part of a "going concern."

Supervising

It is not enough to start the wheels of organization going and then assume that the plans will be well executed. Someone must supervise the process. This includes coaching or training workers so they understand what they are to do and how they are to do it. It includes keeping up the morale of workers. It means revising the plans if they prove faulty. A specific administrator may delegate the function rather than perform it himself. The responsibility to see that there is supervision, however, belongs to the administrator.

Co-ordinating

The various activities of a group need to be co-ordinated so that they result in a unified program. The activities of the various groups in a church need to be co-ordinated so they support each other as parts of the same church. The need here is for proper communication. The larger the church, the more definite must be the provision for this communication. It may take place in the official board, in a cabinet created as a clearinghouse, in informal conversation after the morning worship service, or even on the golf course, at an informal luncheon, or on the way home from work.

Publicizing

We have a great deal to learn about interpreting the program of the church so people will understand and support it. A later chapter is devoted to this subject, but mention must be made of it here for it is an important function of the administrator.

Evaluating

Any church group needs to see what it has done, and how well. Too often we have assumed that whatever is done by a church group is good. Perhaps it is, but is it good enough? We will not carry this subject further, for a chapter is devoted to it.

Evaluation will almost always lead to further planning. So the cycle goes on. If administration is sound, the work of the group improves steadily, and the figure is that of the spiral rather than that of the cycle. There is no stopping place in administration. The ultimate goals are far off. Our efforts are insufficient, but our gains hold promise and they give us hope. Like Paul and Apollos, we are "fellow workmen for God" who is both our goal and our aid.

Democratic Administration

BY FRANK W. HERRIOTT

A study of the nature of Christian development and of the task in which the minister is engaged may produce the conviction that he should draw as many individuals as possible into the active work of the church. But the successful operation of a democratic process is not a simple matter. If he undertakes to function in this way, he will meet difficulties and disappointments which may cause him to wonder if he is on the right track at all. How often it would appear easier to "run the church" himself than to work with and through boards and committees! Before embarking on this path, he should think through carefully just what is meant by democracy in administration and what he will do and avoid doing to conserve the highest values for individuals and for the Christian cause.

What Is "Democracy"?

One of the best working definitions was given some years ago by the late Harrison S. Elliott:

> Democracy seems to me to mean that arrangement of life by which the members of a group, small or large, have opportunity to participate, in proportion to their maturity and ability, in deciding, planning, executing, and evaluating all matters in which the group is concerned, matters both within the life of the group and also in the group's relationship to other groups and the common life of which the group is a part.

Frank W. Herriott, "Christianity Is Learned in a Democratic Church," *The Minister and Christian Nurture*, Nathaniel F. Forsyth, ed. (Nashville: Abingdon Press, 1957), excerpts from pp. 116–126. Used by permission.

Note the essential elements in this definition. Here is participation at every important step of action which affects the group. Those who are to carry out plans are to help make those plans. Even farther back, they are to share in the original decisions out of which the plans came. The final step, evaluation, is not omitted, for at this point some of the most important learnings take place. What was right and what was wrong about it? How would we do it differently the next time? If you have shared in such an evaluation, you are ready to join in future deciding and planning.

Not only do we have in view a total unit of experience and active participation in it, but we are dealing with responsible participation. The members are to carry out the plan as well as make it. Democracy so often falters at this point. There are many people who clamor for a voice in making decisions but leave the work for someone else. In this concept of democracy we are saying that everyone affected by a decision has a right to be in on making it and has an obligation to help carry it out. Democracy means *responsible participation.*

There is a qualifying phrase in this definition: "in proportion to their maturity and ability." This safeguards us from giving completely unwarranted freedom, but it opens the door to an autocratic abuse of the concept, and it certainly brings a host of difficult questions of policy. At what age should children be permitted to make decisions and plans—and about what things? Are there some things which even adults should not be allowed to decide? Obviously we need such an element in our concept of democracy, but it forces a minister back upon his own best judgment in any area where he has the power to grant or withhold freedom of choice.

The need for such responsible participation cannot be too strongly stressed. It is through such experiences that membership in the church takes on new vitality. The depth of our loyalty to a group or an institution depends upon our stake in it, upon our sense of belonging and of sharing responsibility. We find an interesting shift in the way people talk about the problems of the church as they become involved in such a process. At first they are inclined to say, "I wonder what *they* are going to do about that." Later the response changes to, "I wonder what we should do about that." Such experiences not only increase loyalty and depth of commitment but foster growth in spiritual power and in the ability to manage life effectively. There is a peculiar need in these days for the ability to meet with integrity the difficult problems thrown at us by the conflicts and tensions of our society. There is pressure for conformity, for going with the crowd and giving the popular answers. We are told that the French peasants once appeared before their king with the plea: "Sire, what are our opinions?" Members of the Christian fellowship may develop power for independent thought and action by being involved throughout childhood, youth, and adulthood in the making and carrying out of decisions under the challenge of the Christian gospel.

How Make Democracy Work?

As has been said, the conviction that the sharing of power and of responsibility should be the basis of life in the church does not solve all the problems. Carefully evaluated procedures must be developed, always with sensitivity to one's particular local situation. Democratic functioning must be learned by pastor and people alike. It involves a skill not easily achieved. The right of self-government does not bring automatically the ability to make democracy work. Some so-called democratic processes may defeat the very purposes for which they are employed. After such experiences the church members may insist that they prefer the dictatorship of the minister or an oligarchy, such as the "inner clique." Let us consider some of the things to do, or to avoid doing, if one's church is to move forward as members of one body in the true spirit of a Christian community.

Go beyond Representative Government

The procedure for the wide sharing of responsibility will partake more nearly of the nature of the town meeting than of the representative body in the limited sense. Representative government may actually involve only a few individuals who are appointed or elected to represent segments of the membership but who respond to each situation as they personally feel about it, with little opportunity to know the mind of their group. Such sharing of power with a small group has advantages over autocratic control by the minister, but there are ways of making the sharing more inclusive.

Observe, for example, the procedure in a meeting of the congregation which was facing the question of whether or not to build a new building. A small group of church officials might have decided to build and then put on a high-pressure campaign to raise money from the church members in accordance with the decision they had made. Instead, a church meeting was called and the whole problem laid before the people. The board of trustees presented the facts, such as the possible types and sizes and the estimated cost of each, and the pros and cons of the question were thoroughly discussed. Then the meeting broke up into small groups, going off into corners in the few separate rooms the church had, to discover what the membership really favored as a course of action. A few men and women had been briefed in advance to serve as group chairmen, although they actually served as reporters, whose task it was to listen carefully and try to report faithfully when the large meeting resumed just how the individuals in each group felt about the matter. If you are interested in the rest of the story: the church meeting voted against the building project but two years later by an equally democratic procedure decided to go ahead with it.

You may be saying that such a process is fine for a small church (the one reported had 350 members), but how about a much larger organization? This, too, can be managed, especially with regard to important issues on which time for deliberation is necessary. It is possible to have a system of referral to small groups or organizations within the membership who will be affected by the decision, so that the official body which must take the final responsibility can act as truly representative of all. Sometimes this is done by sending out "working papers" of some sort, containing full information on the issue at stake, which can then be thoughtfully discussed and the reactions reported back to the central body. Sometimes the organizational pattern itself provides for such two-way communication between the representative council and the constituent groups. The exact form of the organizational structure is not so important as that it provide some way whereby those who act on behalf of the church can hear the voices of the people of the church, and not have to take their cues from the few with the loudest voices or from the records of what is traditional in the church.

Begin Where the Group Is

This is a sound educational principle which should be applied to the readiness of a group to undertake democratic practices. What have they expected of a leader in the past? Have they the maturity and experience to share constructively in the control of group life?

Here is a boys' camp which has been autocratically controlled for many seasons. A new director inaugurates a full-scale plan for camper control through a camp council. Result: Chaos! The shift was too sudden; the boys were not made ready for it by either past experience or preliminary training.

Here is a church where a great deal of self-reliance has been developed under past leadership. The new minister does not sense the attitudes and abilities of the people and proceeds with one-man planning, followed by scolding because *his* plans are not carried out. Result: sullen resistance by many, emotional outbursts from a few.

Each situation must be examined carefully to determine as accurately as possible where the group is on the scale of leader control—group control. There are times when the minister will *keep control of the situation in the interest of democracy.* An illustration may be drawn from work with children. The mother of a kindergarten child complained that the teacher's relaxation of control had made possible the rise to power of the little tyrant Mary Jane, one of the other children in the group. Each of us can recall similar situations in which the firm hand of some more mature person is needed to make possible a genuine sharing of ideas and growth in the ability to use power responsibly and without tyranny.

Insist upon Facts as well as Opinions

How often have you heard democratic procedure described as the process whereby people "pool their ignorance"! And you may have seen it conducted that way. Nothing could be more of a caricature of true democracy. Not that it is always easy to insist upon a decision's being based upon adequate information. There are times in a discussion, especially that of a controversial issue, when the participants are mainly getting rid of strong feelings. It is the responsibility of the leader in such a situation to point out gently but firmly that there are two types of questions to be asked with reference to this issue: What is *true?* and What is *desirable?* and that a wise decision as to what is desirable is dependent upon knowing the facts as fully as possible. Each person has a perfect right to express his feelings and to give his opinions, but an honest effort must be made to be thoroughly informed. Opinions cannot take the place of facts.

Recognize the Place of the Expert

Decisions as to values and purposes differ from decisions as to effective administration. The setting of goals and purposes should be shared by the members of the group. The making of plans to carry out these purposes and the execution of such plans should also be shared, but at this point it may be essential to use the skill of one with special training or experience. A group wishing to put on a play may put themselves under the authority of an experienced director.

The minister may well be in this role at times. He is then not telling the people what they want or what they ought to want. He is bringing to their service his skill or understanding or the result of his greater opportunity for study, that together the needs of all may be met and the purposes of all be more nearly achieved. The people wish to understand the Bible. The minister should be an expert, able to illumine the Scriptures. The people need a deep experience of worship. The minister is able to plan and conduct a service which will be a vehicle for true worship. The parents wish their children to become familiar with their religious heritage. It is to be hoped that the minister knows where to look for the proper materials. There is no good reason why democracy should lead to mediocrity. Let us recognize the place of the expert in the democratic process.

However, we should be aware of one limitation arising from this policy of turning to experts for guidance in carrying out our programs. We thus overlook the possibility that others might become more expert if they were given training and opportunity. Perhaps such training in some form of apprenticeship should accompany the use of leaders already skilled.

Distinguish between Important Matters of Policy and Smaller Details

Much frustration can be avoided if the entire membership of the church or group is not asked to give its time and energy to working out a detailed implementation of decisions reached. Whether our Christmas celebration is to consist of giving gifts to the Sunday-school children or of their giving gifts to someone else may be a major problem of policy requiring careful deliberation. But we get restive when the next half-hour is spent in deciding what kind of candy to buy and who is going to buy it. Or have you been in a meeting where an important decision had been arrived at and then the whole procedure bogged down in discussing just what phrases to use in the resolution? We may smile at committees and subcommittees, but this is their legitimate function, and their use will make for efficiency with no loss of the co-operative spirit. A committee is asked to do a definite job. It does the job, makes its report, and is discharged with thanks. This is functional organization in operation.

Do Not Discuss a Question if the Answer Is Predetermined

To appear to be giving a choice where there is no choice is a travesty on democracy and violates something precious in our relationships. This is most apt to be a temptation in work with children or youth. It would seem that if the minister can only present the matter in such a way that the group will come to the right decision, then they will feel it is *their* decision, and everything will be lovely. But he knows perfectly well that if they should come out with the wrong decision, he would veto it. If there is to be learning in the process and if the group is to have the unifying experience of searching together earnestly for the best answers, then there must be genuine alternatives, and these alternatives must be realistically presented and honestly faced.

Find Time for Unhurried Deliberation

Those who are asked to share responsibility on boards or committees are sometimes treated as if their only function is to give official approval to decisions and plans which some inner circle of command has already made. They are never permitted to function as a deliberative body, for the time provided is so completely inadequate.

Let us sit in on a meeting of a board or commission on Christian education under the leadership of a layman who prides himself on the efficiency with which he runs the meetings. The board meets at a 12:30 lunch hour. Some come late, so the business session begins about 1:15. However, the chairman's main objective seems to be to close the meeting promptly at two o'clock, no matter what may remain on the agenda. Here is an item of considerable importance, obviously requiring time for questions and discussion if the board is to make a wise decision. But no! The chairman breaks in with, "Now we have no more time for discussion on this question. There are several other items to be covered in the next twenty minutes. What is your pleasure? Will somebody make a motion?"

Such procedure contradicts the basic idea that a responsible board or council should be a deliberative body. The people of your church are doubtless people who do not wish to use more time than is necessary, but they may welcome a suggestion as to scheduling which will give the opportunity for unhurried discussion of important issues. The board mentioned above eventually agreed to meet less frequently but to assign a period of not less than two and a half hours to each meeting. They also agreed to have one meeting a year which would occupy a day and a half and would be held at some out-of-town spot.

This plan for an annual retreat is a familiar one and is to be recommended as providing opportunity for many types of experience together: worship, informal getting acquainted, and the consideration of reports from the past year and plans for the future. Week-end retreats have been conducted by many kinds of groups, such as the church-school teachers and officers, the official boards of the church, or in the case of a small church the entire church membership.

20. DEVELOPING LAY LEADERS

LAY LEADERSHIP represents both the number one problem and the number one opportunity of the Protestant churches. It is a problem because it is hard to develop enough good lay leaders to get the work of the church done. It is an opportunity because it is mostly through lay leaders in the homes and organizations of the church that Christian nurture takes place.

Some people maintain that the church should employ professionally trained workers rather than rely on lay leadership. For most churches an entirely professional staff is impractical because the church could not afford to employ them and because there are not enough trained persons available.

There are, however, two deeper reasons why Protestant churches rely on volunteer leaders: (1) The priesthood of all believers has always been a Protestant principle. Every man is his own priest. Every man is also his neighbor's priest. He is therefore responsible for understanding the faith he professes and for helping others to develop a sustaining faith. By their very nature, Protestant churches are committed to lay leadership. (2) Teaching and learning are not mere mental processes; they take place through relationship. (See chapters 3 and 5.) The nurturing force of relationship is felt in the good church class or group. It is also felt in

558

the home, in the normal contacts of community life, wherever people meet. The church, therefore, is committed to the use of lay leaders. It is also committed to a program of enlistment and training.

Motivation is an important part of any sound effort to develop lay leaders. In addition to the brief treatment of motivation in this chapter, the reader would do well to read now the final quotation in chapter 22.

Principles of Leadership Education

BY LEE J. GABLE

How to develop workers who will exercise this kind of leadership is one of our most difficult problems. The success of our efforts at Christian nurture depends on our ability to solve it. How can we help the church administrator find a solution that will work in his church?

To deal with the problem fully would require a whole book on this subject alone. We must, therefore, limit ourselves to setting forth some basic principles of leadership education.

It is difficult to decide what to list as a principle of leadership education and what not to list. Every principle of Christian education applies also to leadership education. What we say about learning any Christian truth applies to learning the understandings and the skills of leadership. We shall not try to say everything! Rather, we shall try to sort out the principles that deal specifically with the development of leadership, assuming that the church will follow the principles of good Christian education also.

Build the kind of church program that will lay a foundation for Christian service

The best leader is one who is already a committed Christian, who knows the church and its work, and who believes that the world needs the church. This kind of attitude does not grow up overnight, or during a six-weeks course. It grows out of years of Christian experience in home and church. He who has it can be

Lee J. Gable, *Christian Nurture through the Church* (New York: National Council of Churches, 1955), pp. 62–65. Used by permission.

helped to do significant work in a church. He who does not have it is not yet ready for leadership responsibility. Let the church, therefore, lay solid foundations for leadership by developing in all of its members a sense of mission, vocation, and commitment to Christ.

Assign responsibility

A church may succeed in a difficult task like that of developing leadership only if definite responsibility is assigned for it. This assignment should go to the same body that is responsible for over-all educational policy and program. This will usually be the board, commission, or committee on Christian education. It is well to appoint a committee on personnel which can work on leadership concerns between meetings and report periodically to the group as a whole. In the small church, this will be a small committee. It may be only the pastor and the church school superintendent. It is important, however, that the committee be responsible to an overhead body rather than that it should work purely on its own authority.

Provide motivation as well as knowledge and skill

It is not enough to expose a worker to new ideas and new ways in church work. He must somehow feel that these ideas and ways are important. He must want to understand them and use them. A leadership education program, therefore, must include inspiration, prayer, worship, Bible study, and a sense of the guidance of the Holy Spirit. The leader of such a program may not be content with objective presentation of knowledge and procedures. Let him believe in what he is doing with such contagion that people are moved to use what they learn through him.

Equip each person to do the particular job the church has asked him to do

Industrial training programs have served as good examples to church leaders at this point. The industrial trainer analyzes a job to be done into the steps required to do it. He finds trouble spots and works out clues to success. Then he works with the trainees as a group and individually until each is able to do the particular job for which he has been hired.

Church work is not as simple as most of the jobs for which industry trains workers. The objectives of the church are different from the objectives of industry. There are more variables in church work, for we are concerned with the motives and behavior of people, and people are forever changing. It is possible, however, to break down any church task into certain steps. And it is possible to find trouble spots and clues to success. We need to go much further than most of us have gone in the direction of equipping each person to do the particular job the church has assigned to him.

It will be good for a church to work out specific descriptions for each position filled by a volunteer worker. Let these descriptions come from the workers themselves rather than be imposed by the pastor or by the official body of the church. The descriptions should, however, be reviewed by the official body and suggestions for correlation and improvement made by it. The preparation of such job descriptions is not easy. It may be more of a chore than workers will care to assume. If this is the case, secure a prepared job description from your denomination or from the National Council of Churches. Then let workers revise that statement to make it fit them and their church.

Include both content and method

Content and method belong together. It is of doubtful value to help a teacher gain new understandings of the Bible unless the teacher also knows how to help his class gain such new understandings. Ways of teaching are of doubtful value unless they are used to teach a content that is sound from a Christian point of view. But is it not possible to teach content in one leadership education program and method in another? Theoretically it is possible, but practically it does not work too well. A good deal of time may elapse between one program and another. A given worker may attend one program and miss the other entirely. Let the church therefore relate content and method.

Provide experience in good patterns of church work

Each of us follows the pathways that are familiar. We do things the way we have done them or have seen them done. This is true even though we have been told to do them differently. As someone put it, "We teach as we were taught, not as we were taught to teach." The leadership education program, therefore, should include more than reading and talking about new and better ways of doing the work of the church. It should include actual experience.

The best way of providing this experience is through work with an expert. Let the church assign the teacher-in-training to work as an apprentice with a good, experienced teacher. Or let the church send selected workers to laboratory schools where they observe the expert teacher at work and later do practice teaching under his guidance. Observation is another good way, but not so good as guided practice. He who watches the expert at work learns much, especially if there is opportunity to talk with the expert afterwards. Films and filmstrips bring a far-off expert into any church. While they are not so helpful as the expert would be if he could be present in the flesh, they bring good teaching to us in a very real fashion. One advantage is that they can be shown over and over again, and the learner may discover something new each time. Whenever possible, bring actual experience into the training program.

Let the leadership education program itself be a good illustration of group work

Perhaps this is a corollary of the preceding principle, but we believe it deserves separate mention. The concept of leadership that was expressed early in this chapter places great emphasis on the experience of the group. The leader succeeds only if the group succeeds. This is as true of the leadership class as of any other church group. If this class is dominated by the leader, we can only expect that its members will dominate the groups they lead in the church. If the members of this class are responsibly involved, it is likely that they will encourage the same kind of responsible participation in their own church work.

The church that would have the type of leader described here must be able to do two things: find and enlist for service the best workers it has available; and help these workers to develop the commitment, the attitudes, and the skills required in church leadership.

Enlisting Church Workers

BY LEE J. GABLE

Enlisting church workers calls for more than an interview in which someone uses the techniques of salesmanship to get the prospective worker to say "yes." It is necessary to start a good deal further back.

Personnel policy needs to be established, in order that the worker may know the conditions in which he will work, in order that the person doing the interviewing may know what he is asking another to do, and in order that the church may be sure that the worker, once he accepts, will find church service a privilege rather than an unwelcome chore. This personnel policy should cover such items as the following: description of the different positions to be filled by volunteers in the church, tenure of office for each position, a rotation system, assistantships to provide for substitutes as needed and to provide leaders-in-training for the future, a record of potential workers with the interests and abilities of each.

A *personnel committee* should oversee the whole business of enlisting and developing church workers. This committee is selected by the official board or by the board of Christian education. Its purpose is to gather information about potential workers, to help enlist workers for emerging needs in the church, and to clear the requests and needs of different church organizations so needs may be met without friction. It is obvious that the larger the church the greater the need for such a committee. Even the small

Lee J. Gable, *Christian Nurture through the Church* (New York: National Council of Churches, 1955), pp. 65–68. Used by permission.

church, however, needs to have someone acting as a personnel committee.

Advance planning to meet personnel needs is necessary. Unhappy is the church that is constantly "scraping the bottom of the barrel" in its efforts to fill vacant positions. It is not easy to avoid this unhappy position, but advance planning will help a great deal. The church program year usually begins in the fall. That is the time teachers and group leaders are needed in largest numbers. The next greatest need comes a few months later with the beginning of the new calendar year. Let the personnel committee face these needs, not in September or December but in April and May!

Let each organized group in the church indicate in April its probable leadership needs for the following fall and winter. Most of these needs can be anticipated. Any organization can know in advance when terms of office will close, what persons are likely to go away to school or to work, what persons should be relieved of responsibility because of family situations or the pressure of other duties. The church that anticipates its leadership needs can look at all of them together. It can challenge the right person for each job much better than can the church that tries to meet each need as it appears. The individual worker is benefited also. With advance notice of his selection to teach a class or lead a group, a person can observe, read, take training courses, and otherwise fit himself to render acceptable service. Advance planning is the key to many of the church's leadership difficulties.

Where can a church find people to fill its volunteer positions? The best answer is to establish a personnel file. Such a file lists the leaders and potential leaders of the church. It shows their background and training, their previous experience, and the interests and abilities that each is willing to use in the service of the church. This calls for a card file, with a card for each person. It is the task of the personnel committee to establish this file and keep it up to date. Let not the minister or church school superintendent say, "We know our people. We don't need a personnel file." Even the pastor of a small church cannot know and remember all the facts about background and interest of his people, especially the new ones as they move into the community.

The church that has not established its personnel file should lose no time in doing so. Some such device as the *Volunteer Christian Service* card will help. It may be circulated at the time of the every-member canvass, or when a new pastor begins service in a church, or with individual families as they move into the community. Cards or check lists for use in registration may be purchased in quantity from the National Council of Churches or from the denominational boards of Christian education. A church may prefer to print or mimeograph its own form. It should give people an opportunity to check their experience and interest in such types of service as are listed below.

Ushering	Publicity	Departmental
Leading Groups	Telephoning	Superintendent
Camping	Correspondence	Children
Scouting	Typing	Youth
Youth Clubs	Mimeographing	Adult
Hobby Groups	Nursing	Teacher
Directing Music	Cooking	Children
Organist	Decorations	Youth
Instrumental Music	Art Work	Adult
Vocal Music	Crafts	Older Adults
Evangelism	Photography	Nursery Roll
Finance	Audio-Visuals	Home Department
Interchurch	Projectionist	Librarian
Co-operation	Radio-Television	Pianist
Missions	Dramatics	Secretary
Community Welfare	Recreation	Work with Families
Industrial Relations	Athletics	Vacation Church
Intergroup Relations	Folk Games	School Work
Home Visitation	Nature Lore	Weekday Church
Baby Sitting	Church School	School Work
Public Speaking	Superintendent	

From the information which it has assembled the personnel committee, in consultation with the various organizations of the church, selects the people to be invited to serve. Selections should be made in a spirit of prayer, of concern for the work of the groups involved, of concern for the growth of the persons and of concern for the relationships that will result. This is not a casual selection, as one chooses pieces for a jig-saw puzzle. This selection affects the Christian growth of persons. For someone it may be a matter of spiritual life or death. Let the choice be prayerfully and carefully made!

Only when these steps have been taken is the church ready for the *enlistment interview*. The same concerns which apply to selection apply to the interview in which the person selected is challenged to accept responsibility. In addition, there are some techniques which will be helpful. Give the invitation in person. Do not rely on announcements, on letters, or even on phone calls. Go in pairs. Let one person represent the church as a whole and the other person the department or organization to be served. If the person to be interviewed is likely to raise a particular kind of objection, let one of the interviewers be a person who has faced that same objection in his own church service. Be specific and frank about the responsibility involved. Show the person why he is "the man for the job." Show the help which the church is prepared to offer in order that the work may be done well. Help the person know the kind of group and program in which he will work, and the needs and opportunities which it affords. Show the place of the group and its program in the work of the church as a whole. Do not press too quickly for a final answer. Do not let the interview dangle, either. If the person accepts, express your appreciation and that of the church. If the person cannot accept at once, arrange for time when the final answer can be given. Be sure that the new worker knows what the next steps are in his preparation and in his beginnings in service. Let the interview be based on the commitment to Christ and his Church which is involved in church membership and which calls on each to give something of himself in the work of the church.

Opportunities for Church Workers to Improve

"Start Where You Are"

Some churches have a policy that no person shall take a job until he has had some training for it. These are wise churches. God needs skilled workmen in his Kingdom. The opportunity that a leader has to help persons grow in their religious life should challenge him to make careful preparation. Too often teachers and other leaders are grieved that they cannot give more adequate aid to persons who come to them with problems, and these workers will profit greatly from a leadership education program.

The needs of the leaders in a church should determine the kind and extent of the opportunities that will be offered them for increasing their understandings and developing their skills. The church board of education will want to set up a well-rounded program of training, including some steps that can be taken immediately, and some long-range plans that may be revised from time to time in view of emerging needs. Not too much should be attempted at first: "start where you are," get some definite activities under way at once, and add other features as need for them arises. Individuals and committees may be asked to assume certain responsibilities; they may make use of the following suggestions, and may make other plans as the program is carried out.

Training While in Service

One of the most effective means of training is helping persons while they are actually on their jobs. This is true of both workers

And Gladly Serve (New York: National Council of Churches, 1949, revised 1957), adapted from pp. 23–41. Used by permission.

who are just beginning and those who have had long experience. In either instance, it is important to consider the following points that have been discovered through studies and experiments in public schools, since these have significance for Christian education.

- The *workers themselves* must be led to recognize their own problems. Unless they have a sense of need and clearly see and accept a desirable goal, even the most careful efforts to help them will not be successful. These goals should be attainable in the not too distant future in order to prevent undue discouragement, and each teacher should try to begin his improvement at some specific point of need.
- As far as possible, all members of a division or department staff or the whole staff should work together to solve their problems. Group decisions, group planning and group evaluation are essential. Solutions that are handed down by a few persons are rarely adequate and are seldom fully accepted by other workers.
- In attempts to solve problems, the emphasis should be upon the *job* rather than upon the *person* who is doing the job. This approach is significant. Even when personal maladjustments are apparent, a direct attack upon them is less successful than helping a worker understand his role better and perform his task more effectively. Under the stimulus of a group process an individual member of the group may grow and change: he learns to appreciate more fully the implications and demands of his task, and he attempts to improve his personal resources for doing his job.

There are different kinds of "in-service" training for prospective workers and for those who have already had experience. The same principles, such as those stated above, hold in both cases, though there is variance in approach and procedures.

For Prospective Workers: Apprenticeship

There were definite values in the old plan of apprenticeship whereby boys learned a trade by working in a shop or a store or in a law office. This same idea is being followed today in order to help inexperienced young persons and adults learn how to do the work of the church. This is proving to be extremely fruitful. Such training on the job has marked advantage because plans are made and carried through within a short time, under guidance. While persons learn through what they do themselves, experience alone may even be harmful. The learner needs help in discovering what is to be done and why it should be done. He makes his plans, tries them out, evaluates his work so that he may profit from both his successes and his failures. Then he makes better plans for the future. Throughout the process, the person who is serving as apprentice must be willing and eager to learn as much as he can. The plan of apprenticeship is provided for:

Future teachers. An inexperienced person assists an able and experienced teacher for a given period of time. At first, the apprentice simply observes the teacher at work, though he may have certain duties such as keeping the records. He has personal conferences with the teacher before each session to assist in planning the purposes for the lesson, the teaching procedures that may be used, the specific activities in which the pupils may be encouraged to take part. After the session, he has another conference with the teacher to discuss what actually took place, what changes were made in the plans and why they were made, how unexpected incidents were used in achieving the purposes decided upon, and additional methods that could have been used. He gradually takes on more and more responsibility, with the teacher observing his work and making constructive suggestions. Finally the apprentice may take full responsibility for a few class sessions, after preparing his plans with the aid of the teacher. This process helps him achieve insights, gain self-confidence, and develop skills. Instead of learning in one situation some theories about teaching and later putting these theories into practice in another situation (always a questionable procedure), he learns principles *through* practicing them.

Assistants with younger children and in vacation schools. Capable adults may be asked to assume duties as helpers with children in the Sunday school or in additional sessions such as a vacation church school. In addition to observing the teachers, they may arrange the room, provide flowers, and help the children with their wraps. Gradually increased responsibility is assigned, as in the case of an apprentice teacher. Some older high school students may serve in this way. However, it is a good idea for young people under seventeen years of age to remain in classes with excellent teachers: they need further development in their religious experience and maturity in preparation for dealing with persons in church work.

Assistant officers. Often a church board of education appoints assistants to the general church school superintendent and to the superintendents of the divisions and departments. When opportunities are provided for these assistants to carry out some of the duties of such offices, they may replace officers without great loss to the work—and sometimes with profit to the educational program.

"Trainees" on boards and committees. It is wise to give young laymen and laywomen training on boards and committees. Each board and committee of the church should include among its members a number of young adults or older youth with stable personalities and Christian experience. Within a few years they will have the main responsibilities for the work of these organizations. While they are being trained and honored in this way, some of the older men and women who have served long and faithfully may be regarded as "Members Emeriti." Some churches make use of "junior" boards as a means of training in churchmanship.

For Present Workers

While it is important to provide training experiences for prospective workers, a matter of equal urgency and immediate concern is to help those persons who are already in service. Many of them are eager for assistance that will enable them to improve the quality of their work. The principles governing the plan for apprentices are guides in helping present leaders. There are two main types of aid:

Supervision. This term indicates personal guidance on the job; it is a plan whereby an experienced leader counsels with and makes suggestions to a less experienced teacher as they work together on problems. In some churches one or more skilled persons are available as supervisors; frequently, the pastor or a superintendent may serve in this way. Often, the supervisor does some teaching himself, with the regular teacher observing; then they discuss with each other the reasons for doing certain things and make plans for the teacher to acquire greater skill at the points where he needs most help. Also, a supervisor observes a teacher at work and helps him recognize both the strong and the weak features of his procedures.

Coaching in various areas. At intervals, an experienced person may help workers with specific problems; this plan is akin to supervision but may not include either observation or demonstration. Help is often needed in the following areas, among others:

- Lesson Planning. Teachers in public schools are taught to prepare careful plans for each class session; surely, such preparation is even more important in the church school, especially since many of the teachers have not had training at this point. This means that they need help in making teaching plans. Sometimes a supervisor or a pastor or a public school principal may meet with teachers of an age group to help them map out their possible procedures and discover various resources that will enrich a unit.

- Worship. Pastors and other leaders who sense the importance of worship in Christian education are giving careful guidance to individuals or committees planning worship services. If spiritual power is to emerge from such a service, nothing must be left to chance. There are values in worship services being planned and led by young people themselves, but this calls for assistance from adults.

• Music. Accompanists for singing may make or mar the atmosphere of worship. Occasionally a church brings together its accompanists in a "coaching conference" to train them, through practical demonstrations in the art of playing hymns, as to how to secure a climax, to develop an appropriate mood, and to create a spirit of worship.

• Church Visiting. Many churches are successful in enlisting members for visiting. The best results are obtained when the visitors are trained for this service. A number of meetings are held with the pastor in which they discuss such points as the purpose of a visit, how to begin an interview, and topics of conversation.

• Ushering. The ushers have an important place in a church. Often they need help in learning when to seat people and how to secure the cooperation of the congregation so that persons may be seated with little confusion. The pastor may meet with ushers to discuss these and other factors that may improve the service.

• Financing the Church. The act of raising and administering funds may be a positive source of spiritual growth for both the official board and the congregation: the secret lies in the way in which plans for financing the church are made and carried out. Primary consideration should be given to the educational and religious by-products. When a minister sits with the finance committee and uses his influence for wise planning, he is strengthening the leadership in his church.

• The Janitor. The neat appearance of the church building and grounds, and proper heating and ventilation, increase appreciation for the church and add to the comfort of those who attend. Coaching of the janitor is one of the types of training for which the church should provide.

Observation

Opportunities for teachers to observe in public schools, week-day and vacation schools, and in other churches have great possibilities for helping workers improve, provided care is taken at certain points.

- Careful plans should be made so that each person may observe the phases of work with which he is concerned.
- The work observed should be educationally sound in at least some respects; the observers should be helped to evaluate both the fortunate and the unfortunate aspects of it.
- Each observer should know what he wants to look for; "just looking around" will not be fruitful. He may be helped to make a list of points to be considered, comparing the work with that in his own department and noting items that may be tried out in his church.
- Arrangements should be made ahead of time for a conference with the workers observed, for interpretations, explanations, evaluations.

Workers' Conferences

The name itself is significant. These are meetings in which church workers confer with one another, have opportunity for fellowship, gain information, become more inspired, and share in planning their work. All these things are important factors in developing understanding of, loyalty to, and support of the educational program of the church. Throughout, consideration is given to the high purposes of the church and the principles involved in accomplishing these purposes. Most groups find that it is essential to have frequent meetings—many meet monthly, and surely quarterly meetings are seldom enough. The success of a meeting depends upon the care with which the program is worked out and the extent to which each worker is encouraged to participate.

There are various types of these conferences: (1) All the workers in the church school meet to plan together so that they may move forward as a unit. (2) The workers with a given age group consult about how to make their work effective; members of the youth council develop plans in harmony with general objectives of the church. (3) The officers of an organization such as the women's society meet to consider their responsibilities.

Guided Reading

There is a widespread and growing interest in church libraries. Any church, however small, can have a library that includes at least a few books on church school work. The study of a good book, especially when it is discussed with other workers, is a definite form of leadership education.

Visits from a Professional or Semi-Professional Leader

One of the services frequently rendered by a field secretary of Christian education is a visit to a local church. One state secretary secures advance information regarding the local situation, through the use of a survey blank. On a Saturday he meets with the pastor, the general superintendent, and the heads of the departments to discover their main problems; on the next day he observes in the church school, preaches a sermon on some phase of Christian education, and meets with all the workers in the afternoon. Out of this conference come various plans for improvement. The results of the first visit are strengthened if there is a follow-up conference some weeks or months later.

The same principle is employed when a specialist in children's work evaluates the program of the children's division, or a young people's leader surveys the work of the youth division. Such visiting need not always be done by professional leaders; often a capable member of a county or district council of religious education can render helpful service to local churches.

Sending Delegates to Church Meetings

The careful selection of delegates to various leadership enterprises is imperative. They should be serious-minded persons with unusual ability, who have been working in the church school or are willing to serve. A number of workers should go from each church. A lone delegate is frequently frustrated by being unable to convince others of the value of what he learned, and he loses his enthusiasm. A group of delegates who have shared an experience will support each other and keep their spirits afire. Upon their return, they should be asked to interpret to other workers who remained at home their new ideas and suggestions for improvement of the educational program of their church.

The following types of meetings are particularly helpful:

- Summer schools.
- Summer conferences and camps for young people.
- Conventions, institutes, and workshops.

Opportunities for Study

Leadership Education Courses

The Standard Leadership Education Curriculum has been developed over the years by the denominations and councils working together. Information about it is given in the *Leadership Education Handbook,* available through the National Council of Churches and through denominational boards of education. These courses may be offered by individual churches. Leadership schools are held in many communities by churches of the same denomination or of different denominations in cooperation. Some denominations offer courses on a correspondence or home-study basis.

A Laboratory School

In a laboratory school, skilled teachers work with boys and girls, assisted by persons who may have had little training or experience. These assistants not only observe the experienced teacher but also have opportunities to share in the work, help evaluate procedures, suggest changes, and make plans for future sessions— all under the guidance of capable leaders. When adequate arrangements are made for a laboratory school, it is one of the most effective methods of training.

21. EVALUATION IN CHRISTIAN NURTURE

THERE ARE CERTAIN THINGS which a group leader needs to know about the group and its members if he is to work effectively. At the beginning of a program year or of a curriculum unit, or at the beginning of his own term of leadership responsibility, the leader should know such things as these: What do the members know about the coming unit or program series? What experiences have they had with it? How do they feel about it? What are their real desires?

At the close of a program year or of a curriculum unit, the leader should have the answers to similar questions: What have they learned? How have their feelings changed? To what extent have the purposes of the group and of the leader been achieved?

In addition to such program-centered questions, there are questions about the group as a whole and about its members which transcend particular programs, units, or periods of time. What progress are the group and its members making in Christian growth? To what extent is the group fulfilling its purpose in the life and work of the congregation? How satisfactory is the relationship of the group to other groups in the congregation, in the denomination, in the community?

How Effective Is Christian Education?

BY FRANK M. MC KIBBEN

Those who are engaged in aiding in the religious development of persons are participating in a most important aspect of their growth. We dare believe we are "co-workers with God" in the development of human personality. This is a high and holy mission and a tremendous responsibility. Such an interpretation of the role of Christian education is surely warranted. We are dealing with persons at the highest level of their development. In the inner integrity and dominant loyalty of the individual, in his proper relations to his fellows, and in his response to the Eternal all other aspects of his growth find their ultimate meaning. Because these aspects of growth are so important and in many respects so difficult to deal with, we have been discussing throughout this text the ways in which we may make this process of Christian nurture more effective. We have been concerned with improving *our* part in this co-operative task. We are called upon time and again to ask ourselves just how successful have we been? Can we measure the outcomes of our work? This brings us face to face with the necessity and the possibility of evaluation, tests, and measurement in religious education.

The Significance of Measurement in General Education

Remarkable development in the field of testing has taken place in public education in the last quarter century. Such testing has been responsible in part for much of the marked improvement in the

Frank M. McKibben, *Guiding Workers in Christian Education* (Nashville: Abingdon Press, 1953), pp. 135–144, 156. Used by permission.

quality of the work done in the public schools. Beginning with quite elementary efforts in this field, leaders in public education have developed measurement into a science and a most important element in the improvement of teaching. Educators have been concerned to eliminate as far as possible ignorance, guesses, and assumptions about the outcomes of schoolwork. They have engaged in costly research, time- and energy-consuming experimentation to discover more accurately how pupils learn, how they comprehend meanings, the nature and extent of their vocabularies at various stages of their development—also to evaluate more carefully many other aspects of education. Through these studies they have developed norms and standards of achievement. A fifth-grade teacher, for instance, knows what to expect of her pupils in the various subjects through a study of the norms that have been established through testing. She knows whether their performance is average or above or below that which should be expected. The larger school systems have departments of research for training personnel who work steadily at the business of creating and using tests and interpreting the data they reveal. Few schools are without fairly reliable information about the mental ability of each student. The I.Q. is part of the standard information obtained regarding every pupil. In more recent years research has been carried on in the field of aspects of personality and the more intangible outcomes of education. Social adjustment, vocational interests and aptitudes, personality traits, and ethical judgments are typical of the aspects of testing now being developed.

Public educators put religious educators to shame in this regard. Those working in Christian education profess to be dealing with *immortal souls of infinite worth in the sight of God*. Yet their nurture of these "immortal souls" is often characterized by marked carelessness with reference to the information they should have about them and by slovenliness with respect to items of tremendous importance in the development of personality. The public schools do not make such extravagant claims about the infinite worth of individuals, yet their basic concern for the wholesome development of every child in their care bespeaks a sense of the worth of persons that compares favorably with that found in the church or the home or any other institution in society. Every subject and form of activity that enters into the public-school program gains its place there only after critical study and careful experimentation as to its suitability and preference over something else. While these observations are not true of every school, they do represent the direction in which public education has been moving. Public educators have participated in studies of personality development that have been a part of the larger movement embracing psychological research and psychiatric treatment of personality difficulties. All such studies and experimentation may prove invaluable aids to church workers who are sufficiently alert, competent, and genuinely concerned to profit by their findings and procedures.

Can We Test Religious Outcomes?

Something of the same concern must come to characterize Christian education. We all too frequently guess, hope, assume, and pray about the desired results of our work without putting forth the effort necessary to make sure that the outcomes we desire are being realized. Our understanding of the learning process has been superficial. Our knowledge of how personality develops is far too scanty. Our disposition to test for results has been wanting, and our instruments and techniques for measurement we have scarcely begun to develop. *In not a single aspect of Christian nurture can it be said that we have established a norm or standard of measurement.* The Christian Church has long been marked by a passion to *save souls*. In its evangelistic program the church has put forth extraordinary efforts to bring about the commitment of individuals to Christ and his church. True Christian education is and must be thoroughly evangelistic in aim and outcome. But in the educational approach a much longer process is contemplated, and many more factors enter into the nurture of the individual leading to the full stature of Christian discipleship. A full range of educational procedures is engaged in, normal stages of development are recognized, and a wide spread of activities, materials, and relationships enters into educational evangelism. These aspects of education need to be analyzed into their particulars. In addition to using the methods and materials that lead to their proper direction we need to attempt to determine more accurately just how effective those procedures are in securing desired results.

This means that we will need to press constantly for more objective data regarding the effectiveness of our procedures. Various analytical instruments will encourage more exact thinking. The keeping of records of facts on specific phases of given learning situations will furnish a basis for more careful evaluation and a more reliable analysis of elements of success and failure. More of the evaluative, testing attitude will stimulate workers in Christian education along many lines. E. J. Chave has listed the following values of objective measurement:

- It may help to break up a situation into more comprehensive parts.
- It may serve to get more exact data on particular items of the situation.
- It may help to put data in such tabular form that their meaning may be more easily understood and each part seen in perspective.
- It may give more indices to significant effects of the educational program.
- It may serve to check hasty judgment.
- It may uncover weaknesses and permit objective consideration of critical needs.
- It may stimulate definiteness in objectives and determination to get tangible results.
- It may call attention to the complex quality of character and the tremendous task of both general and religious education.

• It may serve to take vague idealism out of some religious education and cause a more thorough study of what is involved.[1]

Difficulties in Testing

Certain questions and problems emerge immediately. It will be recognized that in religious education we do not have a professionally trained personnel. We have the pupils for a very limited amount of time. The investment in time, money, and personnel involved seems to make real testing difficult if not impossible. Furthermore the outcomes we are most concerned with are the most intangible and difficult of measurement. For instance, we should be studying the total personality as it functions in realistic life situations. We can do much by way of observation in this regard, but we have few devices for measuring accurately total personality responses. While we will always necessarily be concerned to identify symptoms and the more superficial reactions of individuals, we should strive to understand more fully and measure more accurately the dynamics of personality. We need to get at the basic motivations of conduct. The ultimate test of any process of Christian nurture is how people think, feel, and act. Yet exact knowledge of how people feel and act is sometimes most difficult to determine. These factors are discouraging and represent serious limitations in any testing program in the church. Yet the situation is by no means hopeless. We will need to begin with what we can safely and helpfully do and proceed further as insights, skills, and instruments become available. We will need to evaluate the results of Christian education on various levels of accuracy and thoroughness. Careful observation of an informal type by various persons identified with the program will constitute the simplest procedure in ascertaining outcomes. Group evaluation will ordinarily be found more reliable than individual judgment. Simpler forms of testing are now being used and can be extended as workers become aware of their values and possibility. The more

---

[1] *Supervision of Religious Education* (University of Chicago Press, 1931), p. 42. Used by permission.

thorough measurement procedures will be undertaken by those professionally trained and who work in situations where conditions are somewhat favorable. Directors, ministers of education, and professors in graduate schools of religion are among those who should attempt to experiment in this field. We will need to borrow heavily from the experience and techniques of public education.

What May We Test For?

Various forms of measurement indicate the extent and definiteness of the knowledge learned by those we teach. While our concern goes far beyond the information we desire pupils to acquire, yet knowledge is the basis of understanding, attitudes, and action. If individuals are expected to have a mastery of certain portions of the Bible, we should be able to determine the extent to which that mastery has been acquired. This can be done only through some form of testing. That will call first of all for some kind of knowledge test. Then we are vitally concerned to know whether students understand what they come to know. How well do they comprehend what they read or study? Do they develop erroneous ideas? Do they fail to understand the true or full meaning? There is one way to find out. That is to administer some form of comprehension test. Usually such tests as are referred to above take the form of pencil and paper tests, such as the essay, the true-false, the multiple choice, the completion, the simple recall, and the matching test. Such tests are not entirely reliable, for there is the problem of using words that are understood by the one being examined and also the reliability of the interpretation of the answers by the examiner. Yet such tests are indispensable in learning how much our pupils come to know and comprehend.

We are likewise concerned over the attitudes of those we teach. Attitudes are very influential in determining conduct. But can we measure attitudes? Certainly we can make a try at it. We can provide opportunities for people to record just how they feel regarding a person, an issue, or a situation. Such a test might take the form of an opinion ballot, a social distance test, or a judgment scale. Such measuring devices are much more difficult to develop than tests about knowledge. They are not infallible, yet they do give all parties concerned a better means of knowing just how people feel and respond. These various forms of testing render both the teacher and the pupil more curious about results; they raise questions and develop an evaluation attitude toward the activities engaged in; they make for definiteness and exactness in teaching and evaluation.

Leaders have for some time been concerned with teacher-counselor descriptions of personality growth, personal reactions, and characteristics of behavior that indicate needs, problems, and achievements. These items are entered upon forms provided for this purpose or are kept in a semiprivate notebook of the teacher. In some cases the forms used constitute a personality inventory or rating chart and may be used by several teachers in studying the growth of the individual pupil.

Ordinarily such efforts will represent the most thoughtful evaluation the teacher or counselor can make of an individual pupil. Only in the more exacting and professional testing will pupils be subjected to a battery of tests of a more scientific nature. Such tests should of course be administered and interpreted by trained persons. The use of such tests is becoming increasingly common in those groups that make a serious attempt to analyze personality and conduct difficulties. It is altogether likely that such forms of testing will become increasingly common. Steadily but surely we are developing instruments to be used and trained research workers qualified to undertake serious investigation. It is interesting to note some of the various devices that are being developed to study, diagnose, measure, and work with personality. The titles of the following instruments, most of them still in an experimental stage, will suggest the kind of efforts being made: Ohio Interest Inventory, Interest-Values Inventory, Social Attitudes Scale, Check List for Determining Attitudes, Pupil Portrait, Personality Growth Book, Ohio Social Acceptance Scale, The Best Thing to

Do, A Test of Personality Adjustment, Self-portrait, Mental Health Analysis, Emotional Maturity Scale, Personal Data Blank. In studying these various forms it is clear that we are not ready to use them in the church. They will require more training in administration and evaluation than most church workers now possess. Their value for us lies in the realization of the efforts of this type that are being made and in the suggestion that ultimately we may hope to make greater use of them in Christian education. If leaders in fields other than Christian education are deeply enough concerned over these more significant aspects of personal growth to engage in exacting research to know better how to aid in personality development, how much more should we who regard each individual as of infinite worth in his own right and as a child of God.

Will Pupils Respond to Testing?

Many people feel that pupils in the church school will not respond to forms of measurement. Who knows? Very little testing has been attempted to date. In most cases where testing has been carried on pupils have responded with enthusiasm. They seem eager to know how well they are mastering the material of the curriculum. Students in the public schools have become accustomed to such procedure. Little difficulty in using more tests will be found in the church. Many leaders have discovered also that when properly motivated and in areas where they are particularly interested adults will respond with some enthusiasm to forms of measurement. A minister was brought into a local church to conduct a six-week course on "Using the Bible in Home and Church School." He lacked acquaintanceship with members of the group and felt the necessity of knowing before beginning something of their understanding and attitude toward the Bible. He asked them to fill out the Northwestern University Religious Beliefs Form in which some twenty questions out of fifty-six deal with the Bible. This they were quite willing to do after he had explained his reasons for suggesting it. It called for careful thinking and the expression of their honest belief on a number of critical questions. As a result he had information regarding attitudes of members of the group and where he might well begin in his discussion with them. They in turn were greatly interested to know just how they compared with other members of the group. The whole procedure quickened interest, lifted up problem areas, and afforded a splendid basis for the further work of the course.

It will be felt, of course, that teachers and counselors will not be interested in or capable of administering tests and measurements. Again let us ask: Who knows? Few have been given the opportunity to try. Certainly they can be trained to use the simpler and more objective tests that will be discussed later. As people are added to the staff who are more fully trained to administer and evaluate tests, many workers in the local church can be interested and trained to participate helpfully in such activities. One of the purposes of this discussion is to make known the various types of measurements that may be used in the local church and those that may be used in situations where there are more ample facilities and trained personnel.

Essentials of a Testing Program

Certain things are essential in any situation where measurement is to be undertaken. *First, there must be an awareness of the importance and value of this kind of activity on the part of Christian educators.* Such a concern as has been expressed in the foregoing pages will motivate those who enter this difficult field. It will lead to the willingness of people to secure the training involved and to spend the time and make the effort necessary in this exacting work. *There will be required a studious evaluative attitude toward all that goes on in Christian education.* Such an attitude will keep workers alert to all possible angles of their work. Careful evaluation cannot be carried on without a fair understanding of the bases of character development and the essentials of Christian nurture. Churches must be willing to experiment with different procedures and materials. They must make whatever financial investment will be required. An objective attitude must be maintained toward all aspects of the program so that prejudices and preconceived notions will not prevail over accurate analyses and critical judgment.

Three further things are highly essential: first, clear-cut objectives; second, criteria for determining if these objectives are being attained; and third, adequate tests for measuring accurately the results secured.

Probably the most significant forms of studying the development of pupils are those which ordinary workers in the program can use and in which they can easily be given training. We refer to actual observation of behavior. So many of the aspects of conduct and personality development we desire to measure are best evaluated in close relation to the situations that call them forth. They cannot successfully be isolated from life and measured by paper tests. In such observation great care should be exercised in recording actual reactions and responses. There is no magic in such data. But if they are recorded in some written form, they may be compared with the observations of others. Such comparisons will help correct excessive subjectivity and prejudiced evaluations. While test forms serve to break conduct down into specific elements and provide devices for scoring, nothing can take the place of firsthand information gained through extended observation of life situations, visitation, and detailed descriptive records of behavior. Even if other forms of testing are used, the results obtained require such a descriptive background for the most meaningful interpretation. Is there any worker in the educational program who cannot be trained to make careful and sustained observation of pupils, to visit them and otherwise to keep in close personal contact with those placed in his care? It will require as much as anything else sheer dogged perseverance to stay at the serious study of individuals long enough to gain clear insights into their interests, needs, problems, and growth possibilities.

Evaluation and Planning by the Teacher

BY BESSIE P. ERB

Jane was embarrassed! She was teaching ninth-graders a course about followers of Jesus and more than half of her class could not answer a simple question asked by the superintendent. "I didn't know that any of my class still thought King Saul and Saul of Tarsus were the same person."

Out of this embarrassing experience Jane took a long step toward becoming a successful teacher. She knew something was wrong with her teaching. She knew she must find out what it was and correct it. As she looked over her plans for the preceding lessons of the course, Jane decided that she had not tested enough. She knew that testing is an important part of teaching; that it is necessary to have weekly and periodic tests. Evaluating activities, too, should be carried out. These are not for the purpose of grading the students but for finding out how well they are learning and how they are growing as Christians. "By testing my pupils I test my teaching," she decided.

Jane realized, of course, that learning information is not the primary goal of Christian education. Information is important only as it leads to a maturing Christian faith and practice, with a commitment to Christ. Yet faith and commitment, if they are to be meaningful and strong, must be informed, intelligent, and well grounded in the facts of Christianity.

Therefore, she must find out first of all what her pupils knew about the lessons studied thus far. The quickest testing activity

Bessie P. Erb, "Evaluate and Plan Again," *International Journal of Religious Education*, May, 1954, p. 20. Used by permission.

she could think of was a question game. She made a list of facts and ideas the pupils should have learned. For each of these she wrote a question on a card. The following Sunday she asked the questions, one by one, and as a pupil answered correctly he was given a card to hold. As the game progressed, she was able to clear up several obscure points and to discover where were the weak spots.

On the basis of what the game revealed Jane planned some evaluating activities. She discovered that Frank had a poor sense of time. She decided that to help him the class ought to develop a time line of the followers of Jesus. Since he liked to draw, Frank might like to illustrate it.

Mary had difficulty placing the "followers" in their proper locations on the map. A wall-map of the world, on which the names of the "followers" with their dates were placed, would help.

Ted attributed ideas and facts to the wrong people. Occasional impromptu dramatizations and role playing would reveal whether the pupils were mixing up the characters and events.

A picture reveals facts and ideas. Perhaps she could get Frank and other members of the class interested in illustrating a triptych on the followers of Jesus for their worship center.

Jane planned to have some kind of short check on every lesson. Formulating intelligent questions is a real test of understanding, so she would continue to use the question game, letting the pupils add their own questions.

To summarize a lesson one must know the facts and ideas. Occasionally she would ask for summaries in the form of telegrams, newspaper headlines, and short newspaper articles.

Jane realized that she should be testing not only for facts and ideas but for Christian attitudes and living. To do this she would listen as often as possible to the conversation of her pupils in and out of class. She would encourage conversations in class, which would range from ideas garnered from the lessons to the everyday life of the young people.

What her pupils did both in and out of class would be a good test of their attitudes. She would try to take a greater interest in their daily lives to see how well they were growing in Christian living.

One important way to evaluate her effectiveness as a teacher would be to maintain closer relationships with the parents and learn from them the needs of the young people, how they responded to what they learned in class, and how she might make her teaching more helpful.

On the basis of what these evaluating activities and checks revealed, Jane knew she could plan her lessons so that her pupils would be learning and growing. She would test not only her pupils but her own teaching. On the basis of such evaluation she would build her plans for the work ahead, and would plan better for her own growth and devotion as a teacher.

Group Program Must Be Constantly Evaluated

BY MARGARET E. KUHN

Evaluation is basic to individual growth and group development. New objectives, new emphases, new projects ought never to be planned until those of the past have been looked at frankly for their good and bad points. This is not a dreary post mortem, but an orderly stock-taking of assets and liabilities, growth or failure to change—in theological terms recognition of human error. Group members and leaders are equally responsible for this appraisal.

Groups should not wait to be confronted with a crisis (loss of members, sharp decrease in attendance or extreme dissatisfaction) before trying to analyze the effects of what the group is doing.

It is important for group leaders and members to realize that some evaluation is going on constantly. Whenever people get together they size up each other's ideas and reactions, they make judgments about situations and problems, and they develop likes and dislikes. It is essential for leaders to know how people are affected or influenced, but it is not always easy to get at their reactions. Usually group members don't express their feelings openly because they do not want to offend others, or because they fear some form of ostracism from the leaders. Even when they are asked for comments and criticisms they frequently hesitate. Because this is so group leaders need to help all the members to see that they aren't spectators on the sidelines, but the moving spirits

Margaret E. Kuhn, "Program Must Be Constantly Evaluated," *You Can't Be Human Alone* (New York: National Council of Churches, 1956), pp. 46–48. Used by permission.

in a co-operative venture. *To have a part in evaluation is to measure up to one's full responsibility in a group.*

When group leaders involve group members in evaluating what they do together and make clear that they expect all members to have ideas about improving the group, in time group members will trust the evaluation process and understand how it helps them to work more effectively toward the goals that they seek. But even more important, they will see the effects of the group activity on the members who participate in it. When members of a group have had a part in evaluating what they do together they will be more ready to make the changes that seem desirable.

In evaluating program groups—

- Study their goals and objectives. Evaluation may point up the fact that group members don't understand too well what their purposes are and what they are trying to do.
- Note what is being done to work toward objectives or goals.
- Analyze whether people in the group are learning as a result of participation, and finding deeper satisfaction and fellowship.
- Discover factors that help or hinder achievement of goals.
- Devise and test out ways of remedying weaknesses in the program, and building on what they have done well.

Evaluation should not be considered a threat to the leader and his status in the group. Rather, it should be considered as a tribute to the leader and his ability to elicit co-operation and team play. Evaluation involves humility and self-criticism on the part of group members as well as the leader. Because it is not easy to face up to our mistakes, evaluation is often omitted. Churchmen might think of evaluation in theological terms. When they neglect it they fail to acknowledge their dependence upon God and the fact that all persons stand under his judgment. No human being or institution can be perfect.

Collecting and Using Data to Improve
Group Efficiency

BY BRADFORD, STOCK, AND HORWITZ

Today guided missiles have a feedback mechanism built into them that continuously collects information about the position of the target in relation to the flight of the missile. When the collected information indicates a shift of the target or a discrepancy in the arc of flight of the missile, the feedback mechanism corrects the flight of the missile.

Most houses with central heating today have a small feedback mechanism, called a thermostat. When the information collected by it indicates the temperature is below a certain point, the mechanism signals the furnace to turn itself on. When information collected by the thermostat indicates that the temperature is too high, it signals the furnace to stop.

Groups need to build in feedback mechanisms to help in their own steering. Such a process of feedback calls for collecting information on the discrepancy between what the group wants to do (its target) and what it is doing (reaching its target) so that it can make corrections in its direction.

Human beings, and therefore groups, not only need continuous self-correction in direction but also (and here they differ from machines) need to learn or grow or improve. Collecting adequate data and using this information to make decisions about doing things differently is one of the major ways of learning.

Leland Bradford, Dorothy Stock, and Murray Horwitz, "Improving Group Efficiency," *Understanding How Groups Work* (Chicago: Adult Education Association, 1955), pp. 41–48. Used by permission.

There are three basic parts to the process of changing group behavior:

Collecting information.
Reporting the information to the group.
Making diagnoses and decisions for change.

Who Should Diagnose?

If a member of a group strives to improve his own behavior in the group so that he can make more useful contributions he will need to make his own personal observations and diagnoses about the group and about his behavior in it. Each member has this individual responsibility.

If the group as a whole is to make decisions about changing its procedures or processes, then the entire group must assume responsibility for collaborative diagnoses of its difficulties and its effectiveness. If the leader takes over this function, he continues to direct and dominate the group—leading them like sheep. If only the leader analyzes group difficulties and acts upon them, only he learns. Similar problems arise if diagnosis is left to any group member; he may too readily use this job to steer the group in the direction he desires.

Each member and the leader may guide and encourage the group toward diagnosis, but the responsibility for self-steering and the opportunities to learn and to grow must remain with the group if it is to improve its operational effectiveness.

Collecting Information

While analysis and evaluation of information and decision about what to do should be carried out by the total group, the collecting of information may be delegated. A number of patterns of delegation are possible.

1. The leader, serving also as observer, can report to the group certain pertinent observations he has made about problems and difficulties of group operation. However, although the

leader may have more experience with groups, to add the function of observer to his leadership responsibilities complicates his job and also tends to create greater dependency upon him.

But when the group is unfamiliar with the process of observation, the leader may play an informal observer role for a few meetings, gradually getting other group members to assume this function.

2. The group may appoint one of its members, perhaps on a rotating basis, to serve as group observer, with the task of noting the manner in which the group works. While a group loses a member as far as work on its task is concerned, it can gain in the growth and improvement of the group.

   Frequently there is a leader-team made up of a discussion leader and observer. The leader and observer work together in behalf of the group, one helping to guide the group and making procedural suggestions, the other watching how it works.

   When a leader-team is formed, it makes possible team planning for each meeting. Between meetings the leader-observer team can look back at the past meeting from two vantage points, and look forward to the next meeting.

3. A third method calls for all group members to be as sensitive as they can, while participating actively, to the particular problems the group faces. Although in mature groups members may raise a question about group procedures or maintenance at any time as a normal contribution to the discussion, in new groups the leader may start a discussion looking at how the group has worked and what its problems are. This may occur at some time during the discussion, when the group has bogged down, or during the last fifteen minutes to half an hour as an evaluation of the entire meeting.

What Information to Collect?

Because of the many group problems and the many causes of these problems there is a wide range of information that a group may need at different points in time. General questions such as these may help get started:

1. What is our goal? Are we "on" or "off the beam"?
2. Where are we in our discussion? At the point of analyzing the problem? Suggesting solutions? Testing ideas?
3. How fast are we moving? Are we bogged down?
4. Are we using the best methods of work?
5. Are all of us working or just a few?
6. Are we making any improvement in our ability to work together?

In any observation of a group more can be seen than can possibly be used for steering, corrective or growth purposes. The following questions may help guide an observer in collecting data about a group:

1. What basic problems does the group seem to have for which information is needed?
2. What is the most important or pertinent information? What information will lead the group into stray paths?
3. What is the essential minimum of material the group needs?

Methods of Observation?

Just as there are many areas of information about group behavior, so there are many possible guides and scales for observation. Frequently groups develop such scales to fit their particular needs. Three techniques of observation are given, each useful for collecting a different kind of information.

1. *Who Talks to Whom*

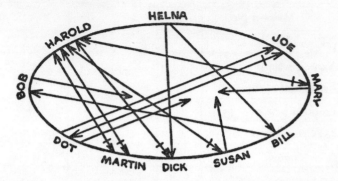

The number of lines made by the observer on this form indicates the number of statements made in a fifteen-minute period—20. Four of these were made to the group as a whole, and so the arrows go only to the middle of the circle. Those with arrows at each end of a line show that the statement made by one person to another was responded to by the recipient.

We see that one person, Harold, had more statements directed toward him than did anyone else and that he responded or participated more than anyone else. The short lines drawn at the head of one of the pair of arrows indicates who initiated the remark. Harold, the leader, in other words had remarks directed at him calling for response from four other people.

2. *Who Makes What Kinds of Contribution*

Member No.	1	2	3	4	5
1. Encourages					
2. Agrees, accepts					
3. Arbitrates					
4. Proposes action					
5. Asks suggestion					
6. Gives opinion					
7. Asks opinion					
8. Gives information					
9. Seeks information					
10. Poses problem					
11. Defines position					
12. Asks position					
13. Routine direction					
14. Depreciates self					
15. Autocratic manner			Based upon observation categories discussed in *Interaction Process Analysis* by Robert F. Bales. Cambridge, Mass.: Addison-Wesley Press. 1950.		
16. Disagrees					
17. Self assertion					
18. Active aggression					
19. Passive aggression					
20. Out-of-field					

This record makes possible the quick rating not only of who talked, but the type of contribution. Individuals in the group are given numbers which are listed at the top of the columns. At the end of a time period it is possible to note the frequency and type of participation by each member.

3. *What Happened in the Group*

1. What was the general atmosphere in the group?
   Formal _____   Informal _____
   Competitive _____   Cooperative _____
   Hostile _____   Supportive _____
   Inhibited _____   Permissive _____
   Comments: _____

2. Quantity and quality of work accomplished
   Accomplishment: High _____ Low _____
   Quality of Production: High _____ Low _____
   Goals: Clear _____ Vague _____
   Methods: Clear _____ Vague _____
                 Flexible _____ Inflexible _____
   Comments: _____

3. Leader behavior
   Attentive to group needs _____
   Supported others _____
   Concerned only with topic _____ Took sides _____
   Dominated group _____ Helped group _____
   Comments: _____

4. Participation
   Most people talked _____ Only few talked _____
   Members involved _____ Members apathetic _____
   Group united _____ Group divided _____
   Comments: _____

This form can be used as a checklist by an observer to sum up his observations, or it can be filled out by all group members to start an evaluation discussion. Forms 1 and 2 can be used only by a full-time observer.

Reporting Information to the Group

The second step is feeding back pertinent information to the entire group. Whether the information is collected and reported by the leader or by the observer, it is very easy to hurt the group rather than help it. The following cautions are particularly pertinent in reporting to the group:

1. Be sensitive to what information the group is ready to use—what will be most helpful to the group now, rather than what was the most interesting point observed.

2. Don't avalanche the group with information. If too much information is given it can't be used. Select only two or three observations which will stimulate thinking and discussion. Let the group ask for more information as they need it.

3. Don't praise the group too much. Learning doesn't take place by being told only when we are on the beam. Mentioning accomplishments is desirable as it helps difficulties get honestly faced.

4. Don't punish or preach or judge. The observer can't play the role of God. He says, "It was interesting that participation was less widespread today than yesterday." He doesn't say, "Some of you dominated the discussion today."

5. It is easier to discuss role behavior than people's behavior. "What role did the group need filled at that time," rather than, "That behavior is bad."

6. Go light on personality clashes. It is usually better to discuss what helped and what hindered the whole group.

Deciding About Change

The third stage is diagnosis from the information reported and the consideration of what the group and its members will do differently in the future. Usually this has a number of steps:

1. The members assess the observations, relate them to their experiences, test to see if they agree with the report.

2. The group examines the reasons. What caused a thing to happen? Could we have recognized it earlier?

3. The group moves to a decision of what to do. What can be done in future similar circumstances? What can individual members do earlier to help? What methods or procedures should be changed? What new directions sought?

This stage is the crucial one if the group is to benefit from its feedback activities. Unless the members are able to gain new insights into the functioning of the group, and are able to find new ways of behaving, the group will not improve its processes and continue in its growth and development.

It is very easy for the time of the discussion to be consumed by the first two steps in this procedure. The leader, as well as the members, needs to be sensitive to this danger and encourage the group to move into the third step of decision. Although the decisions which are made may be quite simple, agreement on future action sets up common expectations for the next meeting and gives a point to the evaluation.

22. THE GROWING LEADER

THE CHURCH GROUP LEADER must be a constantly growing person. Someone has expressed this point aptly in the oft-quoted sentence, "If it is not happening to the teacher it will not happen to the pupil." The truth holds equally well for anyone in a position of leadership—superintendent, pastor, chairman, director of Christian education, adviser, counselor.

Unfortunately, there are many church group leaders who grew for a while in their personal Christian life and in their leadership, but then stopped growing. The fault may not have been theirs, personally. Perhaps they had taken advantage of all the opportunities for growth that were available. The fact remains that the work of many church groups suffers because their leaders have stopped growing.

Only the person himself can start the process of growth anew. A pastor, director, or superintendent cannot do it for him. Much less can a chapter in a book guarantee the growth of its reader. Yet another person may encourage a leader to renew his growth—and even a chapter in a book may help.

Becoming Better Leaders

BY FRANCES C. MC LESTER

None of us is fully satisfied with his work in home or church school. All of us want to become better parents and better teachers and officers. In order to do so each of us should have a definite plan for improvement. A resolution such as the following may be suggestive:

1. I will attempt to do all of my work in the spirit of love that Jesus showed when he was on earth; often each day I will seek communion with God from whom comes the inspiration and the strength to be a follower of his Son; I will diligently study the Bible so that I may more clearly see the Christian way of life and walk therein; I will learn to love the church better and will take more active part in its work.

2. I will try to develop my own personality—to increase the number of my interests; to gain more self-control; to learn how to get along with other people better; to think more of others and less of myself.

3. I will share life with my pupils, whatever age they may be; I will so live with them that I may understand them better; I will take part in their play and work and be interested in whatever concerns them.

4. I will study diligently to become a better teacher; I will read books and take training courses that will help me understand how to teach and what to teach; I will learn more about how to use the

Frances C. McLester, *What Is Teaching?* (Nashville: Abingdon Press, 1932, 1953), pp. 123, 124. Used by permission.

Bible in my teaching; I will develop my appreciation of nature so that I may see more clearly the hand of God in all beauty and order in the world.

5. I will look upon my place in my community as an opportunity to help bring the kingdom of God to our world; I will take an interest in civic affairs, and will vote for laws that will mean justice to all men of every race and in every station in life; I will broaden my interest in human welfare, and will do what I can to further brotherly feeling between nations.

All this and more will I do as a teacher of the religion that Jesus Christ revealed to men through both his teachings and his life.

Some Questions for Teachers of Children

BY PHOEBE M. ANDERSON

As You Work with Children:

Am I serving them or serving myself? Why do I feel this way? What is my real motivation for doing this teaching and this work with parents?

What kinds of experiences provide my emotional satisfaction in this job? When Sunday morning does not go well, when I feel inadequate with a particular child, when I have been told to "go 'way" or "I don't like you," what do I do? How do I feel?

Are there some children I really do not like, and therefore do not love? Why? Is it because I feel defeated in dealing with them? Or has my feeling about their parents anything to do with it?

Which children am I failing? By recognizing this, what new understanding does this give me of myself?

For the most part, do I genuinely enjoy these children and myself when with them? What evidence have I?

As You Work with Other Teachers:

What opportunities for growth am I providing them? In what ways are they becoming more competent with children? What steps have we, as teachers, taken together toward a better understanding and more faithful practice of Christianity?

Do we feel part of a team doing a job together or is it my "show" and they do what I suggest? How personally involved are they? (Writing down the preparation each teacher makes for each

Phoebe M. Anderson, *Religious Living with Nursery Children* (Boston: The Pilgrim Press, copyright, 1956), pp. 148–150. Used by permission.

Sunday, what she does while there, and what she does to clean and straighten the room will help you think this through.)

What exciting and important things are we learning about children? How are we learning—by studying and working through our own experiences, or by someone more expert telling us?

As You Work with Parents:

How do I feel toward parents, in general and in particular? (How I feel about each one will give me a clue as to how I am treating each one.)

Do I strive continually to understand parents—all the parents— as persons trying to do the best they know? (This means I do not judge or condemn them, neither am I patronizing or superior in my attitude toward them.)

How am I performing my job—which is to be of help, of service, to provide ideas, to offer interpretations when asked for them?

Am I inclined to want to tell parents how to deal with their children, or to point out to them what their problems are and how to solve them? Cite the evidence.

How completely am I able to accept each of these parents? Whom do I reject? I wonder why?

As You Consider Yourself:

Am I growing toward Christian maturity myself? How do I know?

What are the marks of my progress?

What methods have I developed by which to take stock of my growth?

A Rating Scale for All Church Workers

Purpose of This Scale

A self-rating scale may help each church worker and leader realize his desires to have a constantly growing and developing personality. By using such a scale a person should be able to keep before himself some qualities which constitute Christian character; to face himself frankly, fairly, prayerfully; and to find renewed determination to grow into full stature in Christ.

This scale is merely an illustration of what a self-rating scale may be. If it is to be used by a group, it may be revised after thorough and free discussion, adopted, and mimeographed.

How to Use This Scale

Read carefully each statement, and then think frankly and objectively about the extent to which you possess the quality or carry out the activity described. Put a check mark in the appropriate column of the three that follow the statement. After you have checked yourself on each item, add up your score by counting each check in the first column as *one,* each in the second column as *two,* each in the third column as *three.*

The highest possible score in this rating scale for all workers is 60. If your score is over 50, you are probably a very successful worker, as far as the items in this particular scale are concerned. If your score is between 40 and 50, you have some good qualities but need to improve in various ways. If your score is less than

And Gladly Serve (New York: National Council of Churches, 1949, revised 1957), pp. 49–51. Used by permission.

608

40, you will want to make strenuous efforts to become a better worker.

Note the points at which you are weakest and direct your main efforts to strengthening these—though you will not want to neglect any of the others. Work out your personal program for improvement. In doing this, refer to the suggestions in this booklet, and seek the advice of your pastor, of an experienced and successful teacher in your church school, of a supervisor in your church or public school, or of some other well-prepared individual. Such a person will be glad to counsel with you about your rating on each item in this scale, and can recommend good books, appropriate leadership, education courses, and other means of developing your possibilities.

I. *My Christian Experience*

A. RELIGIOUS THOUGHT AND LIFE

	Very little	*To some extent*	*To a marked extent*
1. I sincerely try to understand more fully the nature of God and His will for the world	———	———	———
2. I continually strive to live my religion—to make my personal decisions in harmony with the teachings of Jesus	———	———	———
3. I try to serve God and mankind through the use of whatever talents I have	———	———	———
4. My religious convictions and beliefs are positive and strong	———	———	———
5. I read regularly the Bible and other Christian literature for guidance and inspiration	———	———	———

	Very little	To some extent	To a marked extent

B. PARTICIPATION IN CHURCH WORK

1. I give generously to the support of my church

2. I attend regularly and punctually church services and meetings that have bearing on my work

3. I am willing to enlist in any type of Christian service for which I have or may acquire ability

C. PERSONAL AND SOCIAL RELATIONSHIPS

1. I have cordial and friendly relations with other church members

2. I co-operate wholeheartedly with my fellow workers

3. I am just, generous, tactful, and I refrain from hurtful gossip

4. I profit from criticism, acknowledging my mistakes and trying to learn through them

5. I am open-minded and fair toward persons whose opinions and viewpoints differ from my own

6. I recognize that persons of all races and faiths are children of God, and I have increasingly friendly relations with them

7. I cultivate poise, patience, self-control; I am learning

	Very little	*To some extent*	*To a marked extent*
how to get along better with other persons	___	___	___

II. *My Knowledge of the Christian Religion and of the Church*

1. I am increasing my knowledge of the meaning of the Christian religion for my own life   ___ ___ ___

2. I am increasingly able to interpret the Christian message to others   ___ ___ ___

3. I am familiar with the history of the Christian church and its contributions to individuals and to society   ___ ___ ___

4. I am becoming more familiar with Protestant beliefs and with the doctrines of my own denomination   ___ ___ ___

5. Through sharing in the work of my own church I strive to make it a more vital influence in my community   ___ ___ ___

A Rating Scale for Church School Teachers

How to Use This Scale

In order to discover your score as a teacher, follow the directions for the scale in the preceding article.

The highest possible score on this scale for teachers is 90. If your score is over 80, you are probably a very good teacher—though you may still improve. If your score is between 65 and 80, you should develop your attitudes and skills and abilities in a number of ways. If your score is under 65, you need to do many things in order to improve personally and to teach effectively.

Whatever your score may be, note the points at which you are weakest and direct your main efforts toward strengthening these—though you will not want to neglect any of the others. Read the directions for *A Rating Scale for All Church Workers* in the preceding article, and make plans for your own improvement, as recommended therein.

I. *My Knowledge of My Pupils*

	Very little	To some extent	To a marked extent
1. I am vitally interested in my pupils	____	____	____
2. I continually try to understand better the nature and the religious needs of my pupils	____	____	____

And Gladly Serve (New York: National Council of Churches, 1949, revised 1957), pp. 51–54. Used by permission.

	Very little	*To some extent*	*To a marked extent*
3. As I guide each pupil in his growth in religious living, I take into account his environment—his home and community	___	___	___
4. I am keenly aware of the importance of individual differences, and I try to help each of my pupils meet his specific needs	___	___	___
5. I am always ready to give each of my pupils cordial and dependable counsel, in so far as I am able	___	___	___

II. *My Knowledge of and Skill in Using Procedures in Christian Education*

1. I carefully prepare my own plan for teaching each unit or lesson
2. I work out my own purposes for each unit and each lesson, and help my pupils develop purposes of their own for their living as Christians
3. I use in my teaching only those words and ideas that my pupils can understand and thus can make their own
4. I recognize the inherent worth and respect the personality of every member of my group, and I help each pupil to do so
5. I encourage each pupil to take active part in the work

	Very little	*To some extent*	*To a marked extent*

of the group, so that he may develop a sense of "belonging" and of contributing to the group

6. Realizing that each pupil learns best through what he does himself, I help him to select worth-while activities in which he can participate both in and out of class

7. I lead my pupils to think, to reach their own conclusions, to make and carry out plans

8. I prepare leading questions to guide discussion (of youth or adults), and I stimulate each pupil to participate in discussion

9. I use different methods of teaching and experiment with new methods, including use of visual resources

10. I am becoming more skillful in discovering and using printed materials

11. I constantly help each pupil achieve more desirable attitudes and conduct, without resorting to awards for attendance, study, or behavior

12. I try to be fair to each member of my class and to inspire him to have confidence in me

13. I have wholesome and sincere relationships with my pupils, and lead them to de-

	Very little	To some extent	To a marked extent
velop loyalty to the church and its work rather than to individuals or to groups			
14. I cultivate an attractive manner, voice, and appearance			
15. I measure the success of my work in terms of the growth of my pupils in Christian living			
16. I spend time on my preparation for teaching, commensurate with the importance of the work			
17. I am so keenly interested in my work that my enthusiasm is contagious			
18. I continually strive to improve my teaching by:			
a. observing good teachers at work			
b. attending workers' conferences and other meetings			
c. taking leadership education courses			
d. seeking advice from experienced teachers and supervisors			
e. reading pertinent articles in church school periodicals			
f. using teachers' helps prepared by my denomination			
g. studying good books on psychology and education			
19. I am continually trying to improve my personality and to be more Christlike			

How Jesus Developed Leaders

BY LOWELL B. HAZZARD

Jesus developed leaders by choosing followers. . . . When I took down a concordance to discover the words "leader," "lead," and "leadership," I could not discover Jesus ever using these words except when he talked about "blind leaders of the blind," both of whom fall into the ditch. When James and John sought to be leaders, Jesus said, "Not so." No, Jesus, so far as I can discover, never talked about leadership, nor set out to develop any leaders. What Jesus did was to come to a group of people, one here and one there, and to say to them, "Wouldn't you like to follow me?"

I do not know exactly what this says about our process of enlistment and training, except that if we are ever to solve our problem, we must look far behind our leadership training, far behind our enlistment of leaders to basic motivation.

. . .

Even Jesus' wonderful skill in teaching did not make his disciples leaders. It helped, but when Jesus died there wasn't a leader in the group. It was after Peter was graduated that he denied Jesus. No, it took one more thing really to turn the trick.

Jesus died, and rose again, and infused them with his spirit. It was not until Pentecost that Peter stood forth, a marked leader of men. Not until after Pentecost did Peter and John heal the lame man at the temple's Beautiful Gate. Not until then did they stand before the authorities and say, "We must obey God rather than

---

Lowell B. Hazzard, excerpts from an unpublished paper. Used by permission.

men." It was the Christians of the Book of Acts who had actually become leaders, and they served a risen Savior and were possessed of his spirit.

What does that suggest?

That leadership is born out of travail, and not out of books or courses. What had happened to these disciples between the time when they were graduated from the course and the time when they stood forth as leaders? They were *crucified with him* in those dreadful days between Good Friday and Easter, when they were trying to readjust to a world without him. They *rose with him* on the Easter morning when Christ began to be "formed in them."

. . .

I do not know whether Jesus set out to develop leaders or not. He set out to save the world. He got some people to help. And they grew mightily in the process.

We have a world that is desperately needing to be saved. And we have a church that is trying to save it without any major convictions. A new creativity in Christian teaching will require more than new textbooks or new methods. It will require a new passion flaming through our work, a new devotion to all that Jesus stood for and was.

. . .

Only those are qualified to lead who let themselves be led, and the Master—well, the Master is almost out of our sight!

INDEX

INDEX